Individual Labour Rights as Human Rights

Bulletin of Comparative Labour Relations

VOLUME 96

Founding Editor

The series started in 1970 under the dynamic editorship of Professor Roger Blanpain (Belgium), former President of the International Industrial Relations Association. Professor Blanpain, Professor Emeritus of Labour Law, Universities of Leuven and Tilburg, was also General Editor of the International Encyclopedia of Laws (with more than 1,600 collaborators worldwide) and President of the Association of Educative and Scientific Authors Authors. He passed away in October 2016.

General Editor

In 2015 Frank Hendrickx, Professor of labour law at the Faculty of Law of the University of Leuven (Belgium) joined as a co-Editor. Frank Hendrickx has published numerous articles and books and regularly advises governments, international institutions and private organisations in the area of labour law as well as in sports law. He is the Editor-in-Chief of the European Labour Law Journal and General Editor of the International Encyclopaedia of Laws.

Introduction

The Bulletins constitute a unique source of information and thought-provoking discussion, laying the groundwork for studies of employment relations in the 21st century, involving among much else the effects of globalization, new technologies, migration, and the greying of the population.

Contents/Subjects

Amongst other subjects the Bulletins frequently include the proceedings of international or regional conferences; reports from comparative projects devoted to salient issues in industrial relations, human resources management, and/or labour law; and specific issues underlying the multicultural aspects of our industrial societies.

Objective

The Bulletins offer a platform of expression and discussion on labour relations to scholars and practitioners worldwide, often featuring special guest editors.

The titles published in this series are listed at the end of this volume.

BULLETIN OF COMPARATIVE LABOUR RELATIONS – 96

Individual Labour Rights as Human Rights

The Contributions of the European Court of Human Rights to Worker's Rights Protection

Author

Elena Sychenko

Wolters Kluwer

Published by:
Kluwer Law International B.V.
PO Box 316
2400 AH Alphen aan den Rijn
The Netherlands
Website: www.wklawbusiness.com

Sold and distributed in North, Central and South America by:
Wolters Kluwer Legal & Regulatory U.S.
7201 McKinney Circle
Frederick, MD 21704
United States of America
Email: customer.service@wolterskluwer.com

Sold and distributed in all other countries by:
Turpin Distribution Services Ltd
Stratton Business Park
Pegasus Drive, Biggleswade
Bedfordshire SG18 8TQ
United Kingdom
Email: kluwerlaw@turpin-distribution.com

Printed on acid-free paper.

ISBN 978-90-411-8629-4

e-Book: ISBN 978-90-411-8646-1
web-PDF: ISBN 978-90-411-8647-8

Printed in the United Kingdom.

With the most sincere gratitude to my family for their support, understanding and patience and to Prof. Bruno Caruso

Notes on Author

Elena Sychenko is an associate professor at Saint Petersburg State Polytechnic University. She received her PhD degree from the University of Catania in 2016, a master degree with honours from Saint Petersburg State University in 2004. During the last five years she published about twenty articles in peer-reviewed journals in Russian, English, French and Italian and two books in Russian. She is a regular contributor to the French peer-review journal 'Revue de droit comparé du travail et de la sécurité sociale', which reviews the conclusions of the UN Human Rights Committee and the UN Committee on Economic, Social and Cultural Rights relevant to labour law and a contributor to ILO LEGOSH system. She is a member of several professional networks, such as CIELO (Comunidad para la investigación y el estudio laboral y ocupacional), Centre of modern labour law (Tblissi State University, Georgia) and a member of the association 'Lawyers for labour rights' (Moscow, Russia).

Table of Contents

Introduction

'Nations prosper in the global economy...by building their institutional advantages on a floor of fundamental human rights...'
Sir Bob Hepple[1]

In recent years there has been a substantial debate over the interconnection between labour rights and human rights.[2] These debates were mainly conceptual in nature whilst international and regional human rights mechanisms, from a practical perspective, have so far been rather underexplored from the labour rights perspective.[3] My research, as set out in this volume, is largely inspired by a desire to explore how individual labour rights have been referred to in the human rights jurisprudence of the European Court of Human Rights (the Court or the ECtHR). The goal of my analysis is to highlight the Court's views on these rights for the benefit of practitioners working in this area, to show that human rights are not only 'important ideological weapons in the development of labour law,'[4] but can also be practical tools in the legal practice as well.

The aim is to demonstrate that Strasburg 'is not that far'[5] from national labour courts. This international Court has now adopted binding legal positions in respect of discrimination in employment, wages, unfair dismissal, employee's privacy protection, occupational safety. Its legal positions have already changed certain aspects of the national labour laws of some members of the Council of Europe (CoE). The fascinating

1. Bob Hepple. Rights at Work Global, European and British Perspectives. London: Sweet & Maxwell, 2005. pp. 6–7.
2. Keith David Ewing, The Human Rights Act and Labour Law. Industrial Law Journal 27(4) (1998): 275–292; H. Collins, Theories of Rights as Justifications for Labour Law In: G Davidov, B Langillc, editors, 'The Idea of Labour Law'. Oxford: OUP, 2011, 137; G Mundlak, Labor Rights and Human Rights: Why Don't the Two Tracks Meet? Comparative Labor Law and Policy Journal 34 (2012): 237; L Compa, Solidarity and Human Rights. New Labor Forum 18 (2009): 38; K. Kolben, Labor Rights as Human Rights? Virginia Journal of International Law 50(2) (2010).
3. Ebert Franz Christian, Martin Oelz, Bridging the Gap between Labour Rights and Human Rights: The Role of ILO Law in Regional Human Rights Courts. ILO (2012): 2.
4. Bob Hepple, Future of Labour Law. The Comparative Laboratory Law Journal 17 (1995): 626.
5. Lo Faro, Responsabilità e sanzioni per sciopero illegittimo: cambia qualcosa in Italia dopo Laval?, in Giornale di diritto del lavoro e delle relazioni industriali, 2011, n. 3, p. 419.

evolutionary character of the European Convention of Human Rights (ECHR) makes me argue its growing applicability for the protection of wages and of occupational safety.

Substantive individual labour rights (also referred to as 'rights at work' in this volume) are the least researched area of the ECtHR's jurisprudence. These rights include fundamental employment rights such as the right for wages, for protection from unfair dismissal, from discrimination and the right to occupational safety at work. Substantive individual labour rights for the purposes of this research also comprise civil liberties that should be recognised or protected at the workplace, such as the right to freedom of religion, of expression and the right to respect for private life.

The research in this volume is based on the analysis of 347 cases, considered by the Strasburg bodies in the last fifty-three years (from 1963 until October 2016). The cases were considered chronologically in order to establish evolutionary trends in the ECtHR's reasoning and its interconnection with the policy changes in European countries.

The present research comprises four parts, each devised in chapters which are further organised in sections and subsections. Every chapter sets out brief conclusions.

Part I provides research on theories presently dealing with the history, tools and philosophic justification of the integration of social and labour rights in the ECHR. It includes analysis of the ECtHR's perception of the margin of appreciation, the balancing of rights and of the proportionality test as far as these concepts are used in the adjudication of 'employment law' cases.

The remaining three parts are dedicated to the jurisprudence of the ECtHR on protection of the rights at work. My division of the case law into three parts reflects the ECtHR's first cases on 'genuine' ECHR rights which are explicitly relevant to the protection of the rights at work. Accordingly, Part II explores the ECtHR's approach to the prohibition of forced labour (Article 4) and discrimination (Article 14).[6] Part III draws together my research on case law relating to the protection of civil liberties at work; specifically in the areas of the protection of privacy, the right to respect for private life and of the freedoms of religion and expression, including more minor references to freedom of association. Particular focus is drawn to cases about unfair dismissals.

Part IV explores the jurisprudence of the ECtHR on protection of wages and occupational safety at the workplace. These issues were initially outside the scope of the ECHR; however, the evolutionary interpretation of its norms allowed the ECtHR to adopt particular approaches to the relevant rights of employees, which are researched in two chapters. Each of them comprise sections setting out the author's reflections on how the ECtHR's interpretation of the ECHR may be formulated in respect of protection from psychosocial risks (PSR) at work, and in respect of the right to a decent wage.

In Conclusions the most important positions of the ECtHR in respect of the protection of individual labour rights are synthesised to emphasise their current and potential impact on the labour laws of the members of the CoE.

6. References to articles in this volume are to the European Convention on Human Rights, unless otherwise specified.

PART I

The Integration of Labour Rights in the European Convention on Human Rights

This part is devoted to the evolution of the ECHR, and highlights the widening of the scope of protected rights and the emergence of labour law cases before the ECtHR. In order to understand this expansion of the ECHR, which has been vividly described by commentators as an 'awakening of the sleeping beauty',[1] there is a need to trace the history of the Convention. It is also necessary to explore the legal concepts elaborated by the ECtHR for its justification of 'evolutive' interpretation and the use of these concepts in cases concerning labour rights. The ECtHR's approach to the cases concerning the protection of individual labour rights will be researched through investigating the concepts of the margin of appreciation, balancing and proportionality as those concepts have been used by the ECtHR in adjudicating cases.

1. This epithet is usually used to describe the rise of the ECtHR's authority in the 1970s; Jochen Frowein, first used this term in 1984, and it has now been adopted by a number of other scholars. *See*, Jochen Frowein, European Integration Through Fundamental Rights. University of Michigan Journal of Law Reform 5 (1984): 8; Ed Bates. The Evolution of the European Convention on Human Rights: From Its Inception to the Creation of a Permanent Court of Human Rights. New York: Oxford University Press, 2010, p. 277.

CHAPTER 1

History of the Convention: A Long Way to European Quasi-Constitutional Court

In this chapter the fundamental link between the ECHR and the protection of labour rights will be established, starting from the research of premises of social rights protection found in the original drafting of the ECHR. The development of the Conventional system will be traced, focusing on its role in the enlarged CoE after the accession of post-communist countries. In conclusion some reflections about the accession of the European Union ('*EU*') to the CoE will be formulated.

§1.01 DRAFTING OF THE ECHR

It is common to say that the ECHR was designed as an instrument of protection from totalitarianism, being drafted shortly after the fall of Nazi Germany against the background of post-war enlargement of totalitarian Soviet states.[2] As the Ex-President of the European Court noted, 'The Convention was an innovative response, perhaps even revolutionary, to genocide, atrocities and monstrosities of the Second World War and the period that preceded it'.[3] Since the Nuremberg judgments had established a new concept of international responsibility and consequently a new concept of national sovereignty, it was considered necessary to establish effective international guarantees for human rights.[4]

---

2. As W. Churchill put it in a speech in Strasburg on 12 August 1949, 'We have to... protect ourselves against any risk of being overrun, crushed by whatever form of totalitarian tyranny' Available at: http://www.coe.int/aboutcoe/index.asp?page = peresFondateurs&l = en (accessed 1 October 2014).
3. L. Wildhaber, De L'évolution Des Idées Sur Les Missions De La Cour Européenne Des Droits De L'homme in La Promotion de la Justice, Des Droits de L'homme Et Du Règlement Des Conflits Par Le Droit International edited by Marcelo Gustavo Kohen. Martinus Nijhoff Publishers, 2007, p. 644.
4. Gordon L. Weil. The European Convention on Human Rights: Background, Development and Prospects. Leyden: A.W. Sythoff, 1963, p. 22.

The fundamental human rights, listed solemnly in the Universal Declaration of Human Rights (UDHR) in 1948, needed some mechanism by which they could be enforced. By 1949 it had become rather evident to international society that International Covenant, which had to represent the international guarantee of human rights, would be very long in coming (in that time it was not yet clear that the rights would be divided into two separate Instruments[5]). The adoption of the ECHR by the countries of the CoE was a way of implementing the UDHR pending the finalisation of the International Covenant on Civil and Political Rights (ICCPR) and the International Covenant on Economic, Social and Cultural Rights (ICESCR).

In hindsight, it is obvious that the ten founding countries which comprised the CoE in 1949 would represent a more homogenous group of countries than eventually expanded numbers of the members of the UNO. Thus they could more easily reach consensus on what human rights were worthy of international recognition and protection, particularly taking into account that the political and civil rights concerned were already fixed in their domestic legislations.

This is supported by the Preamble of the ECHR, which states expressly that: 'the governments of European countries which are likeminded and have a common heritage of political traditions, ideals, freedom and the rule of law, to take the first steps for the collective enforcement of certain of the rights stated in the Universal Declaration'.

Drafting of the Convention began shortly after the creation of the CoE in 1948. It was not an easy process as even in this 'homogenous' circle of countries there were different views on the due scope of the future Convention, on the mechanism of protection and the possibility of restricting national sovereignty. The main points of dispute were the following: (1) the definition of rights; (2) the list of rights; (3) the process of supervision and the right for individual petition. The discussion around these points of controversy could contribute to the understanding of the roots for future expansion of the ECHR and therefore deserves closer examination.

[A] Dispute on Definition of Rights

According to the Papers of the First Session of the Committee of Ministers[6] held in Strasburg in 1949, the proposal to define each right was opposed by some representatives who argued that the rights mentioned were already 'abundantly dealt with.'[7] The French representative, M. Teitgen, thought that mere enumeration of a statement of principles such as in the UDHR, could be enough to be easily enforced by the European

5. For example, USSR and Syria opposed the idea of placing economic, social, and cultural rights in a separate instrument. *See* J. Whelan Daniel. Indivisible Human Rights: A History. University of Pennsylvania Press, 2011, p. 75.
6. Papers of the First Session of the Committee of Ministers, 1949. Strasbourg. Available at: http://www.coe.int/t/dgal/dit/ilcd/archives/selection/cm/1949Aug.pdf (accessed 1 November 2014).
7. *See* the opinion of the French representative M. Schuman. *Ibid.*, p. 34.

Court.[8] In contrast, and based primarily on their experience in drawing up constitutions for ex-colonies, the British favoured the precise definition of the rights to be included.

The final text of the ECHR ultimately does not provide definitions for each of the Human Rights. This left the Strasburg bodies with significant powers of interpretation which have, with the years, become the driving force of the evolution of the Convention. It may be presumed that the power of interpretation granted to the ECtHR was not intentional. It seems more probable that the rights were not defined as their meanings were already very familiar to the legal system of European states and were, as one party surmised, 'already protected thoroughly'.[9] As fairly noted former Vice-President of the European Commission of Human Rights J. A. Frowein: 'The countries did not expect that the European Convention would go further than their internal system'.[10] Evidently the final version of the Convention, which leaves to the ECtHR the power to interpret each right, is one the secrets of the Court's success. The ability to expand the protection upon certain individual labour rights emerged in case law only thanks to the possibility of particularly broad interpretations, for example, of Articles 3, 8, 11 and Article 1 to the Protocol N 1.

[B] Dispute on the List of Rights

It is remarkable that even at the stage of preparatory work there were ideas to create a 'complete code of all the freedoms and fundamental rights, and all the so-called social freedoms and rights'.[11] The Convention was perceived by some members of the drafting committee as a 'guarantee for further development of social justice in Europe'[12] although it was initially aimed at protecting basic civil and political rights.

The idea to include economic or social rights was in the air but it was rejected. One of the fathers of the Convention, Sir David Maxwell-Fyfe, found these rights to be 'too controversial and difficult of enforcement even in the changing state of social and international development in Europe'. In his view, their inclusion could jeopardise the wider acceptance of the ECHR.[13] This is true; the ECHR could not be ratified by Member States if it included social matters which required dictating the spending of particular states' budgets or other issues which were considered by countries in a very different way. The 'a-la-carte' concept of the European Social Charter and the process of its

8. Gordon L. Weil, *see supra* note 4, p. 28.
9. Ed Bates, *see supra* note 1, p. 114.
10. J.A. Frowein, The Transformation of the Constitutional Law through the ECHR. Israel Law Review 41(3) (2008): 490.
11. These are words said by Pierre-Henri Teitgen while presenting the Draft of the ECHR on 19 August 1949, cited from Ed Bates, *see supra* note 1, p. 59.
12. Words of the Socialist representative cited in Gordon L. Weil, *see supra* note 4, p. 12.
13. *See* Collected Edition of the 'Travaux Préparatoires' of the European ECHR on Human Rights: Preparatory Commission of the Council of Europe, Committee of Ministers, Consultative Assembly, 11 May–8 September 1949. Council of Europe. BRILL, 1975, p. 116.

creation and ratification confirmed the impossibility of fixing social rights in the ECHR in the 1950s.[14]

The approach of the drafters to social rights was vividly expressed by Teitgen:

> Certainly, professional freedoms and social rights, which have in themselves a fundamental value, must also, in the future, be defined and protected; but everyone will understand that it is necessary to begin at the beginning and to guarantee political democracy in the European Union, and then to co-ordinate our economies, before undertaking the generalisation of social democracy?[15]

It is curious to note that Teitgen was one of the judges of the ECtHR in 1978 which considered the case *Tyrer v. The United Kingdom*, where for the first time the European Convention was pronounced to be a 'living instrument'.[16] This approach later permitted the significant widening of the scope of rights guaranteed by the ECHR, including also the 'professional and social rights' as mentioned by Teitgen during the drafting process.

[C] Dispute on Establishment of the Process of Supervision and the Right for Individual Petition

The structure, the powers of relevant bodies and how supervision would be exercised was another area of controversy. The authors of the Conventions completely overestimated the willingness of certain states to create a human rights instrument that threatened their sovereignty; in 1949–1950 the governments of those states had little desire to see an instrument that could, as they saw it, meddle in internal affairs in any way.[17]

The threat to the national sovereignty was (and still is) the most difficult aspect of the ECHR for all Member States – old and new. Understandably, States were more willing to adopt rights that were already fixed in their respective national law but saw a danger in the possibility of external control over domestic legislation. This is why initially only the possibility of interstate claims was provided for in the European Convention. The States were sure that this procedure would be used in very rare cases due to stable diplomatic relations between the European countries. The right for individual claims and the acceptance of the jurisdiction of the ECtHR were only set out as optional clauses in the ECHR.[18]

---

14. On the particularity of the ESC, *see* Khaliq, U. and Churchill, R., The European Committee on Social Sights: Putting Flesh on the Bare Bones of the European Social Charter In: Langford, M, editor. Socio-Economic Rights Jurisprudence: Emerging Trends in International and Comparative Law. New York and Cambridge: Cambridge University Press, 2009, pp. 428–452.
15. Teitgen Report, TP Vol. I at 218, cited from Ed Bates, *see supra* note 1, p. 65.
16. ECtHR, Tyrer v. The United Kingdom (5856/72) 25 April 1978, para. 31. *See also*: Letsas, George, The ECHR as a Living Instrument: Its Meaning and Its Legitimacy (14 March 2012). Available at SSRN: http://ssrn.com/abstract=2021836 (accessed 20 September 2014).
17. Ed Bates, *see supra* note 1, p. 77.
18. *See* more on the acceptance of optional clauses in Ed Bates, *see supra* note 1, pp. 105–107, 133–139.

The adoption of these optional clauses was a very slow process; most of the countries used at the beginning a 'short-term' adherence to these clauses as testing the system and monitoring the activities of the European Commission of Human Rights. The Commission was at that stage the most important player as only single cases were brought before the ECtHR which was established in 1959. Gradually, the consideration of cases by the Commission gained confidence of the States to the Conventional mechanism and finally all members of the CoE accepted the right of individual petition.[19]

The further acceptance of optional clauses by all Member States is to the credit of the Commission, which acted very cautiously, knowing that every mistake it made could bury the bright ideas of the ECHR and transform it to a 'paper tiger'.

§1.02 DEVELOPMENT OF THE CONVENTION SYSTEM

The acceptance of optional clauses opened a new page in the history of the ECtHR. This acceptance allowed violations of human rights to be dealt with in a very bold way. The popularity of the ECtHR grew with the years; gaining authority on both European and world law stages[20] and, as noted by Ed Bated, '[the ECtHR] became more willing to interpret the Convention as a type of European Bill of Rights relevant to contemporary Europe'.[21] The changes brought to the ECHR by Protocol 11[22] created a new permanent Court, abolishing the two-tiered system along with the Commission. The ECHR has started to acquire a 'truly constitutional character for the whole European continent'.[23]

These reforms were particularly important in the context of the CoE expanding to include new Member States, such as Ukraine, Russia, Georgia or Azerbaijan, as these States had a very different history, understanding and perception of human rights compared with the European countries which were the initial adopters of the ECHR. The ECtHR now has a 'missionary function',[24] which is to bring the light of human rights to the most 'obscure' places of the continent. This missionary function is important in protecting labour rights, even if these rights are not directly mentioned in

19. Lecture of the member of the European commission of human rights Henry G. Schermers, Protocol 11 to the European ECHR on Human Rights. Available at: http://europainstitut.de/fileadmin/schriften/317.pdf (accessed 20 October 2014).
20. *See* on the use of the Court's case law by Inter-American court of human rights Gerald L. Neuman, Import, Export, and Regional Consent in the Inter-American Court of Human Rights, The European Journal of International Law 19(1) (2008): 101–123.
21. Ed Bates, *see supra* note 1, p. 151.
22. Protocol No. 11 to the Convention for the Protection of Human Rights and Fundamental Freedoms, restructuring the control machinery established thereby, adopted 11 May 1994, entered in force 1 November 1998.
23. Paul Mahoney, The European Convention On Royal Rights: Royalty, Aristocracy And The European Convention On Human Rights In: Marcelo Gustavo Kohen editor. 'La Promotion de la Justice, Des Droits de L'homme Et Du Règlement Des Conflits Par Le Droit International'. Martinus Nijhoff Publishers, 2007, p. 341.
24. A.W.B. Simpson. The ECHR: the First half Century. University of Chicago Fulton Lecture Series, 2004, p. 12. Available at: http://chicagounbound.uchicago.edu/cgi/viewcontent.cgi?article=1017&context=fulton_lectures (accessed 30 October 2014).

the ECHR. For example, in *Danilenkov and other v. Russia,*[25] the ECtHR required the State to create effective systems to protect trade union members from discrimination, thus demonstrating the values of a true democratic society and teaching Russia to implement laws and principles which were alien for the legal system of the country for the immediately preceding seventy years.

§1.03 ACCESSION OF THE EU TO THE COUNCIL OF EUROPE

The accession of the EU to the CoE might be another step in the development of the Convention system of human rights protection which could have a tangible impact on the protection of labour rights in the EU. The problematic aspects of the accession and of the subsequent expansion of the ECHR over the existing EU institution and laws have already been described by numerous scholars.[26] Most have expressed a hope that accession would raise the status of labour rights within the EU legal order, contribute to the development of anti-discrimination protection[27] and speculated that it might be possible to argue that the decisions of the Court of Justice of the European Union (CJEU) in *Viking* and *Laval* infringe ECHR rights.[28] During the years of negotiations between the EU and the CoE it was difficult to imagine that the CJEU would be an obstacle to the process of integration. The recent opinion of the CJEU has revealed the main non-technical problem of this process.[29] An overt race for power on the part of the CJEU shows that human rights are not treated as a fundamental legal value but are rather treated as being a subsidiary 'thing' to the autonomy of the European legal system.[30] As it is unlikely that the ECtHR would grant the EU special Bosphorus-type

25. ECtHR, Danilenkov and others v. Russia (67336/01) 30 July 2009.
26. Rick Lawson, A Twenty-First-Century Procession of Echternach: The Accession of the EU to the European Convention on Human Rights In: Filip Dorssemont, Klaus Lörcher, Isabelle Schömann, editors. 'The European Convention on Human Rights and the Employment Relation'. Oxford: Hart Publishing, 2013. pp. 47–60; Tobias Lock, EU Accession to the ECHR: Implications for Judicial Review in Strasbourg. European Law Review 6 (2010): 777–798.
27. Nicole Busby, Rebecca Zahn, The EU and the ECHR: Collective and Non-discrimination Labour Rights at a Crossroad? International Journal of Comparative Labour Law and Industrial Relations 2 (2014): 153–174; Niklas Bruun, Prohibition of Discrimination: Article 14 European Convention on Human Rights In: Filip Dorssemont, Klaus Lörcher, Isabelle Schömann, editors. The European Convention on Human Rights and the Employment Relation'. Oxford: Hart Publishing, 2013, p. 377; Olivier De Schutter, The Prohibition of Discrimination under European Human Rights Law Relevance for EU Racial and Employment Equality Directives. European Commission, 2005, pp. 52–53.
28. J. Fudge, Constitutionalizing Labour Rights in Europe In: T. Campbell, K. Ewing & A. Tompkins, editors. 'The Legal Protection of Human Rights: Sceptical Essays'. Oxford: Oxford University Press, 2011, p. 263; Phil Sypris, The Treaty of Lisbon: Much Ado...But about What? Israel Law Review 37(3) (2008): 219–235; Vilija Velyvyte, The Right to Strike in the EU after Accession to the ECHR: A Practical Assessment In: Mark Freedland, Jeremias Prassl, editors. 'Viking, Laval and Beyond'. Bloomsbury Publishing, 2014, pp. 75–94.
29. Opinion 2/13 of the CJEU, adopted 18 December 2014.
30. *Ibid.*, paras 179–200.

deference after accession,[31] the rulings of the CJEU itself could be the subject of ECtHR scrutiny. Therefore, even labour law cases between the EU as employer and employees, which had been rejected by the Strasburg Court earlier,[32] should be considered as admissible if accession takes place.

The reluctance of the CJEU to be bound by the ECtHR's decisions was supported by reference to the autonomy of the EU. The Luxemburg Court stated that the ECHR may affect its powers only if there is no adverse effect on the autonomy of the EU legal order, and it must not have the effect of binding the EU and its institutions, in the exercise of their internal powers, to a particular interpretation of the rules of EU law.[33] One might wonder what is the sense of accession if the legal positions of the ECtHR will not be considered binding for the EU? The arguments of rare defenders of this view, calling for the concerns of the CJEU to be accommodated and to revise the Agreement on the accession of the EU to the ECHR[34] are not satisfactory. The references to constitutional values in cases concerning the ECtHR's authority become more strident when its decisions are uncomfortable for national governments.[35] Regrettably, the opinion of the CJEU is along the same lines. Its unwillingness to become a 'junior' court[36] risks drastically distortion of the initial will to bind the EU institutions to the provisions of the ECHR but also risks the withdrawal from the ECHR of countries which are more concerned with 'sovereignty' than with human rights.

This opinion of the CJEU protracts the process of integrating the EU with the ECHR; the CJEU's remarks render the contents of any future agreement on accession rather unpredictable. Therefore, I will refrain from commenting on the possible impact

31. Olivier de Schutter, Bosphorus Post-Accession: Redefining the Relationship between the European Court of Human Rights and the Parties to the Convention In V. Kosta, N. Skoutaris, V. Tzevelekos, editors. 'The Accession of the EU to the European Convention on Human Rights'. Hart Publishing, 2013, p. 177.
32. ECtHR, Connolly v. 15 Member States of the European Union (73274/01) inadmissible 9 December 2008. *See* more in Lock, Tobias, Beyond Bosphorus: The European Court of Human Rights' Case Law on the Responsibility of Member States of International Organisations Under the European Convention on Human Rights (25 February 2010). Human Rights Law Review 10 (2010): 529–545. Available at SSRN: http://ssrn.com/abstract=1603937 (accessed 12 April 2015).
33. Opinion 2/13 of the CJEU, adopted 18 December 2014, paras 183–184.
34. Halberstam, Daniel, 'It's the Autonomy, Stupid!' A Modest Defense of Opinion 2/13 on EU Accession to the ECHR, and the Way Forward (20 February 2015). University of Michigan Public Law Research Paper No. 439. Available at SSRN: http://ssrn.com/abstract=2567591(accessed 13 April 2015).
35. *See*, for example, the reaction of the Russian authorities to the judgment in Markin case, to Anchugov and Gladkov v. Russia (11157/04 and 15162/05) 4 July 2013, or the British reaction to cases on prisoners' right to vote. *See*, for instance, Marina Aksenova, Anchugov and Gladkov is not Enforceable: the Russian Constitutional Court Opines in its First ECtHR Implementation Case. Published 25 April 2016 at: opiniojuris.org/2016/04/25/anchugov-and-gladkov-is-not-enforceable-the-russian-constitutional-court-opines-in-its-first-ecthr-implementation-case/ (accessed 20 September 2016).
36. *See* the words of UK Lord Chancellor and Minister of Justice, Christopher Grayling, European Scrutiny Committee 30th report, 21 January 2015, cited from Sionaidh Douglas-Scott, Opinion 2/13 and the 'elephant in the room': A response to Daniel Halberstam. http://www.verfassungsblog.de/opinion-213-and-the-elephant-in-the-room-a-response-to-daniel-halberstam/#.VSuho_msVqU (accessed 10 April 2015).

of ECtHR legal positions on EU labour law for the rest of this book, as all these reflections risk being too hypothetical.

Concluding the historical research, the question of the justification of extending the ECHR will be analysed. The ECtHR justifies it by referring to the 'live character' of the ECHR and by stating that there is no 'water-tight division' separating economic and social rights from the field covered by the ECHR.[37] Therefore the theory of indivisible human rights and the concept of the 'live' character of the ECHR are fundamental for the protection of labour rights under the ECHR and would be researched further.

37. ECtHR, Airey v. Ireland (6289/73) 9 October 1979, para. 26.

CHAPTER 2

Integration of Labour Rights into the ECHR

The fascinating history of how the ECHR developed over time provides a unique insight into how an international instrument originally designed to protect classical political and civil rights was expanded, to protect certain social and economic rights. In this chapter, the research will focus on the philosophic roots of the expansion of the ECHR on labour rights, analysing the capabilities theory of Amartya Sen and the interpretation of the ECHR as a 'living instrument'.

Further the ECtHR's perception of the margin of appreciation, granted to its subject States as far as protection of the rights at work is concerned, will be researched and the application of the principle of proportionality in the adjudication of ECHR employment cases will be investigated.

§2.01 INDIVISIBILITY OF HUMAN RIGHTS AND INTEGRATED APPROACH TO THE INTERPRETATION OF THE ECHR

The Vienna Declaration and Programme of Action, adopted at the World Conference on Human Rights in June 1993, proclaims solemnly: 'The international community must treat human rights globally in a fair and equal manner, on the same footing, and with the same emphasis.'[38]

As scholars note, the aim of this principle of indivisibility is to prevent governments from claiming to defend human rights by 'cherry-picking' from the list of rights,[39] and to ensure the treatment of human rights as an interdependent and

38. Vienna Declaration and Programme of Action, adopted by the World Conference on Human Rights in Vienna on 25 June 1993. Available at: http://www.ohchr.org/en/professionalinterest/pages/vienna.aspx (accessed 20 November 2014).
39. Françoise Bouchet-Saulnier, Droits de l'homme, droit humanitaire et justice internationale, Acte Sud 2002, pp. 23 and 27.

indivisible whole, rather than a menu from which one may freely select (or choose not to select).[40]

This principle has, however, largely failed in practice. Although it is widely acknowledged that the basic social and economic rights are 'indivisible from the enjoyment of civil and political liberties,'[41] there is still a significant gap between the level of efficiency of two monitoring systems in particular on the level of the CoE. Economic and social rights are stipulated in the European Social Charter, which, in contrast to the European Convention on Human Rights, does not provide a mechanism for individual applications.[42] This evident shortcoming led the Secretary-General of the CoE Walter Schwimmer, who compared the effects of ECHR and of the European Social Charter, to question rhetorically whether social rights are a less important category of human rights or whether they are even human rights at all.[43]

It must be noted that there were attempts to include certain economic and social rights in the ECHR, which would have provided an efficient mechanism of protection for those rights equal to the protection afforded to civil and political rights. The initiative was eventually rejected by the Committee of Ministers who concluded that the preparation of such a protocol was neither desirable nor expedient.[44] The Airey case,[45] which was mentioned above was a kind of catalyst for practical acknowledgement of the indivisibility of human rights. The ECtHR for the first time in a decision used the integrated approach[46] to the ECHR in order to overcome the initial focus of the ECHR upon political and civil rights to the exclusion of social and economic rights.[47]

In the Strasbourg jurisprudence the integration of rights indicates the ECtHR uncovering new facets of existing rights (e.g., the right to manifest one's religion by wearing a religious symbol at work;[48] or the right to appeal against unfair dismissal on

40. Donnelly Jack. Universal Human Rights in Theory and Practice. Cornell University Press, 2013, p. 28.
41. Indivisible Human Rights: The Relationship of Political and Civil Rights to Survival, Subsistence and Poverty. Human Rights Watch, 1992, p. 76.
42. The same arguments may be found in: Ida Elisabeth Koch. Human Rights As Indivisible Rights: The Protection of Socio-economic Demands Under the European Convention on Human Rights. Martinus Nijhoff Publishers, 2009, p. 324.
43. The speech of the Secretary General of the CoE Walter Schwimmer in Reforming the European Convention on Human Rights: A Work in Progress: a Compilation of Publications and Documents Relevant to the Ongoing Reform of the ECHR, CoE, 2009, p. 31.
44. Koch, *see supra* note 42, p. 321.
45. ECtHR, Airey v. Ireland (6289/73) 9 October 1979.
46. The integrated approach was first mentioned by C. Scott in 1989, referring to the idea of the 'permeability' of human rights norms, *see* Scott, Craig, Interdependence and Permeability of Human Rights Norms: Towards a Partial Fusion of the International Covenants on Human Rights. Osgoode Hall Law Journal 27(3) (1989): 769–878. Cited from M. Magdalena Sepulveda, The Nature of the Obligations under the International Covenant on Economic, Social and Cultural Rights. Intersentia (2003): 53.
47. The Court is rarely unanimous on this matter, for example in the recent case R.M.T. v. UK, Judges Ziemele, Hirvelä and Bianku emphasised in their Joint Concurring Opinion that the States Parties to the Convention have not given the Court the mandate to address the issues concerning their economic and social policies. ECtHR, National Union Of Rail, Maritime And Transport Workers v. The United Kingdom (31045/10) 8 April 2014.
48. ECtHR, Eweida and Others v. the United Kingdom (N 48420/10) 15 January 2013.

political grounds;[49] or the right to strike in solidarity[50]) and incorporates new rights into the original text of the ECHR (e.g., the right to access information concerning risks the employee is exposed to;[51] or the right to be reinstated in case of unfair dismissal[52]).

Philosophical roots of the integrated approach might be found in Sen's concept of freedom.[53] The research of Virginia Montavalou showed that the theory of capabilities may serve as a justification for the integrated approach.[54] An analysis of Strasburg case law on social matters leads us to conclude that the ECtHR's integrated approach is in fact in many aspects consistent with Sen's views on the concept of freedom and the European Convention is used by the ECtHR as an instrument to protect 'the real capacity for human beings to lead lives which we have reason to value'.[55]

Already in 1979, Sen stated that the framework of human rights misses 'some notion of "basic capabilities"'.[56] Basic capabilities are understood as 'the opportunity to achieve valuable combinations of human functioning'.[57] Sen rejects the conceptual differences between blocks of political/civil and economic/social rights,[58] and argues the necessity of protection of all the rights that affect a person's ability to function properly. Sen's attention was always centred to the practical implementation of human rights; to the protection of their validity.[59] In his famous book 'Development As Freedom', Sen noted that the notion of freedom 'involves both the processes that allow freedom of actions and decisions, and the actual opportunities that people have, given their personal and social circumstances'.[60]

This approach may be clearly seen in the Airley case, in which the applicant, who did not have money to pay for legal representation, and therefore was unable to claim for divorce, claimed that the State failed to protect her right to a fair trial. The respondent State argued that the applicant had the right to appear before the relevant judicial body without being represented by a lawyer. The ECtHR considered whether the applicant was in fact capable of obtaining a divorce without legal representation. Taking into account the complexity of the proceedings before the relevant judicial body

49. ECtHR, Redfearn v. United Kingdom, (47335/06) 6 November 2012.
50. ECtHR, The National Union Of Rail, Maritime And Transport Workers v. The United Kingdom (31045/10) 8 April 2014, para. 86.
51. ECtHR, Brincat and others v. Malta (60908/11, 62110/11, 62129/11, 62312/11, 62338/11) 24 July 2014.
52. ECtHR, Oleksandr Volkov v. Ukraine (21722/11) 9 January 2013.
53. It is curious that in Sen's motherland – India – the right for just and humane conditions of work was integrated with the 'right to livelihood'. *See* Ben Saul, David Kinley, Jaqueline Mowbray. The International Covenant on Economic, Social and Cultural Rights: Cases, Materials, and Commentary. Oxford University Press, 2014, p. 280.
54. *See* Virginia Mantouvalou, Labour Rights in the European Convention on Human Rights: An Intellectual Justification for an Integrated Approach to Interpretation. Human Rights Law Review 13(1) (2013): 549–551.
55. Brian A Langille, Core Labour Rights – The True Story (Reply to Alston). European Journal of International Law 16(3) (2005): 432.
56. A. Sen. Tanner Lecture: Equality of What? Stanford University, 1979. Available at: http://tannerlectures.utah.edu/_documents/a-to-z/s/sen80.pdf (accessed 23 November 2014).
57. A. Sen, Elements of a Theory of Human Rights. Philosophy & Public Affairs 32(4) (2004): 332.
58. *Ibid.*, pp. 345–348.
59. A. Sen, Europa e il mondo - Quale sviluppo nel prossimo futuro? Lettera internazionale 2005, 84, p. 9.
60. A. Sen. Development as Freedom. First Anchor Books Edition, 2000, p. 17.

and the 'emotional involvement that is scarcely compatible with the degree of objectivity required by advocacy in court'[61] the ECtHR judged that it was improbable that an applicant could effectively present her own case in circumstances such as these. The ECtHR noted that 'the Convention is intended to guarantee not rights that are theoretical or illusory but rights that are practical and effective,' and found that the applicant's right for fair trial had been violated because although the applicant had the legal right to represent herself before the divorce court, she was not in reality capable of representing herself properly and the State had done nothing to remedy the situation.

Although Sen refrains from listing the basic capabilities,[62] it does not seem outside the realms of possibility to suggest that the ability to properly argue your case before a court might be one of those capabilities. Sen does not list a definitive list of what he considers to be basic capabilities because he argues that the creation of a 'fixed list [of capabilities], emanating entirely from pure theory, is to deny the possibility of fruitful public participation on what should be included and why.'[63]

Sen proposes open public reasoning to be central for the understanding of human rights, and supposes that this is the way to definitively settle disputes about coverage and content.[64] This is another important point for the justification of the integrated approach of the ECtHR. The expansion of the ECHR and its coverage of certain labour rights go hand in hand with the development of human rights protection in European countries. The ECtHR is always very attentive to recent trends in human rights' protection on both national and international levels. When the ECtHR finds that the majority of European countries have achieved consensus in an approach to a certain right, it takes it as a sign to introduce new rights into its interpretation of the ECHR or to reveal new 'facets' of already existing rights. This argument can be illustrated with its decision in the *K. Markin v. Russia* case, where the ECtHR, having undertaken a comparative analysis of the contemporaneous European experience, found that Article 8 (in conjunction with Article 14) provided the right for paternity leave without discrimination. Another example can be found in *Sorensen and Rasmussen v. Denmark,*[65] where the ECtHR held that Article 11 of the ECHR contains a 'negative right of association or, put in other words, a right not to be forced to join an association' and found that the practice of concluding closed-shop agreements violated the freedom of association. In that case much attention was drawn to the legislation of European

61. ECtHR, Airey v. Ireland, para. 24.
62. M. Nussbaum created a list of central human functional capabilities, which in her view 'gives the basis for determining a decent social minimum in a variety of areas'. *See* M. Nussbaum. Women and Human Development. The Capabilities Approach. Cambridge University Press, 2000, p. 79. Available at: http://genderbudgeting.files.wordpress.com/2012/12/nussbaum_women_capab ilityapproach2000.pdf (accessed 27 November 2014).
63. A. Sen. Capabilities, Lists, and Public Reason: Continuing the Conversation, Feminist Economics 10(3) (2004): 77–80.
64. A. Sen. Elements of a Theory of Human Rights, Philosophy & Public Affairs 32(4) (2004): 322.
65. ECtHR, Sorensen and Rasmussen v. Denmark (52562/99 52620/99) 11 January 2006.

countries, the provisions of international instruments and expressed views of the European Committee of Social Rights.[66]

This case is a useful illustration of how the ECtHR can rely on, using Sen's words, 'open public reasoning' to support its conclusions. As a result, the negative aspect of the freedom of association was finally integrated to the Article 11, in spite of the fact that the provision banning compulsory membership in associations was deliberately excluded from the text of the ECHR during the drafting process.[67]

In work prepared for the International Labour Organisation (ILO), Sen focused on the necessity of elaborating basic rights, whether they were legislated or not, as being essential to decent society.[68] Using the integrative approach, the ECtHR seems to elaborate these basic rights which have roots in the text of the original ECHR, as illustrated by the following examples:

(i) *Demir and Baikara v. Turkey*[69] and *Enerji Yapi-Yol Sen v. Turkey*[70] recognises the rights to collective bargaining and to strike.
(ii) *Brincat and other v. Malta* is an example of the ECtHR interpreting Article 8 as providing employees with the right to receive information about working conditions.[71]
(iii) In *R.Sz. v. Hungary*[72] the ECtHR set a rule of wage protection against excessive taxation.
(iv) Finally, in numerous cases the ECtHR has underlined the importance of protection from discrimination in employment and social security relation.[73]

This is a very brief review of basic labour rights which emerges in examining ECtHR jurisprudence and its use of the integrative approach. There is a clear omission regarding the right to work. The ECtHR expressly underlined the absence of this right in several judgments.[74] However, this omission cannot be interpreted as the ECtHR's reluctance to acknowledge the basic or fundamental character of the right to work. The integrative approach has limits of application within the ECHR. It is not easy to outline these limits in the ECtHR's jurisprudence. The right to work could be incorporated into Article 8 by interpreting it as saying that work is an inherent part of private life. As Sen said: 'Employment can be an element of self-respect, and also of the other people's

66. As if the ECtHR was following Sen's advice 'not to confine the domain of public reasoning to a given society only', *see* A. Sen. Elements of a Theory of Human Rights, p. 349.
67. Gordon L. Weil, *see supra* note 4, p. 68.
68. A. Sen, Work and Rights. International Labour Review 139(2) (2000): 122.
69. ECtHR, Demir and Baykara v. Turkey [GC] (34503/97) 12 November 2008.
70. ECtHR, Enerji Yapi-Yol Sen c. Turquie (68959/01), 21 April 2009.
71. ECtHR, Brincat and others v. Malta (60908/11 et al.) 24 July 2014.
72. ECtHR, R.Sz. v. Hungary (41838/11) 2 July 2013, *see also* Á.A. v. Hungary (22193/11) 23 September 2014, P.G. v. Hungary (18229/11) 23 September 2014.
73. *See*, for example, ECtHR, Thlimmenos v. Greece [GC] (No. 34369/97), 6 April 2000, Danilenkov and others v. Russia (67336/01) 30 July 2009, Andrejeva v. Latvia, (55707/00) 18 February 2009.
74. *See* ECtHR, Panfile v. Romania (13902/11) 20 March 2012, Sobczyk v. Poland (25693/94, 27387/95) 26 October 2000, Torri And Others v. Italy (11838/07 2302/07) 24 January 2012.

respect towards a person'.[75] The ECtHR itself once held that 'in the course of their working lives ... the majority of people have a significant, if not the greatest, opportunity of developing relationships with the outside world'.[76]

Therefore, there are both conceptual and jurisprudential premises for integrating right to work into the European ECHR. What keeps the ECtHR from deducing this right? A possible answer is that the right to work is a complex socio-economic right that requires much from the State and touches upon such 'pain points' as employment policy, protection from unemployment, creating of new workplaces, etc. At present, the relevant European States have differing views on these matters, the integration of the right to work to the right for respect for private life would be artificial, unless reached naturally as a result of the domestic development of labour and social security legislations in those states.

These deliberations lead us to the idea that European consensus on issues of human rights acts as a certain limit of application of the integrative approach. Where consensus has been established, the ECtHR can be bolder in protecting those rights even in the absence of there being direct provisions about them in the ECHR.[77]

Concluding the analysis of the integrative approach, it must be said that it is the only effective answer to factual 'divisibility' of human rights. Even if it 'does not by magic dissolve the boundaries between the two sets of rights'[78] it has created one more tool (and the most efficient one) for the protection of certain labour rights which have 'nearness or proximity'[79] to the ECHR.

§2.02 ECHR AS A 'LIVING INSTRUMENT'

It was already noted above that the perception of the ECHR as a 'living instrument' was the key for widening the scope of rights originally guaranteed by the ECHR. The ECtHR's jurisprudence shows that this approach to the ECHR continues to bear fruit. For example, in the recent case of *R.M.T. v. UK*,[80] the ECtHR concluded that the right to secondary strike, although absent from the text of the ECHR itself, was 'an accessory aspect of trade union activity',[81] protected under Article 11.

The words 'living instrument' were used by the ECtHR for the first time *Tyrer v. the United Kingdom*,[82] where the ECtHR underlined the importance of interpreting the

75. A. Sen, Emploi, Institutions et technologie: Quelques problèmes de politique générale, Revue international de travail. vol. 135 (1996), no 3-4, p. 488.
76. ECtHR, Niemietz v. Germany (13710/88) 16 December 1992, para. 29.
77. *See*, for example, the ECtHR's arguments in Markin v. Russia [GC] (30078/06) 22 March 2012, para. 99, for the opposite example where the absence of consensus lead to refusal to find violation, *see* Stec and others v. UK (65731/01, 65900/01) 12 April 2006, para. 64.
78. Koch, *see supra* note 42, p. 280.
79. *Ibid.*
80. ECtHR, The National Union Of Rail, Maritime And Transport Workers v. The United Kingdom (31045/10) 8 April 2014.
81. *Ibid.*, para. 87.
82. ECtHR, Tyrer v. the United Kingdom (5856/72) 25 April 1978, para. 31. *See also*: Letsas, George, The ECHR as a Living Instrument: Its Meaning and its Legitimacy (14 March 2012). Available at SSRN: http://ssrn.com/abstract=2021836 (accessed 20 September 2014).

ECHR in light of contemporaneous conditions, taking into account the then-current development and commonly accepted standards in the concerned sphere. This was a starting point for the 'extensive use of evolutive interpretation'.[83] This method, even without being directly mentioned in the majority of the cases, largely determined the development of the human rights protection under the ECHR.

Scholars note that the application of this concept means that the interpretations of the ECtHR's decisions must be made having regard to the evolving values in European societies and to the new human rights problems brought about by the advances in science and technology which could not have been imagined back in 1950.[84] These adjustments, for instance, lead the ECtHR to expand the protection of private life to take into account rights regarding electronic correspondence and the use of Internet at work;[85] to argue the necessity of applying contemporary protective measures as far as occupational health was concerned.[86]

The roots of this concept might be found both in the text of the ECHR, which was intended as 'the first steps for the collective enforcement of certain of the rights stated in the Universal Declaration'[87] and in the approach of the European judges to the interpretation of the ECHR. Judge Sorensen in 1975 proclaimed the ECHR to be a 'living legal instrument' and emphasised the need to take into account current circumstances of life by using an evolutive interpretation method.[88] The Justice of the Supreme Court of the United Kingdom (UK) suggests that the expression 'living instrument' is reminiscent of the expression '[a] living tree capable of growth and expansion within its natural limits', used by Canadian judge Lord Sankey in 1930.[89]

The evolutive approach to interpretation has never been applied unanimously by the judges of the ECtHR. Moreover, the approach has been consistently criticised by the representatives of State-members and some leading scholars as being illegitimate and leading to unpredictable interpretations of the text of the ECHR which are contrary to the initial will of the States.[90]

83. George Letsas, The Truth in Autonomous Concepts: How To Interpret the ECHR. European Journal of International Law 15 (2004):299.
84. Matti Pellonpaa, Continuity And Change In The Case-Law Of The European Court Of Human Rights in 'La Promotion de la Justice, Des Droits de L'homme Et Du Règlement Des Conflits Par Le Droit International' edited by Marcelo Gustavo Kohen. Martinus Nijhoff Publishers, 2007, p. 409.
85. ECtHR, Copland v. the United Kingdom (62617/00) 3 April 2007.
86. ECtHR, Vilnes and Others v. Norway (52806/09 22703/10) 5 December 2013.
87. Preamble to the ECHR.
88. M. Sorensen, Do the Rights and Freedoms Set Forth in the ECHR in 1950 Have the Same Significance in 1975? In: Pierre-Henri Teitgen editor. 'Forth ECHR Colloquy'. Rome, 1975, pp. 86–106.
89. Brenda Marjorie Hale Justice of the Supreme Court of the United Kingdom. Beanstalk or living instrument? How tall can the European Convention on Human Rights grow? Lecture at Grasham college 16 June 2011.
90. *See*, for example the speech of the British Prime-Minister J. Cameron (http://www.theguardian.com/law/2012/jan/25/cameron-speech-european-court-human-rights-full) or the article of the president of the Russian Constitutional Court V. Zorkin, The limits of pliability (Predel ustupchivosti) Rossyskaya gazeta, 29 October 2010. Available at: http://www.rg.ru/2010/10/29/zorkin.html, accessed 7 October 2013. Bellamy, Richard, The Democratic Legitimacy of International Human Rights Conventions: Political Constitutionalism and the European Convention on Human Rights. European Journal of International Law 25(4) (2014); Lord Hoffman.

Some judges of the ECtHR have emphasised the impossibility of implementing important international obligations when they are not defined sufficiently to enable the States to know exactly what would be involved,[91] and to the fact that the evolutive approach is at odds with the principle of legal certainty.[92] Judge Pinheiro Farinha noted: 'The ECtHR has jurisdiction not to re-draft the Convention but to apply it. Only the High Contracting Parties can alter the contents of the obligations assumed'.[93]

Former judge of the ECtHR, Franz Matscher, stated that the ECtHR has reached the limits of what can be regarded as treaty interpretation in the legal sense and at times has perhaps even crossed the boundary and entered territory which is no longer that of treaty interpretation but is actually legal policy-making.[94]

However, in spite of the critics and criticisms of the 'lack of clarity'[95] with the approach, the ECtHR still interprets each right in accordance with various contemporaneous trends, together with relevant legal and social developments in Europe.[96] This approach has been indispensable in the sphere of protecting labour rights as many of the rights and freedoms are defined in the ECHR in 'too general terms to be fully self executing'.[97] Scholars suppose that the lack of precision in the terms of the ECHR leads to the emergence of the 'creative legislative element' in the ECtHR's power of interpretation, comparable to that of the judiciary in common law countries.[98]

Understanding of the evolutive interpretation of the ECHR is possible through an analysis of the limits of its application and its sources. The ECtHR has faced the necessity of delimiting the use of the evolutive interpretation of the ECHR. In *Johnston and others v. Ireland* it underlined that 'the Court cannot, by means of an evolutive interpretation, derive from these instruments a right that was not included therein at the outset, this is particularly so here, where the omission was deliberate'.[99] However, as we will see further, this statement did not prevent the ECtHR to conclude, for example, the right not to join trade union as being inherent to Article 11, although that negative right was deliberately excluded from the text in the drafting process.[100]

European Human Rights – A Force for Good or a Threat to Democracy? Lecture at the Dickson Poon School of Law, King's College London, 17 June 2014. Available at: http://www.kcl.ac.uk /law/newsevents/newsrecords/2013-14/assets/Lord-Phillips-European-Human-Rights--A-Forc e-for-Good-or-a-Theat-to-Democracy-17-June-2014.pdf (accessed 20 August 2014).

91. ECtHR, Golder v. The United Kingdom (4451/70) 21 February 1975. Separate opinion of Judge Fitzmaurice, para. 30.
92. Joint Concurring Opinion of Judges Villiger, Nussberger and De Gaetano in Lucky Dev v. Sweden (7356/10) 27 November 2014.
93. Partly Dissenting Opinion Of Judge Pinheiro Farinha in Marckx v. Belgium (6833/74) 13 June 1979, para. 4.
94. Judge Franz Matscher, Methods of Interpretation of the Convention In: R.St. J. Macdonald et al., editor. 'The European System for the Protection of Human Rights'. Martinus Nijhoff Publishers, 1993. pp. 69–70.
95. ECtHR, Concurring Opinion Of Judge Ziemele in O'Keeffe v. Ireland (35810/09) 28 January 2014, para. 10.
96. I. Foighel, Reflections of a Former Judge of the European Court of Human Rights In: S Lagoutte et al., editor. 'Human Rights in Turmoil'. Leiden: Brill, 2007, p. 277.
97. H. Waldock, The Effectiveness of the System Set up by the European Convention on Human Rights. Human Rights Law Journal 1 (1980): 9.
98. *Ibid.*
99. ECtHR, Johnston and others v. Ireland (9697/82) 18 December 1986, para. 53.
100. ECtHR, Sorrensen and Rassmussen v. Denmark [GC] (52562/99 52620/99) 11 January 2006.

Another limit might be found in the acknowledgement of the rule that any interpretation must not place an impossible or disproportionate burden on the States. This rule concerns the imposition of the positive obligations on the States to ensure the protection of ECHR rights.[101] For example, in *Brincat and others v. Malta,*[102] the ECtHR referred to this rule in the interpretation of the scope of the State's obligation to ensure the protection of the lives of employees.

The search for common standards, a 'constant thread running through the case law of the Court' is another limit of the application of the evolutive interpretation of the ECHR.[103] Common standards in human rights protection are both the limits and the sources of such interpretations. They limit the ECtHR in being too 'expansive' where common standards cannot be found on the one hand, and on the other, provide the ECtHR with evidence of the development of foreign law (with emphasis on European law), and of the relevant international instruments.

[A] The Use of Other International Instruments and Opinions of Other International Bodies

The possibility to refer to other international instruments has particular importance for the ECtHR's ability to make decisions about the protection of labour rights, given that in recognising the possibility of protecting those rights the ECtHR inevitably faces the lack of entirely appropriate provisions within the ECHR itself. The general basis for the ability to refer to other international instruments in its deliberations was acknowledged in *Cudak v. Lithuania*: 'The Convention, including Article 6, cannot be interpreted in a vacuum. The Court must therefore be mindful of the Convention's special character as a human rights treaty, and it must also take the relevant rules of international law into account'.[104] The Vienna Convention on the Law of Treaties (VCoLT) fixed the possibility to refer to 'other relevant rules of international law' for the interpretation of international treaty (Article 31.3 (C)). The direct reference to this discretion can be found in numerous labour law cases.[105] An analysis of the ECtHR's jurisprudence shows that the ECtHR resorted to Article 31.3 of the VCoLT as a means to support either an expansive or a restrictive reading of the ECHR when substantive issues of fundamental importance for the protection of human rights have presented themselves.[106]

Magdalena Forowicz, author of profound research on the consideration of international law by the ECtHR, noted that the ECtHR finds itself at the apex of two diametrically different judicial paradigms: an open paradigm characterised by a high

101. ECtHR, Koval and others v. Ukraine (22429/05) 15 November 2012, para. 73, between labour law cases –Vilnes and others v. Norway (52806/09 22703/10) 5 December 2013, para. 220.
102. ECtHR, Brincat and others v. Malta (60908/11 et al.) 24 July 2014, para. 101.
103. Sir Nicholas Bratza, Living Instrument or Dead Letter - the Future of the ECHR. European Human Rights Law Review (2) (2014): 124.
104. ECtHR, Cudak v. Lithuania (no. 15869/02), 23 March 2010, para. 56.
105. ECtHR, R.M.T. v. The UK (31045/10) 8 April 2014, para. 76; Demir and Baikara v. Turkey, para. 65, Cudak v. Lithuania, para. 56.
106. Magdalena Forowicz. The Reception of International Law in the European Court of Human Rights. Oxford University press, 2010, p. 59.

level of judicial activism and unhindered references to international law; and the closed paradigm, marked by judicial restraint and few references to international law.[107]

The most vivid application of the 'open paradigm' is represented by the *Demir and Baikara* case. In the Grand Chamber judgment the ECtHR directly stated the following:

> The Court, in defining the meaning of terms and notions in the text of the Convention, *can and must* take into account elements of international law other than the Convention, the interpretation of such elements by competent organs, and the practice of European States reflecting their common values. ...In this context, it is not necessary for the respondent State to have ratified the entire collection of instruments that are applicable in respect of the precise subject matter of the case concerned. It will be sufficient for the Court that the relevant international instruments denote a continuous evolution in the norms and principles applied in international law or in the domestic law of the majority of member States of the Council of Europe and show, in a precise area, that there is common ground in modern societies.[108]

The ECtHR further referred to the norms of the European Social charter, which were not ratified by Turkey, and concluded that the right for collective bargaining was 'an essential element' of the right to freedom of association. This approach triggered a wave of criticism both from judges of the ECtHR and scholars. It was said to be inconsistent with approaches taken by other international tribunals[109] and contrary to the VCoLT.[110]

Judge Wojtyczek in the Concurring Opinion to the judgment in *R.M.T. v. UK* noted:

> The fact that a treaty rule is not binding on at least one Contracting State is an argument against any kind of theological re-interpretation of the Convention in accordance with this rule. In my view, it is illegitimate to transform treaty rules that bind only some members of the Council of Europe into an element of the Convention for the Protection of Human Rights and Fundamental Freedoms, unless unequivocal rules of treaty interpretation require otherwise. In any case, invoking arguments such as a 'continuous evolution in the norms and principles applied in international law' or a 'strong international trend' usually discloses the fact that there are no strong arguments based on international law to support the chosen interpretation.[111]

In fact, the indirect application of norms which a relevant state refuses to ratify evidently cannot be justified in comprehensible legal terms. It must be noted that the *Demir and Baikara* decision remains the only example of such a questionable approach

---

107. Magdalena Forowicz, *see supra* note 106, p. 4.
108. ECtHR, Demir and Baikara v. Turkey, paras 85–86.
109. Ragnar Nordeide, Demir & Baykara v. Turkey - European Court of Human Rights Judgment on Rights of Trade Union Formation and of Collective Bargaining. American Journal of International Law 103(3) (2009): 572.
110. L. Wildhaber, A. Hjartarson, S. Donnely, No Consensus on Consensus? The Practice of the European Court of Human Rights. Human Rights Law Journal 33(7–12) (2013): 252.
111. Concurring opinion of the judge Wojtyczek, The R.M.T. v. United Kingdom (31045/10) 8 April 2014.

to labour law cases. It seems that the ECtHR was too bold in applying international law, based generally on the consent of States, in such an 'innovative' way. As the decision in *R.M.T. v. UK* shows, the ECtHR itself realised that this approach might lead to contradictions and confusion and noted:

> The Court would stress that its jurisdiction is limited to the Convention. It has no competence to assess the respondent State's compliance with the relevant standards of the ILO or the European Social Charter, the latter containing a more specific and exacting norm regarding industrial action.[112]

The ECtHR thus seems to have stepped back from its 'Demir and Baikara methodology,'[113] returning to classical interpretative use of other international instruments based on the VCoLT.

There are frequent references to ratified ILO Conventions and the ESC throughout ECtHR labour law cases. These documents mirror the development in the protection of labour rights and enable the ECtHR to fill certain gaps in the text of the ECHR.[114]

For example, it is acknowledged in the Strasbourg jurisprudence that the term 'forced or compulsory labour', left without definition in Article 4 of the ECHR, is defined in the light of the ILO Convention No. 29 concerning forced or compulsory labour.[115]

The lack of definition of the right to the freedom of association makes the ECtHR refer to the relevant provisions of the ILO Conventions, the ESC and the opinions of ILO bodies and the European Committee of Social Rights.[116] The analysis of these resources, for instance, made the ECtHR conclude the existence of 'core'[117] and 'additional' collective rights.[118]

112. ECtHR, The National union of rail, maritime and transport workers v. UK (31045/10) 8 April 2014, para. 106.
113. *See* more on this method in Klaus Lorcher, The New Social Dimension in the Jurisprudence of the European Court of Human Rights (ECtHR): The Demir and Baykara Judgment, Its Methodology and Follow-up In: Filip Dorssemont, Klaus Lörcher, Isabelle Schömann, editors. 'The European Convention on Human Rights and the Employment Relation'. Oxford: Hart Publishing, 2013, pp. 3–47.
114. *See* more on earlier references of the ECtHR to the ILO and ESC standards in J.G. Merrills. The Development of International Law by the European Court of Human Rights. Manchester University Press, 1988. pp. 202–203.
115. ECtHR, Van Der Mussele v. Belgium (8919/80) 23 November 1983, Siliadin v. France (73316/01) 26 July 2005, Stummer v. Austria (37452/02) 7 July 2011, Graziani-Weiss v. Austria (31950/06) 18 October 2011.
116. ECtHR, Trade Union Of The Police In The Slovak Republic And Others v. Slovakia (11828/08) 25 September 2012, para. 53, Vörđur Ólafsson v. Iceland (20161/06) 27 April 2010, para. 38, Associated Society Of Locomotive Engineers And Firemen (ASLEF) v. The United Kingdom (11002/05) 27 February 2007, para. 67, ECtHR, Veniamin Tymoshenko and others v. Ukraine (48408/12) 2 October 2014.
117. The right for collective bargaining, the negative freedom of association, *see* Demir and Baikara, Sorensen and Rasmussen v. Denmark [GC] (52562/99 52620/99) 11 January 2006.
118. For example, the right for the solidarity strike, *see* ECtHR, R.M.T. v. the UK (31045/10) 8 April 2014. In regard to the right to strike the ECtHR, noting that it was recognised by the International Labour Organisation's supervisory bodies as intrinsic corollary of the right to organise protected by ILO Convention C87, acknowledged its' non-absolute status in the context of the ECHR. *See* Enerji Yapi-Yol Sen c. Turquie (68959/01) 21 April 2009, paras 24, 32.

These international resources aid the ECtHR in its interpretation work, including in relation to the possible restriction of the freedom of association, set out in part 2 of Article 11. For example, in the recent case *Tymoshenko and others v. Ukraine*[119] the ECtHR had to ascertain whether the 'interests of national security or public safety, or the protection of health or morals or the rights and freedoms of others' might justify the prohibition of strikes by pilots of a private company. The ECtHR used references to the provisions of ILO Conventions and the European Social Charter in order to show that the derogative clause must be read in a restrictive way.[120]

It is curious to note that the notion of private life was interpreted by the ECtHR relying on the provisions of the Articles 1 and 2 of the European Social Charter and the interpretation given by the European Committee of Social Rights. In *Sidabras and Dziautas v. Lithuania,*[121] which concerned the restrictions in employment for former KGB officers, the ECtHR found that 'a far-reaching ban on taking up private sector employment does affect "private life"'.[122] The ECtHR attached 'particular weight' in this respect to the text of international instruments and reiterated that there was no watertight division separating the sphere of social and economic rights from the field covered by the ECHR. The wide interpretation of the right for private life opened the way to numerous applications claiming that unfair dismissal was in breach of the ECHR.[123]

Examples of the influence of international instruments on the protection of labour rights by the ECtHR demonstrate that the reference to the ILO Conventions and the European Social Charter is a significant source of further development of the protection of the labour rights under the ECHR. It permits the ECtHR to interpret the ECHR in 'harmony with other rules of international law of which it forms part'[124] and to effectively widen the scope of the ECHR.

[B] The Use of Comparative Research as the Basis of Reasoning

Comparative research helps the ECtHR to determine whether a matter is dealt with consistently by Member States and establishes the consensus among them, which in turn narrows the margin of appreciation in each particular case. References to domestic legislation legitimise the ECtHR's interpretative approach, which allows its decisions to be more easily accepted by Contracting States.[125] Therefore, two main ends might be achieved through comparative analysis – first, harmonisation of the ECHR interpretation with national legislations; and secondly, the enhancement of the authority of the ECtHR's decisions in the Member States.

119. ECtHR, Veniamin Tymoshenko And Others v. Ukraine (48408/12) 2 October 2014.
120. *Ibid.*, paras 32–49.
121. ECtHR, Sidabras and Dziautas v. Lithuania (55480/00 59330/00) 27 July 2004.
122. *Ibid.*, paras 31, 32, 47.
123. ECtHR, İhsan Ay v. Turkey (34288/04) 21 January 2014, Oleksandr Volkov v. Ukraine (21722/11) 9 January 2013, Pay v. UK (32792/05) 16 September 2008 (inadmissible); Schüth v. Germany (1620/03) 23 September 2010.
124. ECtHR, Rantsev v. Cyprus and Russia (25965/04) 7 January 2010, para. 274.
125. Magdalena Forowicz, *see supra* note 106, p. 9.

European consensus

The establishment of the European consensus is usually a sign for narrowing the margin of appreciation in a particular case[126] and means a greater scrutiny of the realisation of the State's positive or negative obligations under the ECHR. The finding of consensus is a very controversial point as even in the cases where it is directly established the ECtHR did not refer to all the members of the CoE. For example, in *Markin v. Russia*,[127] ECtHR found 'European consensus' on the question of men's entitlement to the parental leave even though only twenty-three countries out of forty-seven CoE members were mentioned in the study relied on by the ECtHR in that case.[128]

Eva Brems is right to call the European consensus as 'a rebuttable presumption in favour of the solution adopted by the majority of the Contracting Parties'.[129] Taking into account that the ECtHR is operating on the international stage, where obligations of the States depend on their consent to be bound by those obligations, this approach is highly debatable. Judge Wojtyczek has pointed that when a majority of States adopts a higher standard of protection of a right, it is not (in itself) a sufficient argument for imposing this standard on the minority of States which rejects it.[130] Scholars also criticise this approach as 'unsystematic and unscientific'[131] and lacking legal standards of application in a fair and predictable way.[132]

However this approach also has positive facets as well. It permits the ECtHR to render the ECHR open to the changes of the modern world and imbue it with a truly 'living' character as it creates an 'important link between common European values and the ECtHR's decision-making'.[133] Turning to the use of the European consensus approach in labour law cases it must be noted, that in the majority of cases where a reference to the European consensus can be found,[134] the ECtHR has also established

126. ECtHR, Fernández Martínez v. Spain (56030/07) 12 June 2014, para. 125.
127. ECtHR, Konstantin Markin v. Russia (30078/06) Chamber judgment 7 October 2010, paras 28–29.
128. Bilyaria Petkova noted that the ECtHR in contrast with its historical approach now tends to find European consensus if the particular legal trend among fewer Member States can be established. *See* Bilyaria Petkova, The Notion of Consensus as a Route to Democratic Adjudication? Cambridge Yearbook of European Legal Studies 14 (2011–2012): 663–697, 682.
129. Eva Brems, Human Rights: Universality and Diversity. Martinus Nijhoff Publishers, 2001, p. 420.
130. Concurring Opinion of Judge Wojtyczek, R.M.T. v. UK (31045/10) 8 April 2014, para. 9.
131. Aileen McHarg, Reconciling Human Rights and the Public Interest Conceptual Problems and Doctrinal Uncertainty in the Jurisprudence of the European Court of Human Rights. The Modern Law Review 62 (1999): 671, 687.
132. Brauch, Jeffrey A., The Margin of Appreciation and the Jurisprudence of the European Court of Human Rights: Threat to the Rule of Law (2005). Columbia Journal of European Law 11 (2005): 145.
133. Kanstantsin Dzchtsiaro, Interaction between the European Court of Human Rights and Member States: European Consensus, Advisory Opinions and the Question of Legitimacy In: Spyridōn I. Phlogaitēs, Tom Zwart, Julie Fraser, editors. 'The European Court of Human Rights and Its Discontents: Turning Criticism Into Strength'. Edward Elgar Publishing, 2013, p. 122.
134. ECtHR, R.M.T. v. The UK, Martínez Fernández v. Spain (56030/07) 12 June 2014, Sindicatul 'Păstorul Cel Bun' v. Romania (2330/09) 9 July 2013, Stummer v. Austria (37452/02) 7 July 2011.

the lack of consensus and left to the States a wide margin of appreciation. For example, the States were granted a wide margin of appreciation in relation to the regulation of solidarity strikes in *R.M.T. v. UK*[135] and in relation to the creation of trade unions by employees of a church in *Sindicatul 'Păstorul cel bun' v. Romania.*[136]

The establishment of the European consensus might influence the interpretation of the ECHR only if the right in question is not explicitly fixed in the ECHR. For example in the case *ADEFDROMIL v. France,*[137] which concerned the right of military personnel to form or join a trade union, the ECtHR ignored the respondent's arguments relying on the lack of consensus in this area of law. The ECtHR rejected the European consensus approach in its reasonings in this case, as the right to form and join trade unions was already clearly expressed in Article 11. The 'restrictions' of this right, mentioned in the second part of Article 11 in regard of servicemen, cannot 'impair the essence of the right to organise'.[138]

Comparative research of national approaches to the protection of a particular right is important in the labour law cases. It permits the ECtHR to determine certain trends and to follow them in its judgments, thus ensuring the dynamic interpretation of the ECHR. For example, in *Sorensen and Rasmussen v. Denmark,*[139] comparative research on the admissibility of closed-shop agreements in Member States showed that 'such agreements are not an essential means for securing the interests of trade unions and their members and that due weight must be given to the right of individuals to join a union of their own choosing without fear of prejudice to their livelihood'. The emergence of this trend enabled the ECtHR to overrule the original idea of the drafters of the ECHR in relation to Article 11: according to the 'Travaux Préparatoires', it was considered undesirable to introduce into the ECHR a rule under which 'no one may be compelled to belong to an association' because of the difficulties raised by the 'closed-shop system' in certain countries.[140]

In the earlier case of *Young, James and Webster v. The United Kingdom,* the ECtHR, considering the practice of closed-shop agreements, did not use any references to comparative studies and refrained from reviewing the closed-shop system as it related to the ECHR.[141] Therefore it can be argued that the reference to comparative study is used as a justification of enlarging of the ECHR's scope and overruling of previous jurisprudence. The same use may be found in *Markin v. Russia,*[142] where the decision in *Petrovic v. Austria*[143] was held to be outdated. For another example, *see*

135. ECtHR, R.M.T. v. UK(31045/10) 8 April 2014.
136. ECtHR, Sindicatul 'Păstorul Cel Bun' v. Romania (2330/09) 9 July 2013.
137. ECtHR, ADEFDROMIL c. France (32191/09) 2 October 2014.
138. *Ibid.*, para. 43.
139. ECtHR, Sorensen and Rasmussen v. Denmark (52562/99 52620/99) 11 January 2006, para. 70.
140. Report of 19 June 1950 of the Conference of Senior Officials, Collected Edition of the 'Travaux Préparatoires', vol. IV, p. 262, cited in Young, James and Webster v. The United Kingdom (7601/76 7806/77) 13 August 1981, para. 51.
141. ECtHR, Young, James and Webster v. The United Kingdom, para. 53.
142. ECtHR, Konstantin Markin v. Russia (30078/06) Chamber judgment 7 October 2010.
143. ECtHR, Petrovic v. Austria (20458/92) 27 March 1998.

Christine Goodwin v. The United Kingdom,[144] by which an earlier decision on the protection of the rights of transsexuals were overruled.[145]

One scholar noted that in connection with changes affecting European society, the ECtHR has a mandate to redirect European human rights law.[146] The contrasting approaches highlighted above show that the ECtHR does not redirect the European human rights law itself, but ascertains the trend of redirection which becomes apparent from comparative research of national legislations or an analysis of the relevant international instruments.

§2.03 MARGIN OF APPRECIATION, BALANCING AND PROPORTIONALITY TEST

The concept of the 'margin of appreciation' has become as slippery and elusive as an eel.[147]
Lord Lester

[A] The Margin of Appreciation

The margin of appreciation is the most unclear and controversial concept used by the ECtHR. The aims of this part are to understand the role of the margin of appreciation for the protection of labour rights, and to reveal its interconnection with the process of balancing rights and with the proportionality test.

The margin of appreciation emerged in the jurisprudence of the European Commission of Human Rights ('*Commission*') in the '*Cyprus cases*' (1958) and later in the Commission's presentations to the ECtHR in the *Lawless case* (1961).[148] Its roots can be found in continental administrative law.[149] The concept first appeared on the international scene in 1949, mentioned in proposals made by the European Movement in the debate about the kind of transnational human rights institutions, processes and

144. ECtHR, Christine Goodwin v. The United Kingdom (28957/95) 11 July 2002, para. 86.
145. ECtHR, Sheffield and Horsham v. The United Kingdom (22985/93 23390/94) 30 July 1998, para. 58.
146. Marton Varju, Transition as a Concept of European Human Rights Law. European Human Rights Law Review (2) (2009): 172.
147. QC Lord Lester of Herne Hill, The European Convention on Human Rights in the New Architecture of Europe: General Report, Proceedings of the 8th International Colloquy on the European Convention on Human Rights (Council of Europe) (1995), p. 227 at pp. 236–237 cited from Paul Mahoney, The Doctrine of the Margin of Appreciation Under the European Convention on Human Rights: Its Legitimacy in Theory and Application in Practice. Human Rights Law Journal 19(1) (2001): 1.
148. Yourow. The Margin of Appreciation Doctrine in the Dynamics of European Human Rights Jurisprudence. Martinus Nijhoff Publishers, 1996, p. 16.
149. *See* about the origins of the concept Andrew Legg. The Margin of Appreciation in International Human Rights Law: Deference and Proportionality. Oxford University Press, 2012, pp. 3–4.

norms which should be created in post-war Europe.[150] During the past sixty years, this concept has become one of the most important tools of the ECtHR.[151]

The importance of the concept of the margin of appreciation was recently acknowledged in Protocol 15 to the ECHR. This protocol, if ratified, will add to the Preamble a reference to the margin of appreciation and the subsidiary role of the ECtHR. The Brighton Declaration defines the margin of appreciation in the following way:

> [T]he States Parties enjoy a margin of appreciation in how they apply and implement the Convention, depending on the circumstances of the case and the rights and freedoms engaged. The margin of appreciation reflects that the Convention system is subsidiary to the safeguarding of human rights at national level and that national authorities are in principle better placed than an international court to evaluate local needs and conditions...The margin of appreciation goes hand in hand with supervision under the Convention system.[152]

According to the ECtHR's case law, such supervision concerns both the aim of the measure challenged and its 'necessity', and covers not only the basic legislation but also the decision applying it.[153]

In other words, the States are free to choose the way of implementation, but this freedom has limits which cannot be clearly articulated as it 'depends on the circumstances of the case and the rights and freedoms engaged'.[154]

The words of Lord Lester in this Part's epigraph are illustrative of the concerns of numerous scholars about the ECtHR's use of the concept of the margin of appreciation. In fact, there is no single concept of the margin of appreciation as it is used by the ECtHR.[155] Taking into account the fact that the ECtHR mentions the margin of appreciation in very different contexts, as well as sometimes using it as a mere 'rhetorical device,'[156] it is impossible to find a unified approach to the concept within ECtHR jurisprudence. Scholars note that judges sometimes appear to be applying different standards of necessity according to their view of the merits of the case,

150. Steven Greer, The Interpretation of the European Convention on Human Rights: Universal Principle or Margin of Appreciation? UCL Human Rights Review 3(3) (2010):. Available at: https://www.ucl.ac.uk/human-rights/research/ucl-hrr/docs/hrreviewissue3/greer (accessed 20 January 2015).
151. The text search fulfilled on the official site of the ECtHR found 1744 cases where the margin of appreciation was mentioned out of 43,756 cases present in the database. *See* http://hudoc.echr.coe.int/ (accessed 11 December 2014).
152. Brighton Declaration adopted by the High Level Conference on the Future of the European Court of Human Rights on 19 and 20 April 2012, para. 11.
153. ECtHR, Handyside v. The United Kingdom (5493/72) 7 December 1976, para. 49.
154. As outlined in para. 11 of the Brighton Declaration and in the Draft Explanatory report to Protocol 15 (DH-GDR (2012) R2 Addendum IV, para. 9).
155. Some scholars say that there is no concept at all. *See* Sébastien van Drooghenbroeck, La proportionnalité dans le droit de la Convention européenne des droits de l'homme: prendre l'idée simple au sérieux. Publications Fac St Louis, 2001, p. 485.
156. Yutaka Arai-Takahashi, The Margin of Appreciation Doctrine and the Principle of Proportionality in the Jurisprudence of the ECHR. Intersentia (2002): 128–129.

expressed in terms of a varying margin of appreciation.[157] Articulations of this concept vary from 'the latitude of deference or error which the Strasbourg organs will allow to national legislative, executive, administrative and judicial bodies'[158] to a 'pseudo-technical way of referring to the discretion which the Strasbourg institutions have decided the Convention permits national authorities to exercise in certain circumstances'.[159]

There is a long list of literature on the subject and very little consistency across that literature.[160] Scholars point to the lack of transparency;[161] the unpredictability of the application of this doctrine which questions the legitimacy of the ECtHR;[162] and the fact that it threatens the rule of law.[163] Judges of the ECtHR themselves find this concept to be a 'perennial source of discussion and dissent'[164] and even call on abandoning it.[165]

However, the concept has not been abandoned, and with the passage of time, the ECtHR appears to be giving it more attention, underlining the subsidiary nature of the ECtHR. In order to understand how the concept of the margin of appreciation (if such a concept exists) works in labour law cases there is a need to systematise the use of

157. *See* McHarg, Aileen, Reconciling Human Rights and the Public Interest: Conceptual Problems and Doctrinal Uncertainty in the Jurisprudence of the European Court of Human Rights. The Modern Law Review 62(5) (1999): 671–696. Available at: http://www.elibrary.humanrightshouse.org/library/doc1/7_EC_on_HR_and_its_mechanism_of_HR_protection/general_section/articles_and_books/1097381.pdf (accessed 20 March 2015).
158. H.C. Yourow. The Margin of Appreciation Doctrine in the Dynamics of European Human Rights Jurisprudence. Martinus Nijhoff Publishers, 1996, p. 13.
159. Steven C. Greer. The Margin of Appreciation: Interpretation and Discretion Under the European Convention on Human Rights. Council of Europe, 2000 p. 32.
160. D. Galetta Il principio di proporzionalità dellwomo, fra principio di necessarietà nella convenzione europea dei diritti e dottrina del margine di apprezzamento statale: riflessioni generali su contenuti e rilevanza effettiva del principio, Riv. Ital. Dir. Pubbl. Comunitario – 1999, pp. 743–771, George Letsas, Two Concepts of the Margin of Appreciation. Oxford Journal of Legal Studies 26(4) (2006): 705–732, Jeroen Schokkenbroek, The Basis, Nature and Application of the Margin-of-Appreciation Doctrine in the Case-Law of the European Court of Human Rights. Human Rights Law Journal 19(1) (1998): 30–36; Yutaka Arai-Takahashi, The Margin of Appreciation Doctrine: A Theoretical Analysis of Strasbourg's Variable Geometry In: A. Føllesdal, B. Peters, G.Ulfstein, editors. 'Constituting Europe: The European Court of Human Rights in a National, European and Global Context'. Cambridge University Press, 2013.
161. Jeroen Schokkenbroek, The Basis, Nature, and Application of the Margin-of-Appreciation Doctrine in the Case-Law of the European Court of Human Rights. Human Rights Law Journal 19 (1998): 30.
162. C. Zoethout, Margin of Appreciation, Violation and (in)Compatibility: Why the ECtHR Might Consider Using an Alternative Mode of Adjudication. European Public Law 20(2) (2014): 309–330.
163. Jeffrey A. Brauch, The Margin of Appreciation and the Jurisprudence of the European Court of Human Rights: Threat to the Rule of Law (2005). Columbia Journal of European Law 11 (2005): 117.
164. Words used by the President of the European Court of Human Rights Dean Spielmann in the lecture 'Allowing the Right Margin: the European Court of Human Rights and the National Margin of Appreciation Doctrine: Waiver or Subsidiarity of European Review'? Available at: http://www.echr.coe.int/Documents/Speech_20140113_Heidelberg_ENG.pdf (accessed 20 October 2014).
165. Partly Dissenting Opinion of the Judge De Meyer in Z v. Finland (22009/93) 25 February 1997, para. 4.

'several legal techniques'[166] in the ECtHR's jurisprudence in general. There might be different approaches to the systematisation. Certain scholars entertain two concepts of the margin of appreciation; the 'substantive' concept, which is used to address the relationship between individual freedoms and collective goals; and the 'structural' concept, used to address the limits or intensity of the review of the ECtHR in view of its status as an international tribunal.[167] Another commentator presumes the existence of two types of margins of appreciation; one, as a balancing test between the rights of the individual and collective interests; and two, as a result of the restrictive interpretation of rights.[168]

As noted by Merrills, the concept of the margin of appreciation has been developed on a case-by-case basis,[169] with the result that the ECtHR jurisprudence is the primary source from which one may understand the concept. The ECtHR has reiterated that the application of the margin of appreciation depends on the rights concerned; however, the analysis of case law leads us to the conclusion that it depends even more on the obligations concerned. According to the ECtHR's traditional approach, the State has a negative obligation not to interfere with the rights fixed in the ECHR and an inherent, positive obligation to ensure the effective protection of rights.[170] The classification of the ECtHR's application of the margin of appreciation might be based upon this division.[171]

Where negative obligations are concerned, there is no margin of appreciation unless the article of the ECHR specifies conditions of possible interference with the right.[172] In these cases the margin of appreciation means the freedom of the state to estimate what may be a 'pressing social need' or what is 'necessary in democratic society' and also gives them a certain freedom in balancing competing rights, a kind of interpretative freedom. A judge once noted that states do not enjoy a margin of

166. Eva Brems, *see supra* note 129, p. 361.
167. Letsas George, Two Concepts of the Margin of Appreciation. Oxford Journal of Legal Studies 26(4) (2006): 705–732.
168. Giulio Itzcovich, One, None and One Hundred Thousand Margins of Appreciations: The Lautsi Case. Human Rights Law Review 13(2): 303.
169. J.G. Merrills. The Development of International Law by the European Court of Human Rights. Manchester University Press, 1988, p. 136.
170. A.R. Mowbray. The Development of Positive Obligations under the European Convention on Human Rights by the European Court of Human Rights. Hart, 2004, p. 151.
171. Close classification was proposed in U. Kilkeli, Ye.A. Chefranova, Yevropeyskaya Konventsiya O Zashchite Prav Cheloveka I Osnovnykh Svobod Stat'ya 8. Pravo na uvazheniye chastnoy i semeynoy zhizni, zhilishcha i korrespondentsii. Pretsedenty i kommentarii.(ECHR, Art. 8: Precedents and comments). Rossiyskaya Akademiya Pravosudiya, Moscow, 2001, p. 7; P. Mahoney already proposed that the Nature of the Duty Incumbent on the State is one of the factors of determining the scope of the margin of appreciation, *see* P. Mahouney, Marvellous Richness of Diversity or Invidious Cultural Relativism? Human Rights Law Journal 19(1) (1998): 5.
172. This point was acknowledged, for instance in the report, prepared for the Brighton conference, *see*: Report of the Committee on Legal Affairs and Human Rights for the Draft Protocol No. 15 amending the Convention for the Protection of Human Rights and Fundamental Freedoms. Doc. 13093, Reference 3931 of 21 January 2013. Available at: http://assembly.coe.int/ASP/Doc/XrefViewPDF.asp?FileID = 19542&Language = en (accessed 20 October 2014).

appreciation as a matter of right, but as a matter of judicial self-restraint.[173] This remark, including its reference to administrative self-restraint, represents the role the margin of appreciation can play in matters relating to negative obligations.

Where positive obligations are at stake the margin of appreciation granted to States represents a discretion to choose an appropriate way of implementing the ECHR, in other words, the freedom to act.[174] This use of the margin of appreciation is generally acknowledged to be a broad one.[175]

Different applications of the margin of appreciation in cases depending on whether positive or negative obligations of the States are concerned can be traced in judgments of the ECtHR on labour law matters. For example, in *Brincat and others v. Malta*[176] or *Vilnes and others v. Norway,*[177] the ECtHR considered the death of workers under Article 2 in light of the positive obligation of the state to ensure effective protection of the right to life. It acknowledged that the State should be granted the benefit of a margin of appreciation in its choice of what particular measures it chose to implement in order to provide effective deterrence against threats to the applicants' right to life.[178] In *Danilenkov and others v. Russia*, the ECtHR considered the failure of the State to ensure the protection of trade union members from discrimination. Noting that the State has a certain margin of appreciation in how it would secure this right for the applicants, the ECtHR underlined that the protection of the freedom of association under Article 11 should also involve the protection against discrimination.[179] Thus the positive obligations of the State under Article 11 were complemented with the protection from discrimination. This interpretation led to certain restrictions on the State's reliance on the margin of appreciation in the sphere of protection of freedom of association, as it removes the State's discretion to choose whether to adopt antidiscrimination measures.

As far as negative obligations are concerned, the ECtHR's jurisprudence on Articles 8, 9, 10 and 11 provides numerous examples of the margin of appreciation as the freedom to interpret possible restrictions of the rights to respect for private life, to freedom of religion, expression and association, which are stipulated in the second parts to these articles. According to the ECHR States cannot interfere with the concerned rights unless the proposed interference would be in accordance with the law and satisfy the requirement of necessity.

173. Dissenting opinion of Judge Martens in ECtHR, Cossey v. the United Kingdom (10843/84) 27 September 1990.
174. The court numerously stated that 'where the State is required to take positive measures, the choice of means is in principle a matter that falls within the Contracting State's margin of appreciation', *see* ECtHR, Kolyadenko and Others v. Russia, (17423/05) 28 February 2012, paras 157–161, Fadeeva v. Russia (55723/00) 9 June 2005, para. 96.
175. *See* ECtHR, Gaskin v. The United Kingdom (10454/83) 7 July 1989, para. 40.
176. ECtHR, Brincat and others v. Malta (60908/11, 62110/11, 62129/11, 62312/11, 62338/11) 24 July 2014.
177. ECtHR, Vilnes and others v. Norway (52806/09 22703/10) 5 December 2013.
178. ECtHR, Vilnes and other v. Norway, para. 202, Brincat and others v. Malta, para. 101.
179. ECtHR, Danilenkov and others v. Russia (67336/01) 30 July 2009, para. 123.

Therefore, the ECtHR refers to the concept of the margin of appreciation only if the State's interference is prescribed by law; it would otherwise consider the interference as being incompatible with the ECHR and an unlawful act. For example, in case *Volkov v. Ukraine*[180] the ECtHR did not accept the State's submissions in relation to the margin of appreciation in considering the lawfulness of the interference with the applicant's right to have respect of private life, as this interference was considered by the ECtHR as being incompatible with the relevant domestic law. In another case which concerned negative obligations of the State under Article 11, the ECtHR also did not accept the State's attempt to rely on the margin of appreciation as the banning of strike, which was challenged by the applicants, was not 'prescribed by law.'[181]

Therefore, the need to delineate the margin of appreciation to be allowed to a state emerges when the interference to a ECHR right is prescribed by the state's domestic law. In those circumstances, the ECtHR has to decide whether the interference can be justified by the exceptions permitted by the second parts of the relevant ECHR articles. According to Articles 8, 9, 10, and 11, the interference can be justified if it is necessary in a democratic society and corresponds to the interests of public safety, for the protection of public order, health or morals, or for the protection of the rights and freedoms of others. These general allowances are also supplemented in ways specific to some of the sections, i.e., to protect 'the economic wellbeing of the country' in Article 8; 'for maintaining the authority and impartiality of the judiciary' in Article 10; for 'prevention of disorder or crime' in Article 1. The States are granted a certain margin of appreciation in determining these conditions and how the need for interference with a right might be manifested.[182] The ECtHR is empowered to give the final ruling on whether a 'restriction' is reconcilable with the freedoms protected by the ECHR and whether the margin of appreciation was respected.[183]

In the 'labour law' jurisprudence the ECtHR refers to two possible scopes of the margin of appreciation– the wide margin and the limited one. The wide margin is traditionally applied in relation to matters concerning general social and economic policy.[184] The organisation of the labour market and the adoption of domestic labour laws flow from the economic and social policies of states; therefore, the margin of

180. The case concerning unfair dismissal of the judge of the Supreme Court, ECtHR, Oleksandr Volkov v. Ukraine (21722/11) 9 January 2013, para. 186.
181. ECtHR, Veniamin Tymoshenko and Others v. Ukraine (48408/12) 2 October 2014, paras 79–85.
182. *See*, for instance, ECtHR, Kudeshkina v. Russia (29492/05) 26 February 2009, para. 82, Urcan v. Turkey (23018/04) 17 July 2008, Karacay v. Turkey (6615/03) 27 March 2007, Tüm Haber Sen and Çinar v. Turkey (28602/) 21 February 2006, Kaya et Seyhan v. Turkey (30946/04) 15 September 2009, Eğitim Ve Bilim Emekçileri Sendikasi v. Turkey (20641/05) 25 September 2012, para. 62, Barraco c. France (31684/05) 5 March 2009, para. 42, ASLEF v. The United Kingdom (11002/05) 27 February 2007, paras 46, 52.
183. ECtHR, Ceylan v. Turkey (23556/94) 8 July 1999, para. 32, Eğitim Ve Bilim Emekçileri Sendikasi v. Turkey (20641/05) 25 September 2012, para. 68, Rekvényi v. Hungary [GC] (25390/94) 20 May 1999, para. 42.
184. *See* ECtHR, R.Sz. v. Hungary (41838/11)| 2 July 2013, para. 38, Koufaki et Adedy c. Grèce (57665/12 57657/12) 7 May 2013, para. 31; Stec and Others v. UK (Nos. 65731/01 and 65900/01), 12 April 2006, para. 52.

appreciation should be wider where matters of labour rights are concerned.[185] In certain cases on the protection of trade union rights, the ECtHR has emphasised the wide margin of appreciation in determining how 'the freedom of trade unions to protect the occupational interests of their members may be secured'.[186] Along with stating a wide margin of appreciation in the cases concerning labour rights the ECtHR also acknowledges certain exceptions from this rule, allowing a more limited[187] or narrow margin of appreciation in several cases.

Factors influencing the scope of the margin of appreciation

Scholars propose numerous factors which might reduce the margin of appreciation;[188] including: the state of European consensus over the right concerned; the importance of the right at stake; the text of the ECHR; surrounding circumstances; the reference to other conventions, the existence of a particular local situation, etc. The ECtHR itself has stated that the scope of the margin of appreciation varies according to various factors, including the relevant circumstances, the subject matter and the background of the case.[189] These criteria might be used for further classification of the factors which determine the scope of the margin of appreciation allowed to the states. Research on the application of the margin of appreciation in labour law cases shows that under each of these criteria several factors may be found.

Within the criterion which the ECtHR refers to as *'circumstances of the case'*, the *applicant's vulnerability* plays a role in setting the scope of the margin of appreciation of the state.[190]

This concept of vulnerability appears in the ECtHR's case law on discrimination. Assessing whether the difference of treatment was justified, the ECtHR identified a number of particularly vulnerable groups – for instance, the Roma, homosexuals,

185. Judge Lorenzen noted that the Court has consistently held that the Contracting States enjoy a wide margin of appreciation in the field of labour market relations, *see* ECtHR, Sorensen and Rasmussen v. Denmark, (52562/99 52620/99) 1 January 2006, Dissenting opinion of judge Lorenzen, para. 4.
186. ECtHR, Sorensen and Rasmussen v. Denmark, (52562/99 52620/99) 1 January 2006, para. 58; Vörđur Ólafsson v. Iceland (20161/06) 27 April 2010, para. 75; Schettini and Others v. Italy (29529/95) admissibility decision 9 November 2000.
187. This title is especially questionable as the Court repeats from case to case that the margin of appreciation is never unlimited, *see*, for instance, Handyside v. The United Kingdom (5493/72) 7 December 1976, para. 49, Galstyan v. Armenia (26986/03) 15 November 2007, para. 114, Nosov and others v. Russia (9117/04 10441/04) 20 February 2014, para. 56.
188. Karen Reid. A Practitioner's Guide to the European Convention on Human Rights. Sweet & Maxwell, 2011, p. 60; Brems Eva, The Margin of Appreciation Doctrine in the Case-Law of the European Court of Human Rights. Zeitschrift für ausländisches öffentliches Recht und Völkerrecht 56 (1996), p. 256; P. Mahouney, *see supra* note 23; Jeroen Schokkenbroek, The Basis, Nature and Application of the Margin-of-Appreciation Doctrine in the Case-Law of the European Court of Human Rights. Human Rights Law Journal 19(1) (1998): 31–32.
189. This approach emerged in cases on discrimination, however, it might be used for any other labour law cases. *See* Konstantin Markin v. Russia, para. 100.
190. About the concept of vulnerability in the ECtHR's case law *see* Lourdes Peroni, Alexandra Timmer, Vulnerable groups: The Promise of an Emerging Concept in European Human Rights Convention Law. International Journal of Constitutional Law 11(4) (2013): 1056–1085.

persons with mental disabilities – which had suffered a history of prejudice and social exclusion, in respect of which the state had a narrower margin of appreciation.[191]

In the labour law cases heard by the ECtHR, at least one example highlighting consideration of the applicant's vulnerability can be found: the *I.B. v. Greece.*[192] The applicant argued before the ECtHR that his dismissal on the grounds of being HIV-positive was in breach of the European ECHR. The ECtHR stated that the State's margin of appreciation was substantially narrower in relation to this particularly vulnerable group of society which had suffered considerable discrimination in the past. It consequently found the State in violation of the ECHR.

Turning to the *'subject matter'* criterion, several factors that influence the margin of appreciation of the state may be found in the ECtHR's case law. First, *the nature of the right* is one of the most important factors. For example, in cases concerning the military service of applicants the ECtHR held that the States had a narrower margin of appreciation as far as the respect for private and family life was concerned. It found restrictions (dismissal of service men in the cases of *Lustig-Prean and Beckett v. The UK,*[193] and refusal to grant parental leave in *K. Markin v. Russia*[194]) unjustified.

Another factor is *whether the interference strikes at the core rights*. This point is especially important in relation to the protection of collective labour rights, as the ECHR directly expresses the right to join trade union but does not establish any particular rights of such unions. Therefore, the ECtHR, through interpreting the ECHR in light of the relevant international law (*Demir and Baikara* being the most helpful illustration of this approach), deduces certain rights from the right for the freedom of association, determines the importance of the acknowledged right, which is not provided in the text of the Convention and delineates the margin of the appreciation of the states accordingly to the importance of this right.

In *R.M.T. v. UK* the ECtHR stated:

> If a legislative restriction strikes at the core of trade union activity, a lesser margin of appreciation is to be recognised to the national legislature and more is required to justify the proportionality of the resultant interference, in the general interest, with the exercise of trade union freedom. Conversely, if it is not the core but a secondary or accessory aspect of trade union activity that is affected, the margin is wider and the interference is, by its nature, more likely to be proportionate as far as its consequences for the exercise of trade union freedom are concerned.[195]

This approach was applied by the ECtHR in *Sorrensen and Rassmussen v. Denmark,* when the core character of the negative right to join a trade union was established, reducing the margin of appreciation of the states in this field.[196] In *R.M.T. v. UK*[197] the recognition of the secondary character of the right to secondary strike

191. ECtHR, Kiyutin v. Russia (2700/10) 10 March 2011, para. 48.
192. ECtHR, I.B. v. Greece (552/10) 3 October 2013, para. 78.
193. ECtHR, Lustig-Prean and Beckett v. UK (31417/96 32377/96) 27 September 1999, para. 87.
194. ECtHR, Markin Konstantin v. Russia (30078/06) 22 March 2012.
195. ECtHR, R.M.T. v. UK, para. 87.
196. ECtHR, Sorrensen and Rassmussen v. Denmark [GC] (52562/99 52620/99) 11 January 2006, para. 58.
197. ECtHR, R.M.T. v. the UK, para. 88.

solidarity lead to the acknowledgement of a wide margin of appreciate for the states in regulating this right.

The necessity to balance different rights protected by the ECHR is another factor influencing the margin of appreciation of the states. The complex problem of balancing rights is inherent in the majority of labour law cases. In such cases, taking into account subsidiary role of the ECtHR, the state has to choose adequate means to make this interference proportionate to the aim pursued and is granted a wide margin of appreciation for that.

This approach, for instance, led the ECtHR to conclude that the non-renewal of a contract with the teacher of a Catholic school, because he publicly supported the movement for optional celibacy of Catholic priests, was not in breach of ECHR as the State did not overstep its wide margin of appreciation in balancing church autonomy with the right to the freedom of expression.[198]

The *'background criterion'* is represented by such factors as the European consensus on the regulation of a certain right or the existence of a special regime of regulation of rights.

The European consensus as a factor influencing the scope of the margin of appreciation of the state is raised in many labour law cases.[199] The ECtHR emphasised that the margin of appreciation should be reduced[200] if consensus is established. In cases where the comparative research reveals a lack of consensus the margin of appreciation remains wide.[201] The cases *R.M.T. v. UK*[202] and *Sindicatul 'Păstorul Cel Bun' v. Romania*,[203] referred to in the previous paragraph, are the most illustrative examples of the influence of European consensus on the scope of the margin of appreciation.

A *special regime of the regulation of rights* in relation to certain employees is another background factor determining the scope of the margin of appreciation. The possible exceptions to the protection of the rights to respect for private life, to freedom of expression, religion and association, provided in the second parts of the Articles 8, 9, 10 and 11, can be interpreted as acknowledging the special regime of protection of rights at work in respect of the members of the armed forces, of the police or of the administration of the State. Relevant provisions expressly permit the possibility of restrictions of their rights to the freedom of association, and, indirectly, of the rights guaranteed by Articles 8, 9 and 10 of the ECHR.

198. ECtHR, Fernández Martínez v. Spain[GC] (56030/07) 12 June 2014, *see also* SINDICATUL 'Păstorul Cel Bun' v. Romania (2330/09) 9 July 2013, concerning the right of church employees to form a trade union.
199. *See* more in K. Cavanaugh, Policing the Margins: Rights Protection and the European Court of Human Rights. EHRLR (2006): 422,423.
200. *See* ECtHR, K. Markin v. Russia [GC] (30078/06) 22 March 2012.
201. ECtHR, Schüth v. Germany (1620/03) 23 September 2010, para. 56, Gustafsson v. Sweden [GC] (15573/89) 25 April 1996, para. 45, *see also* non-labour law case, however, very illustrative - Lautsi and others v. Italy [GC] (30814/06) 18 March 2011, para. 70.
202. ECtHR, National union of rail, maritime and transport workers v. The United Kingdom (31045/10) 8 April 2014, para. 86.
203. ECtHR, Sindicatul 'Păstorul cel bun' v. Romania (2330/09) 9 July 2013.

In certain labour law cases the ECtHR, in estimating the margin of appreciation of the States, uses the words 'special context' in relation to those cases. For example, in cases on military service, it was held that the special context of military service leaves a wide margin of appreciation to the states in determining its conditions. In cases on the dismissal of judges, the use of the term 'special context' allowed the ECtHR to conclude that a wide scope of the margin of appreciation should be applied as far as the right for judges to express their religious beliefs was concerned.[204]

However, a narrower margin of appreciation in relation to judges' rights to freedom of expression was found in cases which raise important matters of public interest, 'which should be open to free debate in a democratic society'.[205] Therefore, the margin of appreciation – even in cases concerning applicants with a 'special regime of rights' – might be narrowed if the concerned right has what the Court considers to be crucial importance for democratic society.

The factors reducing the margin of appreciation allowed to states led to the necessity of states to provide 'very weighty reasons for imposing the restrictions in question.'[206] The 'weight' of the reasons for interference is thoroughly balanced by the ECtHR with the requirements of the protection of the individual's fundamental rights.[207]

Flexibility of the margin of appreciation is an important aspect of this tool. French scholars note: 'It is almost unrealistic to assume that it is absolutely necessary to outline a priori the contours of the margin of appreciation afforded to States'.[208] By applying the concept with flexibility, the ECtHR is able to reconcile conflicting supranational and national interests to achieve greater acceptance of its decisions.[209]

The classification of the use of the margin of appreciation in labour law cases represented in this paragraph was based on the main idea of fundamental diversity of cases concerning violations of positive obligations of the state and the negative ones. However there are cases where the nature of obligation cannot be well defined. The ECtHR held that where the boundaries between the State's positive and negative obligations do not lend themselves to precise definition, the applicable principles are nonetheless similar – regard must be had to the fair balance to be struck between the competing interests of the individual and of the community as a whole.[210] Therefore, the balancing and proportionality tests are frequently used tools for determining the margin of appreciation of the state in cases where the nature of the obligation at stake cannot be revealed.[211]

204. ECtHR, Pitkevich v. Russia (47936/99) inadmissible 8 February 2001.
205. ECtHR, Kudeshkina v. Russia (29492/05) 26 February 2009, para. 94.
206. ECtHR, I.B. v. Greece, *see supra* note 179, para. 79.
207. ECtHR, Evaldsson And Others v. Sweden (75252/01) 13 February 2007, para. 55.
208. A.D. Olinga et C. Picheral, La théorie de la marge d'appréciation dans la jurisprudence récente de la Cour Européenne des droits de l'Homme ». R.T.D.H. 1995, p. 567. Available at: http://www.rtdh.eu/pdf/1995567.pdf (accessed 20 November 2014).
209. Giulio Itzcovich, One, None and One Hundred Thousand Margins of Appreciations: The Lautsi Case. Human Rights Law Review 2 (2013): 295.
210. *See* ECtHR, Sorensen and Rasmussen v. Denmark [GC] (52562/99 52620/99) 11 January 2006.
211. On the critics of this approach *see* Matthias Klatt, Moritz Meister. The Constitutional Structure of Proportionality. Oxford University Press, 2012, pp. 87–108. The authors argue that positive

[B] The Proportionality Test

Proportionality[212] is often referred to as the 'general principle in the Convention system'.[213] The principle of proportionality has been named by scholars as the 'other side'[214] or 'contrepoids'[215] of the margin of appreciation, and similar criticisms that the principle 'lack[s] conceptual clarity' has been expressed.[216]

Proportionality is implicitly mentioned in the references to 'necessity in democratic society' in Articles 8–11 of the ECHR. According to the Strasbourg case law, interference can only be justified if it is proportionate to the legitimate aim being pursued. Proportionality in its turn might be found if the rights at stake (or private rights and interests of the state) were fairly balanced.[217]

Before turning to balancing rights there is a need to understand the ECtHR's approach to interpreting the term 'necessity in democratic society'.

Necessary in democratic society

It was already mentioned that Articles 8, 9, 10 and 11 of the ECHR are the main articles serving as the basis of claiming the protection of certain labour rights. All of these articles have a common structure, where the second parts contain possible derogation clauses. Therefore, the right for the respect of private life, freedom of thought, conscience and religion, freedom of expression and association might be subject to limitations which are necessary in a democratic society in the interests of the state (society), as varies from article to article.

The analysis of labour law cases heard by the ECtHR under these articles of the ECHR lead us to presume the existence two types of necessity test: one is 'complete' and consists of several steps; another is 'simplified'. In relation to the 'complete' test, the Court addresses the following issues:

(1) Is there a pressing social need for some restriction of the ECHR?
(2) If so, does the particular restriction correspond to this need?
(3) If so, is it a proportionate response to that need?

---

obligations have a disjunctive structure that differs from the alternative structure of negative obligations, and this difference must lead to the application of different proportionality tests.

212. On the history of this principle *see* Martin Luteran, Towards Proportionality as a Proportion Between Means and Ends In: Cian C Murphy, Penny Green, editors. 'Law and Outsiders: Norms, Processes and "Othering" in the 21st Century'. Bloomsbury Publishing, 2011. pp. 8–10.
213. Pieter van Dijk, Godefridus J.H. Hoof, G.J.H. Van Hoof. Theory and Practice of the European Convention on Human Rights. Martinus Nijhoff Publishers, 1998. pp. 81–82.
214. Mowbray, Alastair, A Study of the Principle of Fair Balance in the Jurisprudence of the European Court of Human Rights (June 2010). Human Rights Law Review 10(2) (2010): 289–317. Available at SSRN: http://ssrn.com/abstract=1617540 (accessed 20 November 2014).
215. Sébastien van Drooghenbroeck, La proportionnalité dans le droit de la Convention européenne des droits de l'homme: prendre l'idée simple au sérieux. Publications Fac St Louis, 2001, p. 485.
216. For example, Jonas Christoffersen, Fair Balance: A Study of Proportionality, Subsidiarity and Primarity in the European Convention on Human Rights, BRILL, 2009, p. 1.
217. ECtHR, Marchenko v. Ukraine (4063/04) 19 February 2009, para. 44.

(4) In any case, are the reasons presented by the authorities, relevant and sufficient?[218]

The simplified necessity test to determining whether the interference was necessary in democratic society is often used when conflict between private interests is at stake. In such cases the ECtHR focuses on balancing the different rights, without answering other questions.[219] When State interests are concerned the ECtHR uses a more complete test, answering whether there was a pressing social need;[220] if interference was proportionate to the legitimate aim pursued;[221] and looks for relevant and sufficient reasons to justify the interference.[222]

To prove a pressing social need it must be demonstrated to the ECtHR's satisfaction that the realisation of rights under the ECHR represents a sufficiently imminent threat to the State or to a democratic society.[223] This point is especially important for the protection of labour rights of civil servants (collective labour rights in particular), as respondent states justify the interference by reference to there being a pressing social need. The ECtHR has in numerous cases acknowledged that the civil service of the applicant does not automatically justify the restrictions of ECHR rights; the State must still prove the existence of the need for the interference.[224]

According to the case law which has developed on this area, the interference with rights, set out in the ECHR, might be justified under the derogation provisions of the Articles 8–10 if it pursued a legitimate aim. Analysis of the labour law jurisprudence demonstrates that the following aims have been previously acknowledged as legitimate in the cases of labour rights violations: defending State democracy;[225] the need to overcome economic hardships;[226] ensuring the loyalty of those charged with safeguarding the public interest;[227] maintaining the independence of the judiciary and the

218. C. Murzea, The European Court of Human Rights and Its Theories of Interpreting the European Convention on Human Rights. Bulletin of the Transilvania 5(54)(1) (2012): 145. Available at: http://webbut.unitbv.ro/BU2012/Series%20VII/BULETIN%20VII%20PDF/18_MURZEA_BUT-1%202012.pdf.

219. *See*, for example, Obst v. Germany (425/03) 23 September 2010, para. 52, Siebenhaar v. Germany (18136/02) 3 February 2011.

220. ECtHR, Wille v. Liechtenstein[GC] (28396/95) 28 October 1999, para. 61, Fernández Martínez v. Spain[GC] (56030/07) 12 June 2014, para. 124, Smith and Grady v. The United Kingdom (33985/96, 33986/96) 27 September 1999, paras 87–89.

221. ECtHR, Lustig-Prean and Beckett v. UK (31417/96 32377/96) 27 September 1999, para. 80, *see also* Pay v. United Kingdom (32792/05) inadmissible 16 September 2008.

222. *See* ECtHR, Enerji Yapi-Yol Sen c. Turquie (68959/01) 21 April 2009, paras 32, 33, Fuentes Bobo c. Espagne (39293/98) 29 February 2000, para. 44, Palomo Sánchez and others v. Spain [GC] (28955/06 et al.) 12 September 2011, para. 63.

223. ECtHR, Tüm Haber Sen and Çinar v. Turkey (28602/) 21 February 2006, para. 40, Sindicatul 'Păstorul Cel Bun' v. Romania, para. 69.

224. ECtHR, Sidabras And Dziautas v. Lithuania (55480/00 59330/00) 27 July 2004; Engel And Others v. The Netherlands (Application nos 5100/71; 5101/71; 5102/71; 5354/72; 5370/72) 8 June 1976, Smith and Grady v. UK (33985/96 33986/96) 27 September 1999, Volkmer v. Germany (39799/98) 22 November 2001.

225. ECtHR, Vogt v. Germany (17851/91) 26 September 1995.

226. ECtHR, Koufaki Et Adedy c. Grèce (57665/12 57657/12) 7 May 2013, para. 38.

227. ECtHR, Naidin c. Roumanie (38162/07) 21 October 2014, para. 61.

credibility of their decisions;[228] preserving the autonomy of religious communities;[229] protection of health;[230] etc. The list of the aims cannot be formulated exhaustively as evidently the scope of the State activities is very wide.

[C] The Balancing Exercise

The analysis of proportionality of the interference is interconnected with striking a 'fair balance' between the interests of the applicant and the community (or the rights of others). The nature of this interconnection can be controversial. The ECtHR often concludes that the requirement of proportionality and of the 'fair balance' have the same meaning.[231] In *James and others v. The UK*,[232] the ECtHR stated that 'the requirement of the reasonable relationship of proportionality between the means employed and the aim sought to be realised ... was expressed in other terms ... by the notion of the "fair balance" that must be struck between the demands of the general interest of the community and the requirements of the protection of the individual's fundamental rights'.[233] Scholars are divided on the connection between proportionality and balancing; there are scholars who distinguish the concept of proportionality from the balancing concept,[234] and others who tend to talk about them synonymously.[235]

The labour law jurisprudence of the ECtHR demonstrates that the process of balancing is the basis of the proportionality test and is another problematic issue in the jurisprudence of the ECtHR. The ECtHR's approach to balancing rights is developed on a case-by-case basis and the jurisprudence does not provide 'a coherent set of tests for determining when rights prevail over the public interest or vice versa'.[236] In the ECtHR's judgments the concept of balancing is often referred to without being

228. ECtHR, Pitkevich v. Russia, Özpinar v. Turkey (20999/04) 19 October 2010.
229. ECtHR, Siebenhaar v. Germany (18136/02) 3 February 2011, Martínez Fernández v. Spain (56030/07) 12 June 2014, Sindicatul 'Păstorul cel bun' v. Romania (2330/09) 9 July 2013.
230. ECtHR, I.B. v. Greece (552/10) 3 October 2013.
231. *See*, for example, ECtHR, Evaldsson and Others v. Sweden (75252/01) 13 February 2007, para. 55, Koufaki et Adedy c. Grèce (57665/12 57657/12) 7 May 2013, para. 32; *see also* Martin Luteran, *supra* note 212, p. 5.
232. ECtHR, James and Others v. The United Kingdom (8793/79) 21 February 1986.
233. *Ibid*., para. 50.
234. J. Christoffersen, for example, supposes that positive obligations are subject to balancing under Art. 8 § 1, whereas negative obligations are subjected to a proportionality appraisal under Art. 8 § 2, *see* Jonas Christoffersen, p. 194, *see also* B. Goold, L. Lazarus, G. Swiney, 'Public Protection, Proportionality, and the Search for Balance' (1007) 10(7) Ministry of Justice Research Series, and Martin Luteran, Towards Proportionality as a Proportion Between Means and Ends In: Cian C Murphy, Penny Green, editors. 'Law and Outsiders: Norms, Processes and "Othering" in the 21st Century'. Bloomsbury Publishing, 2011. pp. 4–23.
235. *See*, for example, Harris O'Boyle and Warbrick. Law of the European Convention on Human Rights. 2nd edn. Oxford: Oxford University Press, 2009, p. 10; Jeremy Mcbride, Proportionality and the European Convention on Human Rights In: Evelyn Ellis, editor. 'The Principle of Proportionality in the Laws of Europe'. Hart Publishing, 1999, p. 24; Stavros Tsakyrakis, Proportionality: An Assault On Human Rights? Jean Monnet Working Paper 09/08. Available at: http://www.jeanmonnetprogram.org/papers/08/080901.pdf (accessed 3 December 2014).
236. Aileen McHarg, Reconciling Human Rights and the Public Interest: Conceptual Problems and Doctrinal Uncertainty in the Jurisprudence of the European Court of Human Rights. The Modem Law Review 62 (1999): 695.

explained. Scholars note that this silence reflects the impossibility of measuring incommensurable values by introducing a mechanistic, quantitative common metric.[237] Still, the principle of legal certainty requires a certain level of predictability in the ECtHR's reasoning and therefore a reliable framework of balancing rights.

The concept of balancing is criticised by leading philosophers of law. Reflecting on the possibility of balancing collective interests versus private ones, Ronald Dworkin argues that balancing state interests and individual rights is a false idea which might be appropriate only in the situation of competing claims of rights.[238] In his view, the precedence of the demands of the majority of the law-abiding community might undermine the whole point of recognising human rights and it is tantamount to declaring that there are no such things.[239] In relation to collective interests, Dworkin emphasises two fundamental ideas of human rights protection – the 'vague but powerful' idea of human dignity; and political equity which must be a kind of limitation for the possible interference with private rights for the sake of collective interests.

Habermas criticised the concept of balancing from another point of view. In his view, the concept of balancing deprives rights of 'strict priority' and the 'the danger of irrational rulings' might emerge as there are no rational standards for balancing.[240]

Olivier De Shuttler and Eva Brems also see dangers in the balancing metaphor. One danger is in the way violations are presented before the ECtHR, as in the case of competing rights 'they do not come before the judge in an equal manner'.[241] Brems goes on to observe that the right that is invoked by the applicant receives the most attention, because the question to be answered by the judge is whether or not this right was violated.[242] Where the private rights are in conflict with State interests – another problem might arise as the 'weight' of the State interest, compared with that of the individual right-holder, will necessarily appear considerable.[243]

In spite of Dworkin's and Habermas's precautions about the danger of balancing, this concept is applied in the adjudication of cases under Articles 8, 9, 10, 11 and Article 1 of Protocol 1 to the ECHR. These norms of the ECHR are structured in a way that makes this process indispensible. In the majority of cases the ECtHR seems to evade the dangers of 'subjectivity' in the perception of rights. Its balancing of the state and private interests is guided by a broad reading of rights and a restrictive reading of

237. Stavros Tsakyrakis, Proportionality: An Assault On Human Rights? Jean Monnet Working Paper 09/08. Available at: http://www.jeanmonnetprogram.org/papers/08/080901.pdf (accessed 3 December 2014).
238. Ronald Dworkin. Taking Rights Seriously. Harvard University Press, 1978. pp. 198, 199.
239. *Ibid.*
240. Jürgen Habermas. Between Facts and Norms. Cambridge: Polity, 1996. pp. 256, 259.
241. *See* E Brems, Conflicting Human Rights: An Exploration in the Context of the Right to a Fair Trial in the European Convention for the Protection of Human Rights and Fundamental Freedoms. Human Rights Quarterly 27 (2005): 305.
242. *Ibid.*
243. Olivier De Schutter, Human Rights in Employment Relationships: Contracts as Power In: Filip Dorssemont, Klaus Lörcher, Isabelle Schömann, editors. 'The European Convention on Human Rights and the Employment Relation'. Oxford: Hart Publishing, 2013, p. 131.

derogations. However, in certain cases the ECtHR gave greater weight to the importance of the state interest at stake and the role of the balancing exercise was diminished. Cases on austerity measures are especially illustrative in this context.

These cases were considered under Article 1 to Protocol 1 of the ECHR. The ECtHR had to consider whether the reduction of pensions and wages was proportionate to the aim of overcoming economic hardships. It used the notion of 'excessive burden' as a test of proportionality. Proportionality, as the ECtHR stated, could not be found 'if the person had to undergo individual and excessive burden.'[244]

This approach seems to be clear and comprehensible, as it underlines the importance of taking into account the personal circumstances of the applicant in striking a fair balance. However, the notion of excessive burden was used by the ECtHR in a superficial way without any analysis of the consequences of the interference for particular applicant, without estimating his needs and expenses.

The ECtHR used in cases such as these a kind of simplified 'quantitative' test of proportionality for revealing whether the interests of the state and the right of applicants were fairly balanced. In cases where reductions were above the level of 50% – it was considered as an excessive burden and the interference was found disproportionate to the aim pursued.[245] In the majority of cases the level of reduction was lower than 50% and the interference was held to be proportionate.[246] This approach to balancing demonstrates the evident emphasis on the importance of the state interests and undermines the significance of the balancing metaphor.

My research of the labour law cases heard under Articles 8, 9, 10 and 11 and in which the ECtHR applied a balancing process, revealed that the following matters might be balanced by the ECtHR: interests of the state against private interests;[247] one Convention right against another in the private law discourse;[248] and the gravity of the imposed disciplinary sanction considering the offence committed by the applicant.[249]

The process of balancing is influenced by the factors that determine the scope of the margin of appreciation (as the nature of the right, circumstances of the case, international consensus etc.).[250] However, it is impossible to create a coherent legal

244. ECtHR, Koufaki Et Adedy c. Grèce (57665/12 57657/12) 7 May 2013, para. 32.
245. ECtHR, R.Sz. v. Hungary (41838/11) 2 July 2013, Á.A. v. Hungary (no. 22193/11), P.G. v. Hungary (no. 18229/11) 23 September 2014, Stefanetti and Others v. Italy (21838/10 et al.) 15 April 2014.
246. ECtHR, Da Silva Carvalho Rico v. Portugal (13341/14) 24 September 2015; Mihăieş and Senteş v. Romania (44232/11, 44605/11) 2 March 2012, Da Conceição Mateus v. Portugal and Santos Januário v. Portugal (62235/12, 57725/12) 8 October 2013, Panfile v. Romania (13902/11) 20 March 2012, Khoniakina v. Georgia (17767/08) 19 June 2012, Maggio and others v. Italy (46286/09 et al.) 31 May 2011.
247. ECtHR, Koufaki and Adedy v. Greece (57665/12 57657/12) 7 May 2013, ECtHR, Vogt v. Germany (17851/91) 26 September 1995.
248. ECtHR, Eweida and Others v. the United Kingdom (48420/10) 15 January 2013; Obst v. Germany (425/03), 23 September 2010; Palomo Sánchez And Others v. Spain (28955/06) 12 September 2011.
249. ECtHR, Kudeshkina v. Russia (29492/05) 26 February 2009; Pay v. The United Kingdom (32792/05) 16 September 2008.
250. *See* on factors that determine the balance in Jeremy Mcbride, Proportionality and the European Convention on Human Rights In: Evelyn Ellis, editor. 'The Principle of Proportionality in the Laws of Europe'. Hart Publishing, 1999, pp. 24–25.

theory on the balancing of rights, and make an exhaustive systematisation of factors, simply by considering the decisions of the ECtHR.

In the context of labour law cases the application of the proportionality test and the balancing concept have their own peculiarities as these cases sometimes concern both the vertical and horizontal applications of the ECHR. As far as horizontal application is concerned, the ECtHR has to verify if the national courts have stuck a fair balance between competing rights.[251] In cases of the vertical application of the ECHR (e.g., where the state acts as an employer) the proportionality test becomes more complex. The interference itself and the lack of due protection of the allegedly violated right by the national court becomes subject to the ECtHR's scrutiny.[252]

Concluding this analysis on theoretical concepts used by the ECtHR in adjudicating labour law cases, it is worth noting that in spite of the ECtHR's sometimes conflicting and ambiguous application of the margin of appreciation, the principle of proportionality or balancing of rights, these concepts still contribute significantly to the protection of individual and collective labour rights and deserved their designation as 'the invisible articles'[253] of the ECHR. The ECtHR develops protection of the rights at work interpreting the value of labour rights as relative values, which, as noted by Prof. Caruso, through the principle of proportionality (but also of equality and legal certainty) are susceptible to being balanced with other goals.[254]

This approach is intended to achieve a better functioning of the system of protecting social-economic rights where the development of labour rights is interconnected with economic growth and the rise of private sector business.

§2.04 CONCLUSIONS

The broadening of the scope of the ECHR through the integration of certain social rights has been criticised by Member States and led to '"vitriolic" fury' [255] directed against the judges of the ECtHR. Prominent scholars pointed that the ECtHR was considering itself the equivalent of the Supreme Court of the United States (US), laying down a federal law of Europe.[256]

The criticism is understandable; the ECtHR was usually reluctant to interfere with social matters; preferring to grant the States a wide margin of appreciation in the sphere

251. ECtHR, I.B. v. Greece (552/10) 3 October 2013.
252. *See*, for example, cases on the dismissal of judges Baka v. Hungary (application no. 20261/12) 27 May 2014, Kudeshkina v. Russia (29492/05) 26 February 2009.
253. AWB Simpson. The ECHR: the First half Century. 2004. University of Chicago Fulton Lecture Series, p. 10. Available at: http://chicagounbound.uchicago.edu/cgi/viewcontent.cgi?article=1017&context=fulton_lectures (accessed 30 October 2014).
254. B. Caruso, New Trajectories of Labour Law In the European Crisis. The Italian Case. Working Paper, Forthcoming in the Comparative Labour Law & Policy Journal. Available at: http://www.labourlawresearch.net/sites/default/files/papers/New%20trajectories%20of%20labour%20law%20in%20the%20European%20crisis%20rev.pdf.
255. Sir Nicolas Bratza, The Relationship between the UK Courts and Strasbourg. EHRLR 505 (2011).
256. Lord Hoffmann. The Universality of Human Rights. Judicial Studies Board Annual Lecture, 19 March 2009. Available at: http://www.brandeis.edu/ethics/pdfs/internationaljustice/biij/BIIJ2013/hoffmann.pdf (accessed 20 January 2015).

of general social and economic policy. It often abstained from judging in favour of the applicants in case of pension or wage cuts due to austerity measures;[257] of the rights to housing;[258] the rights of disabled persons;[259] or of the right to work.[260] However, the most important issues of economic and social policies (such as discrimination, occupational safety, unfair dismissals, right for wage) together with the issues concerning civil liberties at the workplace have become widely covered by the provisions of the ECHR.

The enlarging of the scope of the ECHR seems to address the lack of authority of international bodies created to protect social and economic rights. By interpreting the ECHR in an evolving way, and by referring to other international documents as well as European consensus, the ECtHR has provided certain rights at work with due protection, considering employment cases in the light of fundamental human rights.

ECtHR jurisprudence on the protection of the rights at work shows that the scope of the margin of appreciation granted to states is limited and varies according to the circumstances, the subject matter and the background of the case. In addition, there are additional factors relevant to its use of the margin of appreciation including the applicant's vulnerability, the nature of the right, the European consensus on the matter, and the necessity to balance different rights.

The most important contribution of the ECtHR in this area is the introduction of the proportionality principle, which should be applied by national courts in consideration of employment cases in order to ensure due protection of human rights.

257. ECtHR, Da Silva Carvalho Rico v. Portugal (13341/14) 24 September 2015; Koufaki Et Adedy c. Grèce (57665/12 57657/12) 7 May 2013, Mihăieş and Senteş v. Romania (44232/11, 44605/11) 2 March 2012, Da Conceição Mateus v. Portugal and Santos Januário v. Portugal (62235/12, 57725/12) 8 October 2013, Panfile v. Romania (13902/11) 20 March 2012, Khoniakina v. Georgia (17767/08) 19 June 2012, Maggio and others v. Italy (46286/09 et al.) 31 May 2011.

258. ECtHR, Chapman v. The United Kingdom (27238/95) 18 January 2001, James And Others v. The United Kingdom (8793/79) 21 February 1986, Marzari v. Italy (36448/97) 4 May 1999.

259. ECtHR, Zehnalova and Zehnal v. The Czech Republic (38621/97) 14 May 2002, Botta v. Italy (21439/93) 24 February 1998, Farcaş v. Romania (application no. 32596/04) 30 September 2010.

260. ECtHR, Panfile v. Romania (13902/11) 20 March 2012, para. 18, Sobczyk v. Poland (25693/94 and 27387/95)10 February 2000; Dragan Cakalic v. Croatia (17400/02) 15 September 2003; Torri and Others v. Italy and Bucciarelli v. Italy (11838/07 and 12302/07) 24 January 2012.

PART II

The Prohibition of Forced or Compulsory Labour and Discrimination in Employment

The prohibition of forced and compulsory labour and of discrimination are united under this part as these provisions have direct relevance to the employment law and stipulate the most important, core rules of the labour market.

CHAPTER 3

The Prohibition of Slavery, Servitude, Forced or Compulsory Labour

The prohibition of forced labour is both a classical civil right and the fundamental labour right, as acknowledged by the ILO Declaration on Fundamental Principles and Rights at Work. Article 4 of the ECHR contains a non-derogatory prohibition of slavery, servitude and forced or compulsory labour. It was dictated by the need to protect European society from the reiteration of the terrible experience of concentration camps and forced labour in war times and to ensure the protection of human dignity. The Italian representative in the Consultative assembly of the CoE explained the necessity of this prohibition by referring to 'unbelievable encroachments on our rights: the loss of security of person; arbitrary arrest; forced labour; paralysis of the intelligence and the slow killing of culture'.[1]

According to the preparatory materials to the ECHR, the initial emphasis was placed on the prohibition of slavery and servitude. The first draft of the ECHR, presented by Teitgen in August 1949, did not mentioned forced or compulsory labour. The prohibition of these types of labour was proposed by the representative of the UK in February 1950, and was adopted under the influence of the Preliminary Draft of the International Covenant on Human Rights, adopted by the UN Commission on human rights in its fifth session (1949).[2]

Surprisingly, the ILO Convention on Forced Labour, adopted in 1930, was not mentioned by the representatives of the States while drafting Article 4. However, the reference to this convention may be found in the annex to the Preparatory work on Article 4 as the Secretariat of the Commission decided to append to this document the

1. *See* Preparatory Work on Article 4 of the Convention. Council of Europe, 1962, p. 3. Available at: http://www.echr.coe.int/LibraryDocs/Travaux/ECHRTravaux-ART4-DH(62)10-BIL1712017.PDF (accessed 1 February 2015).
2. Preparatory Work on Article 4 of the Convention. Council of Europe, 1962. Available at: http://www.echr.coe.int/LibraryDocs/Travaux/ECHRTravaux-ART4-DH(62)10-BIL1712017.PDF (accessed 1 February 2015).

abstracts from the Commentary on the Drafts of the Covenant, prepared by the United Nations.[3]

The final text of Article 4 of the ECHR prohibits slavery, servitude, forced and compulsory labour without defining these offences. Its provisions create both positive and negative obligations that states must comply with. Public powers not only have a negative obligation not to enslave; they also have a positive obligation to anticipate these behaviours; to try to eradicate them; and to sanction them whenever they occur.[4] In modern society, the positive obligation of the state to ensure the compliance of private individuals with these norms and to grant effective protection against coercion has gained particular importance. The assumption that slavery-like practices have been eliminated is far from real in the twenty-first century.[5] The concepts of slavery and servitude and the context of forced and compulsory labour have evolved over time[6] and have to now cover matters such as human trafficking and unpaid domestic work which occurs in the relations between private persons.

According to an ILO report, the Developed Economies and EU accounts for 1.5 million (7%) of forced labourers presently working in the world.[7] This has aptly been described as the 'dark side of globalisation'.[8] In the mid-1990s there was a wave of reported trafficking from West Africa, in particular from Ghana and Nigeria; to Italy, the Netherlands and other European countries. Trafficking of women from the Mahgreb and sub-Saharan African countries has also been reported in France.[9]

Therefore, in the twenty-first century the provisions of Article 4 remain more relevant than ever, as international events undermine human dignity and destructively influence the labour market. Citing the new protocol to ILO Convention N 29: 'The suppression of forced or compulsory labour contributes to ensuring fair competition among employers as well as protection for workers'.[10]

§3.01 SLAVERY, SERVITUDE AND HUMAN TRAFFICKING

The lack of a definition for slavery in the ECHR itself has been filled by reference to international instruments on human rights protection and the decisions of international bodies. In particular, the ECtHR has referred to the 1926 Slavery Convention which describes slavery as 'the status or condition of a person over whom any or all of

3. Appendix to the Preparatory Work on Article 4 of the Convention. Council of Europe, 1962, p. 17.
4. Raul Canosa Usera, Prohibition of Slavery and Forced Labour: An Example of Integration of International Treaties (Commentary on Article 4) In: Javier García Roca, Pablo Santolaya, editors. 'Europe of Rights: A Compendium on the European Convention on Human Rights'. Martinus Nijhoff Publishers, 2012, p. 95.
5. Virginia Mantouvalou, Servitude and Forced Labour in the 21st Century: The Human Rights of Domestic Workers. Industrial Law Journal 35(4) (December 2006): 414.
6. International Labour Conference, 89th Session. Stopping forced labour, 2001, para. 21.
7. ILO Global Estimate of Forced Labour. ILO, 2012, p. 16.
8. Daniel Roger Maul, The International Labour Organization and the Struggle against Forced Labour from 1919 to the Present. Labor History 48(4) (November 2007): 477–500, 494.
9. International Labour Conference, 89th Session. Stopping forced labour, 2001, para. 155.
10. Introduction to the Protocol of 2014 to the Forced Labour Convention, 1930 adopted on the 103rd ILC session (11 June 2014).

the powers attaching to the right of ownership are exercised'.[11] Strasbourg bodies also refer to the legal positions taken by the International Criminal Tribunal for the Former Yugoslavia which concluded that the traditional concept of 'slavery' has evolved to encompass various contemporary forms of slavery based on the exercise of any or all of the powers attaching to the right of ownership. Factors relevant to establishing whether an activity comprises a new form of slavery include the control of someone's freedom of movement; control of their physical environment; psychological control; measures taken to prevent or deter escape; force; threat of force or coercion; duration; assertion of exclusivity; subjection to cruel treatment and abuse; control of sexuality and forced labour.[12]

The ECtHR has never found a State to be in violation of the prohibition of slavery in Article 4. However, in several cases heard under Article 4 it has contributed to the legal understanding of this concept. In *Siladin v. France*, a case concerning the unpaid domestic work of an immigrant, the ECtHR noted that the 'genuine right of legal ownership' and the 'reducing of the applicant's status to an "object"' are the main factors of the slavery under the meaning of both European Convention and the Slavery Convention 1926.[13] In *Bulynko v. Ukraine* the ECtHR referred to the voluntary character of performed work and the entitlement to payment as two factors which establish the absence of slavery.[14] In *Rantsev v. Russia and Cyprus*, considering whether slavery encompasses sex trafficking, it was noted that the trafficking of human beings, by its very nature and aim of exploitation, is based on the exercise of powers attaching to the right of ownership. It treats human beings as commodities to be bought and sold and put to forced labour, often for little or no payment. These traits of trafficking have much in common with the traits of slavery. However, the ECtHR refrained from concluding that trafficking constitutes 'slavery'. Instead, it concluded that trafficking itself, within the meaning of Article 3(a) of the Palermo Protocol and Article 4(a) of the Anti-Trafficking Convention, falls within the scope of Article 4 of the ECHR.[15] This approach was criticised for its inherent contradictions, as the ECtHR did not narrow the scope of application to make trafficking synonymous with slavery, but instead expanded the scope of Article 4 beyond its textual boundaries.[16] The ECtHR was criticised for not engaging with the essential elements of what constituted trafficking (its methods, means, or the various lesser servitudes than slavery, including debt bondage and forced labour), thus establishing a very narrow understanding of trafficking.[17]

However there are opposite opinions, which argue that bringing trafficking within the ambit of ECHR Article 4 will provide victims with its absolute protection, including being protected against deportation to a country where they may be at risk of

11. ECtHR, Rantsev v. Cyprus and Russia (25965/04) 7 January 2010, para. 138.
12. *Ibid.*, para. 143.
13. ECtHR, Siliadin v. France (73316/01) 26 July 2005, para. 122.
14. ECtHR, Bulynko v. Ukraine (74432/01) 21 June 2005, para. 22.
15. ECtHR, Rantsev v. Cyprus and Russia (25965/04) 7 January 2010.
16. Allain Jean, Rantsev v Cyprus and Russia: the European Court of Human Rights and Trafficking as Slavery. Human Rights Law Review 3 (2010): 555.
17. *Ibid.*, p. 557.

suffering reprisals from their traffickers or being re-trafficked.[18] Commentators also highly valued the contribution of the ECtHR to the development of 'the human rights approach to trafficking' which they say 'offered a ray of light at the end of the tunnel'.[19] In fact, the ECtHR provided the States with a kind of guidance in order to come out of the tunnel. It emphasised the States' obligation to put in place a legislative and administrative framework to prohibit and punish trafficking.[20] The ECtHR also concluded that the States in cross-border trafficking cases were subject to a duty to cooperate effectively with the relevant authorities of the other States concerned in the investigation of events which occurred outside their territories.[21]

In the recent case *L.E. v. Greece*,[22] concerning the investigation of the criminal complaint of human-trafficking, the Court underlined that criminal proceedings in such cases constitute the appropriate legal remedy.[23] Having established that the national legislation provided the applicant with practical and effective protection the Court pointed significant shortcomings and delays in the relevant procedure. It found that the status of the victim of the human trafficking was granted to the applicant about nine months after the complaint, that operational measures aimed at her protection were insufficient as well as the police attempts to find the main perpetrator of the crime and bring him before the courts.[24] These findings permitted the ECtHR to conclude the violation of the procedural facet of the Article 4.

[A] Definitions

The Strasbourg case law developed the understanding of the Convention prohibition against involuntary servitude. In the earlier case of *Van Droogenbroeck v. Belgium*, which concerned prison labour, 'servitude' was described as a 'particularly serious form of denial of freedom.'[25] In addition to the obligation to perform certain services for others it includes the obligation for the 'serf' to live on another person's property and the impossibility of altering his condition.[26]

In cases concerning the involuntary labour of illegal immigrants two common elements between slavery and being held in servitude can be established: a slave/serf cannot claim wages because the contract is illegal and she cannot report abuse to the authorities for reasons such as for fear of deportation. She is treated like an object,

18. Saadiya Chaudary. Trafficking in Europe: An Analysis of the Effectiveness of European Law. Michigan Journal of International Law 33 (2011): 85–86.
19. Pati, Roza. States' Positive Obligations with Respect to Human Trafficking: The European Court of Human Rights Breaks New Ground in Rantsev v. Cyprus & Russia. Boston University International Law Journal 29(1) (2011): 141.
20. ECtHR, Rantsev v. Cyprus and Russia (25965/04) 7 January 2010, para. 285.
21. *Ibid.*, para. 289.
22. ECtHR, L.E. v. Greece (71545/12) 21 January 2016.
23. *Ibid.*, para. 56.
24. *Ibid.*, paras 77, 83–85.
25. ECtHR, Van Droogenbroeck v. Belgium (7906/77) 24 June 1982, paras 78–80.
26. *Ibid.*

rather than a subject of rights.[27] The main point of difference is the absence of evidence on the exercise of the right of ownership over the serf.

In *Siliadin v. France*, the ECtHR had to determine whether the situation of the applicant, an unpaid domestic worker, fell within the concept of involuntary servitude or slavery. It attached principal attention to the following circumstances:

- the duration of work (almost fifteen hours a day, seven days per week);
- the (in)voluntary nature of the work undertaken (the applicant was a minor, who had been brought to France by relatives and had not chosen to work for her 'employers');
- the restriction of basic freedoms (the applicant had no freedom of movement and no free time, she had not been sent to school); and
- the ability to seek relief (as a minor, she had no resources and no means of living elsewhere other than in the home of her 'employers', as her papers had been confiscated).

Deliberation on these factors led the ECtHR to conclude that although the applicant was clearly deprived of her personal autonomy, the evidence does not suggest that she was held in slavery in the proper sense, as her status was not reduced to an 'object' of rights.[28] It was found that the applicant was held in servitude within the meaning of Article 4 of the ECHR. The reasoning of the ECtHR on this point has been criticised as being too narrow a reading of slavery.[29] The ECtHR was criticised for linking the ECHR prohibition on slavery to traditional chattel slavery and thereby requiring a 'genuine right of legal ownership' before the right could be enlivened.[30] However, the difference between these notions is not of crucial importance for the purpose of protecting the victims of slavery or involuntary servitude. In any case, as will be demonstrated further, the States are obliged to ensure effective protection and prompt investigation of such crimes.

Applications similar to *Siliadin* were considered by the ECtHR in *C.N. and V. v. France*[31] and *C.N. v. The United Kingdom*.[32] In the first case, the ECtHR observed that servitude corresponds with a special type of forced or compulsory labour and called it an 'aggravated' forced or compulsory labour. The fundamental distinguishing feature between involuntary servitude and forced or compulsory labour within the meaning of Article 4 was found in the victims' belief that their condition was permanent and that the situation was unlikely to change. The ECtHR found that belief credible, considering the applicants were illegal immigrants, the threats to denounce them to immigration

27. Virginia Mantouvalou, The Right to Non-exploitative Work In: Virginia Mantouvalou, editor. 'The Right to Work Legal and Philosophical Perspectives'. Hart Publishing, 2015, p. 59.
28. ECtHR, Siliadin v. France (73316/01) 26 July 2005, para. 122.
29. Andrea Nicholson, Reflections on Siliadin v. France: slavery and legal definition. The International Journal of Human Rights 14(5) (2010): 705.
30. *See* H. Cullen, Silihadin v. France: Positive Obligations under Article 4 of the European Convention Human Rights. Human Rights Law Review 6 (2006): 585, cited from Anne T. Gallagher. The International Law of Human Trafficking. Cambridge University Press, 2010, p. 187.
31. ECtHR, C.N. and V. v. France (67724/09) 11 October 2012, para. 91.
32. ECtHR, C.N. v. The United Kingdom (4239/08) 13 November 2012.

authorities[33] and the real potential for them to be sent back to their home country where they would be exposed to dangers that could threaten their lives.[34]

[B] Positive Obligations of the States

In all of these cases on illegal domestic work, the ECtHR found that Article 4 had been breached. The States were held liable as they failed to establish an effective system granting protection and remedy to the applicants in the circumstances of domestic servitude. It is interesting to note in this context that the new Protocol to the ILO Convention N 29[35] includes the obligation of states to ensure that all victims of forced or compulsory labour, irrespective of their presence or legal status in the national territory, have access to appropriate and effective remedies, such as compensation (Article 4-1). As of the date of writing this paper, this Protocol has been ratified only by Nigeria.[36] Therefore, the ECHR is the most efficient international instrument given its provisions are binding on all members of the CoE and the ECtHR's case law has established a set of positive obligations on Member States in relation to the prohibition on slavery and involuntary servitude. The ECtHR has stated that the States must enact domestic law criminalising slavery, involuntary servitude and forced labour and to ensure the effective prosecution of such crimes.[37]

Commentators noticed that Article 4 of the ECHR also sets certain requirements as to the quality of the definitions of these crimes.[38] In *Siliadin* the ECtHR was dissatisfied with the definitions of slavery and servitude in French law as the ECtHR considered they were open to very differing interpretations from one court to another.[39] Above this the ECtHR required a certain quality of investigation of such crimes. Thus in the case of trafficking the ECtHR laid down the following standard which should be spread to slavery and servitude:

> The requirement to investigate does not depend on a complaint from the victim or next-of-kin: once the matter has come to the attention of the authorities they must act of their own motion. For an investigation to be effective, it must be independent from those implicated in the events. It must also be capable of leading to the identification and punishment of individuals responsible, an obligation not of result but of means. A requirement of promptness and reasonable expedition is implicit in all cases but where the possibility of removing the individual from the harmful situation is available, the investigation must be undertaken as a matter of

33. *Ibid.*, para. 80.
34. ECtHR, C.N. and V. v. France (67724/09) 11 October 2012, para. 78.
35. Protocol of 2014 to the Forced Labour Convention, 1930, adopted in Geneva 11 June 2014.
36. *See* the ratification list on the Official site of ILO: http://www.ilo.org/dyn/normlex/en/f?p=1000:11300:0::NO:11300:P11300_INSTRUMENT_ID:3174672 (accessed 27 May 2015).
37. ECtHR, Siliadin v. France (73316/01) 26 July 2005, paras 89, 112.
38. *See* Vladislava Stoyanova. Article 4 of the ECHR and the Obligation of Criminalizing Slavery, Servitude, Forced Labour and Human Trafficking. Cambridge Journal of International and Comparative Law 3(2) (2014): 430.
39. ECtHR, Siliadin v. France, para. 147.

urgency. The victim or the next-of-kin must be involved in the procedure to the extent necessary to safeguard their legitimate interests.[40]

Thus the ECtHR developed its approach to the State's positive obligations under Article 4, focusing on the promptness and efficiency of their implementation. Scholars have praised the ECtHR's contribution to right to be protected against slavery and being held in servitude. It was noted that the ECtHR has set a high standard, reflected in the extent of the positive obligation it imposes on the States.[41] The legal positions expressed in this judgment are hoped to become useful weapons in the armoury of lawyers representing victims of trafficking.[42]

§3.02 FORCED OR COMPULSORY LABOUR

Article 4 of the ECHR states:

1. No one shall be held in slavery or servitude
2. No one shall be required to perform forced or compulsory labour.
3. For the purpose of this Article the term 'forced or compulsory labour' shall not include: (a) any work required to be done in the ordinary course of detention imposed according to the provisions of Article 5 of this Convention or during conditional release from such detention; (b) any service of a military character or, in case of conscientious objectors in countries where they are recognised, service exacted instead of compulsory military service; (c) any service exacted in case of an emergency or calamity threatening the life or well-being of the com-munity; (d) any work or service which forms part of normal civic obligations.

[A] Definition

The concepts of forced or compulsory labour are interpreted by the ECtHR based on the 'guidelines' set out in the third part of Article 4 of the ECHR (referred to below as Article 4-3) and on the ILO Conventions. ILO Convention No. 29 on Forced or Compulsory Labour has been cited in all the cases considered to date under Article 4-2 of the ECHR. According to this instrument the term forced or compulsory labour means all work or service which is exacted from any person under the menace of any penalty and for which the said person has not offered himself voluntarily. ILO Convention No. 29 lists the types of work which are excluded from the term 'forced and compulsory labour'. This list provided in Article 4-3 of the ECHR is largely analogous. However, in contrast with ILO instrument, the ECHR lacks the precision of the meaning of 'emergency' used in this article.

40. ECtHR, Rantsev v. Cyprus and Russia (25965/04) 7 January 2010, para. 288.
41. Andrea Nicholson, Reflections on Siliadin v. France: slavery and legal definition. The International Journal of Human Rights 14(5) (2010): 715.
42. Egan Suzanne, Protecting the Victims of Trafficking: Problems and Prospects. European Human Rights Law Review 1 (2008): 118.

The concepts of forced and compulsory labour are always mentioned together in the ECHR, in the ILO Conventions and are never divided in the jurisprudence of the ECtHR. Interpreting the word 'labour' the ECtHR has noted that it included any work or service, both manual and intellectual.[43]

[B] Elements of Forced or Compulsory Labour

In the earlier case of *I. v. Norway* (called also *Iversen v. Norway*), the Commission stated that forced labour was comprised of two fundamental elements: first, the work or service is performed by the worker against his will; and, secondly, the work or service performed is unjust, oppressive, or involves avoidable hardship.[44] *Iversen* concerned a law passed in Norway in 1956 which provided that dentists could be required to work for a public dental clinic for a period of up to two years. The applicant, who was appointed to work in the northern area of Norway, claimed that this appointment breached the prohibition against forced or compulsory labour. The Commission declared the complaint manifestly ill-founded. The majority of the Commission held that there was no question of forced or compulsory labour, because the service to be rendered was exacted for a limited time, was properly remunerated and was in keeping with the profession chosen by Iversen, while the law in question had not been applied against him in an arbitrary or discriminatory manner.[45] Therefore the points of due remuneration, the temporary character of such work and its social importance made the Commission conclude that the applicant's work in the appointed area did not amount to compulsory labour.

The ECtHR's jurisprudence under Article 4 of the ECHR provides much information on what is not considered as forced and compulsory labour as article was found not to be violated in any of the relevant cases. For instance, in *V.T. v. France*, the ECtHR concluded that the imposition of an obligation to pay family-allowance-contribution on the person who was given aid to stop working as a prostitute, did not necessarily mean that she was forced by the conduct of the collecting agency to continue to work as a prostitute.[46]

[C] Analysis of Cases Considered Under Article 4-3

Clause (a) of article 4-3

According to clause (a) of Article 4-3, any work required to be done in the ordinary course of detention imposed according to the provisions of Article 5 of the ECHR (or during conditional release from such detention) would not constitute forced labour.

43. ECtHR, Van der Mussele v. Belgium (8919/80) 23 November 1983, para. 33.
44. EurCommHR, I. v. Norway (1468/62) inadmissible 17 December 1963.
45. Pieter van Dijk, Godefridus J.H. Hoof. Theory and Practice of the European Convention on Human Rights. Martinus Nijhoff Publishers, 1998, p. 337.
46. ECtHR, V.T. v. France (37194/02) 11 September 2007.

The reference to Article 5 of the ECHR is especially important as this article establishes the rules of lawful detention. The logic of the drafters is evident: the work of a prisoner is not forced only if the imprisonment itself was lawful. In the famous 'vagrancy' case[47] the ECtHR noted that not every breach of Article 5 will automatically lead to the finding that of applicants' work in detention was 'forced' in character. In this case, the Commission of Human Rights found that the work which the applicants were compelled to perform in detention was not justified under Article 4 as, in its opinion, there had been a breach of Article 5-4. The ECtHR agreed with the Commission on the violation of Article 5-4; however, it refrained from deducing a violation of Article 4). The ECtHR interpreted Article 4-3(a) as authorising work ordinarily required of individuals deprived of their liberty under Article 5-1(e). As the violation of this provision was not found and the duty to work imposed on the three applicants had, in the ECtHR's view, not exceeded the 'ordinary' limits within the meaning of Article 4-3(a) of the ECHR, and the work they were required to undertake was aimed at their rehabilitation, the ECtHR concluded that the Belgian authorities did not fail to comply with the requirements of Article 4.[48] This case is a vivid example of the restrictive interpretation of Article 4.

There is a curious difference between the formulation of the provision on prisoners' labour in the ECHR and in the ILO Convention No. 129. The text of the ECHR does not restrict the employment of prisoners in the private sector, which is explicitly prohibited by Article 2-2(c) of the ILO Convention No. 29.[49] The European Commission on Human rights in its earlier jurisprudence on this provision had to refer to the reason of this striking difference. It could find no mention for this discrepancy in the preparatory works on the ECHR. The Commission was left to assume that the drafters, in omitting this clause, had regard to the huge range of prison labour systems prevailing in the European countries; the widespread use of prison labour in conjunction with private enterprise and to the difficulties of the ILO in its ability to reform prison labour systems; finally they had regard to the concerns which were arising even under the ILO Convention at the time as to whether it was really necessary and desirable to exclude the employment of prisoners in conjunction with private enterprise, particularly as it had appeared that such work offered more possibilities of professional training and readaptation that could justify the use of prisoners' labour.[50]

Based on these arguments, the Strasbourg bodies established jurisprudence confirming that low remuneration or the work of prisoners in the private sphere did not constitute a violation of Article 4 of the ECHR.[51] For example, in the case *X. v. The Federal Republic of Germany*, the Commission declared inadmissible the application of

47. ECtHR, De Wilde, Ooms and Versyp ('Vagrancy') v. Belgium (2832/66 et al.) 18 June 1971.
48. ECtHR, De Wilde, Ooms and Versyp ('Vagrancy') v. Belgium (2832/66 et al.) 18 June 1971, paras 88–90.
49. The American convention on Human Rights, in contrast, explicitly prohibits the use of prisoners' labour in private sector (Art. 6).
50. EurCommHR, Twenty-one detained persons v. Germany (3134/67 et al.) inadmissible 6 April 1968.
51. *See* Twenty-one detained persons v. Germany; EurCommHR, R. against the Federal Republic of Germany (1854/63) inadmissible 28 September 1964; V. against Austria (2066/63) inadmissible 17 December 1965.

the prisoner who claimed that he and other prisoners were forced to work forty-two hours a week for private industries but had no right to wages at a time when those private industries paid normal wages to the Bavarian State for the work done by the prisoners but the latter only received between 0.30 DM and 0.80 DM a day.[52]

In respect of prisoners' work, the Strasbourg bodies were reluctant to conclude that the absence of payment constituted a breach of Article 4. In *Twenty-one Detained Persons v. Germany* the Commission observed that Article 4 does not contain any provision concerning the remuneration of prisoners for their work. In recent cases the ECtHR tends to agree with the Commission, noting that the fact that work is unpaid did not in itself 'prevent work of this kind from being regarded as "work required to be done in the ordinary course of detention"' However, in *Zhelyazkov v. Bulgaria,*[53] the ECtHR referred to the 'subsequent developments' in this sphere, reflecting, in particular, on the European Prison Rules 2006, which called for the equitable remuneration of the work of prisoners. This stance gave some hope that in cases concerning unpaid prison work which occurred after 2006, the ECtHR might acknowledge the evolving trends in prison work remuneration, and find a positive obligation on the part of states to remunerate appropriately the work of all detainees in all circumstances.

This hope was dispelled by the decision in *Floroiu v. Romania.*[54] The applicant complained that he had not been paid for the work he had done while in prison. Romanian legislation provided that prisoners could either carry out paid work or, in the case of tasks involving the day-to-day running of the prison, prisoners could undertake unpaid work in exchange for a reduction of their sentence. As the applicant decided to opt for the latter and his sentence was accordingly reduced, the ECtHR concluded that the work he had carried out had not been entirely unremunerated and refused to find that there was a violation of Article 4. It can therefore be seen that the ECtHR grants a particularly wide margin of appreciation to the states in cases dealing with the remuneration of prisoners. From the point of view of a labour scholar, such an approach to remuneration is hardly justifiable; in any case a minimum wage should be granted. Such an approach would be in line with the relevant Recommendation of the Committee of Ministers to Member States on the European Prison Rules.[55]

In the recent case of *Stummer v. Austria*[56] the ECtHR examined a new facet of the notion of forced labour. The applicant had worked in prison for twenty-eight years without affiliation to the old-age pension system. He argued that such work, performed without such an affiliation, could no longer be regarded as work required to be done in the ordinary course of detention and thus violated Article 4 of the ECHR. The ECtHR did not agree with the applicant's interpretation of Article 4 and concluded that the obligatory work he had performed as a prisoner, without being affiliated to the old-age

52. EurCommHR, X. v. The Federal Republic of Germany (2413/65) inadmissible 16 December 1966.
53. ECtHR, Zhelyazkov v. Bulgaria (11332/04) 9 October 2012, para. 36.
54. ECtHR, Floroiu v. Romania (15303/10) 12 March 2013.
55. Recommendation Rec(2006)2 of the Committee of Ministers to Member States on the European Prison Rules, adopted 11 January 2006, para. 26.10. Available at: https://wcd.coe.int/ViewDoc.jsp?id=955747#P6_138 (accessed 20 July 2015).
56. ECtHR, Stummer v. Austria (37452/02) 7 July 2011.

pension system, had to be regarded as 'work required to be done in the ordinary course of detention' within the meaning of Article 4-3(a) of the ECHR and did not therefore constitute forced or compulsory labour.

The Stummer judgment has been hailed by commentators as an 'unfortunate development in the evolution of the case law under Article 4,'[57] particularly in light of the contrary way in which social policies in Europe are developing. Judge F. Tulkens in the partly dissenting opinion noted that more than forty years have passed since such applications by prisoners were ruled inadmissible and prison law – which at that time was virtually non-existent – had developed considerably during the intervening period. Tulkens J emphasised that prisons have gradually been opened up to fundamental rights as the European Prison Rules emphasise the need for equitable remuneration for prisoners and concluded that in the light of current standards in the field of social security, prison work without affiliation to the old-age pension system cannot constitute work which is understood to be 'normally required' in detention.[58]

This judgment was referred to in a later similar case – *Floroiu v. Romania*,[59] mentioned earlier above. There, the applicant claimed that in violation of Article 4 he had been required to perform tasks which were difficult, unpleasant and badly paid, during a total of twenty-five years in prison without being affiliated to the old-age pension system. The ECtHR did not see any particular grounds for departing from its conclusions expressed in the Stummer case.

By refusing on this further occasion to apply a 'living interpretation' to Article 4, the ECtHR effectively confirmed its reluctance to interfere with the social policies of the States and according to its traditions[60] acknowledged a wide margin of appreciation as far as general measures of economic or social strategy are concerned.[61]

A new facet of the derogative clause 4-2 has been recently considered in *Meier v. Switzerland*.[62] For the first time in its case law the Court had to reveal whether the obligation to work imposed on the prisoner after reaching retirement age constituted the violation of the ECHR. Having considered all the circumstances of the case[63] and having attached much weight to the lack of consensus in regulating this matter between the European States the judges were unanimous to conclude that the ECHR was not violated.[64] The Court acknowledged the wide margin of appreciation of the states in determining the conditions of prisoners' work for those who reached the

57. Virginia Mantouvalou, The Prohibition of Slavery, Servitude and Forced and Compulsory Labour under Article 4 ECHR In: Filip Dorssemont, Klaus Lörcher, Isabelle Schömann, editors. 'The European Convention on Human Rights and the Employment Relation'. Oxford: Hart Publishing, 2013, p. 153.
58. ECtHR, Stummer v. Austria (37452/02) 7 July 2011, Partly Dissenting Opinion Of Judge Tulkens, para. 8.
59. ECtHR, Floroiu v. Romania (15303/10) 12 March 2013.
60. ECtHR, Stec and Others v. UK (65731/01 and 65900/01) 12 April 2006, para. 52.
61. ECtHR, Stummer v. Austria (37452/02) 7 July 2011, paras 88, 89.
62. ECtHR, Meier v. Switzerland (10109/14) 9 February 2016.
63. The Court, in particular, pointed that the duty to work had a legitimate aim and that the age and the state of health of prisoners were taken into account while appointing job tasks.
64. ECtHR, Meier v. Switzerland (10109/14) 9 February 2016, paras 30–32, 79.

retirement age since the provisions of the Convention do not indicate that such regulations should be considered as forced labour.

This judgment one more time underlines the importance of comparative research for adjudication of cases which pose new questions before the Court. The reference to European consensus might be considered as a possibility to overrule the judgment in case if the approach of European countries to this matter will significantly change with time and the majority of the states will exclude prisoners of retirement age from obligatory work.

Clause (b) of Article 4-3

Article 4-3(b) states that any service of a military character or, in case of conscientious objectors in countries where they are recognised, service exacted instead of compulsory military service do not fall under the category of forced labour.

Interpretation of military service

In the recent case of *Chitos v. Greece*[65] the ECtHR noted that this provision is formulated differently from ILO Convention No. 29, which only provides an exception in relation to compulsory military service. The applicant, an army officer, argued that the obligation to pay a fee to the State in order to resign before the end of his period of service constituted forced labour. Therefore, this case was a significant opportunity for the ECtHR to delimit specifically the exceptions covered by Article 4-3(b). The ECtHR referred to the European Social Charter, the ILO Convention No. 29 and Recommendation CM/Rec (2010) 4 of the Committee of Ministers to Member States on human rights of members of the armed forces. Based on these international instruments the ECtHR concluded that in accordance with the object and purpose of the ECHR, the provision of the Article 4-3(b) should be read as covering only compulsory military service.[66]

This finding permitted the ECtHR to consider a new facet of forced labour. The ECtHR firstly pointed that the State's desire to secure a return on its investment in the training of army officers justified prohibiting their resignation from the forces for a specified period and to subject them to paying a fee in order to cover the subsistence and training costs.[67] Then it went on to consider the proportionality of the obligation to pay a fee in the sum of EUR 109,527. The ECtHR noted that the applicant was not given the option to pay this sum in instalments, even though he had had an appeal pending before the Court of Audit and noted that significant interest for late payment had been charged. Therefore, the violation of Article 4-2(b) was determined by the shortcomings of the State's procedure for buying back the remaining years of service. This judgment is very important as interprets Article 4-2(b) in a narrow way, excluding from it contractual military service, and introduces the principle of proportionality in the

65. ECtHR, Chitos v. Greece (51637/12) 4 June 2015.
66. ECtHR, Chitos v. Greece (51637/12) 4 June 2015, para. 87.
67. *Ibid.*, para. 94.

relationship between the State and a military officer who wishes to resign before the established term.

Conscientious objections to military service

In earlier case law the Commission was of the view that Article 4-2(b) left it open to the states as to whether they wished to recognise conscientious objectors and, if they did, to provide some substitute service that conscientious objectors could carry out in place of military service. It followed that even in cases of conscientious objections to military service based on religious beliefs, which is protected under Article 9 of the ECHR, Article 4 did not prevent a State which had not recognised a right for conscientious objections from punishing those who refused to do military service on the grounds of being a conscientious objector.[68]

The Chamber of the ECtHR relied on this interpretation in the case of *Bayatyan v. Armenia*.[69] The applicant who was convicted for refusing to perform military service claimed the violation of Articles 4 and 9. He argued that the absence of an opportunity for conscientious objectors to perform alternative service to military service violated the ECHR. The applicant asked the ECtHR to interpret the relevant provisions of Article 4 in an innovative way, departing from the previous case law with regard to significant shifts in the recognition of the rights for conscientious objection to military service in Europe. The Chamber was reluctant to integrate the right for conscientious objections into the ECHR. It placed greater emphasis on the fact that the drafters clearly left the choice of recognising conscientious objectors to each Contracting Party. It also noted that at the material time this right was not fixed in Armenian legislation. Based on these findings, the Chamber concluded that the absence of an opportunity to perform alternative civilian service in Armenia did not constitute the violation of Articles 4 and 9 of the ECHR. It must be noted that the ECtHR's reasoning was not accepted by conscientious objectors and their supporters.[70]

The Grand Chamber, considering this case on 7 July 2011, shifted from the previous approach of examining conscientious objection cases under Article 4 together with Article 9. Its view was that such an approach did not reflect the true purpose and meaning of Article 4. The reference to the travaux préparatoires made the ECtHR presume that the sole purpose Article 4-3(b) was to provide a further elucidation of the notion of 'forced or compulsory labour' and therefore in itself it neither recognised nor excluded a right to conscientious objection. On these grounds it considered the case in light of Article 9, which protects the right to freedom of religion and conscience, and found the violation of that article instead.

This Grand Chamber judgment is a vivid example of an applicant requesting a living interpretation of the ECHR. It also illustrates the impact of domestic trends in

---

68. EurCommHR, Grandrath v. Germany (2299/64) 12 December 1966; G.Z. v. Autriche (5591/72) inadmissible 2 April 1973; Conscientious objectors v. Denmark (7565/76) inadmissible 7 March 1977; A. v. Switzerland the Commission (10640/83) inadmissible, 9 May 1984.
69. ECtHR, Bayatyan v. Armenia (23459/03) 27 October 2009.
70. Özgür Heval Çınar. The Right to Conscientious Objection to Military Service and Turkey's Obligations under International Human Rights Law. Palgrave Macmillan, 2014, p. 76.

human rights protection and of other international instruments upon the ECtHR's reasoning. The Grand Chamber noted that at the time of the alleged interference only five Member States did not provide for the possibility of claiming conscientious objector status.[71] It emphasised that the respondent State also incorporated such norms after the beginning of the proceedings in the ECtHR.

The ECtHR's reasoning that it was necessary to retrospectively apply the evolved right is curious. It referred to the changes in the perception of similar norms of the International Covenant on Civil and Political Rights by the Human Rights Committee, which considered in 1993 that a right to conscientious objection could be derived from Article 18 of the ICCPR.[72] The approach of the EU and of the CoE to this problem was also mentioned as an additional argument for recognition of the right for conscientious objection. It was emphasised that the recognition of such a right was a precondition for admission of new Member States into the CoE and therefore that Armenia should have been aware of the shift in the interpretation of Article 9.[73]

This Grand Chamber judgment, which was called historical by scholars,[74] is remarkable as it brought Strasbourg case law in line with international standards on this point, expanded Article 9 rights[75] and at the same time restricted the application of Article 4-3(b). Legal positions expressed in this judgment must be interpreted as integrating the right for conscientious objection and consequently of the positive obligation of the State to provide the opportunity to perform alternative civilian service. In fact, in the later case of *Savda v. Turkey*,[76] the ECtHR explicitly recognised the positive obligation of the State to establish effective and accessible procedures by which the status of conscientious objector could be recognised.[77]

Clause (c) of Article 4-3

Article 4-3(c) states that any service exacted in case of an emergency or calamity threatening the life or wellbeing of the community would not constitute forced labour. In the ECtHR jurisprudence there is only one case dealing with this provision. The case of *S. v. Germany*[78] concerned an applicant with hunting rights who was required by the State to participate in a program of protection against rabies, which required the gassing of all fox-holes as a measure of controlling against epidemics. The Commission stated that the type of activity required from the applicant was within the scope permitted by the provisions of Article 4-3 and held the application manifestly ill-founded.

71. ECtHR, Bayatyan v. Armenia, para. 103.
72. *Ibid.*, para. 105.
73. *Ibid.*, para. 50.
74. Muzny Petr, Bayatyan v Armenia: The Grand Chamber Renders a Grand Judgment. Human Rights Law Review 12(1) (2012): 135.
75. R. Calo Zachary, Constructing the Secular: Law and Religion Jurisprudence in Europe and the United States. Robert Schuman Centre for Advanced Studies Research Paper No. RSCAS 94 (2014). Available at: http://cadmus.eui.eu/bitstream/handle/1814/32792/RSCAS_2014_94.pdf ?sequence=1 (accessed 25 May 2015).
76. ECtHR, Savda c. Turquie (42730/05) 12 June 2012.
77. ECtHR, Savda c. Turquie (42730/05) 12 June 2012, para. 99.
78. ECtHR, S. v. Germany (9686/82) inadmissible 4 October 1984.

Clause (d) of Article 4-3

According to clause 4-3(d) any work or service which forms part of normal civic obligations are not considered to be forced labour. The ECtHR noted that the understanding of civic obligations must be grounded on the governing ideas of the general interest, social solidarity and what is in the normal or ordinary course of affairs.[79]

These ideas were discussed by the ECtHR in relation to the imposition of the obligation to serve on a jury in *Zarb Adami v. Malta.*[80] In *Karlheinz Schmidt v. Germany,*[81] the ECtHR considered that compulsory fire service such as existed in some German regions was one of the 'normal civic obligations'.

Considering cases under this provision the ECtHR bases its analysis on two main factors. First, whether the work falls outside the ambit of an applicant's normal professional activities and usual work; and secondly, whether the work required of the applicant imposed a disproportionate burden.

Answering the first question, the ECtHR considered the nature of the applicant's professional work and concludes if the imposed work was of the same character. For example, in *Steindel v. Germany*[82] the Court stated that making a private ophthalmologist participate in an emergency-service scheme organised by a public body was to require him to perform work that fell within the applicant's usual professional activities. Therefore, the scope of the professional activities of doctors is perceived in a very broad manner. In *Kovalova v. Czech Republic*[83] the ECtHR found that the applicant's obligation to represent the interests of her deceased's husband's company in tax proceedings was based on an idea of general interest and was within the framework of 'normal civic obligations'.

In several cases the ECtHR has had to consider the civic obligation of lawyers. In 1972 the complaints of an Austrian lawyer about free legal aid had been declared admissible by the Commission, on the ground that 'these complaints raise issues of a complex nature' and could not therefore be declared manifestly ill-founded.[84] These cases led to a friendly settlement, so that the merits of the parties' arguments have not been pronounced on.[85]

In *X. and Y. v. Federal Republic of Germany*[86] the ECtHR considered whether the absence of advance in payment for the work of a state-appointed lawyer amounted to forced labour. The lack of pre-payment was considered as a non-decisive factor in the determination of forced labour, as the States were free to establish their system of remuneration of lawyers. It is interesting to note that the ECtHR interpreted Article 4 in the light of the right for fair trial and the right for legal aid. The Court referred to Article 6-3(c) and reasoned that, since in the ECHR the right to free legal aid has been

79. ECtHR, Van der Mussele v. Belgium (8919/80) 23 November 1983, para. 38.
80. ECtHR, Zarb Adami v. Malta (17209) 20 June 2006.
81. ECtHR, Karlheinz Schmidt v. Germany (13580/88) 18 July 1994.
82. ECtHR, Steindel v. Germany (29878/07) 14 September 2010.
83. ECtHR, Kovalova v. The Czech Republic (57319/00) inadmissible 30 November 2004.
84. ECtHR, Gussenbauer v. Austria (4897/71 and 5219/7) 14 July 1972.
85. Cited from Di Pieter van Dijk, Godefridus J.H. Hoof, G.J.H. Van Hoof. Theory and Practice of the European Convention on Human Rights. Martinus Nijhoff Publishers, 1998, p. 338.
86. ECtHR, X. and Y. v. Federal Republic of Germany (7641/76) 11 December 1976.

recognised, the obligation for a lawyer to give legal aid in a concrete case cannot constitute forced or compulsory labour in the sense of Article 4-2 of the ECHR. Commentators have noted that this conclusion lacks logical approach. The right to legal aid per se does not say anything about the way in which the authorities must give effect to this right and does not necessarily imply that this should be done via an obligation for lawyers to give such legal aid under conditions to be laid down by the authorities.[87] In fact, the submissions made by one party's reference to Article 6 in the context of the application on forced labour seems to be a very artificial and poor argument.

In the later case of *Van der Mussel v. Belgium*,[88] the ECtHR had to decide on the same issue of unpaid lawyer's work. The applicant complained that Article 4-2 had been violated by the failure to pay him for his work as a pupil advocate and because if he refused to work in that capacity he would be liable to sanctions. The ECtHR applied the two-stage test referred to in the cases discussed above and considered the following matters:

> The services to be rendered did not fall outside the ambit of the normal activities of an advocate.
> The student had voluntarily chosen the profession of advocate with knowledge of the practice complained of.[89]
> There was a compensatory factor in the advantages attaching to the profession, including the exclusive right of audience and of representation enjoyed by advocates.
> The services in question contributed to the applicant's professional training and gave him the opportunity to enlarge his experience and to increase his reputation.
> The burden imposed on the applicant was not disproportionate as sufficient time remained for performance of his paid work.[90]

Having regard to the generally prevailing standards in democratic societies, the ECtHR decided that in this case there was no compulsory labour for the purposes of Article 4-2 of the ECHR.

In that case as well as in the more recent *Graziani-Weiss v. Austria*,[91] concerning the appointment of the applicant lawyer as a legal guardian against his will and without payment, the ECtHR tended to interpret the civic obligations of the lawyer broadly. It did not pay sufficient attention to the factor of remuneration for the imposed work. The ECtHR's reference to the 'certain privileges of professional groups of lawyers' is not by itself a sufficient justification of the absence of remuneration.

87. Di Pieter van Dijk, Godefridus J.H. Hoof, G.J.H. Van Hoof. Theory and Practice of the European Convention on Human Rights. Martinus Nijhoff Publishers, 1998, p. 339.
88. ECtHR, Van der Mussele v. Belgium (8919/80) 23 November 1983.
89. *Ibid.*, para. 40.
90. ECtHR, Van der Mussele v. Belgium, para. 39.
91. ECtHR, Graziani-Weiss v. Austria (31950/06) 18 October 2011, paras 41, 42.

[D] The Lack of the ECtHR's Attention to the Factor of Remuneration

In *Ackerl and others v. Austria*[92] the applicants, judges, brought a complaint under Article 4 as they had to assume the work of other judges without receiving supplementary remuneration. The reasoning of the Commission, which declared the application inadmissible, was very brief. It stated that the applicants had freely entered public civil service and had not shown that their individual work-load had increased to such an excessive extent that the obligation to carry it out would have to be considered 'unjust' or 'oppressive'. The Commission, regretfully, did not explain further its perception of just conditions of labour and did not mention that fair conditions of work should, in the first place, ensure the right for due remuneration. It did not consider the fact that the refusal to perform such additional work could lead to disciplinary sanction. Such reasoning might have led the ECtHR to the conclusion that the additional unpaid work was exacted under the threat of penalties being imposed, thus amounting arguably to forced labour.

In *Vnuchko v. Ukraine*,[93] as in many other similar cases against Ukraine, the applicants submitted that unpaid work should be considered as forced labour. In all of these cases the ECtHR used its usual framework of analysis on forced labour cases and decided that the applicants performed the work voluntarily and their entitlement to payment had never been denied. Therefore the ECtHR concluded that the dispute did not disclose any element of forced or compulsory labour within the meaning of Article 4 and rejected the relevant part of the applications as being manifestly ill-founded.[94]

The same conclusion was reached by the Court in the recent case *Radi and Gherghina v. Romania*,[95] where the applicant, a special assistant to her disable nephew, claimed that a very low level of her remuneration amounted to forced and compulsory labour. The Court pointed that she was remunerated for her work and there was no indication of any sort of coercion either on the part of the nephew or on the part of the authorities and found the application inadmissible.[96] The Court did not pay attention to the fact that the applicant was deprived of her right for annual leave as the authorities could not provide her nephew with another assistant in this period. It also remained reluctant to consider such circumstances as the lack of personal assistants in Romania, which meant the necessity to fulfil this job, paid at the level of the minimum wage, by the close relatives of the disabled persons.[97] The Court noted that the applicant accepted her work willingly, as she voluntarily entered into a bilateral contract with the local authorities. But it remains highly questionable whether the work accepted in the lack of choice was entirely a voluntary chosen job, as the non acceptance of such contract would leave her disabled nephew at the mercy of fate without any assistance.

92. EurCommHR, Ackerl and others v. Austria (20781/92) 29 June 1994.
93. ECtHR, Vnuchko v. Ukraine (1198/04) 14 December 2006.
94. ECtHR, Popov v. Ukraine (23892/03) 14 December 2006, para. 14 and Sokur v. Ukraine (29439/02), 26 November 2002.
95. ECtHR, Radi and Gherghina (34655/14) 26 January 2016.
96. *Ibid.*, para. 27.
97. *Ibid.*, para. 18.

These cases yet again demonstrate the lack of willingness of the ECtHR's to expand the interpretation of the forced or compulsory labour, taking into account the monetary aspect of labour. In this context it must be noted that in some countries the concept of forced labour also includes unpaid work, thus attaching more importance to the principle of due remuneration and being more stringent about violations of employees' rights in this sphere.[98]

[E] The Obligation to Accept Any Job as a Criterion of Eligibility for Unemployment Benefits

In a series of cases against the Netherlands, applicants claimed that the obligation to accept any kind of employment in order to receive welfare benefits constituted the violation of Article 4. In 1976 an unemployed specialised building worker complained to the Commission that the obligation imposed on him to accept, in order to receive unemployment benefits, a job offer not in conformity with his qualifications, constituted 'compulsory labour'. Rejecting this complaint, the Commission observed that he was not compelled, by any penalty, to accept such an offer; nor would his refusal constitute an infringement of the law. A refusal would only be penalised by the temporary loss of unemployment benefits.[99] The same conclusion was reached in the later case *Talmon v. The Netherlands*.[100] The applicant, a scientist, complained that the reduction of unemployment benefits for the refusal to perform required work, to which he had a conscientious objection, amounted to forced labour. The Commission declared the application inadmissible as it did not find that the applicant was in any way forced to perform any kind of labour or that his refusal to look for other employment than that of an independent scientist made him liable to any measures other than the reduction of his unemployment benefits.

The ECtHR applied the same approach in considering the complaint of an unemployed philosopher who claimed that due to changes in the relevant legislation she was forced to seek and take up employment which was deemed to be 'generally acceptable' as opposed to being 'suitable', stipulated in the previous legislation.[101] In that case, the ECtHR stated that the obligation to accept any kind of work was in effect a condition for the granting of benefits, and the State, which had introduced a system of social security, was fully entitled to lay down conditions which have to be met for a person to be eligible for benefits under that system. The ECtHR emphasised that Dutch legislation provided that recipients of benefits were not required to seek and take up

98. *See*, for example, Art. 4 of the Russian Labour code. In India a failure to pay the minimum wage was regarded as forced or compulsory labour under the Art. 23 of the Constitution of India. *See* Ben Saul, David Kinley, Jaqueline Mowbray. The International Covenant on Economic, Social and Cultural Rights: Cases, Materials, and Commentary. Oxford University Press, 2014, p. 279.
99. ECtHR, X v. Netherlands, Application 7602/76, (1976) 7 Decisions and Reports 161, cited from Nihal Jayawickrama. The Judicial Application of Human Rights Law: National, Regional and International Jurisprudence. Cambridge University Press, 2002, p. 362.
100. EurCommHR, Talmon v. The Netherlands (30300/96) inadmissible 26 February 1997.
101. ECtHR, Schuitemaker v. The Netherlands (15906/08) inadmissible 4 May 2010.

employment which was not generally socially accepted or in respect of which they had conscientious objections.

This stance of the ECtHR demonstrates that, in spite of the recognition of a wide margin of appreciation of the States in establishing the social security system, certain positive obligations of the State might be deduced. Thus the State, establishing eligibility conditions for unemployment benefits, might be required to ensure that the work proposed to be given to an unemployed person, in circumstances whereas refusal to accept the job will lead to sufficient reduction or abolition of the relevant allowance, would not be in breach of his freedoms of religion, conscience and belief.

§3.03 CONCLUSIONS

The jurisprudence of the ECtHR in relation to Article 4 has both positive and negative aspects. The positive is the emphasis on the necessity of effective protection from slavery and involuntary servitude and including human trafficking within the activities prohibited by this article. The establishment of the qualitative requirements to the measures aimed at the prosecution of these crimes and to the protection of its victims is also a step forward. The negative aspect is the conservatism of the ECtHR's interpretation of forced labour as illustrated by a number of cases, including by *Stummer v. Austria*. The reluctance of the ECtHR to give greater consideration to the remuneration of people obliged to fulfil civic obligations is another criticism.

CHAPTER 4

Prohibition of Discrimination

The ECHR was the first international instrument which fixed an efficient prohibition of discrimination in 1950 after the proclamation of equality in Article 7 of the Universal Declaration of Human rights. Since then the prohibition of discrimination has become one of the most frequently declared norms of international human rights law.[102] The ILO acknowledged the principle of non-discrimination as a fundamental principle of labour law[103] and has created a well-developed system of norms prohibiting discrimination.[104] In this perspective, anti-discrimination law is one of the most mature and symptomatic examples of a global law that unifies and, at the same time, produces plural regulations.[105]

It might seem that discrimination in employment is already abundantly dealt with and that Article 14 of the ECHR is not relevant to labour law matters. However it is very important for the protection of both individual and collective labour rights. The ECtHR is the only international body on the European scene that can issue binding judgments and require the States to remedy discriminatory situations and to create effective systems of protection. For this reason, the applicants in cases concerning the violation of employment rights often refer to this article. Taking into account the fact that the prohibition of discrimination is equally relevant to the rights expressly set out in the ECHR and to the rights which were integrated subsequently as the result of evolutive interpretation, the scope of anti-discrimination protections guaranteed by Article 14 is

102. Anne Bayefski, The Principle of Equality or Non-discrimination in International Law. Human Rights Law Journal 11 (1990/1-2): 1.
103. ILO Declaration on Fundamental Principles and Rights at Work, 1998.
104. The ILO Discrimination (employment and occupation) Convention N 111, The ILO Equal Remuneration Convention N 100, ILO Recommendation concerning Discrimination in Respect of Employment and Occupation, No. 111, 1958, The ILO Vocational rehabilitation and employment (disabled Persons) Convention 1983 (No. 159); The ILO Convention N 169 on indigenous and tribal Peoples 1989; The ILO Convention N 175 on Part-time Work 1994; The ILO Convention N 156 on Workers with Family Responsibilities 1981.
105. Bruno Caruso, Changes in the Workplace and the Dialogue of Global Law in the Global Village. Comparative Labor Law & Policy Journal 28(3) (2007): 509.

very wide indeed. It has been taken to cover unfair dismissal,[106] the right of access to work,[107] wages and pensions (under Article 1 to the Protocol 1),[108] and the realisation at work of the rights expressly provided by Articles 9, 10 and 11 of the ECHR and the procedural aspect of protection of labour rights.[109]

To present the ECtHR's approach to discrimination more harmoniously, this part will consequently address the following topics: the general aspects of the ECtHR's approach to discrimination; research the peculiarities of the indirect discrimination; and analyse positive obligations of the States under Article 14. In all of these sections the research will be based on the case law of the Strasbourg bodies in respect of individual employment rights; the matters relating to the protection of trade unions and certain social security rights will be also taken into account.

§4.01 GENERAL ASPECTS OF THE ECTHR'S APPROACH TO DISCRIMINATION

According to Article 14 of the ECHR, the enjoyment of the rights and freedoms set out in the ECHR should be secured without discrimination on any ground such as sex, race, colour, language, religion, political or other opinion, national or social origin, association with a national minority, property, birth or other status.

The wording of this Article is at the same time broad and restrictive. It is broad insofar as it leaves open the list of discriminatory grounds and provides the ECtHR with a wide discretion as to whether the difference of treatment was discriminatory.[110] The traditional list of discriminatory grounds provided in the European Directives was extended in a number of cases including for example, the status of an adoptive mother. In *Topčić-Rosenberg v. Croatia*,[111] the ECtHR found the violation of Article 14 as the applicant had been denied the right to obtain maternity leave and related allowances after the adoption of her child, even though biological mothers had such a right from the date of the child's birth until its first birthday. The Strasbourg jurisprudence in the sphere of pension rights introduced another new ground such as the applicant's place of residence.[112] Commentators note that the broad approach to the ground of discrimination is advantageous as it helps the ECtHR to deal with complex forms of unequal

106. As the Court integrated to the Art. 8 the right to personal development, and the right to establish and develop relationships with other human beings and the outside world, *see* Oleksandr Volkov v. Ukraine (21722/11) 9 January 2013, Niemietz v. Germany (13710/88) 16 December 1992.
107. ECtHR, Sidabras and Dziautas v. Lithuania (55480/00 59330/00) 27 July 2004, Bigaeva v. Greece (26713/05) 28 May 2009.
108. ECtHR, Valkov and Others v. Bulgaria (2033/04) 25 October 2011, Stec and Others v. UK (65731/01, 65900/01), 12 April 2006.
109. ECtHR, Fogarty v. The United Kingdom (37112/97) 21 November 2001.
110. For example, in non-labour law cases the legal status of the son was found to be a discriminatory ground in ECtHR, Mazurek v. France (34406/97) 1 February 2000, Fabris v. France (16574/08) 7 February 2013 or the size of plot of land - in Chassagnou v. France, No 25088) 29 April 1999.
111. ECtHR, Topčić-Rosenberg v. Croatia (19391/11) 14 November 2013, para. 40.
112. ECtHR, Pichkur v. Ukraine (10441/06) 7 November 2013.

treatment, such as discrimination based on multiple or cumulative grounds or intersectional discrimination.[113]

The restrictiveness of the Article 14 is due to its complementary nature, as it only complements the other provisions of the ECHR and its Protocols which contain the substantive rules.[114]

The adoption of Protocol 12 to the ECHR[115] was intended to provide a wider protection against discrimination without attaching the difference in treatment to the violation of ECHR rights. This Protocol contains a general prohibition of discrimination in the realisation of any right guaranteed by law and might be more applicable in the sphere of labour rights' protection, as employment rights are not explicitly covered by the ECHR. However, it has, as at the date of writing, been ratified by only eighteen states[116] (out of the forty-seven members of the CoE), and its violation had been found only in three cases which were unrelated to labour law.[117]

The text of this Protocol was criticised by certain scholars for the lack of conceptual definitions and for containing ambiguities.[118] Present research of the ECtHR's jurisprudence on discrimination confirms that its provisions are actually not applicable in labour law cases and that Article 14 remains the principal source of anti-discrimination in the Strasbourg system.

As has already been mentioned, the protection against discrimination under Article 14 might be granted if the difference of treatment occurred in the enjoyment of the rights and freedoms fixed in this ECHR. Therefore, the ECtHR treats equality as being auxiliary to substantive rights[119] and tends to interpret this provision in a broad way. Following the legal positions of the Commission,[120] the ECtHR established that it is enough for the discrimination in issue to 'touch the enjoyment of a specific right or freedom,'[121] in other words, 'the facts should fall within the ambit of one or more of the substantive provisions of the Convention and its Protocols.'[122]

113. Janneke Gerards, The Discrimination Grounds of Article 14 of the European Convention on Human Rights. Human Rights Law Review 13(1) (2013): 119.
114. *See*, for example: ECtHR, Bigaeva v. Greece (No. 26713/05) 28 May 2009.
115. Signed in Rome on 5 November 2000.
116. The status of the Protocol N 12 to the ECHR. Available at: onventions.coe.int/Treaty/Commun/ChercheSig.asp?NT=177&CM=&DF=&CL=ENG (accessed 18 February 2015).
117. ECtHR, Sejdić and Finci v. Bosnia and Herzegovina [GC](27996/06, 34836/06) 22 December 2009; Zornić v. Bosnia and Herzegovina (3681/06) 15 July 2014; Savez crkava 'Riječ života' and Others v. Croatia (7798/08) 9 December 2010.
118. Khaliq Urfan, Protocol 12 to the European Convention on Human Rights: A Step Forward or a Step Too Far? Public Law 3 (2001): 457-464.
119. C. Barnard, B. Hepple, Substantive Equality. Cambridge Law Journal 59(3) (November 2000): 567.
120. Opinion of the Commission on human rights in the 'Belgian Linguistic Case' delivered 24 June 1965, cited in ECtHR, 'Relating to certain aspects of the laws on the use of languages in education in Belgium' v. Belgium (1474/62 et al.) 23 July 1968.
121. ECtHR, 'Relating to certain aspects of the laws on the use of languages in education in Belgium' v. Belgium (1474/62 et al.) 23 July 1968, para. 4.
122. ECtHR, Okpisz v. Germany (59140/00) 25 October 2005, para. 30, Willis v. THE UK (36042/97) 11 June 2002, para. 36.

This interpretation of the prohibition of discrimination evidently makes the provisions of Article 14 more applicable in labour law cases. Article 8, for example, does not provide any labour rights, however the ambit of the right to the respect for private life is very 'spacious'. It includes the protection of the moral, psychological and physical integrity of the person[123] and protection of the rights to personal development.[124] Article 8 also protects the right to establish relationships with others, including relationships of a professional nature[125] and to access a profession in the private sector.[126] Therefore, the difference of treatment in the realisation of one of the mentioned rights will fall within the ambit of Article 14. The Strasbourg bodies' broad perception of the 'ambit' is in contrast with the approaches of domestic judges. British judges, for instance, appear to interpret the relevant provisions of the *Human Rights Act 1998* (UK) in light of their perception of Article 14 as 'parasitic,' and conceive it as a slightly extended version of the protective scope of the other more 'substantive' articles.[127]

[A] The Way of Adjudication of Applications Alleging Discrimination

The principle of non-discrimination was filled with meaning by the ECtHR through developing an analytical approach and applying it to individual cases.[128] According to the ECtHR case law, not every difference in treatment would amount to discrimination as prohibited by the ECHR. The ECtHR stated: 'In spite of the very general wording of the French version ('sans distinction aucune'), Article 14 did not forbid every difference in treatment in the exercise of the rights and freedoms recognised'.[129] Only differences in treatment based on an identifiable characteristic, or 'status', are capable of amounting to discrimination within the meaning of Article 14.[130] The ECtHR established the criteria which would enable a determination to be made as to whether or not a given difference in treatment contravened Article 14. It held that 'the principle of equality of treatment is violated if the distinction has no objective and reasonable justification,'[131] and that 'the existence of such a justification must be assessed in relation to the aim and effects of the measure under consideration, regard being had to

123. ECtHR, Brincat and others v. Malta, Raninen v. Finland (20972/92) 16 December 1997; Kyriakides v. Cyprus (39058/05) 16 October 2008.
124. ECtHR, Oleksandr Volkov v. Ukraine (21722/11) 9 January 2013, para. 65.
125. ECtHR, C. v. Belgium (21794/93) 7 August 1996, para. 25.
126. ECtHR, Sidabras and Džiautas v. Lithuania (55480/00, 59330/00) 27 July 2004, para. 47.
127. Baker, Aaron. 'The Enjoyment of Rights and Freedoms: A New Conception of the 'Ambit' under Article 14 ECHR.' The Modern Law Review 69(5) (2006): 714–737. Available at: http://dro.dur.ac.uk/3236/1/3236.pdf (accessed 20 May 2015).
128. Oddný Mjöll Arnardóttir. Equality and Non-Discrimination Under the European Convention on Human Rights. Martinus Nijhoff Publishers, 2003, p. 15.
129. ECtHR, 'Relating to certain aspects of the laws on the use of languages in education in Belgium' v. Belgium (1474/62 et al.) 23 July 1968, para. 60.
130. ECtHR, Valkov and others v. Bulgaria (2033/04 et al.) 25 October 2011, para. 115.
131. For example, the difference of treatment of policemen in regard of the freedom of association was justified with the reference to their special status. *See* Rekvényi v. Hungary (25390/94) 20 May 1999.

the principles which normally prevail in democratic societies.'[132] The difference of treatment in the exercise of a right laid down in the ECHR must pursue a legitimate aim, and there must a reasonable relationship of proportionality between the means employed and the aim sought to be realised.[133]

Therefore the ECtHR's consideration of discrimination cases includes two main steps: the establishment of the difference in treatment; and the finding of an 'objective and reasonable justification' for discriminatory provisions that exists if the difference of treatment pursues a legitimate aim and if there is a 'reasonable relationship of proportionality between the means employed and the aim sought to be realised.'[134]

The ECtHR's approach to the burden of proof[135] in discrimination cases requires the applicant to demonstrate the difference in treatment, and the respondent State to prove that the difference in treatment was justified.[136] The shift of the burden of proof to the defendant in cases of employment discrimination is characteristic for the countries of the EU but is alien to new members of the CoE such as Russia[137] or Ukraine.[138]

In cases concerning indirect discrimination, the ECtHR held that the burden of proof should shift to the respondent State if the applicant establishes the rebuttable presumption that the effect of a measure or practice had been discriminatory.[139] It also noted that it would be extremely difficult in practice for applicants to prove indirect discrimination without such a shift.[140]

In considering whether a relevant difference in treatment existed, the ECtHR tends to compare the situation in question with the treatment of other people in analogous or 'relevantly similar situations'.[141] The requirement to demonstrate an analogous position does not mean that the comparator groups should be identical. An applicant must demonstrate that, having regard to the particular nature of his or her complaint, he or she was in a relevantly similar situation to others treated differently.[142] It must be found that other persons enjoy preferential treatment and that this

132. ECtHR, National union of Belgian police v. Belgium (4464/70) 27 October 1975, para. 46.
133. ECtHR, National union of Belgian police v. Belgium (4464/70) 27 October 1975.
134. ECtHR, Adrejeva v. Latvia [GC] (55707/00) 18 February 2009, para. 81.
135. The distribution of the burden of proof is intrinsically linked to the specificity of the facts, the nature of the allegation made and the Convention right at stake. *See* Nachova and Others v. Bulgaria (43577/98, 43579/98) 6 July 2005, para. 147.
136. ECtHR, I.B. v. Greece (552/10) 3 October 2013, para. 78.
137. *See* more in E. Sychenko, Contradictions of Anti-discrimination Protection of Employees in Russia and the Influence of European Court of Human Rights In: Vladimir Lebedev and Elena Radevich editors. 'Labour Law in Russia: Recent Developments and New Challenges', Issue 6. Newcastle upon Tyne: Cambridge Scholars Publishing, 2014. pp. 289–310.
138. The possibility to shift the burden of proof was recently fixed in the changes to the Law of Ukraine 'On Principles of Prevention and Combating Discrimination in Ukraine' adopted 13 May 2014 No. 1263-VII, however, till now there is no evidence on the results of application of this law.
139. ECtHR, Horváth and Kiss v. Hungary (11146/11) 29 January 2013, para. 108.
140. *Ibid.*
141. ECtHR, Willis v. the United Kingdom (36042/97) 11 June 2002.
142. ECtHR, Valkov and others v. Bulgaria, para. 116.

distinction is discriminatory.[143] In *D. H. and Others v. The Czech Republic*,[144] for example, the ECtHR investigated whether the education of Roma children assigned to special schools was different from the education given to other children in the city of Ostrava. It was found that the applicants had received a substantially inferior education compared to non-Roma children and had therefore been victims of discrimination on the grounds of ethnic origin.

In cases concerning paternity leave the ECtHR compared the treatment of women and men and found that men and women were 'similarly placed' as far as the role of taking care of the child during the period corresponding to parental leave was concerned.[145]

There have been several cases where the ECtHR has rejected discrimination claims on the basis that the applicants were not considered to be in a situation akin to that of another group treated more favourably. In *Carson and Others v. UK*,[146] the applicants (immigrants to South Africa, Australia, Canada) argued that they had been treated differently with regard to pension increases for pensioners living in the UK, as compared to those who had emigrated. The ECtHR did not consider that an act of discrimination had taken place, stating that the conditions of pensioners in UK and those abroad were incomparable in view of the rise of the standard cost of living in the UK.

The choice of comparators can be determinative of the claim.[147] For example, in *Fogarty v. UK*,[148] the applicant claimed that she suffered discrimination on the basis of legislation that conferred immunity in relation to employment-disputes concerning embassy staff. The ECtHR simply asserted that as the legislation in question applied equally to all employment-related disputes within the Embassy there existed no different treatment. Therefore the ECtHR compared the applicant with other employees of the Embassy even though the applicant was referring to the difference in treatment with employees of other employers who were entitled to pursue the claim on discrimination in recruitment processes in the Industrial Tribunal. The status of the employer was the discriminatory ground in this case and the ECtHR had to consider whether the difference in treatment was founded on a 'objective and reasonable justification.'

Whenever a difference in treatment is found, the ECtHR has to determine if there was an objective and reasonable justification. Article 14 does not prohibit distinctions in treatment which are founded on an objective assessment of essentially different factual circumstances and which, being based on the public interest, strike a fair balance between the protection of the interests of the community and respect for the

143. ECtHR, Andrle v. The Czech Republic (6268/08) 17 February 2011, para. 47.
144. ECtHR, D. H. and Others v. the Czech Republic [GC] (57325/00) 13 November 2007.
145. ECtHR, Petrovic v. Austria (20458/92) 27 March 1998, para. 36; Markin Konstantin v. Russia (30078/06) 22 March 2012, para. 132.
146. ECtHR, Carson and others v. UK [GC] (no. 42184/05) 16 March 2010.
147. C. Barnard, B. Hepple, Substantive Equality. Cambridge Law Journal 59(3) (November 2000): 563.
148. ECtHR, Fogarty v. UK [GC] (37112/97) 21 November 2001.

rights and freedoms safeguarded by the ECHR.[149] For example, the establishment of different retirement age for men and women was held by ECtHR legitimate as it was 'rooted in specific historical circumstances' and was aimed at the correction of 'factual inequalities' between sexes.[150]

According to the jurisprudence under Article 14, 'objective and reasonable justification' means that the discrimination in question pursued one or more legitimate aim(s) and there was a reasonable relationship of proportionality between the means employed and the aim sought to be realised.

[B] The Court's Approach to the Legitimate Aim in Cases of Discrimination

The ECtHR tends to interpret 'legitimate aim' in a very broad manner. As such, it has acknowledged in this context the protection of national security,[151] the general interest to avoid fragmentation of trade union organisations,[152] ensuring the loyalty of civil servants towards the democratic regime,[153] providing access to services irrespective of sexual orientation of the person,[154] protecting occupational health,[155] enforcing the uniform code of the employer,[156] etc. The ECtHR's approach to 'legitimate aim' has been criticised as being a 'rhetorical and artificial assertion that has nothing to do with the issues truly deciding the case'.[157] In fact, the examples of accepted 'legitimate aims' mentioned above which have been referred to by the ECtHR are rather traces of reasonable grounds for the difference of treatment rather than being solemn 'legitimate aims'.

In certain cases the ECtHR sets higher standards in order for the legitimate aim to be established.[158] The ECtHR is particularly rigorous in its approach to the justification of discrimination based on gender, or sexual orientation. Where a difference of treatment is based on a person's gender, the margin of appreciation afforded to the State is narrow and in such situations the principle of proportionality does not merely require that the measure chosen should in general be suited to the fulfilment of the aim

149. ECtHR, Zarb Adami v. Malta (17209/02) 20 June 2006, para. 76.
150. *See* ECtHR, Andrle v. The Czech Republic, *see supra* note 143, para. 55; Stec and others v. UK (65731/01, 65900/01) 12 April 2006, para. 61. The Court took into account the move towards establishing the same pensionable age for both sexes.
151. ECtHR, Rainys and Gasparavicius v. Lithuania (70665/01 74345/01) 7 April 2005, Sidabras and Dziautas v. Lithuania (55480/00 59330/00) 27 July 2004, Markin v. Russia [GC](30078/06) 22 March 2012.
152. ECtHR, Wilson, National union of journalists and others v. The UK (30668/96 et al.) 2 July 2002.
153. ECtHR, Naidin v. Romania (38162/07) 21 October 2014.
154. ECtHR, Eweida and others v. The UK (48420/10 et al.) 15 January 2013.
155. *Ibid.*
156. *Ibid.*
157. Oddný Mjöll Arnardóttir, *see supra* note 128, p. 45.
158. Aalt Willem Heringa, Standards of Review for Discrimination. The Scope of Review by the Courts In Titia Loenen, Paulo R. Rodrigues, editors. 'Non-Discrimination Law: Comparative Perspectives'. Martinus Nijhoff Publishers, 1999, p. 30.

pursued, but it must also be shown that it was necessary in the circumstances of the case.[159]

In the recent case of *Emel Boyraz v. Turkey*, the applicant claimed that her dismissal from the post of security officer in the State-run Electricity Company was in breach of the provisions of Articles 8 and 14 of the ECHR. The applicant had been terminated from her job as she did not fulfil the requirements of 'being a man' and 'having completed military service'. The respondent stated that the post in question had been reserved for male candidates in view of the nature of the service and the need to recruit male personnel. The ECtHR accepted that there may be legitimate requirements for certain occupational activities depending on their nature or the context in which they are carried out. However, the mere fact that security officers had to work on night shifts and in rural areas and might be required to use firearms and physical force did not, the Court found, in itself justify the difference in treatment between men and women in this way. In the ECtHR's view, only the personal inability of the applicant to fulfil these tasks might be the legitimate reason for dismissal.[160]

In *Markin v. Russia* the ECtHR agreed with the State that the protection of national security could be regarded as a legitimate aim under Article 14. However, it emphasised that the needs of security cannot be sufficient justification of the difference of treatment per se. Any restrictions of rights are acceptable in this context only where there is a real threat to the armed forces' operational effectiveness that must be 'substantiated by specific examples.'[161]

The ECtHR pointed out that the advancement of gender equality is today a major goal in the Member States of the CoE and very significant reasons would have to be put forward before such a difference of treatment could be regarded as compatible with the ECHR.[162]

[C] The Research on Proportionality of Interference

The research on proportionality of the difference of the treatment comes next after the establishment of the legitimate aim. The assessment of proportionality is influenced by a variety of factors which might be involved in any one case: the type of discrimination; the right concerned; the vulnerability of the applicant.[163] The application of the proportionality test in discrimination cases is not well explained in the labour law jurisprudence of the ECtHR. The judgment of the ECtHR in the famous case of *Eweida and others v. UK*[164] is very illustrative in this context.

Two of four applicants suffered a difference in treatment because their employers did not permit them to wear a cross visibly around their necks. The first applicant, Ms Eweida was an employee of British Airways, which required all their staff in contact

159. ECtHR, Emel Boyraz v. Turkey (61960/08) 2 December 2014, para. 51.
160. *Ibid.*, para. 56.
161. ECtHR, Markin v. Russia, para. 137.
162. ECtHR, Emel Boyraz v. Turkey, para. 51.
163. ECtHR, I.B. v. Greece (552/10) 3 October 2013.
164. ECtHR, Eweida and others v. UK (48420/10 et al.) 15 January 2013.

with the public to wear a uniform and do not display any religious symbol, even discreet ones. The second applicant, Ms Chaplin, was a qualified nurse at the state hospital. After the hospital changed the nurse's uniforms she was requested to remove her cross as it might cause injury if an elderly patient pulled on it. In both cases the ECtHR found that the restrictions were justified by legitimate aims. Having considered the interference's proportionality the ECtHR, however, came to different conclusions in respect of these two applicants.

In the case of Ms Eweida, the ECtHR found the interference to be disproportionate. It stated that national courts did not strike a fair balance as they accorded too much weight to the employer's wish to project a certain corporate image. The Court found no evidence that the wearing of other previously authorised items of religious clothing, such as turbans and hijabs, by other employees, had any negative impact on British Airways' brand or image and concluded that, in the absence of any real encroachment on the interests of others, the domestic authorities had failed to sufficiently protect the first applicant's right to manifest her religion, in breach of the positive obligation under Article 9.

In the case of Ms Chaplin, the ECtHR found that the interference was not disproportionate as the reasons for the restriction were 'inherently of a greater magnitude than that which applied in respect of Ms Eweida'. In addition it was noted that in 'this field' (one can surmise that the ECtHR meant by this hospitals' establishment of uniform policies) the domestic authorities must be allowed a wide margin of appreciation. This way of considering of the proportionality of the interference is a very simplified one as it consists of determining objective reasons for the restriction and the ascertaining of a wide margin of appreciation of the state.

The evaluation of proportionality in cases on trade union discrimination could also be criticised as being rather too cursory. Here, the evaluation of proportionality is substituted by a reference to the national margin of appreciation.[165] For example, in *National union of Belgian police v. Belgium*,[166] the ECtHR had to decide whether the deprivation of the right to be consulted with by the Minister of the Interior constituted a violation of Articles 11 and 14 of the ECHR. The applicant was a union open to municipal and rural police forces, but not to members of the gendarmerie and the police judiciary. To avoid having to deal with too many associations, the number of entities with which the Belgian State, i.e., its Minister of the Interior, had to negotiate was limited by using a criterion of representativeness and the applicant was denied sufficient representation.[167] The ECtHR, having found a certain disadvantage in the applicant's situation, stated that the State had not exceeded the limits of its freedoms to lay down the measures it deems appropriate in its relations with the trade unions and concluded that the disadvantage was not excessive in relation to the legitimate aim

165. Arai, Yutaka, The ECHR and Non-discrimination. Amicus Curiae 7 (1998): 8.
166. ECtHR, National Union Of Belgian Police v. Belgium (4464/70) 27 October 1975.
167. Cited from L. Caflisch, Labour Issues before the Strasbourg Court in ILO. In: The Distinguished Scholars Series, http://www.ilo.org/public/english/bureau/leg/download/series.pdf (accessed 20 February 2015).

pursued.[168] It was found that the principle of proportionality was not offended although it was applied in this case in a very vague manner.

These examples demonstrate that the proportionality test in discrimination cases seem unclear, 'weak' and is not being treated fully.[169]

In spite of certain shortcomings in the reasoning of judgments on employment discrimination, the jurisprudence of the ECtHR nevertheless provides a scheme of adjudication in such cases which might be used by national courts in new Member States of the CoE, such as Russia. The establishment of the legitimate aim and of proportionality could ensure a more flexible approach to discrimination than that provided by Article 3 of the Russian Labour Code. According to its provisions, establishment of distinctions, exceptions, preferences as well as limitation of employees' rights which are *determined by the requirements inherent in a specific kind of work as set by federal laws* or caused by *especial attention of the state to persons requiring increased social and legal protection* shall not be deemed discrimination.[170] This rule is formulated rigidly and does not permit national courts to estimate whether 'positive' discrimination in the particular case was proportionate to the aim of protecting vulnerable persons.[171] In addition, it does not permit employers to allow for preferences or distinctions dictated by the type of work if the particular permission is not explicitly granted by law. As an example, we might refer to the employment of men for work in the men's sauna which is evidently necessary but is not permitted.

The ability to refer to the proportionality and necessity tests in estimating employment discrimination could render these norms more efficient and restrict positive discrimination only to cases where it is reasonably needed.[172]

§4.02 INDIRECT DISCRIMINATION

The ECHR does not mention indirect discrimination, however the ECtHR has developed in its case law protection from this type of discrimination as well. For a long time, the ECtHR was 'rather hesitant' about indirect discrimination,[173] and was criticised for failing to develop an understanding of discrimination that went beyond clear-cut cases of direct discrimination.[174] As the former President of the ECtHR L. Wildhaber once pointed out: 'The ECtHR's attitude has perhaps not been entirely coherent as to the

168. ECtHR, National union of Belgian police v. Belgium, para. 49.
169. Oddný Mjöll Arnardóttir, *see supra* note 128, pp. 55, 192.
170. *See* the English translation of the Russian Labour code on the ILO website: http://www.ilo.org/dyn/natlex/docs/WEBTEXT/60535/65252/E01RUS01.htm (accessed 20 February 2015).
171. See, for example, the Ruling of the Constitutional Court of the Russian Federation No. 617-O-O issued 22 March 2012.
172. *See* more on positive discrimination in Russia and the opinion of the ILO on this subject in Lyutov N.L. Rossiyskoye trudovoye zakonodatel'stvo i mezhdunarodnyye trudovyye standarty: sootvetstviye i perspektivy sovershenstvovaniya.(Russian labor law and international labor standards: conformance and prospects of improvement)Moscow: ANO «Tsentr sotsial'no-trudovykh prav», 2012, p. 49.
173. Christa Tobler, Limits and Potential of the Concept of Indirect Discrimination. European Commission (2008): 14.
174. Rory O'Connell, Cinderella Comes to the Ball: Article 14 and the Right to Non-discrimination in the ECHR. Legal Studies: The Journal of the Society of Legal Scholars 29(2) (2009): 211.

weight to be given to the non-discrimination guarantee'.[175] Recent jurisprudence of the ECtHR can boast of a development in this sphere and demonstrates the potential utility of Article 14 in the context of protection against indirect discrimination in employment relations.[176]

[A] The Definition of Indirect Discrimination

The ECtHR defines indirect discrimination as a 'difference in treatment that takes the form of disproportionately prejudicial effects of a general policy or measure which, though couched in neutral terms, discriminates against a group'.[177] The ECtHR emphasised that a situation may amount to 'indirect discrimination' even in the absence of a discriminatory intent.[178]

A general policy or measure which is apparently neutral but has disproportionately prejudicial effects on persons or groups of persons may be considered discriminatory notwithstanding that it is not specifically aimed at that group, unless that measure is objectively justified by a legitimate aim and the means of achieving that aim are appropriate, necessary and proportionate.[179]

Therefore the ECtHR's approach to indirect discrimination is largely the same as to the direct[180] and is focused on the aim of neutral policy and its proportionality. The ECtHR permits the use of statistical data as evidence in these cases. In earlier jurisprudence it held that statistics are not in themselves sufficient to disclose a practice which could be classified as discriminatory.[181] In the recent case of *Zarb Adami v. Malta*, the ECtHR pointed out that the discrimination potentially contrary to the ECHR may result not only from a legislative measure, but also from a de facto situation which was illustrated by the statistics provided by the applicant.[182]

[B] *Thlimmenos v. Greece* and the Value of the Court's Legal Positions for Russia

Thlimmenos v. Greece[183] is the ECtHR's landmark case on indirect discrimination and deserves to be dealt with in greater detail. In this case, the ECtHR stated that 'the discrimination can be found when States [...] fail to treat differently persons whose situations are significantly different'.[184]

175. Wildhaber Luzius, Protection against Discrimination under the European Convention on Human Rights-A Second-Class Guarantee. Baltic Yearbook of International Law 2 (2002): 71.
176. *See* Eweida and others v. UK (48420/10) 15 January 2013.
177. ECtHR, Opuz v. Turkey (33401/02) 9 June 2009, para. 183; ECtHR, Zarb Adami v. Malta (17209/02) 20 June 2006, para. 80.
178. ECtHR, Horváth and kiss v. Hungary (11146/11) 29 January 2013, para. 105.
179. ECtHR, Oršuš and Others (15766/03) 16 March 2010, para. 150.
180. *See* ECtHR, Eweida and others v. The UK, para. 104.
181. ECtHR, Hugh Jordan v. the United Kingdom (24746/94) 4 May 2001, para. 154.
182. ECtHR, Zarb Adami v. Malta (17209/02) 20 June 2006, para. 76.
183. ECtHR, Thlimmenos v. Greece [GC] (No. 34369/97) 6 April 2000.
184. ECtHR, Thlimmenos v. Greece, para. 44. Similarly, ECtHR, Pretty v. UK (2346/02) 29 April 2002, para. 88.

The applicant was convicted for insubordination because he had refused to wear a military uniform during a general mobilisation. His refusal arose from his religious beliefs as a Jehovah's Witness, which included pacifism as a basic tenet. He was later turned down for the post of chartered accountant because of his previous conviction.

The ECtHR took into account the sentence served by the applicant for his refusal to wear the military uniform and considered the applicant's exclusion from the profession of chartered accountants as an additional sanction which was disproportionate and discriminative. The ECtHR found that the relevant Greek legislation violated the applicant's right not to be discriminated against under Article 9 of the ECHR as it did not treat the applicant differently compared with others convicted for more serious crimes.

In this context, bearing in mind the particular importance of anti-discrimination provisions in the ECHR for non-EU countries in which domestic anti-discrimination provisions are poorly developed, mention should be made of a similar case heard by the Russian Constitutional Court. The applicants claimed that the provisions of the Russian Labour Code prohibiting the appointment of people with past convictions to posts related to teaching activities were unconstitutional.[185] The Constitutional Court examined the case in light of the infringement of the right to work and stated that not every crime listed in Articles 331 and 351.1 of the Labour Code can lead to the unconditional and permanent prohibition of employment in teaching activities. The Constitutional Court affirmed the need to consider different factors such as the severity of the crime or personal characteristics with regard to the employment of people who have been convicted for crimes other than those considered serious and very serious, or crimes against sexual inviolability and sexual freedom. The unconditional and permanent prohibition of working as teacher for those who have committed serious and very serious crimes, crimes against sexual inviolability and sexual freedom was held to be constitutional and must be enforced without any exception.

I suppose that if the applicants had related their claim to the anti-discriminatory provisions of the Constitution and to ECtHR's decision in *Thlimmenos v. Greece*, the decision of the Constitutional Court of Russia might have been different. The Constitutional Court, on the basis of the ECtHR's decision, may have been able to give a broader interpretation of Constitutional norms, including the necessity 'to treat differently' even people who have been convicted of serious crimes.[186]

A review of the cases in which applicants claimed to be victims of indirect discrimination[187] shows that the ECtHR is not 'so sensitive to rules with discriminatory

185. Decision of the Constitutional Court of the Russian Federation N 19-P issued 18 July 2013.
186. In the present decision the Constitutional Court found fair and legal the prohibition of employment connected with teaching activities for persons convicted, for example, for refusal to provide information to the Federal Assembly of the Russian Federation (Art. 287 of the Criminal Code of Russia) or for violation of the rules of safety in the operation of military aircraft, resulting in serious consequences (Art. 351 of the Criminal Code of Russia).
187. ECtHR, Valkov and others v. Bulgaria (2033/04 et al.) 25 October 2011; S.A.S. v. France [GC] (43835/11) 1 July 2014, Gas and Dubois v. France (25951/07) 15 March 2012; Biao v. Denmark (38590/10) 25 March 2014.

effects which are not directly discriminatory'.[188] The ECtHR itself stated that it should be cautious not to extend the breadth of Article 14 too far in developing the principle of protection from indirect discrimination.[189] However, the judgments in *Eweida and others v. UK* and *Thlimennos v. Greece* demonstrate that the ECtHR becomes more sensitive to indirect discrimination in labour law cases where fundamental right are engaged.

The coverage of indirect discrimination by Article 14 is particularly important for countries outside the EU, because European directives already explicitly deal with the problem in the EU. Therefore, the Strasbourg mechanism is especially crucial for the protection from discrimination in employment relations for such countries as Russia, Turkey,[190] Armenia,[191] and Azerbaijan.[192] For example, in Russia there are no cases on indirect discrimination.[193] This is due to the shortcomings of the Russian Labour Code, which does not clearly mention indirect discrimination, and to the peculiarities of the civil procedure that in general does not provide for the ability to reverse the burden of proof. The ECtHR's legal positions on this point can be referred to directly by the legal representatives of applicants in employment cases before domestic courts and they could also serve as an indication of the necessary changes in national legislation.

§4.03 POSITIVE OBLIGATIONS OF THE STATE UNDER ARTICLE 14

In the view of the ECtHR, the prime characteristic of positive obligations is that they in practice require national authorities to take necessary measures to safeguard a right.[194] This approach to ECHR rights was developed in early jurisprudence in such famous

188. Frans Pennings, Non-Discrimination on the Ground of Nationality in Social Security: What are the Consequences of the Accession of the EU to the ECHR? Utrecht Law Review 9(1) (January 2013). Available at: http://www.utrechtlawreview.org/index.php/ulr/article/view/217 (accessed 20 February 2015).
189. ECtHR, The Church of Jesus Christ of Latter-day Saints v. The United Kingdom (7552/09) 4 March 2014, para. 16.
190. At least officially this country has made some progress in prohibiting discrimination in employment due to its status of accession country. *See*, for example, Implementation of EU anti-discrimination law in the Member States: a comparative approach. Available at: http://www.era-comm.eu/oldoku/Adiskri/01_Overview/2011_04%20Chopin_EN.pdf (accessed 20 February 2015).
191. The Committee of Economic, Social and Cultural rights on its session concluded on 24 May 2014 criticised Armenia for the discrimination of women and disabled persons in the labour market. *See* Concluding observations on the combined second and third periodic reports of Armenia. Available at: http://tbinternet.ohchr.org/_layouts/treatybodyexternal/TBSearch.aspx?Lang=en&TreatyID=9&DocTypeID=5 (accessed 29 August 2014).
192. ECRI Report On Azerbaijan Published on 31 May 2011, p. 35. Available at: http://www.coe.int/t/dghl/monitoring/ecri/Country-by-country/Azerbaijan/AZE-CbC-IV-2011-019-ENG.pdf (accessed 20 February 2015).
193. Text search for 'indirect discrimination' was carried out on the sites of the Constitutional court and the Supreme Court of the Russian Federation. *See* http://www.vsrf.ru/, www.ksrf.ru (accessed 23 October 2013).
194. Jean-François Akandji-Kombe, Positive Obligations under the European Convention on Human Rights. A Guide to the Implementation of the European Convention on Human Rights. Human Rights Handbooks, No. 7. Council of Europe, 2007, p. 7.

cases as *Marckx v. Belgium*[195] and *Airey v. Ireland*.[196] Judge Matscher in his opinion to the Marckx judgment noted that 'it was generally accepted that the implementation of many fundamental rights ... called for positive action by the State in the shape of the enactment of the substantive, organisational and procedural rules necessary for this purpose'.[197]

This conclusion must be extended to Article 14 of the ECHR: States are obliged to ensure effective anti-discrimination protection is actually implemented. There is a certain difference between treating discrimination matters in labour law cases arising in the private and public spheres. Cases dealing with discrimination against State employees are considered more rigorously as they concern primarily the negative obligation of the State not to interfere (and therefore not to discriminate).[198] The jurisprudence on anti-discrimination protection in private employment relations shows that the ECtHR gives greater weight to the views of the national courts and determines whether a fair balance had been stuck.[199] Therefore, it examines more closely the State's compliance with its positive obligation to ensure protection from discrimination.

Scholars justifiably note the lack of ECtHR jurisprudence deriving positive obligations from Article 14 of the ECHR.[200] In fact, the judgment in the case of *Danilenkov and others v. Russia*[201] represents almost a unique example of the ECtHR's approach to dealing with the State's positive obligations to provide protection against employment discrimination under Article 14. The applicants were employees of the Kaliningrad Commercial Seaport Co. Ltd. and members of the Kaliningrad branch of the Dockers' Union of Russia (DUR). On 14 October 1997, the DUR began a two-week strike for an increase in wages, better working conditions, and health and life insurance. The strike failed to achieve its goals and was discontinued on 28 October 1997. Subsequently the company management began to harass DUR members, attempting to penalise them for the strike and to get them to renounce their union membership.

DUR members subsequently found themselves reassigned to special work teams, transferred to part-time positions, and ultimately made redundant and dismissed; according to the company these changes in their work arrangements were due to a structural reorganisation of the seaport company.

The applicants responded to these and other actions by bringing a number of cases to local courts where they complained of being subjected to unlawful and discriminatory treatment due to their being union members. Discrimination charges

195. ECtHR, Marckx v. Belgium (6833/74) 13 June 1979, para. 31.
196. ECtHR, Airey v. Ireland (6289/73) 9 October 1979, para. 32.
197. Partly Dissenting Opinion of Judge Matscher in Marckx v. Belgium (6833/74) 13 June 1979.
198. *See* ECtHR, Sidabras and Dziautas v. Lithuania(55480/00 59330/00) 27 July 2004, Zarb Adami v. Malta(17209/02) 20 June 2006, Emel Boyraz v. Turkey (61960/08) 2 December 2014.
199. *See* ECtHR, Eweida and others v. UK (48420/10) 15 January 2013, I.B. v. Greece (552/10) 3 October 2013.
200. Olivier De Schutter, The Prohibition of Discrimination Under European Human Rights Law Relevance for EU Racial and Employment Equality Directives. European Commission, 2005, p. 52.
201. ECtHR, Danilenkov And Others v. Russia (67336/01) 30 July 2009.

were repeatedly dismissed on the grounds that applicants could not prove discriminatory intent on the part of the company. A number of civil courts stated that discrimination could only be established in the framework of criminal proceedings.

The ECtHR's judgment emphasised the importance of the right to challenge discriminatory treatment and being able to exercise the right to take legal action in order to claim damages and other forms of compensation. It attached great weight to the ability to challenge discriminative conduct in civil proceedings. The ECtHR noted that the principal deficiency of a criminal remedy is that, being based on the principle of personal liability, it requires proof 'beyond reasonable doubt'; in this case of direct intent on the part of one of the company's key managers to discriminate against the trade union members.[202] It further held that a criminal prosecution, which depended on the ability of the prosecuting authorities to unmask and prove direct intent to discriminate against the trade union members, could have provided adequate and practicable redress in respect of the alleged anti-union discrimination.

The ECtHR ruled that the State failed to fulfil its positive obligations to adopt effective and clear judicial protection against discrimination on the ground of trade union membership and found the violation of Articles 11 and 14 of the ECHR.[203]

This judgment illuminates the ECtHR's approach to what it considers to be efficient anti-discrimination protection and the corresponding positive obligations it requires of the State in this sphere. The State has an obligation to create a system of judicial protection and to ensure it protects (or creates) the right to bring a *civil* action against discrimination. The applicant should not be required to produce proof 'beyond reasonable doubt' of direct discriminative intent on the part of defendant.

The ECtHR did not, regrettably, develop further its legal position on the appropriate distribution of the burden of proof in relation to discrimination cases. With reference to the European consensus (based on the experience of the EU) it could potentially have established the basic principles of proving discrimination and to require the States to introduce the ability to shift the burden of proof to the defendant in cases where the prima facie discrimination could be demonstrated by the applicant. This conclusion might have provided invaluable support to scholars from developing countries where the civil procedures legislation still does not provide any ability to shift the burden of proof in cases on discrimination. For example, in Russia scholars are calling for such an amendment since the prohibition of discrimination in employment was provided in the new Labour Code of the Russian Federation 2002.[204]

202. ECtHR, Danilenkov And Others v. Russia (67336/01) 30 July 2009, para. 134.
203. *Ibid.*, para. 136.
204. Lyutov N.L. Diskriminatsiya v oblasti truda i zanyatiy: problemy opredeleniya (Discrimination in Employment and Occupation: problems of definition) // Trudovoye pravo v Rossii i za rubezhom. 2011(4), pp. 20–24.

§4.04 CONCLUSIONS

The evolutive approach to the interpretation of the ECHR attaches more potential to widening the scope of anti-discrimination protection under Article 14. It was demonstrated above that the ECtHR examined cases on employment discrimination in the light of States' infringement of both negative and positive obligations. The few cases in which the ECtHR granted protection against indirect discrimination show that 'the jurisprudence has evolved from a formal to a more substantive model of equality'.[205] The ECtHR's authority on the international stage means that it 'can speak with a strong voice on the basis of an over-arching modern principle of substantive equality of opportunity.'[206] It follows the development of European anti-discrimination law[207] and at the same time fulfils a 'missionary function,'[208] spreading the values of equality and arguing the necessity of effective anti-discrimination protections required to be implemented by new members of the CoE.

205. Rory O'Connell, Substantive Equality in the European Court of Human Rights? 107 Michigan Law Review First Impressions 129 (2009), http:// www.michiganlawreview.org/firstimpressions/vol107/oconnell.pdf. (accessed 25 February 2015).
206. Bob Hepple, The Aims of Equality Law. Current Legal Problems. 61(1) (2008): 22.
207. *See*, for example, judgment in Markin v. Russia where, basing on the development of the European legislation, the Court overruled its previous approach, expressed in Petrovic v. Austria. ECtHR, Markin v. Russia (30078/06) 22 March 2012; Petrovic v. Austria (20458/92) 27 March 1998.
208. A.W.B. Simpson. The ECHR: the First half Century. University of Chicago Fulton Lecture Series, 2004, p. 12. Available at: http://chicagounbound.uchicago.edu/cgi/viewcontent.cgi?article=1017&context=fulton_lectures (accessed 30 October 2014).

Part III
Rights of Employees under the ECHR and Unfair Dismissal

The prohibition of forced or compulsory labour under the ECHR has already been dealt with in this paper. The traditional counterpart of this prohibition – the right to obtain work,[1] is not included in the ECHR. Its absence reflects the general bias of the ECHR toward the protection of political and civil rights. In many cases, the ECtHR has emphasised that the ECHR does not guarantee the right to obtain work.[2] However, in several recent cases, the ECtHR was less categorical about the absence of this guarantee and acknowledged the rights of applicants which were closely linked with the right to work. For example, in *Campagnano v. Italy,*[3] the ECtHR found the violation of Article 8 as the applicant was unable to engage in any professional or business activity on account of the entry of her name in the bankruptcy register. In *Mateescu v. Romania*[4] it found the violation of Article 8 as the applicant was not allowed to simultaneously practise two professions in the private sphere. In *Volkov v. Ukraine,*[5] unfair dismissal was found to be in breach of the right to respect of private life with the result that the State was obliged to ensure the applicant's reinstatement.

Therefore the ECtHR implicitly acknowledged certain facets of the right to work, such as the right to choose freely one's occupation or the right to seek remedy when unfairly dismissed. Numerous cases on the protection of employee's freedom of expression, privacy, freedom of religion or association demonstrate that the ECtHR has developed a particular approach to the protection of these rights in employment relations. The ECtHR's jurisprudence has allowed scholars to posit that if a person is

1. Fons Coomans, Education and Work In: Daniel Moeckli, Sangeeta Shah, Sandesh Sivakumaran, editors. International Human Rights Law. Oxford University Press, 2013, p. 252.
2. ECtHR, Panfile v. Romania (13902/11) 20 March 2012, para. 18, Sobczyk v. Poland (25693/94 and 27387/95) 10 February 2000; Dragan Cakalic v. Croatia (17400/02) 15 September 2003; Torri and Others v. Italy and Bucciarelli v. Italy (11838/07 and 12302/07) 24 January 2012.
3. ECtHR, Campagnano v. Italy (77955/01) 23 March 2006.
4. ECtHR, Mateescu v. Romania (No. 1944/10) 14 January 2014.
5. ECtHR, Oleksandr Volkov v. Ukraine (21722/11) 9 January 2013.

dismissed on account of his beliefs or his political opinions or activities, the legitimacy of the decision to dismiss will be subject to review by the ECtHR in light of the various substantive provisions of the ECHR.[6]

This Part will focus on cases where the violation of employees' ECHR rights lead to dismissal or when the dismissal (either the substantive reasons behind the decision to dismiss or the process by which the dismissal was carried out) itself amounted to the violation of the ECHR. Strasbourg jurisprudence on this matter is valuable for the development of domestic labour laws as well as for litigants, as the ECtHR's conclusions might in certain countries result in the need to re-consider the domestic courts' final judgments. It also influences national policy in so far as it establishes the binding interpretation of Convention rights in the context of employment relations.

This Part will consequently deal with the ECtHR's approach to the employee's right to private life, freedom of religion, expression and association with a particular focus on cases of unfair dismissals. The research of these rights is united within this Part as in contrast to rights analysed in Part IV, which were incorporated into the ECHR at a later stage; they represent genuine Convention rights and can be called civil liberties at work.

6. Klaus Samson, The 'Berufswrlwt' problem revisited — Views from Geneva and Starsbourg in Les normes internationales du travail: un patrimoine pour l'avenir: mélanges en l'honneur de Nicolas Valticos edited by Juan Somavía. ILO, 2004, p. 45.

CHAPTER 5

Employee's Right to Respect for Private Life

Article 8. Right to respect for private and family life:

1. Everyone has the right to respect for his private and family life, his home and his correspondence.
2. There shall be no interference by a public authority with the exercise of this right except such as is in accordance with the law and is necessary in a democratic society in the interests of national security, public safety or the economic well-being of the country, for the prevention of disorder or crime, for the protection of health or morals, or for the protection of the rights and freedoms of others.

The right to respect for private and family life is the most complex ECHR right in the context of employment relations. It will be referred to in all parts of this paper as the list of employment rights encompassed by these provisions is very wide. In this chapter these provisions will be dealt with sensu stricto, so far as they establish the employee's right to have her privacy protected and restricting unfair dismissals.

§5.01 PROTECTION OF AN EMPLOYEE'S PRIVACY UNDER ARTICLE 8 OF THE ECHR

The ECtHR has repeatedly stated that it is impossible and unnecessary to attempt an exhaustive definition of what 'private life' in Article 8 means.[7] In fact, over the years it appears to have explored increasing facets of this right. Scholars note that the material scope of the right to privacy as a part of the right to respect for private life has also been

7. ECtHR, Niemietz v. Germany (13710/88) 16 December 1992, para. 29.

extended considerably.[8] However it is interesting to observe that the ECtHR has never stated in any case that the right to privacy was infringed. In the majority of cases, the applicant's claim of a breach of privacy has been interpreted by the ECtHR to mean a violation of the right for personal identity, such as a person's name or picture being disclosed inappropriately,[9] or ensuring protection against the interception of telephone calls made from office,[10] as well the monitoring of personal internet usage.[11] Professor Feldman noted in 1997 that Article 8 does not purport to protect privacy as such, but rather the right to respect for a number of rather more 'concrete' interests (private life, family life, home and correspondence) which are best described as privacy-related rights.[12] It seems that the situation has not changed since then. The term 'privacy' remains alien to the ECtHR. However, it is rather productive for scholars to analyse cases on the gathering and protection of personal data and on prohibitions of interference with private aspects of life in order to understand the Court's approach to workplace privacy.[13]

In the present research both types of interferences with employee's privacy will be dealt with.

[A] Private Life and the Emergence of the Protection of Employee's Privacy on the European Scene

As early as in 1890, the famous Judge Brandeis and Samuel D. Warren wrote that the right to life should be understood in an evolutionary way and include the right to be let alone.[14] The authors justified their conclusion by referring to the intensity and complexity of life, arguing that solitude and privacy had become more essential to the individual due to modern enterprise invading upon his privacy and by which such intrusion subjected an individual to mental pain and distress, such pain being far greater than could be inflicted by mere bodily injury.[15] It is interesting to note that

8. Bart van der Sloot, Privacy as Personality Right: Why the ECtHR's Focus on Ulterior Interests Might Prove Indispensable in the Age of 'Big Data'. Utrecht Journal of International and European Law 31(80) (2015): 25. Available at: http://www.ivir.nl/publicaties/download/1555 (accessed 20 May 2015).
9. ECtHR, Köpke v. Germany (420/07) 5 October 2010.
10. ECtHR, Halford v. The United Kingdom (20605/92) 25 June 1997, para. 44.
11. ECtHR, Copland v. The United Kingdom (62617/00) 3 April 2007, para. 42.
12. Feldman David, The Developing Scope of Article 8 of the European Convention on Human Rights. European Human Rights Law Review (1997): 265–274.
13. *See*, for example, approach of Prof. F. Hendrickx and Aline Van Bever in F. Hendrickx, Aline Van Bever, Article 8 ECHR: Judicial Patterns of Employment Privacy Protection In: Filip Dorssemont, Klaus Lörcher, Isabelle Schömann, editors. 'The European Convention on Human Rights and the Employment Relation'. Hart Publishing, 2013, pp. 183–208. Certain scholars suppose that the right for privacy was acknowledged by the Court in the Niemitz case, *see* Sjaak Nouwt, Berend R. de Vries, Introduction In: Sjaak Nouwt, Berend R. de Vries, Corien Prins, editors. 'Reasonable Expectations of Privacy? Eleven Country Reports on Camera Surveillance and Workplace Privacy'. Cambridge University Press, 2005, p. 4.
14. Samuel D. Warren, Louis D. Brandeis, The Right to Privacy. Harvard Law Review 4(5) (15 December 1890): 193.
15. *Ibid.*, p. 196.

contemporary scholars also refer to the analogous circumstances for urging the protection of privacy, adding globalisation and the threats of terrorism to the mix.[16]

More than hundred years have passed since the publication of that article but neither scholars nor case law have elaborated a unique definition of privacy or private life. It is traditional to criticise existing notions of privacy for being extremely vague and lacking a precise legal connotation.[17] However, there are two predominant understandings of privacy: as a right to liberty, which is characteristic for North Americans,[18] or as being an inherent part of an individual's dignity and autonomy – the prevailing European view.[19] Some European scholars perceive privacy as the logic of self-determination and of informational control on personal data,[20] or as a sphere that ought to be free from state intrusion.[21] These opinions are, however, in line with the understanding of privacy as personal autonomy. The same approach has also been proposed by Russian scholars.[22]

Resolution 428 (1970) of the Consultative Assembly of the CoE defined the right to privacy as the right to live one's own life with a minimum of interference. Thus, the 70th CoE already attached weight to the necessity to protect privacy. Later, its contributions were complemented by the Resolution of the Committee of Ministers on the protection of the privacy of individuals vis-à-vis electronic data banks in the private sector in 1973,[23] and the Resolution on the protection of the privacy of individuals vis-à-vis electronic data banks in the public sector in 1974.[24] In 1981 the Convention No. 108 for the Protection of Individuals with regard to the Automatic Processing of

16. *See* Ugo Pagallo, La tutela della privacy negli Stati Uniti d'America e in Europa: modelli giuridici a confronto. Giuffrè Editore, 2008, p. 37.
17. *See* Sharon Rodrick, Open Justice, Privacy and Suppressing Identity in Legal Proceedings: 'What's in a Name?' and Would Anonymity 'Smell as Sweet'? In: Normann Witzleb, David Lindsay, Moira Paterson, Sharon Rodrick, editors. 'Emerging Challenges in Privacy Law: Comparative Perspectives'. Cambridge University Press, 2014, p. 372; Stéphanie Arnaud, Analyse économique du droit au respect de la vie personnelle: application à la relation de travail en France. Revue internationale de droit économique, 2007, vol. XXI, 2, issue 2, pp. 129–156.
18. James Q. Whitman, The Two Western Cultures of Privacy: Dignity versus Liberty. Yale Law Journal 113 (2003–2004): 1151, 1160, see also Edward J. Eberle, Dignity and Liberty: Constitutional Visions in Germany and the United States. Praeger, 2002, where the author contrasted the countries' alternative visions of human dignity, autonomy or self-determination, and freedom of expression within the constitutional orders of two states.
19. *See*, for instance, Mark Freedland, Data Protection and Employment in the European Union. an Analytical Study of the Law and Practice of Data Protection and the Employment Relationship in the EU and Its Member States. Oxford, 1999. Available at: http://ec.europa.eu/social/main.jsp ?catId = 708 (accessed 20 May 2015).
20. Stéphanie Arnaud, *see supra* note 17, p. 130.
21. Katri Lõhmus, Caring Autonomy: European Human Rights Law and the Challenge of Individualism. Cambridge University Press, 2015, p. 48.
22. T.A. Zykina. The Right of Employees to Privacy (Private) Life (Pravo rabotnika na neprikosnovennost' lichnoy (chastnoy) zhizni). Pravovedeniye. 2007. No. 1. pp. 81–87.
23. Adopted by the Committee of Ministers on 26 September 1973. Available at: https://wcd.coe.int/com.instranet.InstraServlet?command = com.instranet.CmdBlobGet&InstranetImage = 589402&SecMode = 1&DocId = 646994&Usage = 2 (accessed 20 June 2015).
24. Adopted by the Committee of Ministers on 20 September 1974. Available at: https://wcd.coe.int/com.instranet.InstraServlet?command = com.instranet.CmdBlobGet&InstranetImage = 590512&SecMode = 1&DocId = 649498&Usage = 2(accessed 20 June 2015).

Personal Data was adopted by the CoE.[25] The EU adopted the *EU Data Protection Directive 95/46/EC which provided that protecting personal data was one way of ensuring individual privacy.*[26] It included and further developed the general principles of the CoE Convention No. 108, while also providing a unified approach for regulation and control by the relevant data protection authorities.[27]

These instruments demonstrate the shift to the protection of personal data. Increased attention to this facet of privacy protection is understandable as the problem of data storage and of access to such information has been a new challenge for modern society. The ECtHR has largely based its decisions relating to data protection on these documents.[28] It has also referred to Resolution 1165 of the Parliamentary Assembly of the CoE on the right to privacy, adopted on the 26th June 1998,[29] which confirmed that the right to privacy was guaranteed by Article 8 of the ECHR, and concluded that there was no need for the CoE to adopt another Convention dealing with privacy.

Turning to national privacy protection, it must be noted that the right to respect for private life is provided for in most European constitutions. The recognition of this right was also a first step towards the protection of employee's privacy. The introduction of a fundamental rights discourse in labour law and the constitutionalisation of the workplace have enabled privacy rights to develop.[30] General claims for privacy protection have been translated in employment legislations by adopting special legislation, such as in the case of the Finnish Act on Protection of Privacy in Working Life adopted in 2001,[31] or by introduction of relevant norms to main employment laws such as the Statuto dei Lavoratori in Italy in 1970,[32] Estatuto de los Trabajadores in Spain in 1995,[33] or the Labour Code in Russia in 2001.[34] It is interesting to note that French provisions on employment privacy were inspired by a particular publication of

25. Available at: www.conventions.coe.int/Treaty/en/Treaties/Html/108.htm(accessed 20 June 2015).
26. Scholars noticed that this directive often conflict with US interests in workplace transparency and information-flow for security reasons, see Sebastien Ducamp, Cheryl Tama Oblander, Heather Benno, Recent Developments in EU Employee Data Privacy Law. Privacy & Data Security Law Journal (April 2007): 473.
27. Paul De Hert, Hans Lammerant, Protection of Personal Data in Work-related Relations. STUDY. European Parliament, Brussels, 2013, p. 14.
28. ECtHR, Rotaru v. Romania [GC] (28341/95) 4 May 2000, para. 43.
29. ECtHR, Hannover v. Germany (No. 2) (40660/08 60641/08) GC 7 February 2012, Rothe v. Austria (6490/07) 4 December 2012.
30. F. Hendrickx and Aline Van Bever, *see supra* note 13, p. 183.
31. *See* Frank Hendrickx, Protection of Workers' Personal Data in the European Union, 2002. Available at: http://ec.europa.eu/social/main.jsp?catId = 708 (accessed 20 May 2015).
32. Article 4 of Statuto Dei Lavoratori Legge 20 maggio 1970 n. 30) prohibits audio-video methods of workers' surveillance; See also Codice In Materia Di Protezione Dei Dati Personali. Decreto legislativo 30 giugno 2003, n. 196) that sets out requirements to protect personal information including the sphere of employment relations.
33. Article 4 provides for the right of employees to respect for their privacy and dignity. Available at: http://www.boe.es/buscar/doc.php?id = BOE-A-1995-7730 (accessed 29 May 2015).
34. Chapter 14 of the Russian Labour Code 'The protection of employee's personal data' which prohibits any gathering or use of such information without the consent of employee.

Professor G. Lyon-Caen, one of the leading French labour scholars, on computerised forms of monitoring of workers.[35]

The protection of private life in the context of employment relations is a very interesting subject, as the workplace is not a 'private' place in the strict sense. The peculiarity of employment relations, namely the requirement for subordination of the employee and control of the employer over the employee, are other factors highlighting the unique approach that needs to be taken to protecting the private life of an employee. Researching the extent of a worker's right to privacy, Michael Ford noted that it becomes most problematic when the values of privacy collide with property ownership. Prof. Hendrickx pointed that the employee's right for privacy is qualified by the employer-employee relationship and therefore the employee's privacy expectations must necessarily and be accordingly 'reduced'.[36]

By the end of 1990s, national courts were confronted by cases requiring them to rule on employee's rights to privacy. The Spanish Supreme Court, for example, stated that the right to workplace privacy does not prevent employers from monitoring employees.[37] The Spanish Constitutional Court in 2000 acknowledged that video surveillance and video recording of employee could be justified if the employer had detected irregularities in the performance of the employee's contract, and such surveillance and recording did not (in those circumstances) constitute a violation of the employee's privacy if it resulted in an appropriate, necessary and balanced measure for assessing the veracity of the employer's suspicion of serious violations on the part of employee.[38] In France, rules were made as far back as 1987 stating that employer could not open employees' personal lockers unless employees were notified in advance and the lockers were inspected for reasons of periodic cleaning.[39] In 1998, the French Cour de Cassation, in a case concerning secretly installed video cameras in a petrol station cash booth, ruled that the employer was not entitled to rely on evidence obtained in breach of individuals' rights via those cameras so as to justify dismissals.[40] The same line of reasoning can be found in the decisions of Italian Courts. The Supreme Court of Cassation in 2000 stated that photos obtained from cameras installed at the workplace in order to check the fraudulent conduct of the worker, without informing the latter, could not be used as evidence in the proceedings.[41] In later cases, however, Italian

35. Frank Hendrickx, Protection of workers' personal data in the European Union, 2002. Available at: http://ec.europa.eu/social/main.jsp?catId=708 (accessed 20 May 2015).
36. F. Hendrickx and Aline Van Bever, *see supra* note 13, p. 185.
37. Tribunal supremo 4ª, sentencia de 19 July 1999, cited from Colección De Sentencias Relativas A La Actuación De Detectives Privados, APDPE. Sevilla, 2010. Available at: http://apdpe.es/sites/default/files/Jurisprudencia.pdf (accessed 20 May 2015).
38. Sentencia 186/2000 de Tribunal Constitucional, 10 July 2000. Available at: http://www.boe.es/boe/dias/2000/08 November pdfs/T00029-00036.pdf (accessed 20 May 2015).
39. *See* Société Gantois, Conseil d'Etat, 12 June 1987 and Centre Renault Agriculture, Conseil d'Etat, 9 October 1987, cited from Ford Michael, Two Conceptions of Worker Privacy. Industrial Law Journal 31(2) (2002): 146.
40. *Ibid.*
41. Suprema Corte di Cassazione, Sentenza 17 giugno 2000 n. 8250, cited from Monica Gobbato, Controllo dei lavoratori: le pronunce del Garante e la recente giurisprudenza, published 21 July 2006. Available at: http://www.altalex.com/documents/news/2006 July 21/controllo-dei-lavoratori-le-pronunce-del-garante-e-la-recente-giurisprudenza (accessed 20 May 2015).

courts have expressed a more employer-friendly legal position, permitting 'defensive' control of employee's mail in order to establish a behaviour which endanger the employer's business provided that it did not amount to 'significant elimination of any form of guarantee of the employee's dignity and privacy.'[42]

Therefore, by the time the ECtHR was presented with its first workplace privacy dispute – *Halford v. UK*,[43] many European States had already considered how to protect the privacy of employees whilst balancing it against the employer's managerial interests.

The roots of the Strasbourg protection of the employee's private life can be found in *Niemitz v. Germany*, already referred to above. The ECtHR considered the application of the lawyer who claimed that the search of his office amounted to the violation of respect of private life. It acknowledged that the notion of 'private life' should include activities of a professional or business nature 'since it is, after all, in the course of their working lives that the majority of people have a significant, if not the greatest, opportunity of developing relationships with the outside world.'[44] Such an interpretation was found to be consistent with the essential object and purpose of Article 8.[45]

The ECtHR's conclusions, as expressed in *Peck v. UK*,[46] are also valuable for the protection of employees' privacy in so far as this case concerned the protection of privacy in public places. The ECtHR stated that even interpersonal relations conducted in a public context may fall within the scope of 'private life'. Developing a framework for considering cases concerning employees' privacy is the ECtHR's most significant contribution to the protection of employees. As noted above, European countries approached this issue in different ways such that the ECtHR could not create high standards of workplace privacy protection given this would evidently lack the support of European consensus and might even infringe the rights of employers. The focus of the ECtHR on the lawfulness and necessity of interference with an employee's private life, as well as its consideration of the concept of a 'reasonable expectation of privacy', provides national courts with a range of tools by which to consider such cases.

[B] Reasonable Expectation of Privacy

Cases on employee's privacy as adjudicated by the ECtHR can be divided into two main groups –data protection, in which the Court deals with the legality of it being collected, used and disclosed; and the protection from interference with private life by activities such as workplace monitoring using video surveillance, searches of offices and equipment and the interception of workplace telephone calls.

The establishment of the employee's reasonable expectation of privacy is the main instrument for determining the interference with the applicant's private life. It was always used in the adjudication of the second group of cases. In contrast, the

42. Corte di Cassazione, sezione Lavoro, Sentenza 3 aprile 2002, n. 4746.
43. ECtHR, Halford v. UK (20605/92) 25 June 1997.
44. ECtHR, Niemietz v. Germany (13710/88) 16 December 1992, para. 29.
45. *Ibid.*, para. 31.
46. ECtHR, Peck v. The United Kingdom (44647/98) 28 January 2003, para. 57.

ECtHR referred to this factor only briefly in one case dealing with the use of personal information. Thus in *Pay v. UK*,[47] considering the application by a probation officer who was dismissed for being engaged with the activities of bondage, domination and sadomasochism (BDSM) community, the ECtHR stated that when people knowingly participate in activities which may be recorded or reported in a public manner, a person's reasonable expectations as to privacy may be a significant, though not necessarily conclusive, factor.[48]

The concept of a 'reasonable expectation of privacy' came to Strasbourg jurisprudence from the United States of America (USA). It was developed in privacy cases considered under the Fourth Amendment to the US Constitution, which protects its citizens from unreasonable searches and seizures of their persons, houses and belongings which might be carried out by the government. In 1967, the US Justice John Marshall Harlan suggested a test for 'reasonable expectation of privacy' in *Katz v. United States*. He proposed two standards by which it could be determined whether a person had a reasonable expectation of privacy. First, a person must have had an actual (subjective) expectation of privacy in the given situation. Secondly, that society more broadly would accept this expectation as being reasonable (i.e., the objective counterpart).[49] Subsequently, this test has been used in the jurisprudence of other countries, in particular in France, Canada and Australia.[50]

Scholars note that the establishment of the 'reasonable expectation of privacy' by the ECtHR is based on concrete context of a given situation and the relevant facts. The reasonableness of these expectations depends, amongst other things, on the questions of whether the employee was informed about the fact that an interference with his right to privacy was possible; the presence of specific indications of the possibility of such interference; or the (permanent) nature and the impact of the interference.[51] The ECtHR's jurisprudence provides several examples of an employee's 'reasonable expectation of privacy'.

In *Halford v. UK*[52] the ECtHR held that the applicant, who claimed that the interception of telephone calls made from workplace violated her right to respect for private life, had a reasonable expectation of privacy in respect of calls made from her work telephone. The applicant, who was at the relevant time the highest-ranking female police officer in the UK, brought discrimination proceedings after being denied promotion to the rank of Deputy Chief Constable over a period of seven years. She alleged that her telephone calls had been intercepted with a view to obtaining information to use against her in the course of the proceedings, the respondent State did not contested this point.[53] The ECtHR found that telephone calls made from business premises may be covered by the notions of 'private life' and 'correspondence'

47. ECtHR, Pay v. UK (32792/05) inadmissible 16 September 2008.
48. *Ibid.*
49. Sjaak Nouwt, Berend R. de Vries, *see supra* note 13, p. 3.
50. Toby Mendel, Etude mondiale sur le respect de la vie privée sur l'Internet et la liberté: d'expression. UNESCO, 2013, p. 123.
51. F. Hendrickx, A.V. Bever, *see supra* note 13, p. 189.
52. ECtHR, Halford v. United Kingdom (20605/92) 25 July 1997.
53. *Ibid.*, para. 47.

within the meaning of Article 8.[54] In order to establish the expectation of privacy, the ECtHR gave weight to the following details: the applicant was not warned about the possibility that her calls might be intercepted; one of the telephones in her office was specifically designated for her private use; and she had been given the assurance, that she could use her office telephones for the purposes of her sex-discrimination case.

In a similar case considered ten years later, *Copland v. UK*,[55] the ECtHR applied the same line of reasoning to the collection and storage of personal information relating to the use of the telephone, e-mail and internet at the workplace. The applicant was employed by Carmarthenshire College, a statutory body administered by the State. She became aware that enquiries were being made into her use of e-mail at work when her step-daughter was contacted by the College and asked to supply information about e-mails that she had sent to the College. According to the State, the employer was monitoring the applicant's phone calls, e-mails and the internet usage in order to ascertain whether the applicant was making excessive use of College facilities for personal purposes. The State argued that its activities were lawful as the College was authorised under its statutory powers to do 'anything necessary or expedient' for the purposes of providing higher and further education. The ECtHR was not convinced by these arguments. It stated that the applicant had a reasonable expectation as to the privacy of calls made from her work telephone, as well as in relation to her use of e-mail and the internet[56] because she had not been warned about the possibility of this use being monitored,[57] and telephone calls from business premises, e-mails sent from work and information derived from the monitoring of personal internet usage are protected under Article 8. The establishment of the interference with the right for private life required the ECtHR to proceed to consider whether the interference was lawful. As there were no provisions at the relevant time, either in general domestic law or in the governing instruments of the College, regulating the circumstances in which employers could monitor employees' use of telephone, e-mail and internet, the ECtHR concluded that the interference was not 'in accordance with the law' as required by Article 8-2 of the ECHR.[58]

In *Peev v. Bulgary*, the ECtHR applied the test of a reasonable expectation of privacy in a case involving unauthorised searches undertaken by an employer in the applicant's office. The applicant, an expert at the Criminology Studies Council of the Supreme Cassation Prosecutor's Office, wrote a letter which was published in a daily newspaper. In that letter, he criticised the Chief Prosecutor. After the letter was published his office was sealed off and searched. During the search, a draft resignation letter was found and that draft was then used as the basis for formally terminating his employment.

The ECtHR had to consider whether the applicant had a reasonable expectation of privacy at his workplace. In the ECtHR's opinion, the applicant had such an

54. ECtHR, Halford v. United Kingdom (20605/92) 25 July 1997, para. 44.
55. ECtHR, Copland v. the United Kingdom (62617/00) 3 April 2007.
56. *Ibid.*, para. 42.
57. *Ibid.*
58. ECtHR, Copland v. UK, para. 48.

expectation, if not in respect of the entirety of his office, then at least in respect of his desk and his filing cabinets where a great number of personal belongings were stored. The ECtHR presumed that the privacy of a workplace desk was implicit in habitual employer-employee relations. As the employer did not adopt any regulation or policy discouraging employees from storing personal papers and effects in their desks or filing cabinets, there were no arguments to demonstrate that the applicant's expectation was unwarranted or unreasonable.[59]

The ECtHR concluded that this interference with the applicant's right for private life violated Article 8 of the ECHR as it was not in accordance with law; the last because at the relevant time there were no provisions either in general domestic law or in the governing instruments of the employer which permitted it to carry out searches in employees' offices – except in the context of a criminal investigation which clearly did not apply in this case.

In the most recent case of *Köpke v. Germany*[60] the ECtHR, for the first time, found that video surveillance of an employee made without her consent was permissible and not a violation of her rights under Article 8. The applicant, a supermarket cashier, was dismissed without notice for theft, following a covert video surveillance operation carried out by her employer with the help of a private detective agency. The ECtHR, in contrast to its decisions in *Peev*, *Halford* and *Copland,* did not enter into an analysis of the applicant's reasonable expectation of privacy. Instead, it briefly noted that this was not a necessarily conclusive factor. The ECtHR in this case seems to develop the idea, set out earlier in *Copland*, that: 'the monitoring of an employee's telephone, e-mail or Internet usage at the place of work may be considered "necessary in a democratic society" in certain situations in pursuit of a legitimate aim.'[61]

As the applicant was employed by a private employer, the ECtHR considered the case in light of the positive obligation of the State to strike a fair balance between the applicant's right to respect for her private life at work versus both her employer's interest in protecting its property rights, guaranteed by Article 1 of Protocol no. 1 to the ECHR, and the public interest in the proper administration of justice. The ECtHR found that the State did not fail to provide a legal framework for privacy protection, as the relevant domestic courts considered the case in accordance with the developed case law of the Federal Labour Court, which provided a mechanism for striking the balance between competing rights of an employer and those of an employee.

Having satisfied itself as to the reasoning of the State's domestic courts the ECtHR emphasised following factors which they said the State had were correctly evaluated in the process of balancing property rights versus employee's privacy:

(1) The video surveillance was only carried out after losses had been detected during stocktaking in the department in which she worked.
(2) The surveillance measure was limited in time and restricted in respect of the area.

59. ECtHR, Peev v. Bulgary, para. 43.
60. ECtHR, Köpke v. Germany (420/07) inadmissible 5 October 2010.
61. ECtHR, Köpke v. Germany (420/07) 5 October 2010.

(3) The footage obtained was processed by a limited number of persons and used solely for the purposes of terminating the applicant's employment.
(4) The covert video surveillance of the applicant served to clear from suspicion the other employees who were not guilty of any offence.
(5) There had not been any other equally effective means to protect the employer's property rights which would have interfered to a lesser extent with the applicant's right to respect for her private life.

Having regard to the due consideration of all these circumstances by national courts the ECtHR concluded that the domestic authorities had struck a fair balance between the applicant's right to respect for her private life under Article 8 and both her employer's interest in the protection of its property rights and the public interest in the proper administration of justice. It therefore dismissed the application as manifestly ill-founded.

In the final part of its decision, the ECtHR stated that these competing interests might be given different weights in the future, having regard to the extent to which intrusions into private life are made possible by new, more and more sophisticated technologies. This stance might have been understood as the readiness of the ECtHR to find a violation of an employee's privacy, giving less weight to employer's rights, if the interference affects essential aspects of private life or if it is justified by less important arguments. However, in the most recent case, *Bărbulescu v. Romania*,[62] the Court did not attach significant attention to the estimation of the aspects of the applicant's rights affected by the employer's interference.

Mr Bărbulescu, an engineer in charge of sales working for a private company, was dismissed for using the company's Internet for personal purposes during work hours in breach of internal regulations. The case concerned private messages, which were discovered by the employer while monitoring the use of a corporate Yahoo messenger account and its transcripts were used as a piece of evidence in the domestic labour court dismissal proceedings.[63]

As it was demonstrated above, in such cases the Court traditionally investigates whether the applicant had a reasonable expectation of privacy, in other words, whether he might have expected that his communications would not be monitored.

In *Bărbulescu v. Romania*, the Court did not concentrate on the reasonableness of the employee's expectation of privacy. It pointed that the fact of previous notice about the possibility of Yahoo messenger monitoring remained disputable, as the notice, presented by the Government did not bear the employee's signature. Dissenting Judge Pinto De Albuquerque pointed that the lack of previous notice should have a decisive meaning in this case and should lead to the finding of a violation of the applicant's right to privacy.[64] The majority, however, did not attach attention to the lack of a previous

62. ECtHR, Bărbulescu v. Romania (61496/08) 12 January 2016.
63. *Ibid.*, paras 44, 45.
64. Judge Pinto De Albuquerque referred to other international instruments, such as OECD Guidelines, Council of Europe Recommendation No. R (89) 2, ILO Code of Practice, Council of Europe Recommendation Rec (2015), which provide the principle of informed and explicit consent for monitoring procedure.

notice[65] and focused on balancing the applicant's right to respect for his private life and his employer's interests. The Court narrowed the scope of the application to the monitoring of the applicant's communications within the framework of disciplinary proceedings,[66] leaving aside the applicant's arguments that his communications of personal and sensitive nature were disclosed to other employees and were publicly discussed.[67]

The Court further confirmed the conclusion of national courts that the employer did not have another method to verify whether the applicant infringed internal policy as the applicant contested the fact of personal use of the Yahoo messenger. It found that the employer acted within its disciplinary powers and pointed that the monitoring was limited in scope and proportionate.[68]

This judgment seems to be a step back in the protection of employee's privacy. In previous cases, such as Halford or Copland, the Court emphasised the importance of either national or internal regulations, which provide the circumstances in which employers could monitor employees' use of telephone, e-mail and internet. In *Bărbulescu v. Romania* it found that the general ban on personal use of employer's premises constituted sufficient justification for monitoring of employee's private messages in the course of disciplinary proceedings. This approach demonstrates that since *Kopke v. Germany*,[69] where the Court required a much more significant justification of video surveillance of employees for the purposes of disciplinary investigation, the Court has become less rigorous in respect of employers. The present judgment might be read as permitting almost unlimited access to employee's communications during working time made with the use of the employer's premises if such a use is prohibited by internal regulations and therefore fixes the absence of any reasonable expectation of privacy in this respect.

[C] In Accordance with Law

In broadening the scope of private life in *Niemitz*, the ECtHR noted that the coverage of professional activities would not unduly hamper the Contracting States, for they would retain their entitlement to 'interfere' to the extent permitted by Article 8-2.[70] Therefore the interference is permissible if it is in accordance with the law, pursues a legitimate aim and is necessary in democratic society.

The first test is particularly interesting in the cases on protecting an employee's privacy. The ECtHR had stated that the phrase 'in accordance with the law' requires, at a minimum, compliance with domestic law. The quality of that law was also relevant, because it was expected to provide protection against arbitrary interference with individuals' rights under Article 8 and be sufficiently clear in its terms to give

65. ECtHR, Bărbulescu v. Romania (61496/08) 12 January 2016, para. 43.
66. *Ibid.*, para. 55.
67. *Ibid.*, paras 31, 55. Dissenting Judge Pinto De Albuquerque, this point was not disputed by the Government.
68. ECtHR, Bărbulescu v. Romania (61496/08) 12 January 2016, para. 60.
69. ECtHR, Kopke v. Germany(420/07) 5 October 2010.
70. ECtHR, Niemitz v. Germany(13710/88) 16 December 1992, para. 31.

individuals an adequate indication as to the circumstances in which and the conditions on which the State would be entitled to resort to measures affecting those rights.[71] The ECtHR also required that the law in question be accessible to the individual concerned; moreover the individual should be able to foresee the consequences of those laws for him or herself.[72]

In four cases lodged by public servants, the ECtHR found that there had been a lack of provisions aimed at protecting employees against interferences with their rights to respect for private life and correspondence. Accordingly, in all four cases the ECtHR found the violation of Article 8.[73]

In *Köpke v. Germany*, the ECtHR implied that a legal framework must be proportionate to the severity of the threat to human rights; more serious threats required more serious safeguards.[74] It found that as *covert video surveillance at the workplace on suspicions of theft* did *not affect essential aspects* of private life, the requirement of lawfulness could be satisfied by reference to the jurisprudence of the German Federal Labour Court. That jurisprudence elaborated important limits on the admissibility of such video surveillance, safeguarding employees' privacy rights against arbitrary interference by domestic courts.

In *M.M. v. UK*,[75] the ECtHR, taking into account the seriousness of the interference with applicant's private life, conducted a particularly rigorous analysis of the safeguards in the system by which criminal records were retained and could be disclosed. This case is a remarkable example of the application of severe qualitative requirements to the relevant provisions. The applicant was cautioned for kidnapping her grand-son in 2000; this information had to be retained for five years but was later extended to her life-span according to changes in practice of the Police Service in Northern Ireland. In 2006, the applicant was offered employment as a Health Care Family Support Worker, subject to vetting. She was asked to disclose details of prior convictions and cautions. She accordingly disclosed information about her actions in 2000, as well as the fact that she had been cautioned for the incident. As was required by the form she was asked to complete, she also consented to being the subject of a criminal record check. Her potential employer obtained the criminal record check and withdrew the offer of employment, taking into account the caution for child abduction. The applicant argued that retention of the caution data engaged her right to respect for her private life because it had affected her ability to secure employment in her chosen field.

The ECtHR established that there were no relevant domestic statutory provisions on the retention and disclosure of cautions. The recording of cautions in Northern

71. ECtHR, Malone v. The United Kingdom (8691/79) 2 August 1984, para. 68.
72. ECtHR, Madsen v. Denmark (58341/00) inadmissible 7 November 2002.
73. ECtHR, Halford v. The United Kingdom (20605/92) 25 June 1997, para. 44; Copland v. UK, para. 48; Peev v. Bulgaria (64209/01) 26 July 2007, para. 44; Radu v. Moldova(50073/07) 15 April 2014, paras 29–32.
74. Laurens Lavrysen, Protection by the Law: The Positive Obligation to Develop a Legal Framework to Adequately Protect ECHR Rights In: Yves Haeck, Eva Brems, editors. 'Human Rights and Civil Liberties in the 21st Century'. Springer Science & Business Media, 2013, p. 96.
75. ECtHR, M.M. v. UK (24029/07) 13 November 2012, para. 198.

Ireland was made under the police's common law powers to retain and use information for police purposes. The ECtHR noted that both the recording and, at least, the initial retention of all relevant data are intended to be automatic.[76] No distinction regarding how the information was to be stored, or how long it was required to be stored, was made based on the seriousness or the circumstances of the offence, the time which has elapsed since the offence was committed and whether the caution was spent.[77] The ECtHR highlighted the absence of clear legislative framework for the collection and storage of data, the lack of clarity as to the scope, extent and restrictions of the common law powers of the police to retain and disclose caution data, as well as the absence of any mechanism for independent review of a decision to retain or disclose data.

'The cumulative effect of these shortcomings' led the ECtHR to conclude that the retention and disclosure of the applicant's caution data in this instance could not be regarded as being in accordance with the law and therefore violated her rights under Article 8.[78] The ECtHR has thus set a high standard for provisions on retention and disclosure of police data, and underlined the need of flexibility in approach to relevant issues such that different circumstances can be taken into account accordingly. This case can be seen as a kind of development of the 'Thlimmenos rule' to treat differently persons whose situations are significantly different.[79] It is interesting to note that *M.M.* judgment lead to the introduction of a filtering mechanism in Irish police data retention rules, so that old and minor cautions and convictions could no longer be automatically disclosed on a criminal record certificate. Since 2013, disclosure may only be made after taking into account the seriousness and age of the offence, the age of the offender and the number of offences committed by the person.[80]

In *Radu v. Moldova*,[81] which concerned a hospital's disclosure of medical information, on request of the applicant's employer, the Police Academy, about the pregnancy of the applicant who was a lecturer, the ECtHR was not convinced that the State's reference to the domestic law on Access to Information justified the interference. It noted that this law had not been referred to by the Supreme Court of Justice, which had merely stated that the hospital was entitled to disclose the information to the applicant's employer, without citing any legal basis for such disclosure. The ECtHR is emphasised that this law and all the relevant domestic and international laws expressly prohibited disclosure of such information and that in some jurisdictions, such disclosure even amounted to a prima facie criminal offence. Therefore the ECtHR concluded that the interference with the applicant's private life was not 'in accordance with the law' and violated Article 8. Accordingly, there was no need for the ECtHR to go further

---

76. ECtHR, M.M. v. UK (24029/07) 13 November 2012, para. 198.
77. *Ibid.*, para. 204.
78. *Ibid.*, para. 207.
79. ECtHR, Thlimmenos v. Greece [GC] (No. 34369/97), 6 April 2000, para. 44. Similarly, ECtHR, Pretty v. UK (2346/02), 29 April 2002, para. 88.
80. Information about the execution of this judgment is available at official site of the CoE: http://www.coe.int/t/dghl/monitoring/execution/Reports/pendingCases_en.asp (accessed 20 May 2015).
81. ECtHR, Radu v. The Republic of Moldova (50073/07) 15 April 2014.

and to examine whether the interference pursued a legitimate aim or was 'necessary in a democratic society'.

In certain cases, the ECtHR, having established the lack of relevant legislation in the respondent State's domestic legal systems, has been satisfied instead by existing employer's policies which themselves provide some privacy protection to its employees. For example, in cases of obligatory drug tests, such as in *Wretlung v. Sweden*,[82] the ECtHR noted that the requirement of lawfulness in countries where labour issues were mainly regulated by the parties on the labour market can be satisfied by the establishment of relevant provisions in collective agreements or the employer's policy.[83] In this case, the applicant who worked as a cleaner at the nuclear plant claimed that the compulsory drug testing was in breach with Article 8 of the ECHR as an employee's refusal to undergo the tests could lead to his or her dismissal from the job. It is interesting to note that the central collective agreement in force did not provide for the conducting of any drug or alcohol tests on the employees by employers. On the other hand, the local collective agreement which introduced at the plant a drug policy programme, involving (*inter alia*) compulsory drug and alcohol tests, was not signed by the applicant's trade union. However, the employer subsequently issued a policy, containing the same obligations of all employees as did the local collecting agreement which the applicant's trade union had not signed.[84]

The ECtHR did not, in this case, give weight to the refusal of applicant's trade union to sign the relevant provisions of collective agreement. It relied completely on the approach of Swedish Labour Court which recognised the employer's right to manage and organise the work as a general legal principle. The right to carry out control measures was deduced from the right to manage and organise the work.

In the most recent case, *Karabeyoğlu v. Turkey*,[85] the ECtHR found that the use in disciplinary proceedings of the data obtained during a criminal investigation in the telephone surveillance operation in respect of a public prosecutor was in violation of Article 8. This conclusion was made on the basis of analysis of the lawfulness of the interference during which it was established that Turkish law did not permit telephone surveillance in disciplinary investigation. Moreover, the law explicitly required the authorities to *destroy the information gathered in criminal proceedings after the end of investigation.*[86]

The ECtHR's broad approach to the perception of 'lawfulness' in the context of interference with applicants' privacy provides countries with multiple possibilities in handling employee's privacy and facilitates the reconciliation of the employee's right for private life and the management rights of the employer. The ECtHR's case law in this area demonstrates that the States, in order to comply with either positive or negative obligations under Article 8, have to do at least one of the following: introduce relevant legislation to protect employees' privacy; elaborate a particular approach of

82. ECtHR, Wretlund v. Sweden (46210/99) inadmissible 9 March 2004.
83. Similar conclusions can be found in ECtHR, Madsen v. Denmark (58341/00) inadmissible 7 November 2002.
84. ECtHR, Wretlund v. Sweden (46210/99) inadmissible 9 March 2004.
85. ECtHR, Karabeyoğlu v. Turkey (30083/10) 7 June 2016.
86. *Ibid.*, paras 114-116.

national courts to this issue; or to ensure the adoption of relevant policies or rules on the enterprise or local level.

[D] Necessary in Democratic Society

Where the lawfulness of an interference has been established, the ECtHR will turn to an analysis of its necessity in democratic society. This test enables the ECtHR to balance the rights concerned (usually the employee's privacy versus employer's right to manage the activities) taking into account the particular circumstances of the case.

Two similar cases discussed below concern data protection, in the context of the employer's ability to gather urine samples for drug and alcohol tests. Some scholars refer to this type of cases as centring on the protection of so-called 'bodily privacy'.[87] The ECtHR's reasoning in these cases matters for Europe because in the majority of European countries there are no express provisions in relation to bodily privacy and approaches differ significantly between jurisdictions. In the UK, for example, work drug testing is increasing in importance:[88] the Employment Practices Data Protection Code, issued by the Information Commissioner, states that testing for drugs and/or alcohol must be proportionate to the aim to be achieved and should only be carried out on workers whose drug or alcohol consumption would put at risk the safety of others.[89] In Italy, a Workplace Drug Testing (WDT) law took effect from 2008 and applied to workers involved in public/private transportation, oil/gas companies, and explosives/fireworks industry with the aim to ensure public safety for the community.[90] In Poland and the Czech Republic, workplace drug and alcohol testing is generally prohibited.[91]

The ECtHR's approach to the necessity of conducting drug tests on employees could provide general guidelines for finding a balance between the employee's right to privacy and the employer's rights, and help members of the CoE create a framework of protection based on the interpretation of the ECHR.

The fact scenarios in *Madsen v. Denmark*[92] and *Wretlund v. Sweden* are quite similar. In both applications the employees argued that the obligatory testing system itself amounted to the violation of their right for private life. In *Madsen* the applicant,

87. *See*, for instance, Constance E. Bagley, Managers and the Legal Environment: Strategies for the 21st Century, 8th ed. Cengage Learning, 2015, p. 332; more on bodily privacy in Stefano Scoglio, Transforming Privacy: A Transpersonal Philosophy of Rights. Greenwood Publishing Group, 1998. pp. 109–112.
88. Alain G. Verstraete, Anya Pierce, Workplace drug testing in Europe. Forensic Science International 121(1) (2001): 2–6.
89. Alain Verstraete. Workplace Drug Testing. Pharmaceutical Press (2011): 114.
90. Kazanga, Isabel, et al., Prevalence of Drug Abuse Among Workers: Strengths and Pitfalls of the Recent Italian Workplace Drug Testing (WDT) Legislation. Forensic Science International 215(1) (2012): 46–50.
91. Danielle Urban, U.S. Drug-Testing Rules Do Not Translate Overseas. Published 12 August 2014. Available at: www.shrm.org/hrdisciplines/global/articles/pages/us-drug-testing-rules.aspx (accessed 30 May 2015).
92. ECtHR, Madsen v. Denmark (58341/00) inadmissible 7 November 2002.

a passenger assistant in a Danish shipping company, argued that employer's requirement for employees to pass random control measure (by means of providing a urine sample) violated Article 8. In *Wretlund*, the applicant was an office cleaner at a nuclear plant who had no access to sensitive areas of the plant, and he claimed that the compulsory drug testing program instituted by his workplace was in breach of Article 8.

In both cases, the ECtHR attached great weight to the legitimate aims of 'public safety' and 'the protection of the rights and freedoms of others'. Both applicants argued that they were not directly responsible for the safety of the ship nor the nuclear plant respectively. The ECtHR pointed out in *Wretlund* that in cases of emergency the applicant could be required to perform tasks with importance for the safety of the plant. In *Madsen*, the ECtHR found that all crew members on board were part of the safety crew and had to be able to perform functions related to the safety on board at any time. The Court also noted that domestic courts had found the use of drugs by other employees of the Shipping company. Therefore a legitimate aim had been established in each of the cases.

Examining the proportionality of interference, the ECtHR took into account the following circumstances, as established by the national courts:

- Employees were appropriately informed about the possibility of such tests being conducted.
- The frequency of tests (once a year in *Madsen* and once in three years in *Wredlund*).
- Advance notice (In *Wredlund* employees were notified about a week in advance of the test; employees were not notified in advance in *Madsen*).
- Coverage of all employees without any exception.
- The way of testing and any further use of obtained data (in both cases, testing had to be performed in private and the results were disclosed only to persons involved in the drug policy for the purpose of detecting the employees' possible consumption of alcohol and drugs).

An examination of the factors set out above led the ECtHR to conclude that the assumed interferences were, in these instances, justifiable on the basis that they were 'necessary in a democratic society,' and declared each of the applications as being manifestly ill-founded. These decisions were criticised for the application of proportionality test in the same way as national courts do.[93] However, this point is an advantage of the ECtHR's review as it demonstrates to the countries, where proportionality test is not applied, a valuable tool for adjudication of disputes on employee's privacy.

In *Leander v. Sweden*, the ECtHR touched upon an important facet of informational privacy – the right to access one's personal information. Mr Leander complained that he had been prevented from obtaining permanent employment and had been

93. J. Mouly, J-P. Marguénaud, L'alcool et la drogue dans les éprouvettes de la CEDH: vie privée du salarié et principe de proportionnalité, Recueil Dalloz Sirey: hebdomadaire, No. 1 (2005), p. 36.

dismissed from provisional employment on account of certain secret information held by the terminating employer, which allegedly named him as a security risk. The information related to his security risk assessment had not been disclosed him. Mr Leander complained that he should have been provided with the information in question. The application was lodged under Articles 8, 10 and 13 of the ECHR. The jurisprudence of the ECtHR demonstrates that applicants are more successful in seeking access to their data (as stored by the public sector)[94] when they applicants combine their right to receive information, set out in Article 10, with a demonstrated connection that failure to receive the information about themselves allegedly interferes with their right to respect for private or family life as set out in Article 8.[95]

In *Leander* the ECtHR began by establishing the necessity in collecting personal information and the fact that it was stored in registers not accessible to the public. In addition, the information was only used for the purpose of assessing the suitability of candidates for employment in posts important to national security. It stated that the lack of communication of the information in question could not by itself warrant the conclusion that the interference was not 'necessary in a democratic society in the interests of national security', as non-communication was aimed at the efficacy of the personnel control procedure. The ECtHR did not explain how the communication of information could influence the personnel control procedure and proceeded with answering the question of whether the Swedish personnel control system provided the applicant with necessary safeguards in order to meet the requirements of Article 8-2, concluding that the State did not violate Article 8. Considering the case in light of Article 10, the ECtHR observed that the right to freedom to receive information does not provide a right of access to a register containing information on the applicant's personal position, nor does it embody an obligation on the State to impart such information to the individual.[96]

In such situations, when public security overweighs the applicant's right to respect for private life, the existence of an effective remedy in case of an interference occurring becomes particularly important. However, the ECtHR by four votes to three found that 'the aggregate of the remedies' (the control procedure by the National Police Board, the control by the Chancellor of Justice and the Parliamentary Ombudsman and the possibility of making an appeal to the Government) satisfied 'the conditions of article 13 in the particular circumstances of the case' even in the absence of the

94. There are opinions that a positive obligation to provide information could be deduced from Art. 10 only in theory, *see* Wouter Hins, Voorhoof Dirk, Access to State-Held Information as a Fundamental Right Under the European Convention on Human Rights. European Constitutional Law Review 3(01) (2007): 114–126. Available at: http://www.coe.int/t/dghl/standardsetting/media/ConfAntiTerrorism/HinsVoorhoofBackground.pdf (accessed 30 May 2015).
95. *See* ECtHR, Leander v. Sweden (9248/81) 26 March 1987, Gaskin v. United Kingdom (10454/83) 7 July 1989, Guerra and others v. Italy (14967/89) 19 February 1998.
96. In later cases the ECtHR was less rigorous and clarified that if a secret service file was used to justify restrictive measures against an individual, it must contain information making it possible to verify whether the secret surveillance measures taken were lawfully ordered and executed or not. Cited from Franziska Boehm. Information Sharing and Data Protection in the Area of Freedom, Security and Justice: Towards Harmonised Data Protection Principles for Information Exchange at EU-level. Springer Science & Business Media, 2011. pp. 78–79. *See*, for example, ECtHR, C.G. and others v. Bulgaria (1365/07) 24 April 2008.

impartial and independent Court. Judges Pettiti and Russo noted in their Partially Dissenting Opinion that an independent authority should be able to determine the merits of an entry in the register and even whether there has been a straightforward clerical error or mistake of identity – in which case the national-security argument would fail. The dissenting judges in this case emphasised that the State could not be the sole judge in its own cause in this sensitive area of human-rights protection and held that there had been a breach of Article 13.

This case had a very interesting follow up which proved that the dissenting judges were absolutely right. The applicant obtained access to the materials in question in 1997 and found out that his having been categorised as a security risk was based solely on the grounds of his belonging to the movement against the Vietnam War and that the State had, at the time of the case being adjudicated, completely misled the Commission and the ECtHR.[97]

On 27 November 1997, the Swedish Government made a statement officially stating that there was not, in 1979 nor then, any grounds on which to label Mr Leander a security risk; that it was wrong that he was dismissed from his job as a carpenter at the museum; and, as compensation for the unjust infringement of his rights, awarded him compensation of 400,000 Swedish crowns.[98]

The conclusion to the Leander story might teach the ECtHR to be more cautious with concluding that the lack of communication of the information cannot not by itself warrant the conclusion that an interference was 'necessary in a democratic society'. This case demonstrates the need to undertake a more detailed analysis of the necessity of interference. It also highlights the need to have impartial reviews of similar applications by independent bodies, such as the Supreme Administrative Courts in Belgium, France and Italy.[99] Control over the processing of personal data has in fact become 'a precondition for the effective protection of other civil, social and political rights',[100] and labour rights in particular. The ECtHR's approach to this subject is crucial because in certain legal systems national courts are obliged to follow it. For example, the Constitutional Court of Latvia viewed the denial of access to an investigation file, in the case of dismissal of a public servant, as a restriction on the right to respect for private life and justified such an interference with the reference to the Leander judgment.[101]

In 2015 the ECtHR complimented its vision of due balancing of the employee's right to respect for private life and the state's interests. In *Sõro v. Estonia*[102] it considered the application of former KGB driver, who argued that public disclosure of

97. The Leander Case: Challenge to European Court Decision. Statewatch: Monitoring the State and Civil Liberties in the UK and Europe, 7(6) (November–December 1997). Available at: http://www.statewatch.org/subscriber/protected/sw7n6.pdf (accessed 30 May 2015).
98. *Ibid.*
99. As pointed out by Dissenting Judges Pettiti and Russo in their Partially Dissenting Opinion in Leander v. Sweden (9248/81) 26 March 1987.
100. Giorgio Resta, Dignità, persone, mercati. Giappichelli Editore, 2014, p. 156.
101. *See* ECtHR, Ternovskis v. Latvia (33637/02) 29 April 2014, para. 26. It is interesting to note that in this case the lack of access to secret files was one of the submissions which led the Court to conclude the violation of the right for fair trial (*see* paras 72, 74).
102. ECtHR, Sõro v. Estonia (22588/08) 3 September 2015.

his past employment as a driver at the KGB breached his right to respect for his private life. This is one of the long list of cases against post-Soviet states, where different measures 'to dismantle the heritage of former communist totalitarian systems'[103] were adopted.

Considering the necessity of the interference the Court pointed that Estonian legislation provided the publication of information about all employees of the former security services, regardless of the specific function they had performed and without distinction between different levels of past involvement with the KGB.[104] Taking into account that after the publication the applicant was derided by his colleagues and was forced to quit his job it found that the dissemination of the information about the past employment constituted the interference with Mr Sõro's right to respect for his private life and was disproportionate to the legitimate aims pursued by the State.

This is the first case among similar cases concerning lustration process in post-Soviet states considered under Article 8, where the applicant won even if he was neither dismissed nor refused employment, having proved that his reputation was affected.

[E] Positive Obligations of the States

The majority of cases considered in this section concerned public employees. In these judgments and decisions the ECtHR outlines in some detail the acceptable scope of state interference with its employee's privacy, i.e., the limits of permissible negative interference. The establishment of the state's positive obligations in the sphere of privacy protection is especially valuable for the development of relevant national policies and should be examined further.

The ECtHR's approach to the positive duties of the States can be summarised as imposing an obligation to adopt regulations (the duty to regulate) and to provide for their effective implementation (the duty to act).

The duty to regulate

The ECtHR's requirements as to the quality of a State's legal framework dealing with privacy protection can be understood as requiring the State to adopt regulations of employee's privacy protection either by introducing relevant legislation or through case law, soft law or employer's regulations. The choice of those methods is left to the States. However, the Court has implied that that a more intrusive interference should be regulated by law.[105]

103. ECtHR, Matyjek v. Poland (38184/03) 30 May 2006, para. 36.
104. ECtHR, Sõro v. Estonia (22588/08) 3 September 2015, para. 61.
105. *See* ECtHR, Kopke v. Germany(420/07) 5 October 2010, M.M. v. UK (24029/07) 13 November 2012.

The State should ensure that in case of conflict between the rights of an employee and those of the employer, a proper balancing exercise taking all relevant circumstances into consideration should be undertaken.[106]

The general quality requirement to these regulations was formulated in the *Malone* case[107] as precision, certainty, and foreseeability. In *M.M. v. UK* the ECtHR went further and said that States needed to ensure there were clear, detailed rules governing the scope and application of measures interfering with the right for private life and providing minimum safeguards concerning, *inter alia*, duration, storage, usage, access of third parties, procedures for preserving the integrity and confidentiality of data and procedures for their destruction, thus providing sufficient guarantees against the risk of abuse and arbitrary use.[108] In respect of data protection the ECtHR emphasised that appropriate and adequate safeguards which reflect the principles elaborated in applicable data protection instruments and prevent arbitrary and disproportionate interference with Article 8 rights must be ensured at each stage of data processing.[109]

Duty to act

As far as the informational privacy of public employees is concerned, the State has a positive duty under Article 8 to implement effective methods of data protection. This facet of privacy protection was developed by the ECtHR in *I. v. Finland*.[110] The applicant worked on fixed-term contracts as a nurse in the polyclinic for eye diseases in a public hospital; being HIV-positive she herself attended the polyclinic for infectious diseases at the same hospital as a patient as well. At that time, hospital staff had unfettered access to the patient register which contained information on patients' diagnoses and their treating doctors. The applicant's colleagues thus became aware of her disease. Upon her request, the hospital's register was amended so that only the treating clinic's personnel had access to its patients' records. The applicant complained before the ECtHR that there had been a failure on the part of the hospital to guarantee the security of her data against unauthorised access, or, in ECHR terms, a breach of the State's positive obligation to secure respect for her private life by means of a system of data protection rules and safeguards.[111] The ECtHR noted that the mere fact that the domestic legislation provided the applicant with an opportunity to claim compensation for damages caused by an alleged unlawful disclosure of personal data was not sufficient to protect her private life. The State had to provide the practical and effective

106. *See*, for instance, Kopke v. Germany (420/07) 5 October 2010, or Madsen v. Denmark (58341/00) 7 November 2002, Wretlund v. Sweden (46210/99) inadmissible 9 March 2004.
107. ECtHR, Malone v. The United Kingdom (8691/79) 2 August 1984.
108. ECtHR, M.M. v. UK (24029/07) 13 November 2012, para. 195.
109. *Ibid.*
110. ECtHR, I. v. Finland (20511/03) 17 July 2008, *see also* Råman Jari, European Court of Human Rights: Failure to Take Effective Information Security Measures to Protect Sensitive Personal Data Violates Right to Privacy–I V. Finland, No. 20511/03, 17 July 2008. Computer Law & Security Review 24(6) (2008): 562–564.
111. ECtHR, I. v. Finland (20511/03) 17 July 2008, para. 37.

protection to exclude any possibility of unauthorised access to her personal data stored by her employer.[112]

The judgment was met by scholars with much enthusiasm. Certain scholars supposed that as a result of the *I. v. Finland* judgment, signatory states to the ECHR could be found liable for failing to ensure that private parties had taken positive steps to prevent privacy violations by other private parties.[113] This opinion seems too optimistic at first glance; however, it might become true once applications by private employees are lodged claiming shortcomings in the State's control over employee privacy protection.

[F] Conclusions

A former President of the ECtHR, R. Ryssdal, once wrote that cases on privacy protection suggest that Article 8 might develop towards a right of informational self-determination as the collection, storage and handling of personal information by public powers might constitute an interference with the right enshrined in the first paragraph of Article 8.[114] Scholars have noted that the willingness of the Strasbourg Court to adapt the ECHR to take account of the potential dangers that new or uncontrolled forms of data processing create for individual liberties is the most positive aspect of the case law on Article 8.[115]

In fact, in this area at least the ECtHR is responding to the challenges of the modern world. The jurisprudence of the Strasbourg Court reveals that the right to privacy is continuously engaged when authorities seek, collect, store, process, compare, or disseminate personal information about a data subject.[116]

The protection of personal data has, within the most recent twenty years, been included in the legislation of a large majority of members of the CoE.[117] However, certain countries have intrinsic difficulties with privacy protection at work. One leading Russian labour scholar noted that, as nothing could be 'private' in the Soviet Union, the idea of privacy did not penetrate easily into the citizens' consciousness nor

112. *Ibid.*, para. 47.
113. Purtova Nadezhda, Private Law Solutions in European Data Protection: Relationship to Privacy, and Waiver of Data Protection Rights. Netherlands Quarterly of Human Rights 28 (2010): 179. Available at: https://pure.uvt.nl/portal/files/1247976/Purtova_PRIVATE_LAW_SOLUTIONS_IN_EUROPEAN_DATA_PROTECTION_100712.pdf (accessed 25 May 2015).
114. R. Ryssdal, Data Protection and the European Convention on Human Rights In: Data Protection, Human Rights and Democratic Values, Proceedings of the 13th Conference of Data Protection Commissioners held 2–4 October 1991 in Strasbourg, Strasbourg: CoE, 1992, p. 42.
115. Lee A. Bygrave, Data Protection Pursuant to the Right to Privacy in Human Rights Treaties. International Journal of Law and Information Technology 6(3) (1998): 284.
116. Feldman D., Civil Liberties and Human Rights in England and Wales. 2nd edn. Oxford: Oxford University Press, 2002, p. 530, cited from Benjamin J. Goold, Daniel Neyland, New Directions in Surveillance Privacy. Routledge, 2013, p. 80.
117. *See* information on national laws providing data protection on the official site of the Council of Europe: http://www.coe.int/t/dghl/standardsetting/dataprotection/National%20laws/National_laws_en.asp (accessed 30 June 2015).

the State's legal systems.[118] The ECtHR's legal positions on protection of an employee's privacy (both in respect of data protection and protection from interference with his private life at the workplace) might serve as a kind of vector for the development of relevant national legislations and case law.

As there is a general trend towards broadening the roles of personal information use[119] as well as towards constant surveillance of employees' activities with the use of diverse equipment,[120] the ECtHR's jurisprudence on the lawfulness and necessity of the interference with an employee's privacy has particular value. The American experience, where more than one fourth of all employers have fired workers for misusing e-mail and nearly one third have fired employees for misusing the internet,[121] demonstrates that the ECtHR is absolutely right to confirm that an employee's telephone calls, e-mail, correspondence, use of internet from work premises, personal items stored at the workplace, and personal information should be protected against unnecessary interference under Article 8, and requiring that such interferences with the right for privacy should be in accordance with the law and proportionate to the legitimate aim pursued by the employer.

§5.02 DISMISSAL AND THE VIOLATION OF THE RIGHT TO RESPECT FOR PRIVATE LIFE

It is not controversial that every dismissal affects the private and family life of persons. However, the ECtHR is generally reluctant to ensure the protection from unfair dismissal – recognising that it constitutes a violation of the applicant's private life, but without finding the violation of any other Convention right.

The attempt to find a general approach to the ECtHR's adjudication of cases on unfair dismissal revealed a lack of coherency in the legal positions taken from case to case. For example, in the *Nenkova-Lalova v. Bulgaria*[122] case, which dealt with the dismissal of a journalist, the ECtHR stated that first of all it should ascertain whether the disciplinary dismissal amounted to an interference with the exercise of a ECHR freedom, or whether it lay within the sphere of the right to employment, a right not secured in the ECHR or its Protocols. However, eight years earlier, the ECtHR ruled that

118. A. Lushnikov, Protection of employee's personal data: comparative and legal comments of chapter 14 of the Russian Labour Code (Zashchita Personal'nykh Dannykh Rabotnika: Sravnitel'no-Pravovoy Kommentariy Gl.14 Trudovogo Kodeksa Rf) Upravlenie personalom. 2009, № 17. Available at: http://www.top-personal.ru/issue.html?2150 (accessed 20 May 2015).

119. Mark Freedland, Data Protection and Employment in the European Union. An Analytical Study of the Law and Practice of Data Protection and the Employment Relationship in the EU and Its Member States. Oxford, 1999. Available at: http://ec.europa.eu/social/main.jsp?catId=708 (accessed 20 May 2015).

120. Rowena Rodrigues, The Surveillance Industry in Europe In: David Wright, Reinhard Kreissl, editors. 'Surveillance in Europe'. Routledge, 2014. pp. 101–149.

121. Electronic Monitoring & Surveillance Survey (2007). Available at: http://press.amanet.org/press-releases/177/2007-electronic-monitoring-surveillance-survey/ (accessed 20 April 2014).

122. ECtHR, Nenkova-Lalova v. Bulgaria (35745/05) 11 December 2012, para. 50.

some aspects of the right to employment affects 'private life'[123] and considered the case on the ban on taking up private sector employment in the light of Article 8 of the ECHR. The same year, the ECtHR had considered as admissible the application made by a cook who had been dismissed from his job cooking at an airport restaurant for (according to the respondent State) security reasons. The ECtHR considered his application admissible, rejecting the State's submission that the right to work is not guaranteed by the ECHR.[124] Since then, the ECtHR has repeatedly found that dismissal from a work position amounted to the interference with the right to respect for private life.[125] In the most recent case on the dismissal of professor,[126] it was even reluctant to investigate the nature of dispute and adjudicated the case in spite of its evident 'employment law' grounds.

The lack of clarity in determining whether the dispute on unfair dismissal could be legitimately considered under the provisions of the ECHR has caused concern among some ECtHR's judges about 'the risk of transforming the ECtHR into a higher-instance labour court adjudicating on the merits of labour disputes'.[127] However, some clarity might be revealed through the systematisation of unfair dismissal cases considered under Article 8.

Unfair dismissal and the right to respect for private life might be linked in several ways. This right might be infringed when the information used to justify the dismissal was of private character – in this situation the violation of the right for private life precedes the dismissal, determines it and the link with human right is direct. In the second situation, the right is infringed as a consequence of unfair dismissal, which was unfair due to the violation of some other ECHR provision and as a result, affected the dismissed person's right to establish and develop relationships with others. The link with the right for private life can be referred to as a consequential link in these circumstances.

[A] When the Reason of Dismissal Amounts to the Interference with the Right for Private Life

The cases considered in this subparagraph have a couple of fact scenarios in common: in the first fact scenario; the employer, who after becoming aware of some aspect of the employee's private life, came to the conclusion that the employee could no longer continue to be employed under new circumstances. In some cases, this inability for the employee to continue to be employed was prescribed by law – when it concerned

123. ECtHR, Sidabras and Dziautas v. Lithuania (55480/00 59330/00) 27 July 2004, para. 47.
124. ECtHR, Jonasson v. Sweden (59403/00) admissibility decision 30 March 2004.
125. ECtHR, İhsan Ay v. Turkey (34288/04) 21 January 2014, Oleksandr Volkov v. Ukraine (21722/11) 9 January 2013, Özpınar v. Turkey (20999/04) 19 October 2010.
126. ECtHR, Rubins v. Latvia (79040/12) 13 January 2015.
127. ECtHR, Rubins v. Latvia, Dissenting Opinion of Judges Mahoney and Wojtyczek, para. 16.

homosexuality of military personal in the UK,[128] for example, or in the case of the collaboration of civil servants with the GDR Ministry of National Security in Germany.[129] In other scenarios, the information of private character received by the employer affected the employer's reputation, and revealed the lack of the employee's loyalty; for example, 'unsuitable' clothing and make-up of a judge,[130] or in relation to the BDSM activities of a probation officer who in his job worked with sex offenders.[131]

According to Article 8-2 of the ECHR, the right to respect for a person's private and family life might be restricted in accordance with the law if it is necessary in a democratic society in the interests of national security, public safety or the economic wellbeing of the country, for the prevention of disorder or crime, for the protection of health or morals, or for the protection of the rights and freedoms of others. This clause is traditionally read by the ECtHR as imposing upon national authorities and courts the obligation to balance fairly the rights or freedoms concerned.

Therefore, in adjudicating cases under Article 8 the ECtHR answers the following questions: whether the interference was prescribed by law and pursued one or more legitimate aim(s); if it was necessary in democratic society; and if the restriction of the right was proportionate to the aim pursued. Thus in the *Knauth v. Germany*[132] the ECtHR, considering the application of a nursery-school teacher who was dismissed for having collaborated with the GDR Ministry of National Security, held the dismissal to be proportionate to the legitimate aim pursued. This conclusion was reached as the ECtHR found it legitimate for the employer to dismiss the applicant from the civil service, after examining each individual case of employees who had collaborated with the GDR Ministry of National Security, and above all those who had lied about their collaboration to their new employer as had occurred in the case before them.

In *Ihsan Ay v. Turkey,*[133] the ECtHR noted that the dismissal of the applicant, a teacher, in the result of security check pursued legitimate aim, but was disproportionate to it. The applicant was dismissed as the employer's investigation revealed an erased criminal conviction. The Court pointed that the teacher was convicted for acts no longer considered to be criminal offences and which had been committed more than twenty years earlier. On this basis it concluded that the interference was not necessary in a democratic society.

In the majority of cases concerning unfair dismissal, the ECtHR considers whether the employer could have applied a less restrictive sanction to the employee, and takes into account particular circumstances of the employee's situation.

The cases on dismissal of church employees illustrate this approach. In *Schüth v. Germany,*[134] the ECtHR stated that an employer whose ethos is based on religion or on

128. ECtHR, Lustig-Prean and Beckett v. UK (31417/96, 32377/96) 27 September 1999; Smith and Grady v. UK (33985/96, 33986/96) 27 September 1999; Perkins and R. v. UK (43208/98 and 44875/98) 22 October 2002; Beck, Copp and Bazeley v. UK (48535/99, 48536/99 and 48537/99) 22 October 2002.
129. ECtHR, Knauth v. Germany (41111/98) inadmissible 22 November 2001.
130. ECtHR, Özpınar v. Turkey (20999/04) 19 October 2010.
131. ECtHR, Pay v. UK(32792/05) inadmissible 16 September 2008.
132. ECtHR, Knauth v. Germany (41111/98) inadmissible 22 November 2001.
133. ECtHR, Ihsan Ay v. Turkey (34288/04) 21 January 2014.
134. ECtHR, Schüth v. Germany (1620/03) 23 September 2010.

a philosophical belief may impose specific duties of loyalty on its employees; however, a decision to dismiss based on a breach of such duty cannot be subjected only to a limited judicial scrutiny without having regard to the nature of the post in question and without properly balancing the interests involved in accordance with the principle of proportionality.[135] In this case the applicant argued that his dismissal from the post of organist and choirmaster in a Catholic parish on the grounds that he had violated the basic regulations of the Catholic Church on employment with the Church, by engaging in an extra-marital relationship with another woman who was expecting his child, was in breach with the respect for his private life. Although the applicant was employed by a private organisation the ECtHR held that the State had a positive obligation to ensure the respect for private life fairly balancing it with the church's autonomy in considering the employment dispute.[136] The same approach was taken by the ECtHR in the *Obst v. Germany*[137] case, where the applicant was dismissed from the post of director of public relations of the Mormon Church for Europe for adultery.

A careful scrutiny of the national ECtHR's judgments in *Schüth* reveals that due attention was not paid to the circumstances of the case, including factors such as the nature of the post, the good reputation of the applicant during fourteen years of church service, and the limited opportunities of finding another job. However, all these details were considered by the German tribunals in *Obst*: national judgments explained why the Church had not been obliged to inflict a less severe penalty, and the consequences of dismissal were analysed taking into account relatively young age of the applicant.[138]

In *Schüth* the ECtHR stated that the duty of loyalty cannot be interpreted as a 'personal unequivocal undertaking to live a life of abstinence in the event of separation or divorce,'[139] whilst in *Obst* it underlined the necessity of absolute fidelity to the spouse within the Mormon Church, and the particular importance of the duty of loyalty of representatives of the Church.[140]

These judgments demonstrate that the ECtHR's consideration of dismissals in the private sphere is limited to an analysis of the national judicial system's adjudication of the employment dispute. As it noted in *Schüth*:

> by putting in place both a system of employment tribunals and a constitutional court having jurisdiction to review their decisions, Germany has in theory complied with its positive obligations towards citizens in the area of labour law, an area in which disputes generally affect the rights of the persons concerned under Article 8 of the Convention.[141]

In contrast to dismissals of private employees, applications by civil servants about having been unfairly dismissal are considered in a deeper way as the ECtHR revises the

135. *Ibid.*, para. 69.
136. ECtHR, Schüth v. Germany(1620/03) 23 September 2010, paras 66–69.
137. ECtHR, Obst v. Germany (425/03) 23 September 2010.
138. ECtHR, Obst v. Germany (425/03) 23 September 2010, para. 48.
139. ECtHR, Schüth v. Germany, para. 71.
140. ECtHR, Obst v. Germany, paras 50, 51.
141. ECtHR, Schüth v. Germany, para. 59.

grounds and the procedure of dismissal verifying compliance with the negative obligations of the state under Article 8.

In this context, the cases on the dismissal of homosexual military men are of particular interest as the whole policy of the British Armed Forces was considered in the light of ECHR and was found to be in breach of Article 8.[142] The ECtHR found it striking that the absolute and general character of the policy of dismissal in these cases took into consideration only their innate personal characteristics.

In *Lustig-Prean and Beckett v. United Kingdom* the applicants were dismissed based on the results of an investigation which included detailed interviews on their sexual orientation, sexual practices and even searches of the second applicant's locker. The ECtHR decided that these investigations and the consequent administrative discharge of the applicants on the sole ground of their sexual orientation interfered directly with the applicants' rights to respect for their private lives. Considering whether this interference might be justified the ECtHR noted that the State might impose restrictions on an individual's right to respect for his private life where there is a real threat to the armed forces' operational effectiveness which must be 'substantiated by specific examples,'[143] which were not provided by the State. The investigation process was found to be of 'an exceptionally intrusive character' incompatible with Article 8 of the ECHR; thus the 'privacy' facet of the case was outlined. The impact of the dismissal on the right guaranteed by Article 8 was also considered. The ECtHR noted the profound effect of the disciplinary discharges on the careers and prospects of the applicants as they would have difficulties in transferring essentially military qualifications and experience to civilian life.[144] Therefore the ECtHR's conclusion on the violation of Article 8 was substantiated by two types of arguments – the intrusive character of the investigation of the applicants' private lives and the consequences of their dismissal.

Investigations into an employee's private life was scrutinised by the ECtHR in other civil servant dismissal cases. Thus in *Özpınar v. Turkey*, the ECtHR found the violation of the Article 8 in the case of the dismissal of a judge for inappropriate conduct, because during the disciplinary procedure against him the applicant was not provided protection against arbitrariness as required by Article 8 of the ECHR. Therefore, the ECtHR integrated a 'procedural' facet to Article 8 which is particularly important for unfair dismissal cases. It also mentioned that the reputation of the applicant was at stake in this case and reiterated that the right of a person to protect his reputation is covered by Article 8 as part of the right to respect for private life.[145]

Evaluating the scope of the protection of a judge's private life, the ECtHR noted that the ethical duties of a magistrate may impinge on privacy, when private conduct affects the image or reputation of the judiciary.[146] However, the public servant must be able to predict, to some extent, the consequences of private actions and, if necessary,

142. ECtHR, Lustig-Prean and Beckett v. UK (31417/96, 32377/96) 27 September 1999, paras 86, 98.
143. *Ibid.*, para. 82.
144. *Ibid.*, para. 85.
145. ECtHR, Lustig-Prean and Beckett v. UK (31417/96, 32377/96) 27 September 1999, para. 47.
146. ECtHR, Özpinar c. Turquie (20999/04) 19 October 2010, para. 71.

to receive adequate safeguards.[147] Here, the applicant did not receive the report of the disciplinary investigation and was not able to familiarise himself with the witness testimony before the dismissal; furthermore, many aspects of her private life which were examined in the report had no relevant connection with her professional activities. Based on these findings, the ECtHR concluded that the interference was not proportionate to the legitimate aim pursued. The attention of the ECtHR both to the 'quality' of the dismissal procedure and to the content of the private life information which served as a basis of the dismissal is an important feature of this judgment.

In the case *Pay v. the UK*[148] the ECtHR considered inadmissible an unfair dismissal application made by a probation officer who worked with sex offenders. The applicant was dismissed from his post for being closely engaged with the activities of a firm which advertised itself as the builder and supplier of products connected with 'BDSM' and as an organiser of BDSM events and performances. He argued that the dismissal was disproportionate to the legitimate aim of protecting the reputation of the Probationary Service. As in the *Özpınar* case the ECtHR agreed that the dismissal of a specialist public servant was a very severe measure and affected his reputation.[149] However, this sanction was found to be justified and proportionate as the duty of loyalty, reserve and discretion dictated some restriction of private life activities for probation officers who had to maintain the respect of the offenders placed under their supervision, the confidence of the public in general and victims of sex crimes in particular. The ECtHR also took into account the initial unwillingness of the applicant to accept that his BDSM activities could damage the reputation of his employer and to remove pictures of himself on the internet site of his business. Commentators noted that if the applicant had voluntarily severed his links with the BDSM organisation, the ECtHR could have decided the application admissible and rule that the dismissal was a disproportionate measure.[150]

Scholars opine that the ECtHR should apply the test of proportionality in a way to justify dismissal on the ground of off-duty conduct only if there was a clear and present impact or a high likelihood of such impact on work, and that a speculative and marginal danger does not suffice.[151] In this case, in the opinion of V. Mantovalou, the dismissal of Mr Pay should have been deemed unlawful, 'because the sole reason that led to it involved his engagement in conduct that he considered fulfilling in his life after work, in his private time', and no stringent test was employed in scrutinising the employer's decision.[152]

147. *Ibid.*, para. 76.
148. ECtHR, Pay v. UK(32792/05) inadmissible 16 September 2008.
149. The same approach was used in ECtHR, Ihsan Ay v. Turkey (34288/04) 21 January 2014, para. 31.
150. H. Collins, V. Mantouvalou, Private Life and Dismissal: Pay v UK (2009) Industrial Law Journal 38: 138.
151. Virginia Mantouvalou, Human Rights and Unfair Dismissal: Private Acts in Public Spaces. The Modern Law Review 71(6) (2008): 935–936.
152. *Ibid.*, p. 937.

In my opinion, this decision demonstrates that the ECtHR applied the test of proportionality in a rather detailed manner, bringing sufficient reasons for the justification of the employer's decision to dismiss the applicant.

[B] When the Consequences of Dismissal Amount to an Interference with the Right for Private Life

The first reference to Article 8 in the context of the consequences of dismissal may be found in the Commission's decision in the *C. v. The United Kingdom.*[153] The applicant impugned his dismissal stating, among other things, that it caused the loss of his home (being tied to the job) and much distress to himself and his family and thus violated Article 8. The Commission assumed that the dismissal 'could be said to have involved an interference with the applicant's Article 8 rights', but it was justified as being 'necessary in a democratic society' for the protection of the rights and freedoms of the applicant's employer. The Commission thus established a logical link between the fairness of dismissal and the absence of an interference with the right for private life.

Further development of the ECtHR's approach to unfair dismissal took place in 2004, when the ECtHR considered the case *Sidabras and Dziautas v. Lithuania.*[154] The ban on former employees of the Secret Service being employed in various private sector activities was considered in the light of the ECHR. The applicants were dismissed from public service for collaborating with the Secret service at the time of the USSR, and could not find employment in the private sphere due to prohibitions under new legislation. Therefore, the case was more about access to employment than about unfair dismissal. However, as it will be demonstrated further, the ECtHR's reasoning here is valuable for the cases on unfair dismissal.

The State in this case argued principle inadmissibility of the application as it concerned the right for employment which is not guaranteed in the ECHR. The ECtHR stated that the right for private life secures to the individual a sphere within which he or she can freely pursue the development and fulfilment of his or her personality. Citing the *Niemietz v. Germany* case,[155] it emphasised that respect for private life must also comprise to a certain degree the right to establish and develop relationships with other human beings. It is interesting to note that the judgment includes a reference to Article 1 § 2 of the European Social Charter as a kind of justification of integration of the right to establish and develop relations with others.

The above-mentioned arguments led the ECtHR to conclude that the right for respect of private life was affected, but not violated. According to the Strasbourg jurisprudence it was enough to find that the discrimination was in the ambit of Convention rights to begin a consideration of the case under Article 14. This pattern was used in the *Sidabras* case, thus the ECtHR left a highly controversial 'integrative' road and considered the impugned ban on employment in light of the prohibition of

153. EurCommHR, C. v. The United Kingdom case (11882/85) inadmissible 7 October 1987.
154. ECtHR, Sidabras and Dziautas v. Lithuania (55480/00 59330/00) 27 July 2004.
155. ECtHR, Niemietz v. Germany (13710/88) 16 December 1992, para. 29.

discrimination.[156] It found a violation of Article 14 in conjunction with Article 8 as the applicants were discriminated on the basis of being 'former KGB collaborators'.

The ECtHR's conclusion was criticised for dealing unsatisfactorily with the material scope of the ECHR, and for refraining from undertaking a thorough analysis of the importance of work for one's private life.[157] However, although the ECtHR did not go deeper into the interconnection between the right for respect of private life and the right to work, it laid down the foundation for considering cases on unfair dismissal as for the first time it linked the right to develop relations with the right to work, thus 'substantially expanding the scope of the Court's control'.[158]

This approach was further applied in the case of unfair dismissal which was largely similar with the Sidabras case. In *Rainys and Gasparavicius v. Lithuania*,[159] the applicants impugned the violation of their rights as a result of the application of the Law on the Evaluation of the USSR State Security Committee and the Present Activities of Permanent Employees of the Organisation. Under the provisions of this Law, the first applicant was dismissed from a private telecommunications company where he had worked as a lawyer and the second applicant was disbarred because they were 'former KGB officers'.

The applicants complained that the loss of their jobs *and* the ban on their finding employment in various private-sector spheres breached Article 8 of the ECHR, taken alone and in conjunction with Article 14. In contrast with *Sidabras*, the applicants here argued that their dismissals were in breach of Article 8 of the ECHR. Unfortunately, the ECtHR decided it was unnecessary to consider the application under Article 8 taken alone. In order to establish the link with Article 14 it stated that *the dismissal affected directly the applicants' right to respect for their private lives*[160] and further found the violation of Article 14 in conjunction with Article 8.[161] This is the first explicit reference to the right for respect of private life in the case of an unfair dismissal, which paved the

156. Three judges in this cases stated that it should be considered only under Art. 8 of the ECHR, *see* opinions of Judges Mularoni, Loucaides, Thomassen in Sidabras and Dziautas v. Lithuania (55480/00 59330/00) 27 July 2004.
157. Virginia Mantouvalou, Work and Private Life: Sidabras and Dziautas v. Lithuania (2005). European Law Review 30 (2005): 575.
158. Sophie Garcia-Jourdan, De La Transition Démocratique En Lituanie À La Consécration Du Droit D'exercer Une Activité Professionnelle Dans Le Secteur Privé. Revue trimestrielle des droits de l'homme, 2005, vol. 16, p. 369.
159. ECtHR, Rainys and Gasparavicius v. Lithuania (70665/01 74345/01) 7 April 2005.
160. ECtHR, Rainys and Gasparavicius v. Lithuania, para. 35.
161. It is interesting to note that in 2015 the Court considered the applications from Sidabras, Dziautas and Rainy who complained about Lithuania's failure to repeal legislation ('the KGB Act') banning former KGB employees from working in certain spheres of the private sector, despite ECtHR judgments in their favour in 2004 and 2005. The Court found the violation of Art. 14 taken in conjunction with Art. 8 only in respect of Mr Rainy, whose claim of reinstatement was refused by the domestic courts as provisions prohibiting the employment of former KGB officers in the private sphere were in force. The violation in respect of other applicants were not found as, in the opinion of the Court, they did not demonstrate that they had been discriminated against after the ECtHR judgments in their case. *See* ECtHR, Sidabras and Others v. Lithuania (50421/08) 23 June 2015.

way for the appeal of unfair dismissals under the provisions of the ECHR and the reference to Article 8 is now usual practice in such applications.[162]

There are three cases which are particularly interesting for a detailed analysis: The first, *I.B. v. Greece*,[163] is an example of the violation of Article 14 in conjunction with Article 8. The applicant, who was HIV-positive, was dismissed from a private company following complaints by co-workers unwilling to work with him. A lower domestic court acknowledged a violation of the applicant's rights, but the Court of Cassation quashed this decision, finding that the termination of an employment contract was not abusive if it was justified in the employer's interests. The Strasbourg Court found that there was an interference with the employee's right for respect of private life as the dismissal resulted in his stigmatisation and uncertainty surrounding his search for a new job. It further stated: 'The fact that the applicant did find a new job after being dismissed does not suffice to erase the detrimental effect of his dismissal on his ability to lead a normal personal life'.[164] Based on the judgment in *Kiyutin v. Russia*,[165] the ECtHR acknowledged the vulnerable status of HIV-positive persons which should result in narrowing of the margin of appreciation of the States. The ECtHR's analysis of the consideration of the case by national courts was rigorous: it pointed out cursory argumentation of the Court of Cassation and found that the competing interests were not balanced carefully and thoroughly. As the Greek Court did not adequately explain why the employer's interests prevailed over those of the applicant, the ECtHR decided that the State failed to weigh up the rights of the two parties in a manner required by the ECHR. It is interesting to note that this conclusion was additionally justified by the reference to the experience of other States in this sphere which showed that there was a clear general tendency towards protecting HIV-positive persons from any discrimination in the workplace.

In other cases, the ECtHR has stated that employment disputes generally affect the rights of the persons concerned under Article 8 of the ECHR.[166] *I.B.* demonstrates that the reference to Article 8 in the application of discriminative dismissal entitles the person to seek relief in the ECtHR. This conclusion might in theory be spread also to other claims on discrimination in employment. Therefore, Article 8 has high antidiscrimination potential, in particular it is evident in cases of unfair dismissal where the right for respect of private life is affected the most.

The judgment in *Fernández Martínez v. Spain*[167] also demonstrates the potential of Article 8 in the context of employment relations. This case concerned the non-renewal of a contract with a teacher of religion because he violated his obligation to fulfil his duties 'without risking scandal'. The applicant was a Roman Catholic priest

162. ECtHR, Žičkus v. Lithuania (26652/02) 7 April 2009; Beçaj v. Albania (1542/13) inadmissible 24 June 2014; Milojević and others v. Serbia (43519/07 et al.) admissibility decision 3 September 2013, still pending.
163. ECtHR, I.B. v. Greece (552/10) 3 October 2013.
164. *Ibid.*, para. 72.
165. ECtHR, Kiyutin v. Russia (2700/10) 10 March 2011.
166. For example, Schut v. Germany(1620/03) 23 September 2010, para. 59, Bigaeva v. Greece (26713/05) 28 May 2009.
167. ECtHR, Fernández Martínez v. Spain (56030/07) 12 June 2014.

who applied for a dispensation from celibacy and then married. He taught the Roman Catholic religion and morals in a state high school; his contract had to be renewed annually by the Bishop. He was a member of the Movement for Optional Celibacy ('*MOCEOP*'). In 1996, a newspaper published an article about this movement where the applicant expressed his views on celibacy which were in contrast with the Church rules; photos of the applicant and his family were published as well. In 1997 the Vatican dispensed him from celibacy but stated that anyone so dispensed was barred from teaching the Catholic religion in public institutions unless the local bishop decided otherwise according to his own criteria and provided that there was no scandal. In September 1997, the local bishop decided not to renew the applicant's teaching contract.

It is evident that this case encompassed several ECHR rights: the rights for the freedom of expression (Article 9), the right to express opinions about official Church doctrines (Article 10) and the right to be a member of an organisation holding specific views on issues concerning religion (Article 11). In the ECtHR's view, however, the main issue in the present application lay in the non-renewal of the applicant's contract which affected his private and family life. Both the Chamber and the Grand Chamber reviewed the case solely in light Article 8 of the ECHR, integrating to some extent the elements of protection of other ECHR rights but at the same time reducing the level of their protection.

It is curious to note that the consideration of the non-renewal of applicant's contract under Article 8 was substantiated by the reference to the employee's presumption of renewal as long as he fulfilled the conditions of employment and there were no circumstances that might justify its non-renewal under canon law.[168] Therefore, non-renewal constituted a sanction entailing serious consequences for his private and family life.[169] The ECtHR's conclusion on the non-violation of Article 8 was in its turn determined largely by the conduct of the applicant, who had knowingly placed himself in a situation that was incompatible with the Church's precepts.[170] This argument creates doubt as to whether the applicant could have had a presumption of the contract being renewed of contract if he had not voluntarily made public his views and his membership of MOCEOP. It seems that the consideration of the case in light of Article 8 was a weak part of this decision, as it did not permit the applicant to count upon developed standards of protection of the freedom of expression which, in my opinion, was violated in this case.[171]

The ECtHR's assessment of the State's compliance with Article 8 was based on an estimation of the applicant's conduct and his compliance with the duty of loyalty towards the Church, which was the consequence of the autonomy of religious communities. It balanced the right for autonomy of religious communities and the

168. ECtHR, Fernández Martínez v. Spain, para. 112.
169. *Ibid.*, para. 145.
170. *Ibid.*, para. 146.
171. *See* in contrast Lombardi Vallauri v. Italy (39128/05) 20 October 2009 where the non-renewal of contract with professor of Catholic University was found to be in breach with the Art. 10 of the Convention.

applicant's right guaranteed by Article 8 and came to the conclusion that the interference with the right for respect of private life was not disproportionate in this case. It stated that a less restrictive measure for the applicant would certainly not have had the same effectiveness in terms of preserving the credibility of the Church.[172]

This judgment was criticised as indicating that church authorities have reduced obligations to respect the fundamental rights of their personnel[173] and for giving disproportionate weight to the autonomous existence of religious communities, possibly excluding particular employees from protection against discrimination under employment law.[174] Another point of criticism might be added to these comments: the ECtHR seems to have overestimated the loyalty due to the Church owed by a public school teacher. It could have adopted the approach established in the *Vogt v. Germany*[175] case where it took into account that the applicant did not spread her political views in class. *Schut and Obst v. Germany* could be helpful as the ECtHR stated a less strict duty of loyalty was owed by employees who did not represent the Church. This case shows that the use of Article 8 as a kind of 'rubber' clause might indirectly cause the tolerance of violations of other ECHR rights.

In *Oleksandr Volkov V. Ukraine*,[176] the ECtHR took a very wide approach to the protection of social rights and for the first time in its practice required the State to ensure the reinstatement of the unfairly dismissed applicant.

The applicant was a judge of the Ukrainian Supreme Court. In 2009, two members of the High Council of Justice ('*HCJ*') conducted preliminary inquiries into possible misconduct by Mr Volkov. They concluded that he had reviewed decisions delivered by Judge B., his wife's brother, and that he had made gross procedural violations. Following these inquiries, the President of the HCJ submitted two applications to Parliament for dismissal of Mr Volkov from his post. In 2010, the applicant was dismissed by Parliament. He complained before the ECtHR that Article 6 had been breached because the proceedings before the HCJ had lacked impartiality and during the electronic vote in Parliament those who were present had used absent peers' voting cards to skew the vote. The applicant concluded that his dismissal from the post of judge had been an interference with his private and professional life under Article 8.

It is interesting to note that the State, perhaps for the first time for this type of case, did not contest that there was a violation of the right for respect of private life. The traditional approach of the respondent states was to deny any connection between an applicant's dismissal and his or her private life.

The ECtHR established numerous violations of Article 6 in the way in which the dismissal was carried out. In regard to Article 8, it stated:

172. ECtHR, Fernández Martínez v. Spain, para. 146.
173. Kristin Henrard, The Effective Protection of the Freedom of Religion: The ECtHR's Variable Margin of Appreciation Regarding Religion–State Relations and the Rule of Law In: Marie-Claire Foblets et al., editors. 'Belief, Law and Politics: What Future for a Secular Europe?'. Ashgate Publishing, 2014, p. 162.
174. Stijn Smet, Fernández Martínez v. Spain: Towards a 'Ministerial Exception' for Europe?, http://strasbourgobservers.com/2012/05/24/fernandez-martinez-v-spain-towards-a-ministerial-exception-in-europe/ (accessed 20 April 2015).
175. ECtHR, Vogt v. Germany (17851/91) 26 September 1995, para. 60.
176. ECtHR, Oleksandr Volkov v. Ukraine (21722/11) 9 January 2013.

> the dismissal of the applicant from the post of judge affected a wide range of his relationships with other persons, including relationships of a professional nature. Likewise, it had an impact on his 'inner circle' as the loss of his job must have had tangible consequences for the material well-being of the applicant and his family. Moreover, the reason for the applicant's dismissal, namely breach of the judicial oath, suggests that his professional reputation was affected.[177]

This finding was further substantiated by the reference to the evident shortcomings of the disciplinary procedure. It was stated in particular that there was no practice establishing a consistent interpretation of the notion of 'breach of oath', no adequate procedural safeguards had been put into place to prevent arbitrary application of the relevant provisions. In addition to this, the national law had not provided any time-limits for proceedings to be taken against a judge for a 'breach of [his] oath', which had made the discretion of the disciplinary authorities open-ended and undermined the principle of legal certainty. The absence of am appropriate scale of sanctions for disciplinary offences of judges was also mentioned.

These arguments of the ECtHR can be regarded as a development of the procedural guarantees under Article 8 which are particularly important for disciplinary procedures. Legal positions of the ECtHR can be read as establishing certain criteria of disciplinary procedures under Article 8: the specificity of the charge, the right of employees to read the materials that present the case against them, the adoption of set time-limits for these procedures, and the elaboration of an appropriate scale of disciplinary sanctions.

The ECtHR's justification of why the State had to reinstate the applicant is another interesting feature of this case. The shortcomings of the national system of disciplinary procedure in respect of judges caused the ECtHR to establish the need of reforming the system of judicial discipline. This conclusion lead to the consideration that the reopening of domestic proceedings would not constitute an appropriate form of redress for the violations of the applicant's rights. The ECtHR stated that by its very nature the situation found to exist in this case did not leave any real choice as to the individual measures required to remedy the violations of the applicant's ECHR rights. Having regard to the urgent need to put an end to the violations of the ECHR, it held that the respondent State *shall secure the applicant's reinstatement to the post of judge of the Supreme Court* at the earliest possible date.

Since this judgment was handed down, Ukraine has made some steps in order to fulfil the general measures requested by the ECtHR.[178] The applicant was reinstated on 5 February 2015.[179]

The remedy required from the State in this case is evidently revolutionary. On the one hand the possibility of such a prescription might render the protection of the rights

177. ECtHR, Volkov v. Ukraine, para. 166.
178. A. Ashchenko, Y. Zaikina, L. Ibadova, N. Okhotnikova, V. Chovgan, The Implementation of Judgments of the European Court of Human Rights in Ukraine (Ispolneniye resheniy Yevropeyskogo suda po pravam cheloveka v Ukraine). Khar'kov, Izdatel'stvo 'Prava Lyudini', 2014, p. 127.
179. *See* information on the official site of the Ukrainian Supreme Court: http://www.scourt.gov.ua/clients/vsu/vsuen.nsf/(documents)/40758947BA3FE9EAC2257DE00054D6B5?OpenDocument&year=2015&month=02& (accessed 20 April 2015).

of unfairly dismissed applicants more efficient. On the other hand, it creates doubt as to whether the ECtHR remained within its subsidiary role as an international body. As such, it gives support to those opponents of the ECtHR who claim the need for a restrictive approach to the interpretation of the ECHR.

In *Şahin Kuş v. Turkey*[180] the Court established that the annulation of the recognition of foreign diploma and the subsequent dismissal of a teacher was in violation of Article 8. It is remarkable that the Court decided to consider the case in the light of Article 8 though the applicant did not refer to any of the Convention provisions. It acknowledged that the interference affected the possibility for the applicant to exercise the teaching profession, and had an impact on a lot of relationships with others, particularly in the professional field. It also underlined that the dismissal had an impact on his 'inner circle', as the loss of his job has inevitably led to a negative impact on his material well-being and that of his family.[181] The Court expressed doubt as to the lawfulness of the interference, however proceeded with examining its necessity. It further established that the annulment of the recognition of the foreign degree in theology was a general measure that was implemented without taking into account personal circumstances of each teacher. The applicant worked as a teacher for four years after the recognition of his diploma, received his master degree in Turkey and was never reproached by school authorities.[182] Thus, in the opinion of the Court, the applicant had a right to plan with confidence his future considering the pursuit of his teaching career for granted. Dissenting Judge Karakaş did not agree with such a broad interpretation of Article 8. He pointed that the application of Article 8 to professional or public activities is not unconditional and expressed doubt that this article could be applied arbitrarily to each and every dismissal, noting in particular, that the applicant did not refer to these provisions and did not demonstrate the effects of the interference on his private life.[183]

I suppose that this judgment illustrates the positive trend of the further evolution of the Court's approach to dismissal which started in *Volkov v. Ukraine*. Now it perceives dismissal, in particular when it is connected with the impossibility to pursue the career in the same professional field, as an interference with the right to respect for private life, without requiring the applicant to demonstrate the violation of another Convention rights or bring evidence of the grave consequences of the interference.

The same line was followed in the most recent case, *Milojević and Others v. Serbia*,[184] where the Court clearly stated that the dismissal from office can constitute an interference with the right to respect for private life. The applicants, police officers, were dismissed from police pending criminal proceedings against them and had not been reinstated despite their ensuing acquittal. They claimed the violation of Article 6 and 8 of the ECHR. The Court pointed that the Ministry of Interior Act was not formulated in a clear and precise way, leaving to the complete discretion of the Ministry

180. ECtHR, Şahin Kuş v. Turkey (33160/04) 7 June 2016.
181. *Ibid.*, paras 35, 36.
182. *Ibid.*, paras 50–52.
183. *Ibid.*, dissenting opinion of the Judge Karakaş.
184. ECtHR, Milojević and Others v. Serbia (43519/07, 43524/07, and 45247/07) 12 January 2016.

the decision about the dismissal of the officers against whom criminal proceedings were under way. It did not provide instruction as to the consequences of the acquittal of the police officers and thus did not correspond to the requirement of foreseeability, imposed by the Court to the law in question.[185] The ECtHR found the violation of Article 8 in respect of two applicants, as others were dismissed before the day the Convention came to force in Serbia.

The Court in this case did not investigate the consequences of dismissal for the applicants, taking for granted that the dismissal could also have had an impact on their 'inner circle', as the loss of job must have had tangible consequences for the material well-being of the applicants and their families.[186]

§5.03 CONCLUSIONS

The research of the ECtHR's jurisprudence under Article 8 demonstrates that the Strasbourg bodies have created the basis for the protection of employees' privacy, and indisputably acknowledged a link between private life and employment, stating that unfair dismissal might violate the right to respect for private life. This acknowledgment 'can shield an individual employee against employer domination', a possibility that was absent in countries such as the UK before its incorporation of the ECHR.[187]

It is important to note that the judgments considered in this section contributed not only to the protection of the rights of the applicants, but forced the States to adopt certain changes into their national labour law, enhancing the level of protection of the right to respect for private life at the workplace. In addition, the ECtHR provided domestic courts with the framework to determine the violation of this right. It urged states to adopt a clear legislative framework for the collection and storage of personal data, and for the protection of employees' privacy at the workplace.

The ECtHR's approach to the private life of employees has becomes wider with the years and there is an obvious trend of enlarging the scope of the ECHR upon employment relations with the use of this article. This observation permits us to argue that Article 8 of the ECHR has a great potential in the field of employment law.[188] In particular, it might be referred to in cases of harassment or violations of occupational health and safety (OHS) rules by the employer. This idea will be developed in the last chapter of the present work.

185. *Ibid.*, paras 65–67.
186. *Ibid.*, para. 59.
187. Virginia Mantouvalou, Human Rights and Unfair Dismissal: Private Acts in Public Spaces. The Modern Law Review 71(6) (2008): 939.
188. This point of view is shared by other scholars, *see*, for example, Rory O'Connell, The Right to Work in the European Convention on Human Rights. European Human Rights Law Review (2) (2012): 176–190; Virginia Mantouvalou, The Protection of the Right to Work through the European Convention on Human Rights. Cambridge Yearbook of European Legal Studies 16 (2013–2014).

CHAPTER 6

Employees' Freedom of Thought, Conscience and Religion and Unfair Dismissals

Article 9 of the ECHR is formulated largely in the same manner as Article 8 and protects the freedom of thought, conscience and religion.

According to this article, everyone has the right to freedom of thought, conscience and religion; this right includes the freedom to change one's religion or belief and freedom, either alone or in community with others and in public or private, to manifest one's religion or belief, in worship, teaching, practice and observance. Freedom to manifest one's religion or beliefs shall be subject only to such limitations as are prescribed by law and are necessary in a democratic society in the interests of public safety, for the protection of public order, health or morals, or for the protection of the rights and freedoms of others.

Turning to the employment cases considered in the light of this article, the focus will be on the definitions of employee's freedom of thought, conscience and religion (Subsection §6.01), and how applications under Article 9 are adjudicated (Subsection §6.02). The employee dismissal cases considered in light of the violation of the freedom of religion can be divided into two main groups: cases regarding the manifestation of religious beliefs of the employee at the work-place, which will be dealt with in the Subsection §6.03; and cases concerning the failure of the employee to satisfy the requirement of loyalty towards a particular religion imposed by his or her employer (Subsection §6.04).

§6.01 DEFINITIONS OF EMPLOYEES' FREEDOM OF THOUGHT, CONSCIENCE AND RELIGION

The ECtHR has in numerous cases emphasised the fundamental nature of the rights guaranteed in Article 9. In *Kokkinakis v. Greece*, it noted that Article 9-2, unlike the second paragraphs of Articles 8, 10 and 11, which cover all the rights mentioned in the first paragraphs of those articles, that of Article 9-1 refers only to the 'freedom to manifest one's religion or belief.'[189] Therefore the freedom to hold beliefs and convictions is unconditional; the only limitation - specified in Article 9 itself - concerns the way in which this freedom is exercised.[190]

Should this article be read as providing absolute freedom of thought, conscience and religion of the employee at the workplace? This question will be answered in respect of the freedom of religion in the first place and then it will be analysed in respect of the employee's freedom of conscience.

The freedom of religion

The wording of Article 9-1 emphasises the primary importance of the right to freedom of thought, conscience and religion and the fact that a State cannot dictate what a person believes or take coercive steps to make him change his beliefs.[191] In *Ivanova v. Bulgaria*, the ECtHR acknowledged the applicant's absolute freedom of religion. In this case, the applicant was a swimming pool manager who was dismissed from her post because she (ostensibly) lacked the required higher education. The ECtHR established that the dismissal in fact took place on account of her religious beliefs and affiliation with the organisation Word of Life, thus constituting an interference with her right to freedom of religion in violation of Article 9 of the ECHR.[192] It expressed a very important legal position: the fact that the applicant's employment was terminated in accordance with the applicable labour legislation - by introducing new requirements for her post which she did not meet - failed to eliminate the substantive motive for her dismissal.

The ECtHR analysed the circumstances of the cases which were not taken into account by national courts, such as the persecution of the members of the Word of Life and the earlier dismissal of the director of the same school who had been affiliated with this religious organisation. It concluded that the dismissal constituted a violation of Article 9 as the employment of the applicant had been terminated on account of her religious beliefs. Thus the ECtHR acknowledged the absolute right of employee for the freedom of religion.

The freedom of conscience

The ECtHR and the former European Commission of Human Rights refrained from acknowledging the absolute character of the employee's freedom of conscience. In the early case of *Grandrath v. Germany*,[193] which concerned a Jehovah's Witness who

189. ECtHR, Kokkinakis v. Greece (14307/88) 25 May 1993, para. 33.
190. Jean-François Renucci, Article 9 of the European Convention on Human Rights: Freedom of Thought, Conscience and Religion. Human Rights Files, 2005, No. 20. Available at: http://www.echr.coe.int/LibraryDocs/DG2/HRFILES/DG2-EN-HRFILES-20%282005%29.pdf (accessed 12 April 2015).
191. ECtHR, Ivanova v. Bulgaria (52435/99) 12 April 2007.
192. ECtHR, Ivanova v. Bulgaria, para. 84.
193. EurCommHR, Grandrath v. Germany (2299/64) 12 December 1966.

sought to be exempted both from military and from substitute civilian service, alleging a violation of his freedom of conscience, the Commission found it superfluous to examine any questions of interpretation of the term 'freedom of conscience and religion' used in Article 9 and concluded that that provision had not been violated.[194] The ECtHR appears to have followed this approach and to consider applications on the violation of an employee's freedom of conscience only in light of other freedoms. In *Blumberg v. Germany*,[195] the applicant complained that the dismissal violated his freedom of conscience. He was dismissed from his job as a doctor, for refusing to perform a medical examination because of a 'moral dilemma'. The ECtHR did not consider the case in respect of freedom of conscience and noted that Article 9 primarily protects the sphere of personal beliefs and religious creeds. Further, it went on to ascertain the scope of protection of personal beliefs. The judgment in *Maestri v. Italy*[196] is another example of the ECtHR's shift from the protection of the freedom of conscience of employees. The applicant, a judge, alleged that the imposition of a sanction on him for being a Freemason amounted to a violation of Articles 9, 10 and 11 of the ECHR. The ECtHR stated that the applicant's complaints fell most naturally within the scope of Article 11 of the ECHR and considered them under that provision only.

The application of Ms Ladele in *Eweida and others v. UK* is the most vivid and the most recent example of the ECtHR's unwillingness to grant protection to the employee's freedom of conscience under Article 9. Ms Ladele was employed by the London Borough of Islington, a local public authority, from 1992. The applicant held the orthodox Christian view that marriage is the union of one man and one woman for life. The Civil Partnership Act 2004, which provided for the legal registration of civil partnerships between two people of the same sex, came into force in the UK on 5 December 2005. The employer decided to designate all existing registrars of births, deaths and marriages as civil partnership registrars. The applicant believed that same-sex unions were contrary to God's will and that it would be wrong for her to participate in the creation of an institution equivalent to marriage between a same-sex couple. Because of her refusal to agree to be designated as a registrar of civil partnerships, disciplinary proceedings were brought, culminating in the loss of her job. The applicant relied on Articles 14 and 9 of the ECHR and claimed that she was discriminated on the ground of her religious beliefs as she was not treated differently. The majority of European Judges considered the case in the light of the freedom to manifest one's religious beliefs and Article 14. It stated that the State had a wide margin of appreciation in striking balance between two competitive rights and this margin was not exceeded.

Dissenting Judges Vučinić and De Gaetano proposed another approach to the protection of Ms Ladele's rights which better corresponded to the circumstances of the case. The Judges noted that this case was not so much one of freedom of religious belief as one of freedom of conscience. Further, they emphasised a principle which is

194. *Ibid.*, paras 32–33.
195. ECtHR, Blumberg v. Germany (14618/03) inadmissible 18 March 2008.
196. ECtHR, Maestri v. Italy (39748/98) 17 February 2004.

particularly important for employment relations: no one should be forced to act against one's conscience or be penalised for refusing to act against one's conscience. The case of Ms Ladele was about conscientious objection. In the opinion of the dissenting Judges, once a genuine and serious case of conscientious objection is established, the State is obliged to respect the individual's freedom of conscience both positively (by taking reasonable and appropriate measures to protect the rights of the conscientious objector) and negatively (by refraining from actions which punish the objector or discriminate against him or her).

This conclusion of Judges Vučinić and De Gaetano has some common points with the new approach of the ECtHR to conscientious objection. In *Baratyan v. Armenia*,[197] a case on conscientious objection to military service, the Grand Chamber overruled the judgment of Chamber and for the first time found Article 9 applicable to conscientious objectors, unlike the Commission, which refused to apply that Article to such persons. The Commission, dealing with similar cases, concluded that the right to conscientious objection was not included among the rights and freedoms guaranteed by the ECHR.[198] In *Baratyan* the Grand Chamber stated that although Article 9 does not explicitly refer to a right to conscientious objection, the opposition to military service, where it is motivated by a serious and insurmountable conflict between the obligation to serve in the army and a person's conscience or his deeply and genuinely held religious or other beliefs, constitutes a conviction or belief of sufficient cogency, seriousness, cohesion and importance to attract the guarantees of Article 9.[199] Therefore, the ECtHR acknowledged that the right for conscientious objection could be protected under Article 9 but didn't recognise it as a part of a freedom of conscience. The dissenting Judges in *Ladele* went further and stated that when an employee has a conscientious objection it must be satisfied by the State as a part of its positive duties under Article 9. It is interesting to note that the American Supreme Court decided as far back as in 1965 that when Congress provided a 'conscientious objection' exemption from military service for men whose religion would not allow them to serve, an atheist whose moral convictions also prohibited service did qualify for the objection.[200]

All of the above-mentioned cases demonstrate that the ECtHR appears to be uncomfortable with the protection of employees' freedom of conscience under Article 9 and tends to rely on the elaborated case law on the protection of the manifestation of religious beliefs. This approach can clearly be explained, as the acknowledgement of the absolute right for conscientious objections within the context of employment relations would inevitably lead to the conflict of rights (rights of employers, rights of others; it would be in conflict even with public interests).

Therefore, the possibility to claim protection for employees' conscientious objections under Article 9-2, as in the cases of opposition to military service, could be a large step forward in the development of the protections granted under Article 9. It is

197. ECtHR, Bayatyan v. Armenia (23459/03) 7 July 2011.
198. EurCommHR, X v. Germany, (7705/76) 5 July 1977; Conscientious Objectors v. Denmark (7565/76) 7 March 1977; A. v. Switzerland (10640/83) 9 May 1984.
199. ECtHR, Baratyan v. Armenia, para. 110.
200. Cited from Ronald Dworkin, Religion without God. Harvard University Press, 2013, p. 4.

interesting to note that a number of countries have recognised the conscientious objections of officials like Ladele, when introducing comparable legislation; in addition, national courts in the Netherlands upheld the claims to exemption on the grounds of conscientious objections.[201]

§6.02 THE ADJUDICATION OF EMPLOYMENT CASES UNDER ARTICLE 9

Employment cases under Article 9 tend to be adjudicated in a way consisting of a number of steps. First, the ECtHR investigates whether there was an interference with the right to manifest the employee's religion or belief. It determines the person's religion[202] or belief. An individual must show that the particular practice, for which he or she wishes to obtain protection as a 'manifestation' of religion or belief, is necessary to, or mandated by, the religion or belief system espoused.[203]

In *Kosteski v. Former Yugoslav Republic of Macedonia*,[204] the ECtHR stated that requiring the applicants to prove they were Muslims was not unreasonable or disproportionate as he was making a claim to a privilege or exemption to which he was not entitled unless he was a member of the faith concerned and in circumstances which arguably gave rise to doubts as his entitlement.[205]

The forms of manifestations are listed in Article 9: worship, teaching, practice and observance. The ECtHR has stated on numerous occasions that this article does not protect every act motivated or inspired by a religion or belief.[206] Thus in the case *Skugar and others v. Russia*,[207] where the applicants sought to have their taxpayers' numbers cancelled on the ground that their attribution was tantamount to marking them with the 'mark of the Beast' and thereby alienating them from the Orthodox Church, the ECtHR pointed that acts or omissions which do not directly express the belief concerned or which are only remotely connected to a precept of faith fall outside the protection of Article 9.

In *X. v. Denmark*, the Commission stated that the freedom of religion does not include the right of a clergyman to set up his own conditions for baptising.[208] Therefore, Article 9 does not always guarantee the right to behave in the public sphere in any and all ways dictated by one's personal beliefs. This principle has been

201. Ian Leigh, Andrew Hambler, Religious Symbols, Conscience, and the Rights of Others. Oxford Journal of Law and Religion 3(1) (2014): 9.
202. Lucy Vickers, Religious Freedom, Religious Discrimination and the Workplace. Oxford: Hart, 2008, p. 107.
203. Ian Leigh, Andrew Hambler, Religious Symbols, Conscience, and the Rights of Others. Oxford Journal of Law and Religion 3(1) (2014): 10.
204. ECtHR, Kosteski v. 'The Former Yugoslav Republic Of Macedonia' (55170/00) 13 April 2006.
205. *Ibid.*, para. 47.
206. ECtHR, Kalaç v. Turkey (20704/92) 1 July 1997, para. 26, EurCommHR, Arrowsmith v. the United Kingdom (7050/75) 12 October 1978; Leyla Şahin v. Turkey [GC] (44774/98) 10 November 2005, para. 105.
207. ECtHR, Skugar and others v. Russia (40010/04) 3 December 2009.
208. EurCommHR, X. v. Denmark (N° 7374/76) inadmissible 8 March 1976.

confirmed by the ECtHR in numerous cases.[209] The ECtHR has held that the freedom of thought, conscience and religion denotes views that attain a certain level of cogency, seriousness, cohesion and importance[210] and are therefore worthy of respect in a democratic society.[211] However, the States, according to the Strasbourg jurisprudence, have an obligation of neutrality and impartiality, which is incompatible with any power on the State's part to assess the legitimacy of religious beliefs.[212]

The ECtHR has never provided a thorough explanation of what 'cogency, seriousness and cohesion' means in this context. However, it has developed a broad approach to the interpretation of religious beliefs, which enables it to accept, in principle, that its protection extends to Druidism, pacifism, veganism, the Divine Light Zentrum and the Church of Scientology.[213]

British Courts have elaborated their understanding of the necessary level of cogency, seriousness, cohesion and importance of beliefs under the ECHR and the Human Rights Act 1998. Lord Nicholls in the case of *Williamson v. Secretary of State for Education and Employment* said that while private belief (the forum internum) could be of any kind, any beliefs which are manifested must meet what he described as 'modest, objective minimum requirements': first, they must be consistent with basic standards of human dignity or integrity (thus ruling out beliefs which would involve subjecting others to torture, etc.), and secondly, they must be coherent, in the sense of being capable of being understood.[214]

In another case considered by the British Employment Appeal Tribunal ('EAT') the applicant's views on climate change were found to be cogent, serious, cohesive and important as they affected the way he lived his life, and his hopes and fears for the future. In addition, a certain amount of emphasis was given by the EAT to the fact that these views were worthy of respect in society.[215]

Interference with an employee's freedom of religion would constitute a violation of the ECHR if was not in pursuit of a legitimate aim, or if the interference was disproportionate to the aim pursued. Therefore, establishing a legitimate aim and conducting a balancing exercise are the next steps taken by the ECtHR in adjudicating cases under Article 9.

According to this article, the interference does not amount to the violation of the ECHR if it was prescribed by law and was necessary in a democratic society in the interests of public safety, for the protection of public order, health or morals, or for the

209. ECtHR, Porter v. the United Kingdom (15814/02) 8 April 2003, and Zaoui v. Switzerland (41615/98) 18 January 2001.
210. ECtHR, Leyla Sahin v. Turkey [GC] (44774/98) 10 November 2005; Leela Förderkreis e.V. and Others v. Germany (58911/00) 6 November 2008.
211. ECtHR, Chassagnou and others v. France [GC] (25088/94 et al.) 29 April 1999, para. 114.
212. ECtHR, Jakóbski v. Poland (18429/06) 7 December 2010, para. 44; Campbell and Cosans v. the United Kingdom (7511/76, 7743/76) 25 February 1982, para. 36.
213. Bob Hepple, Tufyal Choudhury, Tackling Religious Discrimination: Practical Implications for Policy-Makers and Legislators. Home Office Research Study 221, p. 9. Available at: http://www.religionlaw.co.uk/reportae.pdf (accessed 12 April 2015).
214. Cited from Pitt Gwyneth, Keeping the Faith: Trends and Tensions in Religion or Belief Discrimination. Industrial Law Journal 40(4) (2011): 384.
215. Cited from Lucy Vickers, Religious Discrimination in the Workplace: An Emerging Hierarchy? Ecclesiastical Law Journal 12(03) (2010): 290.

protection of the rights and freedoms of others. The list of legitimate aims can be very lengthy as each of these aims might be interpreted in a very broad manner. One commentator noted that the ECtHR has not endeavoured to define carefully the profiles of those concepts and utilised them with in determination and even vagueness.[216] This problem influences how the cases are considered, as the ECtHR, having established a legitimate aim, will go on to balance the proportionality of the interference to the importance of the aim pursued. Therefore, it seems particularly important to conduct this balancing exercise with a correctly defined aim in place.

Let us return to the case of dismissal of Ms Ladele in *Eweida and others v. The UK*. The ECtHR, considering the proportionality of the interference, balanced the right of the applicant to manifest her religious beliefs with the legitimate aim to provide a service of registrating civil partnerships without discrimination (therefore against the right of others to be registered without discrimination). This right of others was called 'abstract' by dissenting Judges Vučinić and De Gaetano as there was no actual complaint on the violation of this right by the applicant or her employer. In fact, it would be more appropriate for the ECtHR to balance the right of the applicant with the right of her employer to manage his staff, as the applicant was not the only registrar in the Islington Borough Council. According to the arguments of the applicant, the employer was not required to designate all existing registrars of births, deaths and marriages as civil partnership registrars. Some other UK local authorities took a different approach, and allowed registrars with a sincerely held religious objection to the formation of civil partnerships to opt out of designation as civil partnership registrars.[217] Therefore Ms Ladele's employer could have ensured that he delivered the required service of same-sex civil union registrations without imposing on the applicant an obligation to register such partnerships.[218] In other words, Islington Borough Council could accommodate applicant's religious beliefs by substituting Ms Ladele in cases of registering same-sex couples, or leaving her in the post of registrar of deaths and births whilst assigning others to deal with registering civil union partnerships and marriages. The attention to these circumstances should have led the ECtHR to a different balancing exercise to the one they actually undertook. The right of Ms Ladele to manifest her religion should have been weighted against the right of employers to manage their staff.[219] It is unlikely that as a result of such a balancing test the ECtHR could have found that the dismissal of Ms Ladele was proportionate to the legitimate aim pursued and that Article 9 of the ECHR was not violated.

Turning now to the balancing exercise undertaken by the ECtHR in such cases, the focus will be on the details which attract the ECtHR's attention. Considering the circumstances in which the employee's freedom to manifest his or her religion has been restricted, the ECtHR establishes whether this restriction was of crucial importance for the employer. Thus in the case of Ms Eweida the ECtHR referred to the prohibition to

216. Martínez-Torrón Javier, Limitations on Religious Freedom in the Case Law of the European Court of Human Rights. Emory International Law Review 19 (2005): 633–634.
217. ECtHR, Eweida and others v. UK (48420/10) 15 January 2013, para. 25.
218. The same idea was expressed by Lucy Vickers, *see supra* note 202, pp. 280–303.
219. As, for example, in Matúz v. Hungary (73571/10) 21 October 2014, para. 34 (the case on protection of whistleblowers).

wear a Christian cross visibly and considered that there was no evidence that the wearing of other, previously authorised, items of religious clothing by other employees had any negative impact on British Airways' brand or image. It also took into account further changes in the uniform code, which allowed the wearing of visible religious symbolic jewellery.[220] Basing on these facts, the ECtHR held that prohibiting Ms Eweida from wear her cross was not of crucial importance for the employer to carry out its business. Therefore, balancing the applicant's right with the right of the employer to establish a uniform code, the ECtHR gave priority to the rights of Ms Eweida.

In contrast, in considering the application of Ms Chaplin, a nurse who was prohibited from wearing a cross due to safety and health reasons, the ECtHR found that the aim of interference was inherently of a greater magnitude than that which applied in respect of Ms Eweida. The interference with the applicant's right to manifest her religious beliefs at work was therefore found to be proportionate in that case.

Considering overall the adjudication of employment cases under Article 9, it must be noted that the majority of applications were either held inadmissible or the violation of the ECHR was not established. In the majority of such decisions and judgments, the ECtHR referred to the wide margin of appreciation of the State in such cases. Regretfully, such references sometimes implies a refusal or avoidance to more deeply analyse cases which could lead to troublesome conclusions, such as the necessity to accommodate employees' conscientious objections in cases exemplified by that of Ms Ladele.

§6.03 THE RIGHT OF AN EMPLOYEE TO MANIFEST HIS OR HER RELIGION

The approach of Strasbourg bodies to protecting the manifestation of one's religion or belief in the work-place has significantly changed with the years. The former European Commission on Human Rights had a steady line of jurisprudence showing that it was unwilling to provide protection against dismissals of persons whose employment was terminated because they came to work late or left early on a regular basis in order to comply with a prescript of their religion.[221] Although it acknowledged that a dismissal could, in certain circumstances, raise an issue under Article 9, in the Commission's opinion this right could have been protected by the ability of the employee to resign from his or her post.[222]

220. ECtHR, Eweida and others v. UK (48420/10) 15 January 2013, para. 95.
221. Henrard Kristin, A Critical Appraisal of the Margin of Appreciation Left to States Pertaining to 'Church-State Relations' Under the Jurisprudence of the European Court of Human Rights. In: M.C. Foblets, K. Alidadi, Vrielink, editors. 'Test of Faith? Religious Diversity and Accommodation in the European Religious Diversity and Accommodation in the European Workplace'. Ashgate, 2012. Available at SSRN: http://ssrn.com/abstract=2307845 or http://dx.doi.org/10.2139/ssrn.2307845. *See*, for example, EurCommHR 3 December 1996, Konttinen v. Finland (24949/94) 3 December 1996.
222. EurCommHR, Knudsen v. Norway (11045/84) inadmissible 8 March 1985; *see also*, Konttinen v. Finland (24949/94) inadmissible 3 December 1996; Stedman v. the United Kingdom (29107/95) inadmissible 9 April 1997.

The Commission was very reluctant to acknowledge the link between an employee's refusal to fulfil employment obligations and the right to manifest his or her religious beliefs. For example, in *Konttinen v. Finland*[223] an employee of the Finnish State Railways was dismissed for failing to respect his working hours, on the basis that to work after sunset on a Friday was forbidden by the Seventh-Day Adventist Church, of which he was a member. The Commission held in this case that the applicant was not dismissed because of his religious convictions but for having refused to respect his working hours; although the refusal was motivated by religious convictions, such a situation did not give rise to protection under Article 9-1. The Commission emphasised that the applicant had failed to show that he was pressured to change his religious views or prevented from manifesting his religion or belief. In *X v. UK*, the Commission decided that the obligation imposed on a teacher to observe normal working hours, which clashed with his attendance at Friday prayers, was compatible with Article 9.[224]

In *Stedman v. UK*,[225] the Commission considered the application of an employee who was dismissed from a private company for refusing to work on Sundays. The application was also considered inadmissible as the Commission held that the applicant was dismissed for failing to agree to work certain hours and not for the expression of her religious belief.

Recent case law of the ECtHR demonstrates that, in contrast with the approach of the Commission, it is developing the 'better approach' by properly considering the proportionality of any interference. In *Eweida and others v. UK* it stated:

> Given the importance in a democratic society of freedom of religion, the ECtHR considers that, where an individual complains of a restriction on freedom of religion in the workplace, rather than holding that the possibility of changing job would negate any interference with the right, the better approach would be to weigh that possibility in the overall balance when considering whether or not the restriction was proportionate.[226]

Thus the ECtHR has abandoned the Commission's view that the freedom to manifest one's belief might be protected by resigning from the post and has started to balance the freedom of the employee to manifest his or her religion in the workplace as against the rights of his or her employer, referring to the possibility to resign as only one additional factor in the overall balance. The balancing test which was absent from the early decisions of the Commission was applied by the ECtHR in *Dahlab v. Switzerland*,[227] concerning a primary school teacher who was prohibited from wearing an Islamic headscarf (*hijab*) in the performance of her teaching duties. The ECtHR weighed the right of a teacher to manifest her religion against the need to protect pupils by preserving religious harmony. It gave weight to the tender age of the children for whom the applicant was responsible as a representative of the State and concluded that

223. EurCommHR, Konttinen v. Finland (24949/94) inadmissible 3 December 1996.
224. Cited from Riza Tiirmen, Freedom of Conscience and Religion In: Marcelo Gustavo Kohen, editor. 'La Promotion de la Justice, Des Droits de L'homme Et Du Règlement Des Conflits Par Le Droit International'. Martinus Nijhoff Publishers, 2007, p. 594.
225. EurCommHR, Stedman v. UK (29107/95) inadmissible 9 April 1997.
226. ECtHR, Eweida and other v. UK (48420/10) 15 January 2013, para. 83.
227. ECtHR, Dahlab v. Switzerland (42393/98) 15 February 2001.

the authorities had not exceeded their margin of appreciation and that the measure they took was therefore not unreasonable.[228] This decision is in line with other more recent cases concerning the wearing of conspicuous religious symbols where the ECtHR held that the relevant ban was aimed at preserving the 'secular nature of the institution concerned.'[229]

In the most recent case *Ebrahimian v. France,*[230] *the Court estimated the proportionality of the interference with the employee's freedom of religion in case of non-renewal of the contract because of the refusal to stop wearing* an Islamic headscarf at work. The applicant was a social assistant in the psychiatric hospital. The principles of secularism and neutrality of public services in France constituted the leitmotiv of the judgment.[231] The Court agreed with the applicant that there had been an interference with the freedom to manifest her religion. This interference, in opinion of the majority, had a legal basis. Such a basis was found in the principle of secularism, fixed by the French constitution, and in the decision of the Conseil d'Etat, issued about six month before the non-renewal of the contract with the applicant. This decision concerned the veil ban established for the teachers in public schools. The ECtHR ruled that the restrictions outlined in it were clearly enough and provided that the refusal to remove her veil constituted a disciplinary offence.[232] Actually this finding is in contrast with the traditional requirement of the Court to the legal provisions, which have to be formulated with precision, certainty, and should be foreseeable.[233]

The Court then took a careful balancing exercise, considering such factors as the right of patients of the psychiatric hospital,[234] the wide margin of appreciation of the states in this field,[235] and the fact that the applicant enjoyed all the guarantees in the disciplinary procedure. The Court also took into account the fact that the applicant was included in the list of candidates for the post of social assistant, but did not participate in it. These finding led the Court to conclude that the interference was proportionate to the legitimate aim pursued by the State and the application was declared inadmissible.

It is curious to note that this case, where much attention was paid to the right of the patients, and the decision in *Dahlab* represent a contrast to the famous *Lautsi* case, where the ECtHR seemed unconcerned about the potential influence a crucifix displayed in the classroom might have upon the pupils.[236]

228. *Ibid.*
229. ECtHR, Leyla Sahin [GC] v. Turkey (44774/98) 10 November 2005, para. 116.
230. ECtHR, Ebrahimian v. France (64846/11) 26 November 2015.
231. *Ibid.*, paras 21–31.
232. This point was not divided by the Judge O'Leary, who issued a partly concurring and partly dissenting opinion, and was criticised by scholars. E. Brems, in particular, found that the Court might establish the violation in this case on the basis of legality, without having to engage in the proportionality analysis. *See* Eva Brems, Ebrahimian v. France: headscarf ban upheld for entire public sector, https://strasbourgobservers.com/2015/11/27/ebrahimian-v-france-headscarf-ban-upheld-for-entire-public-sector/ (accessed 20 October 2016).
233. ECtHR, Malone v. The United Kingdom (8691/79) 2 August 1984.
234. ECtHR, Ebrahimian v. France (64846/11) 26 November 2015, paras 53, 62, 63.
235. *Ibid.*, paras 64, 65.
236. Lucy Vickers, Freedom of Religion and Belief, Article 9 ECHR and the EU Equality Directive In: Filip Dorssemont, Klaus Lörcher, Isabelle Schömann, editors. 'The European Convention on Human Rights and the Employment Relation'. p. 213.

Eweida and other v. UK is still the only case in which the ECtHR has touched upon the necessity to accommodate an employee's religious beliefs. The word 'accommodation' was not used in the conclusions of the ECtHR. However, the North American experience in this sphere, and further reliance on Article 14 as requiring the State to treat differently persons whose situations are different,[237] together with previous case law on the accommodation of prisoners' religious dietary requirements,[238] altogether leads to the conclusion that the ECtHR is moving towards the recognition of such a right within Article 9 of the ECHR. This conclusion is particularly important taking into account the fact that, in general, European legislatures and courts have been very reluctant to accept reasonable accommodation as a legally binding principle.[239]

The analysis of the various applicants' claims considered in the case of *Ms Eweida and others v. UK* demonstrates that the ECtHR's approach to the accommodation of employees' religious beliefs lacks consistency. For example, it paid significant attention to the voluntary acceptance of a job or role which did not accommodate the practice in question in respect of Mr McFarlan (another applicant) and Ms Ladele. However, the ECtHR did not find the violation of the ECHR in any of the cases although Ms Ladele was constrained to fulfil employment obligations which were in contrast with her religion, while Mr McFarlane must have known that the job of counsellor in a private organisation which provided confidential sex therapy might include the counselling of same-sex couples.

The finding of a violation of Article 9 solely in relation to Ms Eweida causes us to assume that the absence of influence of such accommodation on the rights of others was a decisive factor in this case. Commentators were very optimistic with this judgment, supposing that it had become clear that many of the accommodations sought by employees, such as the meeting of dietary requirements, time off for religious observance, and uniform codes, could be viewed as manifestations of religion and thus be potentially protected by Article 9.[240] I would be less optimistic as the Courts tends to interpret broadly the impact of the accommodation on the rights of others, which evidently would lead to acknowledgment of such a right only in exceptional cases where the refusal to accommodate one's religious beliefs could not be justified with the reference to Article 9-2.

According to the ECtHR's case law, certain restrictions on the freedom to manifest one's religion or belief might be justified by the requirements of a particular job. Thus in *Pitkevich v. Russia*[241] the ECtHR emphasised that the States have a wide margin of appreciation in determining whether the interference with a judge's freedom to manifest his religion was proportionate to the aim of maintaining the authority and impartiality of the judiciary.

237. ECtHR, Eweida and others v. The UK, para. 88.
238. ECtHR, Vartic v. Romania (No. 2) (14150/08) 17 December 2013; Jakóbski v. Poland (18429/06) 7 December 2010.
239. Heiner Bielefeldt, Freedom of Religion or Relief: Anachronistic in Europe? In: Zeynep Yanasmayan, Katayoun Alidadi, Jørgen S Nielsen, Marie-Claire Foblets, editors. 'Belief, Law and Politics: What Future for a Secular Europe?'. Ashgate Publishing, 2014 (55–67), p. 61.
240. Lucy Vickers, *see supra* note 215, p. 212.
241. ECtHR, Pitkevich v. Russia (47936/99) inadmissible 8 February 2001.

In this case, the applicant argued that her dismissal from the post of a judge was in breach of Article 9, as her termination was based on her membership in the Living Faith Church and on her expressions of her Christian religious beliefs in the workplace. The ECtHR observed that the applicant was dismissed for specific activities (praying publicly during court hearings, promising certain parties to proceedings a more favourable outcome on their cases if they joined the Church) which were found to be incompatible with the requirements for judicial office. These activities, although connected with her religious beliefs, were found relevant to establishing the applicant's unsuitability as a judge and the consequent dismissal.

In *Kalaç v. Turkey*,[242] the ECtHR considered the application of a former judge advocate who claimed that his compulsory retirement on the ground of his holding unlawful fundamentalist opinions violated Article 9. The ECtHR noted that the system of military discipline by its very nature implied the possibility of placing constraints on certain rights and freedoms of members of the armed forces; constraints which would not need to be imposed on civilians. It was established that the applicant, within the limits imposed by the requirements of military life, was able to fulfil the obligations which constituted the normal forms through which a Muslim practises his religion. The ECtHR concluded that the applicant's compulsory retirement did not amount to an interference with the right guaranteed by Article 9 since it was not prompted by the way the applicant manifested his religion, but rather by his conduct and attitude.

§6.04 DISMISSALS FROM RELIGIOUS ORGANISATIONS DUE TO THE LACK OF LOYALTY

The freedom of religion is read by certain scholars as including the right to create religiously homogenous workplaces.[243] In fact the Strasbourg cases on dismissal for lack of loyalty towards a religious community always include a balancing exercise between this right of the employer and ECHR freedoms of employees. This jurisprudence outlines another facet of Article 9, namely, the scope of the rights of religious organisations to determine their own employment requirements.[244]

In order to provide a more systematic approach to this issue within this paragraph, the focus will be on cases considered under Article 9 while similar cases considered in the light of other articles will be also mentioned. In the previous parts, several judgments concerning dismissals for the lack of loyalty were already discussed (*see*, for example, *Obst v. Germany*, *Schüth v. Germany*, *Fernández Martínez v. Spain*). In these cases, as well as in others concerning employment relations between religious organisations and their employees, the ECtHR granted to the States a wide margin of appreciation in determining the fair balance between the rights of the church and those

242. ECtHR, Kalaç v. Turkey (20704/92) 1 July 1997.
243. Mark R. Freedland, Lucy Vickers, Religious Expression in the Workplace in the United Kingdom. Comparative Labor Law & Policy Journal 30(3) (2009): 601.
244. Lucy Vickers. Religious Freedom, Religious Discrimination and the Workplace. Oxford: Hart, 2008, p. 107.

of its employees. The ECtHR has also provided support for religious ethos organisations, such as religious hospitals or schools, to determine their employment requirements along religious lines.[245]

An understanding of the Strasbourg approach to the cases concerning employment in religious organisations is possible through analysis of the ECtHR's perception of the State's neutrality, the church's autonomy, and the employee's loyalty towards his or her employer.

It might seem that the neutrality of the States, recognised by many national constitutions and acknowledged by the ECtHR,[246] should preclude the ECtHR from finding violations of the ECHR in the sphere of employment relations between an employee and religious organisations. In fact, judicial authorities across Europe have traditionally declared that they lack the power to review decisions of religious organisations and the processes underpinning those decisions, because these entities enjoyed religious autonomy.[247]

Strasbourg bodies, however, understand the State's neutrality in a more restrictive way: neutrality does not mean the absence of positive obligations of the State to protect employee in the case of conflict between church autonomy and the ECHR freedoms of an individual employee. As Judge Tulkens once pointed out: 'Neutrality does not have to be equivalent to indifference'.[248]

In *Rommelfanger v. The Federal Republic of Germany*,[249] the Commission acknowledged the obligation of the State to ensure that national courts in relevant employment cases have weighed the freedom of an employee against the freedom of the employer and to establish that no unreasonable demand of loyalty had been made. In subsequent cases the ECtHR has broadened this approach and acknowledged the necessity to provide procedural safeguard to the employee in cases of dismissals for a lack of loyalty.

In this context, the case of *Lombardi Vellauri*[250] is particular interesting as the ECtHR found that the State's refusal to consider the applicant's application for a renewal of his employment contract as a professor of a Catholic University, was in breach of the ECHR due to the lack of procedural safeguards around the refusal. The ECtHR pointed out that the applicant did not receive any explanation of the university's decision; had no possibility of administrative appeal against that decision, and was denied an appeal in Italian courts, which embraced the traditional jurisdictional approach to church autonomy.[251]

Therefore, state neutrality, according to the ECtHR, means the State must ensure the fair trial standards provided in Article 6 of the ECHR applies to disputes between

245. *Ibid.*, p. 111.
246. ECtHR, S.A.S. v. France [GC] (43835/11) 1 July 2014, para. 127.
247. Ioana Cismas. Religious Actors and International Law. Oxford University Press, 2014, p. 133.
248. Françoise Tulkens. European Convention on Human Rights and Church-State Relations Pluralism vs. Pluralism, Cardozo Law Review 30 (2008): 2575, 14.
249. EurCommHR, Rommelfanger v. The Federal Republic of Germany (12242/86) inadmissible 6 September 1989.
250. ECtHR, Lombardi Vallauri c. Italie (39128/05) 20 October 2009.
251. I. Cismas. Religious Actors and International Law, Oxford University Press, 2014, p. 136.

employees and the religious organisations that employ them.[252] At the very least, this includes the employees knowing the case against them and having a chance to respond to it. This guarantee provides employees with a degree of protection from malice, unsubstantiated rumour and baseless accusations.[253]

The autonomy of churches and other religious organisations was deduced by the ECtHR as a result of interpreting Article 9 in light of Article 11, which safeguards associative life against unjustified state interference.[254] The ECtHR has emphasised that the autonomous existence of religious communities is indispensable for pluralism in a democratic society and is an issue at the very heart of the protection which Article 9 affords.[255] Autonomy has several facets, such as the establishment of the inner domain of faith, doctrine and polity and administration of religious organisations. Commentators note that although there are areas of collective religious autonomy which have obtained more protection by the ECtHR, it is impossible, at this stage, to determine whether certain spheres of forum internum of religious communities are completely shielded from state interference.[256] As pointed out above, the ECtHR acknowledged that the State's positive actions are necessary in the sphere of protecting church employees. It has thus moved away from traditional European approaches to religious autonomy issues, which was effectively a jurisdictional approach,[257] and determined certain limits of the church's autonomy in this field. These limits were classified by scholars into groups of procedural and substantial limitations.[258] Procedural limitations were already dealt with in the example of the *Lombardi Vellauri* case. Substantive limitations might be illustrated by this citation from the *Fernández Martínez v. Spain* Grand Chamber judgment:

> Mere allegation by a religious community that there is an actual or potential threat to its autonomy is not sufficient to render any interference with its members' rights to respect for their private or family life compatible with Article 8 of the Convention. In addition, the religious community in question must also show, in the light of the circumstances of the individual case, that the risk alleged is probable and substantial and that the impugned interference with the right to respect for private life does not go beyond what is necessary to eliminate that risk and does not serve any other purpose unrelated to the exercise of the religious community's autonomy. Neither should it affect the substance of the right to private and family life. The national courts must ensure that these conditions are satisfied, by

252. *See*, for example, ECtHR, Ahtinen v. Finland (48907/99) inadmissible 23 September 2008.
253. Cited from Carolyn Evans, Anna Hood. Religious Autonomy and Labour Law: A Comparison of the Jurisprudence of the United States and the European Court of Human Rights. Oxford Journal of Law and Religion (2012): 25.
254. ECtHR, Siebenhaar v. Germany (18136/02) 3 February 2011, para. 41.
255. ECtHR, Sindicatul 'Păstorul Cel Bun' v. Romania [GC] (2330/09) 9 July 2013, para. 136.
256. Merilin Kiviorg. 'Religious Autonomy in the ECHR.' Derecho y Religión IV (2009): 131–144. Available at: http://www.deltapublicaciones.com/derechoyreligion/gestor/archivos/07_10_31_124.pdf (accessed 20 May 2015).
257. Carolyn Evans, Anna Hood. Religious Autonomy and Labour Law: A Comparison of the Jurisprudence of the United States and the European Court of Human Rights. Oxford Journal of Law and Religion 2012 (1–27): 16.
258. *Ibid.*

conducting an in-depth examination of the circumstances of the case and a thorough balancing exercise between the competing interests at stake.[259]

Therefore, religious organisations and domestic Courts should take into account the rights of employees while deciding cases on dismissals for the lack of loyalty, giving attention to the particular circumstances of each applicant, including to factors such as the duration of employment with the religious organisation,[260] the ability to find another job, or whether any unemployment benefit is available,[261] the nature of the restricted right.[262]

The main consequence of giving religious communities autonomy is so that they may demand a certain degree of loyalty from those working for them or representing them.[263]

Duty of loyalty

The ECtHR has on numerous occasions acknowledged that the employees of religious organisations have a higher duty of loyalty towards their employer.[264] It means that certain restrictions of their freedoms of religion, expression or association would not necessarily held to be in breach of their ECHR rights insofar as those restrictions were clearly set out in their employment contracts and could therefore be anticipated by the employees. The demand for loyalty is reasonable as far as it touches on an issue of crucial importance for the religious organisation (such as an opinion on abortions[265] or the celibacy of priests[266]). It is also reasonable in cases where the position of the employee, who infringed the duty of loyalty, could influence the image of the religion that the organisation is affiliated with or represents (as in cases of teachers[267] or university professors[268]).

In the case mentioned earlier, *Rommelfanger v. The Federal Republic of Germany*, the Commission recognised that the ECHR permitted contractual obligations where an employee accepts a duty of loyalty towards the Church which limits his ECHR freedoms to a certain extent. In other cases, the ECtHR has emphasised the importance of the employee's ability to anticipate the restrictions dictated by the duty of loyalty.[269] Thus in *Siebenhaar*, the case in which a kindergarten teacher was dismissed from her position by the Protestant Church because of her active commitment to another religious community, the ECtHR attached weight to the fact that the applicant should

259. ECtHR, Fernández Martínez v. Spain (56030/07) Chamber Judgment 15 May 2012, para. 132.
260. ECtHR, Siebenhaar v. Germany, para. 44.
261. ECtHR, Fernández Martínez v. Spain [GC] (56030/07) 12 June 2014, para. 124.
262. ECtHR, Schüth v. Germany (№1620/03) 23 September 2010, para. 131.
263. *See*, for example, Fernández Martínez v. Spain (56030/07) Chamber Judgment 15 May 2012.
264. EurCommHR, Rommelfanger v. The Federal Republic of Germany (12242/86) inadmissible 6 September 1989, Fernández Martínez v. Spain (56030/07) Chamber Judgment 15 May 2012, para. 86.
265. EurCommHR, Rommelfanger v. The Federal Republic of Germany (12242/86) inadmissible 6 September 1989.
266. ECtHR, Fernández Martínez v. Spain (56030/07) Chamber Judgment 15 May 2012.
267. *Ibid.*, *see also* Siebenhaar v. Germany (18136/02) 3 February 2011.
268. ECtHR, Lombardi Vallauri c. Italie (39128/05) 20 October 2009.
269. ECtHR, Fernández Martínez v. Spain, para. 119.

have been aware of this duty as it was directly stated in her employment contract and the relevant regulations – all of which she ought to have read before signing the employment documents and entering that employment. Therefore, it found that the applicant should have been aware that membership in the Universal Church and its teaching activities were inconsistent with her employment duties.[270]

According to the ECtHR's findings, Ms Siebenhaar's dismissal for lack of loyalty had been necessary to preserve the Church's credibility, which outweighed her interest in keeping the job. It was noted that the domestic courts had given more weight to the interests of the Protestant Church than to those of Ms Siebenhaar. This finding, however, did not preclude the ECtHR from *concluding that there had been no violation of Article 9.*

This judgment, together with *Fernández Martínez*, demonstrates that the ECtHR, where it has found that the duty of loyalty should have been known by the applicant, becomes very reluctant to protect employees from dismissal in cases where it did not strike core ECHR rights as for example in *Schüth*. The ECtHR's approach to the cases of dismissal for the lack of loyalty is very narrow, as on many occasions it leads the ECtHR to accept the restriction on an employee's ECHR rights and the fact that national courts gave more weight to the interests of the Church, although a more thorough balancing exercise should have led to the opposite conclusion. Thus the interplay between the state's neutrality, religious autonomy and the employee's loyalty leaves, in fact, little space for the protection of individual ECHR rights of such employees.

However, a positive facet could be established here as well. The judgments mentioned in this section contributed to the understanding of the limits of the autonomy of religious organisations as employers and urged domestic courts to conduct a careful balancing exercise to address conflicts between the collective religious rights of organisations and individual human rights in a way that duly respects both sides, allowing them to co-exist.[271] It is interesting to note that after the judgments in *Schüth* and *Obst* were handed down, a labour court in Germany decided that the dismissal of a doctor from a Catholic hospital, following his civil divorce and his remarriage, was unlawful.[272] This example vividly illustrates the positive impact of the jurisprudence of the ECtHR upon national courts in the sphere of protecting the employees of religious organisations.

§6.05 CONCLUSIONS

The ECtHR's achievements in the sphere of protecting employees' freedom of religion are rather modest. The majority of applications on the violation of employees' freedom

270. ECtHR, Siebernhaar v. Germany, para. 46.
271. Eva Brems, Loures Peroni, Religion and Human Rights: Deconstructing and Navigating Tensions In: Silvio Ferrari, editor. 'Routledge Handbook of Law and Religion'. Routledge, 2015. pp. 145–160, 153.
272. Cited from Van der Vyver, Johan D. State Interference in the Internal Affairs of Religious Institutions. Emory International Law Review 26 (2012): 1. Available at: http://law.emory.edu /eilr/_documents/volumes /26/1/recent-developments/vandervyver.pdf (accessed 20 May 2015).

of religion were either held inadmissible or the violation of the ECHR was not established. One of the main reasons for these conclusions was the repeated reference to the wide margin of appreciation allowed to the States in such cases.

However, several judgments of the ECtHR demonstrate a remarkable step forward in this sphere of establishing basic employee rights. In contrast with the former European Commission of Human Rights, the ECtHR, instead of holding that the ability for applicants to change jobs negates any interference with their freedom of religion, balanced the rights of employees against the rights of employers to manage the staff and assessed the proportionality of any interference.

The ECtHR's judgment in respect of Ms Eweida moved forward to recognise a right for employees to religious accommodation at the workplace. This is a very important step for the members of the CoE as European legislatures and courts did not acknowledge such a right. The ECtHR's refusal to find a violation in the case of Ms Ladele in turn illustrates that the right for accommodation might be acknowledged in particular cases, when such accommodation does not infringe any broadly interpreted rights of others.

In *Baratyan v. Armenia* the Grand Chamber acknowledged the right of conscientious objection to military service, absent from the text of Article 9, thus establishing a common standard for the countries of the CoE.

In numerous cases brought by the employees of religious organisations, the ECtHR outlined the scope of the rights of religious organisations to determine their own employment requirements. Relying on the concepts of a state's neutrality and the church's autonomy, the ECtHR tended to interpret broadly the duty of loyalty of such employees and granted to the States a wide margin of appreciation in determining the fair balance between the rights of the religious organisation and those of the employee. The positive facets of the Strasbourg jurisprudence in this sphere can be represented by the following requirements of the ECtHR:

(1) The employee's ability to anticipate or know the restrictions dictated by the duty of loyalty.
(2) To provide procedural safeguards to the employee in cases of dismissal for lack of loyalty.
(3) To ensure that 'no unreasonable demand of loyalty was made'.

The recent case considered by a German court, referred to in this section, is an example of the adoption of the above rules by domestic court and represents the practical impact the ECHR may have on the human rights of employees on the national level.

CHAPTER 7

The Employee's Freedom of Expression and Association

'Without publicity, no good is permanent;
under the auspices of publicity, no evil can continue'.
Jeremy Bentham[273]

The freedoms of expression and association are considered by scholars to be essential for the enjoyment of all other freedoms included in the ECHR.[274] In this section, the focus will be on the protection of the employee's freedom of expression and the freedom of association as far as the protection of personal opinions is also 'one of the objectives of the freedoms of assembly and association as enshrined in Article 11'.[275]

The freedom of association understood as a set of collective labour rights, as elaborated by the ECtHR,[276] is outside the scope of the present research:

> Article 10: 1. Everyone has the right to freedom of expression. This right shall include freedom to hold opinions and to receive and impart information and ideas without interference by public authority and regardless of frontiers. This Article shall not prevent States from requiring the licensing of broadcasting, television or cinema enterprises.

273. Cited from Gerald J. Postema, The Soul of Justice: Bentham on Publicity, Law, and the Rule of Law In: Xiaobo Zhai, Michael Quinn, editors. 'Bentham's Theory of Law and Public Opinion'. Cambridge University Press, 2014, pp. 40–62, 46.
274. Thilo Marauhn, Freedom of Expression, Freedom of Assembly and Association In: Dirk Ehlers, Ulrich Becker, editors. 'European Fundamental Rights and Freedoms'. Walter de Gruyter, 2007 (97–129) p. 98.
275. ECtHR, Volkmer v. Germany (39799/98) inadmissible 22 November 2001.
276. See among others: ECtHR, Young, James and Webster v. the United Kingdom (7601/76 7806/77) 13 August 1981; Sorensen and Rasmussen v. Denmark (52562/99 52620/99) 11 January 2006; Wilson, National Union Of Journalists and others v. the United Kingdom (30668/96 30671/96 30678/96) 2 July 2002; Demir And Baykara v. Turkey (34503/97) 12 November 2008; Enerji Yapi-Yol Sen c. Turquie (68959/01) 21 April 2009; National Union Of Rail, Maritime and transport workers v. The United Kingdom (31045/10) 8 April 2014.

> 2. The exercise of these freedoms, since it carries with it duties and responsibilities, may be subject to such formalities, conditions, restrictions or penalties as are prescribed by law and are necessary in a democratic society, in the interests of national security, territorial integrity or public safety, for the prevention of disorder or crime, for the protection of health or morals, for the protection of the reputation or rights of others, for preventing the disclosure of information received in confidence, or for maintaining the authority and impartiality of the judiciary.

The list of possible restrictions is wider than in the Article 8 or 9; the drafters explicitly stated that this freedom may be subject to such formalities, conditions, restrictions or penalties as are prescribed by law. The complexity found within the right to freedom of expression owes much to the jurisprudence of the Strasbourg Court.[277] The ECtHR stated that the freedom of expression, as enshrined in Article 10, is subject to a number of exceptions which, however, must be narrowly interpreted and the necessity for any exceptions must be convincingly established.[278]

The scope of employees' freedom of expression is narrower as employment relations impose the duty of loyalty which also means certain restrictions on employees' ECHR freedoms (the restriction on their freedom of religion was already illustrated above). Should employees be permitted to express negative opinions about their employers or to criticise the quality of product made by their employers? Might an employee participate in a political party and express political opinions in contradiction with the policy of her employer? Can a civil servant disclose publicly confidential information on the basis of the public interest and be expected democratic society to protect him? These are the most challenging questions for the domestic courts in this context.

Disputes over the employee's freedom of expression have become much more frequent in the last decade as the growing use of social networks such as Facebook made the expression of an employee's opinion, which was previously more easily hidden from the employer and difficult to prove, easily accessible. It is not surprising that people are dismissed for the publications of photos or comments in Facebook or other similar systems. Thus the British Employment Tribunal stated that the manager of a pub had been fairly dismissed for gross misconduct after posting negative comments about customers on her Facebook page.[279] In another case, the British tribunal upheld the dismissal of an Apple retail store employee, who posted negative comments about Apple products on her private Facebook page,[280] since friends could copy and pass on the information thus making it public. French courts are more

277. Jean-Francois Flauss. European Court of Human Rights and the Freedom of Expression. Indiana Law Journal 84 (2009): 809. Available at: http://www.repository.law.indiana.edu/cgi/viewcontent.cgi?article=1124&context=ilj (accessed 16 May 2015).
278. ECtHR, Steel and Morris v. The United Kingdom (68416/01) 15 February 2005, para. 87.
279. Preece v. JD Wetherspoons plc ET/2104806/10, *see* Sarah James. 'Social Networks' at Work–Employment Law and the Facebook Generation. Human Resource Management International Digest 19(6) (2011).
280. Crisp v. Apple Retail, cited from Daniel Ornstein. Social Media Usage in the Workplace around the World–Developing Law and Practices. Business Law International Journal 13 (2012): 195.

rigorous in deciding whether Facebook publications can amount to gross misconduct and they tend to overrule decisions of lower courts which have upheld such dismissals as lawful.[281] These cases demonstrate that new technologies increasingly erase the clear borders between public and private expression of opinions and the protection of the freedom of expression granted by the ECHR may become particularly valuable in this context.

The ECtHR's approach to the most complicated issues in addressing the employee's freedom of expression will be analysed on the basis of its numerous judgments. In particular, emphasis will be drawn to the criteria for balancing the freedom of expression of the employee, bound by the duty of loyalty, against the right of employers to manage their staff. The limits of the freedom of expression, and the protection of whistle-blowers will be also researched.

This Section will be divided into several subsections. Subsection §7.01 will deal with the duty of loyalty and discretion as it is a basic notion for understanding the ECtHR's case law on restricting employees' freedom of expression; subsection §7.02 will focus on criticisms of employers, the disclosure of information of public interest and standards of whistle-blower protection. Subsection §7.03 will research the most interesting cases on dismissal considered in the light of Articles 10 and 11.

§7.01 THE DUTY OF LOYALTY AND DISCRETION

The majority of the Strasbourg jurisprudence on the violation of Article 10 in the context of employment relations concerns the rights of public servants. The ECtHR has reiterated repeatedly that employees owe to their employer a duty of loyalty, reserve and discretion.[282] The research of relevant case law does not allow us to define these notions separately and clearly. In the majority of cases, these duties are listed in order to remind us of the special character of employment relations in general and of public servants in particular, attaching particular weight to the special fiduciary character of employment relations especially as far as public servants being representatives of the state are concerned.

However, the ECtHR has pointed that the requirement to act in good faith in the context of an employment contract does not imply an absolute duty of loyalty towards the employer or a duty of discretion to the point of subjecting the worker to the employer's interests.[283] The scope of these obligations depends on the particular

281. Arrêt de la Cour d'appel de Douai du 16 décembre 2011, L'arrêt de la Cour d'appel de Versailles était attendu le 22 février 2012 cited from Anthony Bem, Les « licenciements Facebook »: évolution et dernières actualités jurisprudentielles. Available at: http://www.legavox.fr/blog/maitre-anthony-bem/licenciements-facebook-evolution-dernieres-actualites-7765.htm#.VXVixs_tmkp (accessed 7 June 2015).

282. See ECtHR, Langner v. Germany (14464/11) 17 September 2015, para. 43; Vogt v. Germany (17851/91) 26 September 1995, para. 53; Matuz v. Hungary (73571/10) 21 October 2014, para. 32; Pay v. The United Kingdom (32792/05) inadmissible 16 September 2008.

283. ECtHR, Palomo Sánchez and others v. Spain[GC] (28955/06 et al.) 12 September 2011, para. 76.

position of the employee, on the public interest in the disclosed information (in case of disclosure) and even on the historical background of a particular country.[284]

The duty of loyalty emerged in the Strasbourg case law in a series of cases against Germany, where public servants (mostly teachers) alleged that their dismissal for lack of loyalty to the German Constitution violated the ECHR. In *Kosiek v. Germany*,[285] the applicant, a probationary lecturer at a State Technical College, claimed that his dismissal for lack of loyalty violated Article 10 of the ECHR. The employer stated that Mr Kosiek had not proved himself during the probationary period as he was an official of a political party, whose aims were inimical to the German Constitution. The ECtHR in this case perceived the duty loyalty as one of the conditions of eligibility for the post of a teacher. As the right for access to civil service was not enshrined in the ECHR, the ECtHR did not proceed any further into an evaluation of the proportionality of such a requirement. Despite pointing out that his status as a probationary civil servant did not deprive him of the protection afforded by Article 10,[286] the ECtHR decided that there had been no breach of Article 10 because access to the civil service, which was not guaranteed by the ECHR, lay at the heart of the issue.[287] This was a dangerous line of reasoning as it suggested that the dismissal involved no prima facie breach of the ECHR.[288] Such a conclusion could lead to the general neglect of employment rights' protection under the ECHR. Judge Cremona in the Concurring Opinion to the judgment in *Glasenapp*[289] correctly pointed that the civil service status provided no more than the general background, whereas the dominant feature in the foreground is a prejudice suffered because of the holding and expression of opinions.[290]

It is remarkable that both the ECtHR and the Commission in *Kosiek* and other similar cases such as *R.Q.* or *Glasenapp v. Germany* refrained from assessing the necessity of an interference with the rights of the applicants, ignoring each of the relevant applicant's arguments on this matter.[291] In the opinion of the dissenting Judge Spielmen in *Kosiek*, the question of the necessity of the interference in a democratic state (in other words, of its proportionality) was of crucial matter in such a case and should lead the ECtHR to an opposite conclusion than the one they arrived at.[292] A more considered approach to the duty of loyalty as the basis for restricting an employee's freedom of expression or association might be found in *Vogt* case, where the ECtHR for the first time found that the dismissal of a school teacher, for being a member of a political party, was in breach of both Articles 10 and 11 of the ECHR. The

284. See ECtHR, Vogt v. Germany, also Joint Dissenting Opinion of Judges Bonello, Strážnická, Bîrsan, Jungwiert and Del Tufo in Maestri v. Italy (39748/98) GC 17 February 2004.
285. ECtHR, Kosiek v. Germany (9704/82) 28 August 1986.
286. *Ibid.*, para. 36.
287. *Ibid.*, para. 39.
288. Lucy Vickers, Freedom of Speech and Employment. Oxford University Press, 2002, p. 79.
289. ECtHR, Glasenapp v. Germany (9228/80) 28 August 1986.
290. The Concurring Opinion of Judge Cremona in Glasenapp v. Germany.
291. See EurCommHR, R.Q. v. the Federal Republic of Germany (10942/84) 9 December 1987, see also ECtHR, Otto v. Germany (27574/02) inadmissible 24 November 2005 (on the refusal to promote a civil servant with the police on account of political activities).
292. See Partly Dissenting Opinion of Judge Spielmann, Kosiek v. Germany (9704/82) 28 August 1986.

ECtHR distinguished the Vogt case from previous similar cases because the applicant in this case had been a permanent civil servant for a number of years. However, as pointed out, Ida Koch, Glasenapp and Kosiek (the applicants in the cases referred to above) also had their permanent appointments annulled, and the difference between the cases was more modest than the ECtHR appeared willing to acknowledge.[293]

What *did* make the ECtHR step from the *Kosiek* and *Glasenapp* approach to the protection of public servants' freedom of expression? An examination of the necessity of the interference in a democratic society emerged in this case, and was also undertaken subsequently in similar cases such as *Volkmer v. Germany*[294] and *Petersen v. Germany*.[295] The ECtHR progressed from simply framing such cases as being about the right to access the public service, and actually undertook a proper analysis of the scope of the duty of loyalty, taking into account more relevant circumstances. In *Vogt*, it found the absolute nature of the duty of loyalty as construed by the German courts striking, and criticised such an approach in the following way:

> It (the duty of loyalty) is owed equally by every civil servant, regardless of his or her function and rank. It implies that every civil servant, whatever his or her own opinion on the matter, must unambiguously renounce all groups and movements which the competent authorities hold to be inimical to the Constitution. It does not allow for distinctions between service and private life; the duty is always owed, in every context.[296]

This is a remarkable statement of the ECtHR attempting to outline the limits of the loyalty civil servants owed to their employers, the State. According to the majority of the Grand Chamber, the duty of loyalty, as far as political views and membership in political parties are concerned, cannot be equally spread to all employees without taking into account his or her particular circumstances. It was pointed out that the States should ensure the distinction between an imposed duty of loyalty in the employee's professional versus private life. As a former Judge of the ECtHR J.A. Frowein once wrote, human nature should be taken into account in the adjudication of such cases.[297]

Having established these points the Grand Chamber further weighed circumstances of the *Vogt* case such as the political neutrality of the applicant at the workplace; her previous appointment to the permanent post in spite of the then-existing membership to the political party, which pursued, in opinion of the State, unconstitutional goals; the legality of the political party of which the applicant was a member. The Concurring Judges also took into consideration these factors; however, they came to the opposite conclusion, considering that particular circumstances of

293. Ida Elisabeth Koch, Human Rights as Indivisible Rights: The Protection of Socio-economic Demands under the European Convention on Human Rights. Martinus Nijhoff Publishers, 2009, p. 229.
294. ECtHR, Volkmer v. Germany (39799/98) inadmissible 22 November 2001.
295. ECtHR, Petersen v. Germany (39793/98) inadmissible 22 November 2001.
296. Vogt v. Germany (17851/91) 26 September 1995, para. 59.
297. J.A. Frowein, How to Save Democracy from Itself? In: Y. Dinstein Domb, editor. 'Israel Yearbook on Human Rights'. Martinus Nijhoff Publishers, 1996, p. 212.

German history taken together with the possibility of '"hidden" ways in which political and moral values "creep into" academic language and logic'[298] justified the disciplinary measure of dismissing the teacher.

It is remarkable that the ECtHR tends to interpret more broadly the duty of loyalty of public or municipal servants as far as such pain points as racism or terrorism are concerned, as if it is willing to restrict any speculation on these topics. Thus in *Kern v. Germany*,[299] the ECtHR declared inadmissible the application by an environmental engineer with the Lübeck municipality, who had been dismissed for the publicly expressed support of the attacks on the World Trade Centre and the Pentagon in 2001 in the USA. The ECtHR put great weight on the employee's duty to recognise the free democratic order. It is interesting to note that the contents of a press release issued by the applicant on behalf of a right-wing extremist group, on the day after the terrorist attacks, were not considered to be evidence of the lack of loyalty or as a refusal to recognise the free democratic order by the Labour Court. The first instance domestic court found that the applicant had basically condemned all terrorist attacks and expressed his sincere condolences to all innocent victims of the attacks and that he had merely expressed his anti-American feelings. The European ECtHR, however, had another view of the contents of the press release. Taking into consideration statements in it, which approved of the terrorist attacks and assumed the existence of a 'Zionist oligarchy' as well as the impact of those statements on the civil service, it found that the dismissal was not an excessive restriction on the freedom of expression of civil service employees. The ECtHR agreed with the Court of Appeal that it was unacceptable for the employer to continue the applicant's employment, as it could not expect the applicant to respect the free democratic order in the future. This conclusion is rather surprising, as the text of the press release does not provide any grounds on which the applicant's views on the democratic order can be assessed.

In two cases concerning a teacher and a university professor respectively, the ECtHR noted that if the employees' expressed opinions infringed the basic values of the ECHR, such expression might be excluded from protection under Articles 10 and 17. The propaganda of racist ideas[300] and opinions which could 'sow doubts in the importance of the extermination of Jews and other groups stigmatized during the Second World War'[301] were evaluated as possible examples of such exemption.

The ECtHR's approach to the duty of loyalty and discretion owing by public servants has, with time, matured and developed to differentiate between applicants who might be military men, judges and members of parliament. Scholars suppose that this differentiation reflects the different scopes of the margin of appreciation afforded to the states in cases about the protection of various types of speech.[302]

298. Dissenting opinion of Judge Jambrek in ECtHR, Vogt v. Germany (17851/91) 26 September 1995.
299. ECtHR, Kern v. Germany (26870/04) inadmissible 29 May 2007.
300. ECtHR, Seurot v. France (57383/00) inadmissible 18 May 2004.
301. ECtHR, Gollnisch v. France (48135/08) inadmissible 7 June 2011.
302. Lucy Vickers, *see supra* note 215, p. 103.

Military men and police

The ECtHR's approach to military men's freedom of expression was first established in *Grigoriades v. Greece,* [303] where the conviction of an officer accused of 'insult to the army' was found to be in breach of Article 10 of the ECHR. The basis for his conviction was a letter he had written to his commanding officer, which contained certain strong and intemperate remarks in respect of army life and the army as an institution. The ECtHR stated: 'Article 10 does not stop at the gates of army barracks and applies to military personnel as to all other persons within the jurisdiction of the Contracting States'.

According to the ECtHR, States are entitled to impose restrictions on freedom of expression where there is a real threat to military discipline;[304] however, this right should not be used for the purpose of frustrating the expression of opinions, even if these are directed against the army as an institution. The conclusion of the majority was criticised by the dissenting judges[305] as undermining military discipline 'for the benefit of an aggravating interpretation of the freedom of expression'.[306] Scholars, however, supported the majority's view and considered that the ECtHR had been able to balance the interests of the State with the fundamental rights of the individual.[307]

The ECtHR's support of military personnel's freedom of expression was also expressed in *Vereinigung Demokratischer Soldaten Österreichs and Gubi v. Austria,*[308] where the second applicant, a soldier of the Austrian army, was prevented from distributing a newspaper containing critical articles about army life. It is remarkable that Mr Gubi, during the several months before these events, had lodged complaints and published open letters criticising the number of fatigue duties to which he was assigned. The State in this case argued that by ordering him to cease distributing the newspaper, his commanding officer had sought to prevent Mr Gubi from destabilising his fellow soldiers even further given he was already responsible for the friction existing at the time in his barracks. The ECtHR found that the interference with Mr Gubi's right to freedom of expression was disproportionate as the newspaper articles did not call into question the duty of obedience or the purpose of service in the armed forces. The newspaper was aimed at criticising and putting forward proposals for

303. ECtHR, Grigoriades v. Greece [GC] (24348/94) 25 November 1997.
304. See also ECtHR, Jokšas v. Lithuania (25330/07) 12 November 2013, para. 70. *See also* Kirchner Stefan, Vanessa Maria, The Freedom of Expression of Members of the Armed Forces under the European Convention on Human Rights in Jokšas V. Lithuania. Baltic Journal of Law and Politics 7(1) (2014): 12–28.
305. See Dissenting opinions of judges Sir John Freeland, Mr Russo, Mr Valticos, Mr Loizou, Mr Morenilla, joint dissenting opinion of Mr Gölcüklü and Mr Pettiti and dissenting opinion of Mr Casadevall. Grigoriades v. Greece.
306. Cited from Jean-Francois Flauss, European Court of Human Rights and the Freedom of Expression. Indiana Law Journal 84 (2009): 809.
307. Rowe Peter, Control Over Armed Forces Exercised by the European Court of Human Rights. Geneva Centre for the Democratic Control of Armed Forces. Working paper series 56 (2002), p. 67.
308. ECtHR, Vereinigung Demokratischer Soldaten Österreichs and Gubi v. Austria (15153/89) 19 December 1994.

reform in the army, and the freedom to express those views, in the ECtHR's opinion, had to be protected under ECHR.

The ECtHR's approach to the expression of political opinions by members of the armed forces is stricter. In this respect, it emphasised that the 'duties and responsibilities' referred to in Article 10-2 assumed a special significance, which justified leaving to the national authorities a certain margin of appreciation in determining whether the impugned interference was proportionate to the above aim.[309] Based on this argument, the ECtHR declared inadmissible the applications of soldiers who were dismissed from the army for being part of political parties which pursued 'unconstitutional' goals.[310]

The same approach, attributing major significance to the loyalty of policemen, can be traced in *Trade Union of the Police in the Slovak Republic and Others v. Slovakia*,[311] which concerned the freedom of expression of police trade unions. The applicants, members of the police trade union, spontaneously called for the Government to step down during a public meeting, and displayed a banner which read: 'If the State doesn't pay a policeman, the mafia will do so with pleasure.' Subsequently, the Minister of the Interior criticised the meeting and its organisers and removed one of the applicants from his post as a director in the police force. In deciding this case, the ECtHR placed great weight on the police's duty of loyalty to the State, which played a fundamental role in ensuring internal order and security and fighting crime.[312] Refusing to rule in favour of the applicants, it upheld the requirement that police officers should act in an impartial manner when expressing their views, so that their reliability and trustworthiness in the eyes of the public was maintained.[313]

However, in spite of the broader duty of loyalty imposed on policemen, the prohibition on them joining any political party or of engaging in any political activity has been found to be in breach of Article 10. In *Rekvényi v. Hungary*,[314] the ECtHR stated that that this prohibition, because it curtailed the applicant's involvement in political activities, interfered with the exercise of the applicant's right to freedom of expression. The ECtHR had recognised the establishment of a politically neutral police force as a legitimate aim of the interference.[315] Considering the necessity of the interference it drew attention to the peculiarity of Hungarian history as only five years had passed since the collapse of the communist regime.[316]

309. ECtHR, Erdel v. Germany (30067/04) inadmissible 13 February 2007(Call-up of reserve officer revoked owing to membership of a political party suspected of disloyalty to the constitutional order).
310. *Ibid.*, Lahr v. Germany (16912/05) inadmissible 1 July 2008 (Early termination of a conscript's military service on the ground of his membership of an extremist party).
311. ECtHR, Trade Union of the Police in the Slovak Republic and Others v. Slovakia (11828/08) 25 September 2012.
312. See also ECtHR, Lahr v. Germany, para. 69.
313. ECtHR, Trade Union of the Police in the Slovak Republic and Others v. Slovakia, para. 70.
314. ECtHR, Rekvényi v. Hungary [GC] (25390/94) 20 May 1999.
315. *Ibid.*, para. 46.
316. Judge Fischbach, in contrast with the majority, found that it was essential that change be accompanied by an approach fostering awareness of democratic pluralism through divergent political views that fuel debate over ideas in the police as well. Partly Dissenting Opinion of Judge Fischbach, Rekvényi v. Hungary.

Scholars noticed that the ECtHR gave considerable weight to the circumstance of the State's transition from that communist regime in conducting its balancing exercise.[317] The special regard paid to the length of this period reflected, in the opinion of certain commentators, the fact that in respect of dangers to democracy the ECtHR does not allow States to use the argument of special circumstances of transition for a very long time.[318] Besides this factor and with more depth, the ECtHR also considered the scope of the prohibition.

Comparing the case with *Vogt*,[319] the Grand Chamber in *Rekvényi* found that the wording of the relevant article in the Hungarian Constitution might prima facie suggest that it required an absolute ban on the political activities of policemen. However, an examination of the relevant legislation showed that police officers had in fact remained entitled to undertake some activities enabling them to articulate their political opinions and preferences. Notably, whilst sometimes subject to restrictions imposed in the interest of the service, police officers had the right to expound on election programmes, including to promote and nominate candidates, organise election campaign meetings, vote in and stand for elections to Parliament, local authorities and the office of mayor, participate in referenda, join trade unions, associations and other organisations, participate in peaceful assemblies, make statements to the press, participate in radio or television programmes or publish works on politics.[320] In these circumstances, the scope and the effect of the impugned restrictions on the applicant's exercise of his freedom of expression were found to be proportionate to the aim of protection of national security and public safety and the prevention of disorder.[321]

The ECtHR's reasoning as to the interference with the applicant's rights under Article 11 was brief. Referring to its analysis in relation to Article 10, the ECtHR stated that the interference with the applicant's freedom of association was justified under Article 11-2 which did not prevent the imposition of lawful restrictions on the exercise of these rights by members of the armed forces, of the police or of the administration of the state.[322]

This Grand Chamber judgment, in spite of having failed to find a violation, provides important guarantees of policemen's freedom of expression on political matters as it extends the main conclusion of the *Vogt* judgment – the freedom to express political opinions cannot be banned absolutely.

317. Varju Marton, Transition as a Concept of European Human Rights Law (19 January 2009). Available at SSRN: http://ssrn.com/abstract=1329978 (accessed 1 June 2015).
318. Antoine Buyse, The Truth, the Past and the Present: Article 10 ECHR and Situations of Transition In: Antoine Buyse, Michael Hamilton, editors. 'Transitional Jurisprudence and the ECHR: Justice, Politics and Rights'. Cambridge University Press, 2011, p. 136.
319. It's worth noting that Judge Jambrek in the Vogt case argued that the ban was not absolute. See Dissenting Opinion of Judge Jambrek, Vogt v. Germany (17851/91) 26 September 1995, para. 6.
320. ECtHR, Rekvényi v. Hungary, para. 49.
321. ECtHR, Rekvényi v. Hungary [GC] (25390/94) 20 May 1999, paras 41, 50.
322. *Ibid.*, para. 61.

Judges

The ECtHR has on many occasions emphasised the special role of the judiciary, which, as the guarantor of justice, must enjoy public confidence.[323] In order to maintain public confidence, judges are required to show restraint in exercising their freedom of expression in all instances where the authority and impartiality of the judiciary were likely to be called in question.[324] Public criticism of the judiciary on the part of judges themselves obviously undermines the public's confidence in this branch of Government. In these types of cases, the ECtHR has had to decide whether such a freedom of expression, which is evidently in contrast with the duty of loyalty, might be justified by the public interest and should be permitted in democratic society.

In *Wille v. Lichtenstein*,[325] the ECtHR protected the right of the judge to hold personal opinions on political matters and even to share it publicly in spite of the State's arguments that the nature of judicial office required the applicant to exercise a particularly high degree of self-restraint in making public pronouncements which had a political flavour.[326] The Chamber judgment in *Baka v. Hungary* protected the right of the president of the respondent's Supreme Court to criticise judicial reforms; in *Kudeshkina v. Russia*[327]- the right of judges to make whistleblower disclosures.

Therefore, the duty of loyalty and discretion imposed on judges, although rather wide, could be restricted in favour of the freedom of expression insofar as public interests in democratic societies were concerned.[328] In the cases of some Italian judges, punished for being members of mason organisations, the ECtHR did not consider the necessity of such an interference under either Articles 10 or 11 of the ECHR, having found that such a sanction lacked foreseeability and thus violated the ECHR for that reason.[329] The *Maestri* case had a strong dissent; the dissenting opinions of five judges drew especial attention to the specific historical background of mason organisations being connected with the mafia, finding that the disciplinary sanctions imposed by the State was not in breach of the ECHR. These dissenting opinions show that judges' duty of loyalty might be read as precluding them from expressing views or against membership in organisations which might influence public's view of judicial impartiality.

323. ECtHR, Kudeshkina v. Russia (29492/05) 26 February 2009, para. 86.
324. ECtHR, Wille v. Liechtenstein[GC] (28396/95) 28 October 1999, para. 64, Kudeshkina v. Russia, para. 86.
325. ECtHR, Wille v. Liechtenstein[GC] (28396/95) 28 October.
326. *Ibid.*, para. 59.
327. ECtHR, Kudeshkina v. Russia (29492/05) 26 February 2009.
328. See also ECtHR, Pitkevich v. Russia (47936/99) inadmissible 8 February 2001, where the Court considered the judge's freedom of expression which did not serve any public interest.
329. ECtHR, Maestri v. Italy (39748/98) 17 February 2004; N F v. Italy (37119/97) 2 August 2001.

Members of parliament

In the recent case of *Karácsony and others v. Hungary,*[330] the ECtHR underlined that the right of democratically elected parliamentary representatives to the freedom of expression deserves a very high level of protection, because it is necessary to ensuring democratic principles and an open process, in addition to exemplifying the principles of pluralism.[331] In this case, which concerned the imposition of fines on members of Parliament,[332] the ECtHR did not agree with the State, which argued that speeches in Parliament did not fall under the ordinary standards of speech as they entailed special responsibilities of parliamentarians. The ECtHR found the violation of Article 10 in this case.[333]

In *Zdanoka v. Latvia,*[334] the ECtHR acknowledged that parliamentarians' duty of loyalty could not be identical or even similar to that required of other members of the public service.[335] It emphasised that candidates for legislature, which is based on the idea of political pluralism, cannot be required to be 'politically neutral'.

It further found that the State, having ruled on the applicant's ineligibility to stand for parliamentary election in Latvia due to her former membership of a political party and expression of certain political views, violated Article 11 of the ECHR.

In *McGuinness v. The UK,*[336] the ECtHR ruled inadmissible the applicant's claim that his Article 10 rights had been violated because his Northern Irish republican beliefs were in contrast with the prescribed oath of allegiance to the British monarchy. The ECtHR pointed out that the requirement for elected representatives of the House of Commons to take an oath of allegiance to the reigning monarch could reasonably be viewed as an affirmation of loyalty to the constitutional principles that support, *inter alia,* the workings of representative democracy in the respondent State. The alleged denial of access to services and facilities in the precincts of the House of Commons did not prevent the applicant from expressing his views and thus did not violate Article 10 of the ECHR.

Therefore, parliamentarians' duty of loyalty, although rather limited compared with the analogous duty imposed on other public servants, is indisputable as far as basic constitutional principles are concerned.

330. ECtHR, Karácsony and others v. Hungary (42461/13) 16 September 2014, the case was referred to the Grand Chamber, which upheld the judgment. ECtHR, Karácsony and Others v. Hungary (42461/13 and 44357/13) 17 May 2016 [GC].
331. *Ibid.*, para. 66.
332. The applicants were fined for conduct which was considered to be gravely offensive to the parliamentary order: during a Parliament sessions they presented a banners with the words 'FIDESZ [the governing party]. You steal, you cheat and you lie' and 'Here operates the national tobacco mafia'. *Ibid.*, paras 7–10.
333. ECtHR, Karácsony and others v. Hungary (42461/13) 16 September 2014, paras 40, 69.
334. ECtHR, Zdanoka v. Latvia (58278/00) 17 June 2004.
335. *Ibid.*, para. 85.
336. ECtHR, McGuinness v. UK (39511) inadmissible 8 June 1999.

Private employees

In *Predota v. Austria*,[337] the ECtHR determined that a State Company employee, who did not exercise any public authority and whose employment relationship was governed by private law, and whose employment disputes were subject to the jurisdiction of the domestic Labour Courts, could not claim the violation of the State's negative obligations. Therefore, all private employees as well as employees falling within the category specified in the *Predota* decision can refer only to the violation of the positive obligation of the State, when seeking protection of their to the freedom of expression in the workplace. The ECtHR's approach to the loyalty of private employees is much more superficial in contrast to the above-mentioned cases in respect of public servants.

In *Van der Heijden v. Netherlands*,[338] the applicant appealed against his dismissal from the Limburg Immigration Foundation due to his being a member of a political party which was hostile to the presence of foreign workers in the Netherlands. In dismissing this claim, the Commission noted the evident tension between the aims of the employer and the views of the applicant, concluding that the employer should have some discretion concerning the composition of his staff. Although the Commission refrained from considering the employee's loyalty, this decision demonstrates the factors which can have particular importance for establishing proportionality of an interference and therefore for outlining the limits of an employee's loyalty. It took into account the professional duties of the applicant, who was a regional director of a Foundation, and the specific nature of his work, which was aimed at protecting the rights of immigrants. The application was declared inadmissible, as in the view of the Commission, the employer could reasonably take account of the adverse effects which the applicant's political activities might have on the Foundation's reputation.

It is interesting to note that the Commission decided it was unnecessary to consider whether the views of the applicant influenced his professional activities, thus attaching high standards of loyalty to the employee without distinguishing between private life and professional activities.

The same approach may be seen in the *Rommelfanger* case,[339] in which the applicant, a doctor at a Catholic hospital, argued that his dismissal, based on his having expressed an opinion about abortion in the press that was not in conformity with the position of the Catholic Church, violated his freedom of expression. The Commission noted that by entering into contractual obligations vis-à-vis his employer the applicant had accepted a duty of loyalty towards the Catholic Church, which limited his freedom of expression to a certain extent. The Commission arrived at this conclusion without undertaking any analysis as to the actual harm which might be caused to the Hospital, or reflections of the public value of the applicant's opinion.

337. ECtHR, Rudolf Predota v. Austria (28962/95) inadmissible 18 January 2000.
338. EurCommHR, Van der Heijden v. Netherlands (11002/84) inadmissible 8 March 1985.
339. EurCommHR, Maximilian Rommelfanger v. Federal Republic of Germany (12242/86) inadmissible 26 June 1986.

In the recent decision of *Lichtenstrasser v. Austria*,[340] the ECtHR was reluctant to protect the freedom of an employee to express his opinion and refrained even from the necessity test. The applicant in this case was forced to sign a mutual agreement on dismissal because his views as to the impossibility of his self-development at work and his desire to develop his own business had been raised in an interview published in the newspaper. The ECtHR noticed that there was no public interest in the dissemination of this information. Referring to the margin of appreciation of the state, it briefly concluded that 'the dispute was an ordinary labour contract dispute, which did not disclose any inappropriate limits to the applicant's freedom of expression within the meaning of Article 10 of the Convention' as the applicant had a duty of loyalty towards his employer and was not under pressure when he signed the agreement to terminate his employment.[341]

The *Lichtenstrasser* decision makes us remember the judgment in *Ivanova v. Bulgaria*[342] where the ECtHR, despite there being a lawful reason for the applicant's dismissal, overruled the decisions of the national Courts, and found that it was in breach of the ECHR as it violated the applicant's freedom of religion. Therefore, the ECtHR on occasions goes much deeper into its analysis of what an 'ordinary labour contract dispute'[343] might constitute on a national level.

This finding leads to the presumption that as far as private employees are concerned, the States have a particular wide margin of appreciation in their estimation of the duty of loyalty.[344]

Concluding this subsection on employees' duty of loyalty in the context of the freedom of expression or association, the main contribution of the ECtHR to the protection of the rights of employees should be emphasised. The ECtHR has elaborated a detailed approach to the scope of the obligation of loyalty and discretion in respect of different public servants; it has urged States to balance in all cases the duty of loyalty with the right to freedom of expression and association, paying particular attention to the rigorous examination of the necessity of the interference.

§7.02 PUBLIC CRITICISM OF ONE'S EMPLOYER, DISCLOSURE OF INFORMATION AND STANDARDS OF WHISTLE-BLOWER PROTECTION

Public criticism by an employee evidently affects the reputation of his or her employer and is in contrast with the employee's duty of loyalty; this has already been discussed above. However, the ECtHR in many cases has acknowledged that an employee has the

340. ECtHR, Lichtenstrasser v. Austria (32413/08) 7 October 2014.
341. ECtHR, Lichtenstrasser v. Austria (32413/08) 7 October 2014, para. 30.
342. ECtHR, Ivanova v. Bulgaria (52435/99) 12 April 2007.
343. The case Rubins v. Latvia is another example of a deeper scrutiny of employment disputes. ECtHR, Rubins v. Latvia (79040/12) 13 January 2015.
344. See in this respect Collins, Hugh. On the (In)compatibility of Human Rights Discourse and Private Law. LSE Law, Society and Economy Working Papers 7/2012. Available at: http://www.lse.ac.uk/collections/LAW/wps/WPS2012-07_Collins.pdf (accessed 20 May 2015).

right to publicly criticise his or her employer if the criticism contributes in some way to the development of a democratic society, and is expressed in an appropriate form. The main questions that the ECtHR poses to consider such cases are: who, whom, why and in what form? In the first subsection, the ECtHR's approach to all these factors will be discussed. In the second subsection, the standards of whistle-blower protection will be dealt with.

[A] Factors Influencing the Adjudication

WHO?

Deciding whether an interference with the employee's freedom of expression was necessary in a democratic society, the ECtHR puts significant weight to the social or workplace position held by the applicant.[345] Generally, the ECtHR tends to give more protection to the right of higher management personnel, leading public officials, journalists, trade union leaders to freely express themselves, especially if the applicant could have a 'complete vision of the situation concerned'.[346]

Higher management

In case of *Bathellier v. France* the applicant, a state electric company human resources ('*HR*') chief, was dismissed for reporting to the prefect of the city the shortcomings in company which, in his opinion at the time, presented a serious danger to public security. The ECtHR, declaring the application inadmissible, pointed out (amongst other things) that the applicant, due to the peculiarity of his post, could not have a complete vision of technical aspects of the problem he was complaining of.

Thus the ECtHR implicitly established the requirement that an employee seeking protection under this provision had to be duly competence in his or her public criticism of the employer, or over the substance of the disclosed internal information. Another example of this approach by the ECtHR, focusing on an applicant's 'complete vision of the situation', is found in *Predota v. Austria*.[347] In this case, the applicant, a switch cleaner of the Austrian federal railway company, was dismissed for publicly criticising the railway service and the way prices were regulated. The ECtHR declared this application inadmissible as it imputed that the employee's main motivation was to damage the employer's reputation. However, taking into account that the terms used by the applicant were emotional rather than excessive, the ECtHR could have come to the opposite decision if the same information was spread by one of the leading managers who had access to the relevant information.

345. ECtHR, Di Giovanni v. Italy (51160/06) 9 July 2013, para. 75.
346. ECtHR, François Bathellier v. France (49001/07) inadmissible 12 October 2010.
347. ECtHR, Predota v. Austria (14621/06) inadmissible 18 January 2000.

Public officials

The right of public servants' to publicly criticise their employer, the State, is granted in exceptional situations when the ECtHR considers that the information made public has indisputable social value and must be known to the citizens. In such cases, the ECtHR always balances the public official's freedom of expression on the one hand against the resultant damage to the State's reputation. Public prosecutors and judges have particular roles amongst public officials. In respect of prosecutors, the ECtHR has widened the admissible limits of public criticism, acknowledging that they can play a 'crucial role in the administration of justice'.[348]

As far as judges' freedom of expression is concerned, the ECtHR has stated that judges are expected to show restraint in exercising this freedom in all cases where the authority and impartiality of the judiciary were likely to be called in question.[349] This restraint is an essential factor for ensuring the public's confidence in the judiciary which 'involves a belief in the fairness and impartiality of the tribunal.'[350] On these grounds, the freedom of criticism is protected only when the information has factual basis and was directly known to the judge who made the criticism.[351]

Journalists

The ECtHR has acknowledged the special character of journalists' duty of discretion, 'given that it is in the nature of their functions to impart information and ideas'. It has found, for instance, that the penalty imposed on journalists for publicly criticising the management and programming policy of public broadcasting organisations constituted a violation of Article 10.[352] However, the ECtHR pointed out that a broad acceptance to the discretion and loyalty of journalists as employees did not mean that they are automatically entitled 'to pursue, unchecked, a policy that ran counter to that outlined by employer, to flout legitimate editorial decisions.'[353] In cases concerning the right of other employees (not journalists) to publicly criticise their employers, the ECtHR pointed out that the applicants did not have a role to inform and alert the public, nor to impart information and ideas on matters of public concern and therefore restricted their freedom of expression, finding their applications inadmissible.[354]

The ECtHR's perception of the scope of journalists' freedom to criticise was expressed in *Wojtas-Kaleta v. Poland*, where it upheld the applicant's argument that as a journalist, an employee had a right and an obligation to comment on matters of public interest.[355]

348. ECtHR, Kayasu v. Turkey, para. 91.
349. ECtHR, Wille v. Liechtenstein, para. 64.
350. Arthur Selwyn Miller. Public Confidence in the Judiciary: Some Notes and Reflections. Law and Contemporary Problems (1970): 69–93. Available at: http://scholarship.law.duke.edu/cgi/viewcontent.cgi?article=3277&context=lcp (accessed 17 June 2015).
351. Compare the ECtHR's judgments in Di Giovanni v. Italy and Kudeshkina v. Russia.
352. ECtHR, Wojtas-Kaleta v. Poland (20436/02) 16 July 2009 and Fuentes Bobo v. Spain (39293/98) 29 February 2000; Matuz v. Hungary.
353. ECtHR, Nenkova-Lalova v. Bulgaria (35745/05) 11 December 2012, para. 59.
354. ECtHR, Balenović v. Croatia (28369/07) inadmissible 30 September 2010.
355. ECtHR, Wojtas-Kaleta v. Poland, para. 47.

Trade union leaders

The freedom of expression of trade union leaders is 'the oxygen which gives associative rights their vitality'[356] and forms a part of the freedom of association granted by Article 11. The ECtHR has on numerous occasions confirmed that the members of a trade union must be able to express to their employer the demands by which they seek to improve the situation of workers in their company.[357] European judges emphasised that this right is an essential and indispensable aspect of the right of association, a prerequisite to the fulfilment of the goals of associations and trade unions.[358]

However, this freedom is not unlimited and must be balanced with the necessity to protect the reputation of the employer. Trade unions of public servants are more subject to such limitations as even in their role as a trade union leader or member these public servants need to act with loyalty and restraint.

Thus, in *Szima v. Hungary* the ECtHR justified the criminal conviction of a police trade union leader for 'accusatory opinions which undermine the trust in, and the credibility of, the police leadership'.[359] The ECtHR emphasised that the applicant, who had considerable influence over other servicemen, should have had to exercise her right to freedom of expression in accordance with the duties and responsibilities which that right carries with it, in the specific circumstances of her status and in view of the special requirement of discipline in the police force.

The ECtHR's criticism of the applicant's internet publications shows that there would have been more likelihood of the ECtHR finding in her favour had the applicant's statements been more related to trade union activities and more than being a 'pure value judgment' to actually having a clear factual basis. The ECtHR noted the fact that the applicant, in domestic legal proceedings, was deprived of the ability to submit evidence to support her statements; however, this finding did not change the general direction of the judgment. Commentators noted that such a refusal, in itself, to be barred from giving evidence or proof in court to show the factual basis of certain allegations, has been considered by the ECtHR in other cases to constitute a breach of Article 10 of the ECHR.[360]

This judgment was criticised by scholars as largely restricting the freedom of expression of a trade union leader in respect of an ordinary staff member who would have been granted whistleblower protections.[361] In my opinion, the lack of attention to the facts asserted by the applicant is the problematic point of this judgment. Ms Szima's

356. M. O'Boyle, Right to Speak and Associate under Strasbourg Case-Law with Reference to Eastern and Central Europe. Connecticut Journal of International Law 8 (1993): 282.
357. ECtHR, Palomo Sanches and others v. Spain, Szima v. Hungary, Vellutini v. France.
358. Joint Dissenting Opinion Of Judges Tulkens, Davíd Thór Björgvinsson, Jočienė, Popović And Vučinić in Palomo Sanches v. Spain.
359. ECtHR, Szima v. Hungary, para. 32.
360. Dirk Voorhoof, New Judgment on Trade Union Freedom of Expression, 7 November 2012. Available at: strasbourgobservers.com/2012/11/07/new-judgment-on-trade-union-freedom-of-expression/#more-1853 (accessed 2 June 2015).
361. Filip Dorsscmont, Collective Action against Austerity Measure In: Niklas Bruun, Klaus Lörcher, Isabelle Schömann, editors. 'The Economic and Financial Crisis and Collective Labour Law in Europe'. Bloomsbury Publishing, 2014, pp. 153–170, 162.

allegations, even if they were 'indeed capable of causing insubordination since they might discredit the legitimacy of police actions', could have been justified under Article 10 if they were based on hard facts. Therefore, the ECtHR's main mistake in this case (taken in the context of Article 10) is failing to take into account the refusal of national courts to consider any evidence the applicant should have been able to bring to prove her accusations, and the reluctance to consider such relevant evidence in Strasbourg.

Returning to the scope of a trade union's right to criticise an employer, it is worth referring to the *Vellutini* judgment.[362] In *Vellutini*, the ECtHR found that the conviction of the President and the General Secretary of the municipal police officers' union ('*USPPM*') for public defamation of the mayor, on the basis of statements made in their capacities as union officials, violated their rights under Article 10. It is interesting to note that trade union leaders were not, in this case, expected to prove their statements as rigorously as journalists have been in other cases.[363]

The ECtHR thus attached great significance to the fact that the applicants had made their statements in their capacities as union officials and in connection with the professional situation of one of the union's members. The mayor, even if directly named in the leaflet spread in the town by the applicants, was criticised only in connection with his professional duties. As the applicants' remarks had been made in response to the mayor's accusations about the professional personal conduct of a member of their union, the ECtHR was willing to justify on their part 'a degree of exaggeration, or even provocation' and their use of immoderate language.[364] It stated that the impugned remarks had not been offensive or hurtful to a degree that went beyond the framework of trade union discourse.

In the Grand Chamber judgment of *Palomo Sanches and others v. Spain*,[365] the ECtHR, in contrast, stated that the applicants, whose criticism of their employers were formulated in a very offensive manner, exceeded the limits of the trade union's freedom of expression and justified the dismissal of trade-union members for publishing articles offending their colleague.[366]

This case law demonstrates that the trade union's freedom to express criticism is more protected[367] but still cannot overstep normal ethical rules.

Academic staff

The peculiarities of the Court's approach to public criticism by academic staff can be illustrated in two recent cases: *Aurelian Oprea v. Romania*[368] and *Kharlamov v. Russia*.[369] Both concerned civil actions taken against university professors who publicly disclosed information about the shortcomings in their universities.

362. ECtHR, Vellutini et Michel v. France (32820/09) 6 October 2011.
363. ECtHR, Vellutini et Michel v. France (32820/09) 6 October 2011, para. 41.
364. *Ibid.*, para. 39.
365. ECtHR, Palomo Sánchez and Others v. Spain [GC] (28955/06 et al.) 12 September 2011.
366. *Ibid.*
367. See also Wojtas-Kaleta v. Poland (20436/02) 16 July 2009, para. 45.
368. Aurelian Oprea v. Romania (no. 12138/08) 19 January 2016.
369. ECtHR, Kharlamov v. Russia (application no. 27447/07) 8 October 2015.

In *Aurelian Oprea v. Romania* the applicant, an associate professor at the University of Agronomical Sciences and Veterinary Medicine, delivered a speech at a press conference concerning corruption in Romanian universities, criticising specifically his university's deputy rector for encouraging a plagiarised book, for his management of a programme of publicly funded scientific research and for accumulating too many management positions. These accusations were later repeated in an article published by the weekly newspaper. In civil proceedings Mr Oprea was held liable for the way in which he had presented his accusations about the deputy director to journalists.

Considering this case the Court pointed that the applicant endeavoured to demonstrate that his statements had been well-founded by submitting extensive documentary evidence in national proceedings and domestic court noted that he had acted not with the intention of harming the Deputy Rector. It was established that the applicant informed the rector of the University and the Ministry of Education about the shortcomings perceived by him in the management of the department lead by the Deputy Rector before disclosing them to the press, however it did not change the situation.

The most interesting conclusion was made in respect of Deputy Rector, who, in opinion of the Court, 'was expected to tolerate a greater degree of public scrutiny than a private individual, even though it may have had a negative impact on his honour and reputation'.[370] All these findings in totality lead the Court to conclude that the order to pay compensation to the Deputy Rector in the sum EUR 7,470 violated the applicant's freedom of expression as this interference was not 'necessary in a democratic society'.

In *Kharlamov v. Russia*,[371] the applicant, a university professor in physics, was sued in defamation after he had criticised the election procedure of the university's senate.

The Court emphasised that a measure proscribing statements criticising the acts of an elected body can be justified with reference to 'the protection of the rights or reputations of others' only in exceptional circumstances.[372] The Court took special account of the academic context as it presumed the academics' freedom to express their opinion about the institution.[373] The issue raised by the applicant concerned a matter of general interest, according to ECtHR's case law very strong reasons are required for justifying the restrictions of such debates. The Court mainly focused on shortcomings of the national civil proceedings, noting that the domestic courts did not perform a balancing exercise between the need to protect the University's reputation and the applicant's right to impart information on issues of general interest. Then the Court, in contrast with domestic courts, found that the applicant's allegations on illegitimacy of the University Senate were a value judgment, not a factual accusation, and even if he had recourse to a certain degree of hyperbole the limits of admissible criticism were not overstepped.

370. ECtHR, Aurelian Oprea v. Romania (no. 12138/08) 19 January 2016, para. 74.
371. ECtHR, Kharlamov v. Russia (application no. 27447/07) 8 October 2015.
372. *Ibid.*, para. 27.
373. *Ibid.*

These findings lead the Court to conclude that the interference was not necessary in the democratic society and violated Article 10 of the ECHR.

This judgment is a an important contribution to the protection of the academics' freedom of expression as the Court one more time emphasised its broader scope as far as it concerns public interest and reiterated the need to balance the employer's right to reputation with the employee's freedom of expression. It is significant to note that the applicant's allegations were found groundless by domestic court, however the Court judged in favour of the applicant as his opinion had some factual basis and was expressed in public interest.

WHOM?

The ECtHR attaches great significance to the position of the criticised person, as this factor helps to establish the limits of permitted criticisms. Thus in *Kudeshkina v. Russia*, the ECtHR pointed out that the freedom of expression targeted at criticising the judiciary should be more restricted taking into account the importance for judges to enjoy public confidence to fulfil their duties.[374] However, the social value of the disclosed information permitted the ECtHR to broaden the freedom of expression of the applicant and decide in her favour nevertheless in this case.

In several cases the ECtHR has pointed out that criticism of high-ranking officials, as, for instance, the deputy Prosecutor-General, should be granted more scope than in relation to a private individual.[375] The status of private individuals, in the opinion of the ECtHR, enlarged the zone of interaction, which may fall within the scope of private life and therefore narrows the scope of acceptable criticism.[376]

In two cases concerning the criticism of doctors, the ECtHR recognised that medical practitioners enjoy a special relationship with patients based on trust, confidentiality and confidence. However, the special fiduciary character in such relationships is not interpreted as preventing doctors from criticising other doctors' professional activities,[377] even those who have a superior position,[378] as far as it is aimed at protection of the rights of others.

WHY?

It is generally established that the criticism of one's employer or the disclosure of information would be protected by Article 10 if the employee's criticism or disclosure was motivated by acknowledged social goods, such as the maintenance of the impartiality of the judiciary;[379] reporting violations of democratic principles;[380]

374. ECtHR, Kudeshkina v. Russia, para. 86; Di Giovanni v. Italy, para. 81, Poyraz v. Turkey (15966/06) 7 December 2010, para. 77.
375. ECtHR, Raichinov v. Bulgaria (47579/99) 20 April 2006.
376. ECtHR, Marin Stănciulescu v. Romania (14621/06) 22 November 2011.
377. ECtHR, Frankowicz v. Poland (53025/99) 16 December 2008, para. 49.
378. ECtHR, Sosinowska v. Poland (10247/09) 18 October 2011.
379. ECtHR, Kudeshkina v. Russia (29492/05) 26 February 2009.
380. ECtHR, Matuz v. Hungary (73571/10) 21 October 2014, reporting about censorship in the state telecommunication company.

reporting the abuse or misuse of powers and other irregularities in the employer's activities;[381] or more broadly advancing the protection of the rights of others.[382]

If the motive of an employee was to harm the reputation of his employer or of other employees – such criticism or disclosures are generally not protected under Article 10.[383] However, the intention to harm is not always objectively ascertainable. The ECtHR tends to find it in cases where the criticism or disclosure of information followed, or was made in the course of, a conflict between an employer and its employees. Thus in the recent case of *Langner v. Germany*, it referred to the conclusions of the national court, which found that the employee's allegations regarding his superior's illegal conduct was motivated by personal misgivings arising from the prospect of the impending dissolution of the applicant's sub-division at work (the city council).[384]

In the case of *De Diego Nafria v. Spain,*[385] the ECtHR found that the dismissal of the Spanish Bank's employee, who sent a letter to the Vice-President of the bank accusing its Governor and other senior officials of various irregularities, was not in breach of Article 10 because there had been pre-existing conflict between the employee and bank

In *Fuentes Bobo v. Spain*, the ECtHR also established that the employee, dismissed from the state telecommunication company for the criticism of the employer in non-ethical terms, was motivated by an intention to harm its reputation.[386] It took into account the harsh criticism he made of his employer in the radio interview leading to his dismissal was made in the course of a conflict between he and his employer after the cancelling of a TV programme on which the applicant had worked. However, seeing the social importance of the topic (the management of state telecommunications), the ECtHR focused its attention on the proportionality of the sanction and found that the employer should have chosen a less severe penalty.[387]

In *Predota v. Austria* the ECtHR, having established the employee's intention to harm the reputation of his employer, did not consider the proportionality of the dismissal.[388] In *Rubins v. Latvia,*[389] the ECtHR acknowledged that the motives of the

381. ECtHR, Guja v. Moldova [GC] (14277/04) 12 February 2008, also Rubins v. Latvia (79040/12) 13 January 2015.
382. ECtHR, Sosinowska v. Poland, Heinisch v. Germany (28274/08) 21 July 2011.
383. ECtHR, Diego di Naria v. Spain(46833/99) 14 March 2002, para. 35; Predota v. Austria (28962/95) 18 January 2000; Stănciulescu v. Romania (14621/06) 22 November 2011, paras 31–32.
384. ECtHR, Langner v. Germany (14464/11) 17 September 2015, para. 47.
385. ECtHR, De Diego Nafría v. Spain (46833/99) 14 March 2002.
386. ECtHR, Fuentes Bobo v. Spain (39293/98) 29 February 2000.
387. Dissenting Judges Caflisch and Makarczyk, in contrast to the majority, supposed that the employer could not have been required to choose another sanction as a less severe disciplinary penalty was already used against the applicant. See Opinion dissidente de mm. les Juges Caflisch et Makarczyk, arrêt Fuentes Bobo v. Spain (39293/98) 29 February 2000.
388. ECtHR, Predota v. Austria(28962/95) 18 January 2000.
389. ECtHR, Rubins v. Latvia (79040/12) 13 January 2015.

applicant, who was dismissed for an unethical letter sent to the employer, were relevant for the assessment of the proportionality of the interference. However it refrained from conducting an in-depth analysis of this factor. The ECtHR concluded that the dismissal of Mr Rubins, a professor who was threatening to the Rector of the University that he would disclose public information on certain irregularities in order to keep his post, violated Article 10. In *Balenović v. Croatia*,[390] the ECtHR paid much greater attention to the motives of the applicant. The applicant in that case had publicly accused the management of the State oil company of mismanagement and fraud. Having established the lack of a factual basis for such statements, it noted that the applicant was motivated by a concern to publicise her own professional grievances.

These cases demonstrate that the ECtHR has not elaborated a coherent theory of how it regards or considers 'the motive factor'. In some cases it seems to have a major importance for dismissing the application, in others it serves only as one of many other factors, and does not significantly influence the overall conclusion either way.

IN WHAT FORM?

The ECtHR has repeatedly stated that Article 10 is applicable not only to 'information' or 'ideas' that are favourably received or regarded as inoffensive or as a matter of indifference, but also to those that offend, shock or disturb the State or any sector of the population.[391] However, Article 10 protects the expression of such 'shocking' or 'disturbing' information only if it is made in appropriate terms, the form of expression corresponds with the circumstances of the case (depending on factors including the people concerned and the reasons for which the disclosures are made, as has been looked at in the immediately preceding paragraphs), and must have a factual basis.[392] The criticism must be more than a 'pure value judgment'[393] and the more serious allegation requires the more solid the factual basis.[394] Criticism of employers or the disclosure of information is generally more protected if it forms a part of political speech or advances recognised public interests.[395]

The general approach to the role played by the form of the criticism can be found in *Palomo Sánchez and others v. Spain*, where the ECtHR found that the opinions which are expressed in grossly insulting or offensive terms cannot be protected under Article 10.[396]

This approach is largely justified as the use of grossly offensive vocabulary tends to reveal an intention to humiliate, rather than to contribute to the social debate.

390. ECtHR, Balenović v. Croatia (28369/07) inadmissible 30 September 2010.
391. ECtHR, Handyside v. The UK (493/72) 7 December 1976, para. 49; Raichinov v. Bulgaria, para. 48; Kudeshkina v. Russia, para. 82.
392. EurCommHR, Eliane Morissens v. Belgium (11389/85) inadmissible 3 May 1988.
393. ECtHR, Szima v. Hungary (29723/11) 9 October 2012, para. 30.
394. ECtHR, Balenović v. Croatia (28369/07) 30 September 2010.
395. ECtHR, Kudeshkina v. Russia (29492/05) 26 February 2009; Matuz v. Hungary (73571/10) 21 October 2014, see also Nilsen and Johnsen v. Norway [GC] (23118/93) 25 November 1999, para. 46.
396. ECtHR, Palomo Sánchez and others v. Spain [GC] (28955/06 et al.) 12 September 2011, para. 76.

However, the ECtHR is not always clear in its analysis dealing with the form of an employee's freedom of expression. Returning to the case of the railway employee in *Predota v. Austria*,[397] it must be mentioned that, in the ECtHR's opinion, the terms used by the applicant revealed that his main intention was to damage his employer's reputation, so the dismissal was considered necessary in a democratic society and proportionate to the aim pursued.

This decision leads us to consider which words or terms, used by the employee, could have led the ECtHR to such a conclusion. It is worth reproducing here an extract of the leaflet distributed by the applicant:

> Very often our railways are of no use, stairs too high, connections bad (often there are none), uncomfortable (ugly) waiting rooms, stations too far from the towns, trains not suitable for handicapped people and so on...
>
> Prices too high; rates too complicated; soon nobody will understand.
>
> Practical personnel are diminishing; useless bureaucracy is increasing.
>
> Showing off instead of comfort and the clients feel angry.
>
> (Political) party posts paralyse ideas; practical and friendly co-operation becomes more and more meaningless.

These statements are evidently emotional, but it is conceivable that they still contribute to the social debate, in contrast with the ECtHR's views as expressed in the case. It can be argued that the railway has become an essential part of everyday life for almost every citizen; therefore the quality of the service, the transparency of prices are matters of legitimate public concern. The ECtHR did not take into account the previous suggestions and critical comments sent by the applicant to his employer and his further transfer to a lower post. It did not consider whether another sanction could have achieved the employer's goals.

In contrast, the ECtHR in *Kudeshkina v. Russia* protected a judge's freedom of expression in spite of the fact that they found she had 'allowed herself a certain degree of exaggeration and generalisation.'[398] The importance of the information she disclosed, which was absent in *Predota*, made the ECtHR conclude that her statements should not be regarded as a gratuitous personal attack but as a fair comment on a matter of great public importance.

An analysis of the jurisprudence reveals that the ECtHR assesses more rigorously written expressions of criticism and public criticisms. It has found that criticism of higher-level officials was protected by the ECHR as the criticism was 'apparently made in the course of an oral exchange and not in writing, after careful consideration'.[399] In *De Diego Nafria*, the ECtHR found that the dismissal of the Spanish Bank's employee, who sent a letter to the Vice-President of the Bank accusing the Governor and other senior officials of various irregularities, was not in breach of Article 10. It noted that the accusations were 'expressed in complete serenity and clarity in substance and form'.[400]

397. ECtHR, Predota v. Austria (14621/06) inadmissible 18 January 2000.
398. ECtHR, Kudeshkina v. Russia, para. 95.
399. ECtHR, Raichinov v. Bulgaria, para. 52.
400. ECtHR, De diego Nafria v. Spain, para. 35, see also Aguilera Jiménez And Others v. Spain (28389/06) 8 December 2009, para. 35.

In *Langner v. Germany*, the ECtHR pointed out that the applicant's oral allegations of his supervisor's illegal conduct were subsequently substantiated in writing; therefore, Mr Langner had time to reflect on the impact of his allegations and had the opportunity to verify their legal significance.[401] Basing on these findings, the ECtHR concluded that the dismissal of the applicant did not violate his freedom of expression.

The ECtHR distinguishes between written forms of employees' criticisms 'means which have a broad and immediate impact',[402] such as newspapers or leaflets,[403] and others which have less impact, such as letters written to the organisation itself, and applies a more rigorous analysis in the case of the former when determining the social value of the information concerned versus any harm caused to the employer's reputation by the publication of that information.

Considering cases on criticism of employers, the ECtHR urged national courts to assess the truthfulness of the respective employee's statements.[404] Thus in *Di Giovanni v. Italy*, the ECtHR decided that the disciplinary sanction imposed on a judge was a proportionate measure for the State to take as the information related in her newspaper interview was not grounded in facts and at that time, presented a rumour, subsequently discredited, as a well-founded public opinion.[405]

In contrast, the ECtHR found in *Kudeshkina v. Russia* that the dismissal of a judge for criticising the Court to be in breach of Article 10, as the information disclosed in the radio interview which comprised the criticism was directly known to the applicant and had been confirmed by other testimonies.[406]

The approach of the ECtHR to the various forms of criticism can be summarised as follows: a more public expression of criticism requires a more solid factual basis and must be justified by the social interest in democratic society. The cases considered above show that the ECtHR has elaborated a complex approach to the cases of public criticism or disclosure of information. The set of questions used by the ECtHR (who is making the disclosure, whom are the subject of the disclosures being made, why are the disclosures being made and in what form the disclosures are publicised) might provide a very helpful framework for national courts in consideration of employment disputes where the employee's freedom of expression is engaged. Even though the application of this test, on occasions, lacks coherence and clarity, it still provides a practical tool for the determination of violations of employees' right to the freedom of expression.

---

401. ECtHR, Langner v. Germany (14464/11) 17 September 2015, para. 50.
402. ECtHR, Balenović v. Croatia (28369/07) inadmissible 30 September 2010.
403. ECtHR, Predota v. Austria(28962/95) 18 January 2000.
404. ECtHR, Sosinowska v. Poland (10247/09) 18 October 2011.
405. ECtHR, Di Giovanni v. Italy (51160/06) 9 July 2013, para. 79. The applicant stated in the interview that a member of the examining body, established for the recruitment of judges and public prosecutors, had used his influence to help a relative to pass the competition.
406. ECtHR, Kudeshkina v. Russia, para. 92.

[B] Standards of Whistleblowers Protection

The protection of whistleblowers has gained particular public attention in recent times, especially after the disclosures made by Edward Snowden. The UN High Commissioner for Human Rights, Navi Pillay, said that national legal systems must ensure that there are adequate avenues afforded to individuals disclosing violations of human rights to express their concern without fear of reprisals.[407] However, the research of the domestic European State's laws shows that most EU countries fail to adequately protect whistleblowers even though their value in anticorruption and crime-fighting efforts has long been proven.[408]

Only about half of the members of the CoE have ratified the Termination of Employment Convention no. 158 of the International Labour Organisation, which contains provisions on whistleblower protection.[409] Twenty countries have not ratified the Criminal Law Convention on Corruption adopted by the CoE on 27 January 1999.[410] Therefore, on the European stage there was no unified approach to this problem and an elaboration of the framework for such protection is the main contribution of the ECtHR to support whistleblowing. The Commission, in contrast to the ECtHR, was rather reluctant to protect employees who disclosed important information.

Thus in *Patrick Haseldine v. UK*,[411] where the applicant argued that his dismissal for writing a published letter to the Guardian newspaper criticising the British Prime Minister was in breach of Article 10. The Commission did not analyse the public interest of the information presented in the letter. It focused on the duties of the applicant as a civil servant in a sensitive governmental post and considered that the applicant's action in criticising the policies of the Government to whom he was responsible as an employee was incompatible with his position. The application was further declared inadmissible as the dismissal was found to be a proportionate sanction.

The ECtHR developed a more considered approach to whistleblowing in *Guja v. Moldova*.[412] The circumstances of the case can be summarised as follows: after a public call by the President of Moldova on law enforcement officers to disregard undue pressure from public officials the applicant, who was then the head of the press department of the Prosecutor General's Office, gave the newspaper two letters received

---

407. UN High Commissioner for Human Rights, Navi Pillay, Mass Surveillance: Pillay Urges Respect for Right to Privacy and Protection of Individuals Revealing Human Rights Violations (published 12 July 2013). Available at: hhtp://www.ohchr.org (accessed 20 June 2015).
408. Mark Worth, Whistleblowing in Europe Legal Protections for Whistleblowers in the EU. Report. 2013. Available at: https://whistlenetwork.files.wordpress.com/2014/01/whistleblowing-in-europe-report-november-2013.pdf (accessed 20 June 2015). *See also* Sándor Léderer, Tivadar Hüttl, Whistleblower Protection in the Central and Eastern Europe Region, Final Study. www.whistleblowing-cee.org/summing-study/ (accessed 20 June 2015).
409. The list of countries that have not ratified this Convention is available at: www.ilo.org/dyn/normlex/en/f?p = NORMLEXPUB:11310:0::NO:11310:P11310_INSTRUMENT_ID:312303:NO (accessed 20 June 2015).
410. Ratification list is available at: http://conventions.coe.int/treaty/en/Treaties/Html/173-1.htm (accessed 20 June 2015).
411. EurCommHR, Patrick Haseldine v. UK (18957/92) inadmissible 13 May 1992.
412. ECtHR, Guja v. Moldova [GC] (14277/04) 12 February 2008.

by the Prosecutor General's Office, neither of which bore any sign of being confidential, which revealed the attempt of the Deputy Speaker of Parliament and of the Vice-Minister to influence the process of criminal investigations in respect of policemen. After the publication of these letters the applicant was dismissed on the grounds that, among other things, the letters had been secret and that he had failed to consult the heads of other departments of the Prosecutor General's Office before handing over the letters, in breach of the press department's internal regulations.

The applicant had in fact breached his employment obligations and the ECtHR had to determine where it was the case of whistleblowing, which should attract particular protection to the employee's freedom of expression by waiving his duty of loyalty and discretion towards his employer.

The ECtHR noted that a civil servant, in the course of his work, might become aware of in-house information, including secret information, the publication of which corresponds with a strong public interest. The exposure of illegal conduct or public misconduct in the workplace should, in the opinion of the ECtHR, s enjoy protection under Article 10 in certain circumstances.

The ECtHR further set out a list of factors which should be taken into account in considering such cases:

- First, it attached great significance to the role of the applicant in this case, pointing that such protection should only be granted in cases where the employee was the only person, or part of a small category of persons, who was aware of what was happening at work and was thus best placed to act in the public interest by alerting the employer or the public at large.[413]
- The sequence of disclosure was considered relevant and it was emphasised that disclosure should be made in the first place to the person's superior or some other competent authority and could be disclosed to the public without such prior notification only if such notification was clearly impracticable.[414] In any case, the ECtHR had to determine whether there were any other effective means of remedying the wrongdoing which the applicant intended to uncover available to him.[415]
- The research of the public interest which would be advanced by the disclosed information should also form part of adjudication process in order to determine whether it was so strong as to override even a legally imposed duty of confidence.[416]
- The information disclosed should be genuine and any person who chooses to disclose information must carefully verify, to the extent permitted by the circumstances, that it is accurate and reliable.[417]

413. ECtHR, Guja v. Moldova, para. 71.
414. *Ibid.*, para. 73.
415. *Ibid.*
416. *Ibid.*, para. 74.
417. *Ibid.*, para. 75.

- The damage from disclosure should be assessed to see whether it would outweigh the public interest in having the information revealed.[418]
- The motive behind the actions of the reporting employee is another relevant factor in deciding whether a particular disclosure should be protected or not. The ECtHR directly stated that an act motivated by personal grievance or a personal antagonism, or to gain a personal advantage, including pecuniary gain, would not justify a particularly high level of protection.[419]
- The proportionality of the sanction imposed on the applicant (its severity and the availability of other less severe penalties) should be considered, as well as the consequences of imposing each of those sanctions where options are available.

Having considered the case in the light of these principles the ECtHR found that the dismissal constituted a violation of the applicant's right to impart information.

Later, these principles were expressed in Recommendation 1916 (2010), adopted by the Parliamentary Assembly of the CoE, which invited all Member States to review their legislation concerning the protection of whistleblowers.[420]

The same principles were upheld to lead the ECtHR to its conclusions in *Kudeshkina v. Russia*. Considering the applicant judge's motives in making public accusations against the President of the Moscow City Court, the ECtHR noted that the accusations were made during the applicant's election company for the post of the deputy of the State Duma. It pointed out that political speech should enjoy special protection under Article 10.[421] In assessing the proportionality of the sanction, it noted that the dismissal of the applicant could undoubtedly discourage other judges in the future from making statements critical of public institutions or policies, for fear of loss of judicial office.[422] Therefore, as in the *Guja* case,[423] the ECtHR weighed the possible 'chilling effect' of the sanction, 'which works to the detriment of society as a whole,'[424] and attached much significance to this factor.

In *Heinisch v. Germany*,[425] it stated that the State has a positive obligation to protect the right to freedom of expression, even in private employment, and concluded that the applicant's dismissal from a state-owned limited liability company specialising in health care, on account of her criminal complaint against her employer and upheld by the German courts, constituted an interference with her right to freedom of expression. The applicant was dismissed for publicly disclosing information about the

418. *Ibid.*, para. 76.
419. ECtHR, Guja v. Moldova, para. 77.
420. Recommendation 1916 (2010), adopted by the Parliamentary Assembly of the Council of Europe, adopted on 29 April 2010. Available at: http://assembly.coe.int/nw/xml/XRef/Xref-XML2HTMLen.asp?fileid=17852&lang=en (accessed 20 June 2015).
421. ECtHR, Kudeshkina v. Russia, para. 95.
422. *Ibid.*, para. 98.
423. ECtHR, Guja v. Moladova, para. 95; see also Heinisch v. Germany, para. 91; Bucur et Toma c. Roumanie (40238/02) 8 January 2013, para. 119.
424. ECtHR, Guja v. Moladova, para. 99.
425. ECtHR, Heinisch v. Germany (28274/08) 21 July 2011.

alleged deficiencies in the care provided by the public health institution where she worked as a nurse.

The ECtHR affirmed that 'the public interest in being informed about the quality of public services outweighs the interests of protecting the reputation of any organisation.' In order to justify external reporting by means of a criminal complaint it found that she had made sufficient numbers of internal complaints before. As an additional argument, the ECtHR noted that German law did not provide for a particular enforcement mechanism for investigating a whistleblower's complaint and seeking remedial action from the employer.[426] In these circumstances, the ECtHR concluded that the dismissal violated Article 10 of the ECHR.

In *Bucur and Toma v. Romania*,[427] the first applicant, who worked for the Romanian Intelligence Service ('*RIS*'), was convicted for breaching official secrecy as he stated at a press conference that the RIS unlawfully tapped the phones of a large number of journalists, politicians and businessmen.

It is particularly interesting that the ECtHR reproached the respondent's national courts for the refusal to verify that the divulged information was indeed classified as 'top secret'. In its opinion, the domestic courts should have examined whether maintaining the confidentiality of the information outweighed the public interest in knowing about any illegal interceptions.[428] Therefore, the ECtHR established that the national courts should examine the content of the classified information and satisfy itself as to the legitimacy of its claims to confidentiality before making a decision in such cases.

The ECtHR granted protection to the applicant in this case, in spite of the fact that the accusations were not reported internally before the press conference. It pointed out that given the irregularities the applicant had discovered concerned directly his superiors, it was unlikely that any internal complaints could have stopped the unlawful practices in question. The ECtHR also stressed the fact that at the time of the disclosure being made, the new laws providing a legal framework for whistleblowing had not yet been adopted by the State.[429]

The most recent confirmation of the whistleblowing protection available under Article 10 of the ECHR can be found in *Matuz v. Hungary*.[430] The applicant, a journalist at the State TV company, had published a book with numerous in-house letters comprising exchanges concerning alleged censorship by the cultural director of the company. After the publication he was dismissed for breaching the confidentiality clause in his employment contract. The domestic courts upheld the dismissal, having found that the applicant had indeed breached his contract by means of the unauthorised publication of his former employer's internal documents.

The ECtHR noted that the national courts failed to consider the case in the light of the applicant's right to freedom of expression, and the respondent's Supreme Court

426. *Ibid.*, para. 75.
427. ECtHR, Bucur et Toma c. Roumanie (40238/02) 8 January 2013.
428. *Ibid.*, para. 111.
429. ECtHR, Bucur et Toma c. Roumanie, para. 99.
430. ECtHR, Matúz v. Hungary (73571/10) 21 October 2014.

had even expressly excluded from its scrutiny the question of whether the applicant's freedom of expression justified a formal breach of his employment contract. The ECtHR further stressed that the absence of an effective judicial review of the impugned measure may also lead to a violation of Article 10 and the degree of the margin of appreciation afforded to the authorities will necessarily be narrower if the reasoning of the national courts demonstrates a lack of sufficient engagement with the general principles of the ECtHR under Article 10 of the ECHR.[431]

In spite of the difference between such a journalist employed by the State television company and a public servant who discloses illegal conduct, the ECtHR's approach in addressing the respective disclosures of confidential information to advance the public interest was largely the same.[432] The ECtHR used the framework elaborated in the *Guja* judgment and considered: (a) the public interest involved in the disclosed information; (b) the veracity of the information disclosed; (c) the damage, if any, suffered by the employer as a result of the disclosure in question; (d) the motive of the reporting employee in making the disclosure; (e) whether, in light of the duty of discretion owed by an employee towards his or her employer, the information was made public as a last resort, following disclosure to a superior or other competent body; and (f) the severity of the sanction chosen to be imposed.[433]

Having considered the relevant circumstances, the ECtHR concluded that the interference violated Article 10. This judgment was applauded for raising awareness about the lack of whistleblower protection in many European states.[434] Indeed, it raised significant attention to the need to support whistleblowing on the national level and reminded national courts to take into consideration the fundamental rights element when considering labour disputes.

In the most recent case *Soares v. Portugal*[435] the Court developed its views on due sequence of whistleblowing. The applicant, the chief corporal in the National Republican Guard, sent an email to the General Inspectorate of Internal Administration on the subject 'Suspected misuse of money', in which he made reference to an alleged misuse of money by Commander M.C. of territorial post in accordance with what he had heard in a conversation with colleagues. He was convicted by the domestic courts for aggravated defamation as none of the three different entities which investigated his allegations were able to establish their veracity.[436]

The Court pointed that the applicant, knowing that his allegations were based on a rumour, made no attempt to verify their authenticity before reporting them.[437] It also underlined that Mr Soares was aware of internal channels within the hierarchy of the

431. *Ibid.*, paras 16, 35.
432. ECtHR, Matúz v. Hungary, para. 33.
433. *Ibid.*, para. 34.
434. Dirk Voorhoof, Whistleblower Protection for Journalist Who Alarmed Public Opinion about Censorship on TV. 25 November 2014. Available at: http://strasbourgobservers.com/2014/11/25/whistleblower-protection-for-journalist-who-alarmed-public-opinion-about-censorship-on-tv/ (accessed 20 June 2015).
435. ECtHR, Soares v. Portugal (79972/12) 21 June 2016.
436. *Ibid.*, para. 47.
437. *Ibid.*, para. 46.

National Republican Guard to which he could have reported the rumour, however did not use this channel without any convincing explanation, preferring to notify the General Inspectorate. The ECtHR found that the applicant did not comply with the chain of command and denied his hierarchical superior the opportunity to investigate the veracity of the allegations.[438] These circumstances led the Court to conclude that the interference with the applicant's freedom of expression was not disproportionate and thus did not violate Article 10.

An example where the severity of the sanction imposed on an employee for making a disclosure was the main point of the Court's scrutiny can be found in *Marchenko v. Ukraine.*[439] The applicant argued that his criminal conviction for publicly accusing his superior of misappropriation and for requesting an official investigation was in breach with Article 10. Mr Marchenko, a teacher and the head of a trade union, had lodged criminal complaints against the director of his school about misuse of school property, which were dismissed for lack of evidence. Later, he organised picket at the local administration offices and displayed banners with slogans accusing the director of professional misconduct and abuse of office. The director sued the applicant for defamation and was successful in obtaining a judgment against the applicant.

The ECtHR considered the letters demanding investigations into the director's official conduct and the banner slogans exposed during the picket separately. It found that the letters were written in good faith as he had acted on behalf of his trade union and presented various materials in support of his allegations. The banner slogans, however, were found to be defamatory and undermined the director's right to be presumed innocent of the allegations made by the banners' messages, particularly as the slogans were phrased in particularly strong terms directly accusing her of misappropriating school property. In these circumstances, the ECtHR accepted that the domestic authorities had reasonable grounds for convicting the applicant of defamation. Considering the proportionality of the sanction imposed, it reminded us that the protection of the reputation of others should not unduly hinder public debate concerning matters of public concern, such as the misappropriation of public funds.[440] The imposition of a prison sentence, even if it was suspended, would inevitably have a chilling effect on public discussion and therefore was not necessary in democratic society. This judgment also separately emphasises the necessity of determining the public interest factor and of the balancing exercise, expanding whistleblowing protection to include criminal cases based on defamation actions.

Prof. Dirk Voorhoof once wrote that the ECtHR had 'manifestly helped to create an added value for the protection of freedom of expression'.[441] The elaboration of a clear framework for the adjudication of cases on whistleblower protection, a careful

438. *Ibid.*, para. 48.
439. ECtHR, Marchenko v. Ukraine (4063/04) 9 February 2009.
440. ECtHR, Marchenko v. Ukraine, para. 52.
441. Voorhoof Dirk, The Right to Freedom of Expression and Information Under the European Human Rights System: Towards a More Transparent Democratic Society. EUI Working Paper RSCAS 2014/12. Available at: http://cadmus.eui.eu/bitstream/handle/1814/29871/RSCAS_2014_12.pdf?sequence=1 (accessed 20 June 2015).

consideration of the employee's freedom of expression in the context of employment relations, the emphasised value of information disclosed in the public interest – these are the priceless contributions of the ECtHR to the construction of domestic whistle-blower protection, a protection which is presently missing in many members of the CoE.

In Russia, for example, Article 9 of the Law 'On Combating Corruption' imposes a duty on all civil servants and municipal employees to 'notify the employer, the prosecution authorities or other state agencies of all cases referred to it to any person in order to induce him to commit corruption offenses'. However, there are still no provisions on the protection of such whistleblowers from dismissal or disciplinary sanctions.[442] Considering that in 2014 alone, six thousand people reported corruption in Russia, there is an obvious need to create a system to protect whistleblowers.[443]

Whistleblowing, even if disturbing to employers and undermining their reputations, serves to ultimately benefit society and even, in the opinion of certain scholars, advances 'the moral good of the employer'.[444]

§7.03 UNFAIR DISMISSAL AND THE PROTECTION OF THE FREEDOM OF EXPRESSION AND FREEDOM OF ASSOCIATION AT THE WORKPLACE

The majority of cases considered above concerned unfair dismissal when used as a sanction against employees exercising their freedom of expression. However, very little was said about the positive obligations of the State in case of unfair dismissal on the grounds of political beliefs or affiliations. In addition, several cases, very briefly considered in the previous subsections, pose a very interesting question: whether the adjudication on the merits of labour law disputes by the ECtHR leads to 'the risk of transforming it into a higher-instance labour court'.[445]

This section addresses these queries. The first subsection will deal with the positive obligations of the state, developed in *Redfearn v. UK*.[446] The second researches the 'borders of adjudication' of labour disputes under the ECHR, thus setting out certain limits for the human rights impact on labour law.

442. The draft of such a law is still pending. See the draft of the federal law 'On the protection of persons reporting corruption offenses from persecution and violation of their rights and legitimate interests', presented for discussion in the Civic Chamber of the Russian Federation on the 15 May 2015. Available at: https://www.oprf.ru/ru/1449/2133/1537/2192/newsitem/29263?PHPSESSID=pgp301g98n02muckpmoro9p3b6 (accessed 26 June 2015).
443. Victor Khamraev, The Reporting of a Bribe Will Be Facilitated (Chinovnikam oblegchat sdachu vzyatki).16 May 2015. Available at: www.kommersant.ru/Doc/2728291 (accessed 26 June 2015).
444. Varelius Jukka, Is Whistle-Blowing Compatible with Employee Loyalty? Journal of Business Ethics 85(2) (2009): 263–275.
445. ECtHR, Rubins v. Latvia (79040/12) 13 January 2015, Dissenting Opinion of Judges Mahoney and Wojtyczek, para. 16.
446. ECtHR, Redfearn v. UK (47335/06) 6 November 2012.

[A] Positive Obligation of the State

The judgment in *Redfearn v. UK*[447] demonstrates the ECtHR's development of the law regarding States' positive duties under Article 11. Mr Redfearn, a driver in a private company, was responsible for transporting people with disabilities, the majority of whom were Asian in origin. He was elected to the position of local councillor with the British National Party and was consequently dismissed from his job. His employer referred to the possible harm to its reputation, as well as the potential health and safety risks which might arise from the applicant's continued employment because his remaining in the role could give rise to considerable anxiety among his passengers. Under British law at the time, the applicant had been employed for less than a year, so he could not bring a claim on unfair dismissal on the grounds of political views.

The ECtHR noted that the State had a positive obligation to protect employees against dismissal by private employers where the dismissal was motivated solely by an employee affiliation with a particular political party. It accepted that the consequences of his dismissal were serious and capable of striking at the very substance of his rights under Article 11 of the ECHR.[448] The main question at stake, in the ECtHR's view, was whether the qualifying period provided in the then British law for applicants to seek review of an unfair dismissal in such circumstances, was reasonable and appropriate in protecting the applicant's Article 11 rights. The ECtHR noted that such a time requirement deprived the applicant of the only means by which he could effectively have challenged his dismissal on the ground that it breached his fundamental rights at the domestic level.[449] Assessing the qualifying period in general, it agreed that it was both reasonable and appropriate for the respondent State to bolster the domestic labour market by preventing new employees from bringing unfair dismissal claims. However, the ECtHR further noted that in practice, the one-year qualifying period did not apply equally to all dismissed employees and certain employees were exempt from this rule.[450] It found that domestic tribunals should be allowed to decide whether or not, in the circumstances of a particular case, the interests of the employer should prevail over the Article 11 rights asserted by the employee, regardless of the length of the latter's period of employment.[451] The ECtHR left to the States a choice as to the measures it could effect in order to comply with this interpretation of Article 11: to either adopt a further exception to the one-year qualifying period; or to permit a free-standing claim for unlawful discrimination on the grounds of political opinion or affiliation.[452] Because the British legislation was found to be deficient in this respect, the State was held responsible for the violation of Article 11 of the ECHR.

The dissenting Judges in this case wrote that the majority of the ECtHR had 'pressed the positive obligation too far' and that the states should have a wide margin

447. ECtHR, Redfearn v. UK (47335/06) 6 November 2012.
448. *Ibid.*, para. 47.
449. *Ibid.*, Para. 52.
450. Redfearn v. The UK, para. 54.
451. *Ibid.*, para. 56.
452. *Ibid.*, para. 57.

of appreciation in determining the exceptions from the qualification period rule.[453] Scholars, in contrast, supported the majority, pointing out that 'it is not within the states' margin of appreciation which grounds of discrimination they may prohibit within employment',[454] and praised the push for higher levels of positive obligations on the part of the States to ensure employees' political views/affiliations could remain protected in the workplace.[455] It is interesting to note that the respondent reacted promptly to this judgment and by 2013 had already introduced amendments to its Employment Rights Act 1996, stating that the qualifying period of employment does not apply if the reason for the dismissal is, or relates to, the employee's political opinions or affiliation.[456]

This case one more time demonstrates the importance of the ECtHR jurisprudence for labour law, particularly in respect of procedural norms which should also comply with the fundamental rights of employees.

[B] Should There Be Limits on the ECtHR's Ability to Adjudicate Labour Law Disputes?

This question is addressed within the chapter dealing with the protection of employees' freedom of expression and association, as judgments in this area have made the author query whether the ECtHR has taken too profound approach to labour disputes, which might be difficult to justify in respect of an international Court.

In the majority of cases which considered the dismissals of employees under Article 10, the ECtHR tends to determine whether the dismissal amounted to an interference with the applicant's right to exercise his or her freedom of expression, or whether it lay strictly within the sphere of employment rights, the latter not being secured by the ECHR nor its Protocols.[457] In order to answer that question, the ECtHR considers the appropriateness of the dismissal by putting it in the context of the specific facts of the case and of the relevant legislation establishing a casual link between the expression of the employee's opinion and the sanction which followed that expression.[458]

453. Joint Partly Dissenting Opinion Of Judges Bratza, Hirvelä And Nicolaou, para. 4. Redfearn v. The UK.
454. G. Letsas, Redfearn v. UK: Even Racists Have the Right to Freedom of Thought. UK Const. L. Blog (13 November 2012). Available at: http://ukconstitutionallaw.org (accessed 20 June 2015).
455. Lourdes Peroni, Redfearn v. the United Kingdom: Protection against Dismissals on Account of Political Belief or Affiliation (11 December 2012). Available at: www. strasbourgobservers.com /2012/12 November redfearn-v-the-united-kingdom-protection-against-dismissals-on-account -of-political-belief-or-affiliation/ (accessed 20 June 2015).
456. Enterprise and Regulatory Reform Act 2013: http://www.legislation.gov.uk/ukpga/2013/24/ contents/enacted.
457. See ECtHR, Nenkova-Lalova v. Bulgaria, para. 50; Glasenapp v. Germany, para. 50; Wille v. Liechtenstein, para. 43.
458. For example this link lacked in the Nenkova-Lalova v. Bulgaria and the ECtHR did not find the violation of Art. 10 (ECtHR, Nenkova-Lalova v. Bulgaria, para. 61).

Taking the subsidiary role of the ECtHR into account, there is a need to determine the depth of the consideration of employment disputes by the ECtHR. It was established already in the Belgian linguistics case that the ECtHR cannot assume the role of the competent national authorities, for it would thereby lose sight of the subsidiary nature of the international machinery.[459] In recent cases on Article 10, the ECtHR affirmed that it is for the national authorities, notably the courts, to interpret and apply domestic law;[460] and that it cannot question the way in which the domestic courts have interpreted and applied national law except in cases of flagrant non-observance or arbitrariness.[461]

In the opinion of scholars, this subsidiarity means that the ECtHR should not only follow the national system in procedural terms but also take into account the substance of the decision taken at a national level.[462] Prof. Sandra Fredman once wrote that the ECHR presupposes a full-blooded role for national courts.[463] It was noted by other scholars that the ECtHR generally refrains from interpreting domestic laws and it defers to national courts' assessments on the credibility of witnesses and the relevance of evidence to the issues in the case, and only in exceptional cases where Member States insufficiently investigate credible claims of serious human rights violations, might the ECtHR might reconsider the case on its merits.[464]

Striking the right balance between conducting an effective review and recognising the primary role of national courts to interpret national law is obviously difficult.[465] However, moving the discourse into the labour law field, such a problem becomes less evident. Thus many unfair dismissal applications have been declared to be inadmissible. Alternatively, the violation of the ECHR was not found as the ECtHR accepts the findings of the national courts which established that there was a reasonable ground for the dismissal.[466] The ECtHR tended to find violations only in the cases where the national courts did not take into account the applicants' claims on violations of

459. ECtHR, Case 'Relating to certain aspects of the laws on the use of languages in education in Belgium' v. Belgium (Merits) (Belgium Linguistic case) (1474/62, 1677/62, 1691/62, 1769/63, 1994/63, 2126/64) 23 July 1968, para. 10.
460. ECtHR, Perinçek v. Switzerland (27510/08) 17 December 2013, para. 66; Delfi As v. Estonia [GC] (64569/09) 16 June 2015, para. 127.
461. ECtHR, Yordanova and Toshev v. Bulgaria (5126/05) 2 October 2012, para. 41.
462. Kanstantsin Dzehtsiarou. European Consensus and the Legitimacy of the European Court of Human Rights. Cambridge University Press, 2015, p. 166.
463. Sandra Fredman. From Deference to Democracy: The Role of Equality Under the Human Rights Act 1998. Oxford Legal Studies Research Paper No. 5/2006; Law Quarterly Review 122 (2006): 53–58. Available at SSRN: http://ssrn.com/abstract=894252.
464. Laurence R. Helfer, Embeddedness as a Deep Structural Principle of the European Human Rights Regime. European Journal of International Law 19(1) 2008: 142–144: 142–144.
465. Geranne Lautenbach. The Concept of the Rule of Law and the European Court of Human Rights. Oxford: Oxford University Press, 2013, p. 85.
466. ECtHR, Pitkevich v. Russia (47936/99) 8 February 2001, Lichtenstrasser v. Austria (32413/08) 7 October 2014; Nenkova-Lalova v. Bulgaria (35745/05) 11 December 2012; Balenović v. Croatia (28369/07) 30 September 2010; Pay v. UK (32792/05) 16 September 2008; Leander v. Sweden(9248/81) 26 March 1987; Knauth v. Germany (41111/98) 22 November 2001.

fundamental rights, or when it determined that the State had incorrectly assessed the proportionality of the sanction.[467]

Therefore, the ECtHR has developed a particular subsidiary approach to labour cases where the consideration of the case was firmly restricted to an evaluation of the national judgment in the light of ECHR principles. In taking such an approach, which evidently respects the subsidiarity of the international court, the ECtHR should obviously not consider the employment dispute on its merits. However, in two recent cases the ECtHR appears to have overstepped these limits on international adjudication, dealing with the applications as if it was a higher-instance labour court.

Baka v. Hungary

Mr Baka was elected to the post of President of the Supreme Court of Hungary for a six-year term in 2009. In his capacity as President of that court and of the National Council of Justice, the applicant expressed his views on various legislative reforms affecting the judiciary on a number of occasions in the period from April to November 2011. The Fundamental Law of 25 April 2011 established that the highest judicial body would be the Kúria. The transitional provisions of the new Constitution provided that the Kúria would be a legal successor of the Supreme Court and that the mandate of the President of the Supreme Court would end, following the new Constitution taking effect. In October 2011, a criterion for the election of the new president of the Kúria was adopted. As the applicant did not satisfy the new requirements (candidates were required to have at least five years' experience as a judge in Hungary), he was ineligible for the post of President of the new Kúria and was instead appointed as a judge. He argued that the early termination of his employment breached Article 6, as he was deprived of any ability to seek judicial review of his termination; and of Article 10, as the dismissal was in response to his criticism of the proposed judicial reforms. In this unanimous judgment, referred later to the Grand Chamber, which upheld the judgment by fifteen votes to two.[468]

In both judgments the ECtHR acknowledged that the premature termination of the applicant's role had in fact been a reaction for the views he expressed publicly in his professional capacity. The Court found this to have violated Article 10 of the ECHR. The ECtHR said that the crux of the case they had to determine was whether the applicant's mandate as the President of the Supreme Court was ended solely as a result of the reorganisation of the judiciary in Hungary, as the State claimed, or whether, as the applicant argued, it was due to the views he expressed publicly on legislative reforms affecting the judiciary. Despite the absence of any direct evidence[469] on the casual link between the expression of his opinions and the termination of his employment, the

467. ECtHR, Kudeshkina v. Russia (29492/05) 26 February 2009, Ihsan Ay v. Turkey (34288/04) 21 January 2014; Schüth v. Germany (1620/03) 23 September 2010; Özpinar c. Turquie (20999/04) 19 October 2010.

468. ECtHR, Baka v. Hungary (20261/12)GC judgment 23 June 2016.

469. As for the example in Wille v. Liechtenstein, where the non-appointment to the post of the President of the Administrative Court on the grounds of the applicant's political views was proved by the letter written by the Prince of Liechtenstein announcing the intention not to reappoint the applicant. See Wille v. Liechtenstein, para. 50; in the case of Kudeshkina v.

ECtHR found it persuasive that the proposals to terminate his mandate; as well as the new eligibility criterion for the new post were submitted to Parliament after he had publicly expressed his views on the legislative reforms, and were adopted by Parliament subsequently within an extremely short period of time.[470]

The Grand Chamber, facing the lack of evidence, referred to its case law under Articles 2 and 3 and admitted that the proof may follow from the coexistence of sufficiently strong, clear and concordant inferences or of similar unrebutted presumptions of fact.[471] Having considered 'the sequence of events in their entirety', and documents submitted by the applicant, such as articles published in both the Hungarian and foreign press and the texts adopted by CoE institutions, the Court came to conclusion that there was *prima facie* evidence in favour of the applicant's version and shifted the burden of proof to the Government.[472] This stance was criticised by dissenting judge as not being in conformity with the standards of procedural justice.[473]

Estimating the evidence provided by the Government, the ECtHR was not convinced by the arguments that the impugned measure was a necessary consequence of the fundamental structural changes to the supreme judicial authority in Hungary. It was not convinced either by the decision of the Hungarian Constitutional Court, which had considered an application by the Vice-President of the Supreme Court in relation to the premature termination of *his* employment also purportedly as a result of the judicial reforms. The Constitutional Court had rejected the then Vice-President's complaint, stating that the premature termination of the claimant's term of office had not violated the Fundamental Law, since it was sufficiently justified by the wholesale reorganisation of the judicial system and the broadened tasks and competences of the President of the Kúria.[474] The ECtHR, whose mission is to supervise and not to substitute national authorities, did not consider the necessity of the new criterion and did not consider the fact that the applicant still worked as a judge of the new Kúria[475] and the point that his criticism concerned mostly the changes to retirement age of the judges, and, due to his age, he was among those whose position would be affected by new provisions.

The Grand Chamber referred to the independence of judiciary more than 200 times in its 140-pages judgment, while forgetting to analyse the independence of the State in adopting the Constitution and establishing the criteria for public service. Judges Pinto de Albuquerque and Dedov pointed in their joint concurring opinion: 'The Court seems to take for granted its jurisdiction to assess the compatibility of constitutional provisions with the European Convention on Human Rights (Convention),

Russia, the applicant was dismissed in the result of disciplinary proceedings organised after the expression of critical remarks in respect of the court she worked at.

470. ECtHR, Baka v. Hungary, para. 94.
471. ECtHR, Baka v. Hungary (20261/12) GC judgment 23 June 2016, para. 143.
472. *Ibid.*, para. 148.
473. ECtHR, Baka v. Hungary (20261/12) GC judgment 23 June 2016, Dissenting opinion of the Judge Wojtyczek, para. 10.
474. *Ibid.*, para. 46.
475. It was superficially considered in para. 95 of the Chamber judgment, Grand Chamber judgment did not pay sufficient attention to this factor.

without explaining the grounds and breadth of its remit'.[476] Dissenting judge Pejchal emphasised that no court (including an international court) can review, in the framework of the democratic rule of law, the reasons for the votes cast by the Members of Parliament in a free election.[477] This position is evidently more coherent with the international law.

The ECHR as signed by members of the CoE is about the protection of human rights and not about how the States should organise its domestic judicial arrangements. The States alone should have the right to determine for themselves the eligibility criteria for judicial appointees and the ECtHR does not have a mandate to interfere with this process unless there is a direct and significant evidence of abuse which led to human rights violations. Where the circumstances of the case do not permit to establish with certainty that causal link, the State should not be held responsible for any alleged violation of the ECHR. The State's margin of appreciation in the sphere should be limited only in very exceptional cases where it can be demonstrated beyond any doubt that the negative obligation under the ECHR was violated.[478] ECtHR's judgments in Baka case seem to demonstrate that the ECtHR has crossed the borders of legitimate international adjudication and make us remember the words of Prof. David Kennedy: 'When we invoke human rights against state power, we are pounding ... also on sovereign privilege and constitutional right'.[479]

Rubins v. Latvia

This case is an example of the ECtHR's high level attention paid to the circumstances of a case, which had little relevance to the employment dispute in the opinion of the national courts. The applicant was a professor and Head of the Department of the State University. The latter position was abolished as a result of the merging of two Departments of the faculty. After the decision to abolish his position, the applicant sent an email to the Rector of the University and to several other recipients, including to the members of the Senate, criticising the lack of democracy and accountability in the

476. These judges, however, voted with the majority and their separate opinion was aimed at filling the gaps of the judgment through establishing the legal basis for ruling against the Constitutional provisions. They concluded that on the basis of the Convention, the Council of Europe may put forward a strong European constitutional claim, if need be, against any contradicting domestic constitutional claim, regardless of the size of the supporting political majority. See paras 1, 25 of the joint concurring opinion of Judges Pinto de Albuquerque and Dedov, ECtHR, Baka v. Hungary (20261/12) GC judgment 23 June 2016.
477. ECtHR, Baka v. Hungary (20261/12) GC judgment 23 June 2016, Dissenting Opinion of Judge Pejchal.
478. Previous case law demonstrates that the ECtHR's scrutiny of the applications of judges was limited to the consideration of the fairness of the disciplinary sanctions and proceedings: see ECtHR, Kudeshkina v. Russia, or Volkov v. Ukraine, Harabin v. Slovakia (58688/11) 20 November 2012; Olujic v. Croatia (22330/05) 5 February 2009; Maestri v. Italy (39748/98) 17 February 2004; N.F. v. Italy(37119/97) 2 August 2001; Juričić v. Croatia (58222/09) 26 July 2011.
479. Kennedy David, The International Human Rights Regime: Still Part of the Problem? In: Rob Dickinson, editors. 'Examining Critical Perspectives on Human Rights'. Cambridge University Press, 2012, p. 25.

leadership of the university, using unfavourable terms when speaking about several university managers.

In another letter titled 'Settlement agreement,' sent to the Rector of the University, the applicant proposed to withdraw all his appeals if the University revoked all the orders and decisions of the Senate concerning the merger of his Department, or paid him a compensation in the sum of EUR 123,000. The Rector refused and the following day, 23 March 2010, the national news agency published the applicant's views about the alleged shortcomings in the management of the university. After an investigation of the applicant's conduct was carried out by an *ad hoc* investigative committee and the university's ethics committee, the applicant received a notice informing him that his employment at the university was terminated. The notice stated, *inter alia*, that the 'settlement agreement' was one of the reasons for dismissal as it was considered as absolutely contrary to good morals.

Mr Rubins appealed to the District Court, which held that an unethical email sent to one's employer was not a legitimate reason for being dismissed from one's job, and ordered the applicant's reinstatement with back-payment of his salary. The Appeal Court quashed the first-instance court's judgment. It considered that the applicant had invited the Rector to carry out 'unlawful actions', namely to annul a decision of the Senate of the University concerning the merger of two departments. The Appeal Court emphasised that the letter sent to the Rector evidenced the applicant's wish to act for a selfish cause, namely to retain his position as head of department, contrary to the Senate's decision on reorganisation, and to receive substantial financial compensation. It also pointed out that the applicant did not attempt to inform society and the relevant authorities about the alleged violations by the University before the decision to abolish his post was made.

The form of the letter and the motives of the applicant were considered to be in breach of ethical norms by both national courts. The public criticism of the University was mentioned as only one of the facts which in totality led the Court of Appeal to conclude that the applicant had contravened the obligation to treat the staff of the university with respect.

Notwithstanding the foregoing, the ECtHR remained reluctant to accept the State's submissions on the inadmissibility of the application. The Government stated that the application concerned the dismissal of an employee for a violation of ethical norms, which is not covered by the ECHR. Moreover, it emphasised that in his civil claim of 11 May 2010, the applicant had not made any allegations that his freedom of speech had been impinged. The ECtHR largely ignored these submissions. It briefly acknowledged that 'the crux of the employment dispute was the allegedly unethical manner of expression used by the applicant in communication with his employer,'[480] and then shifted to analyse the information that the applicant was going to disclose and did actually disclose.[481] All the subsequent reasoning of the ECtHR was of little

480. ECtHR, Rubins v. Latvia, para. 45.
481. *Ibid.*, para. 84.

relevance to the employment dispute at stake, and largely concerned the information disclosed, which was a misstep.[482]

Why was this way of consideration a misstep? The case was about the dismissal of a professor for unethical behaviour (for writing and sending his employer a threatening letter). The Court of Appeal considered that the further disclosure of information was a relevant fact in the case but did not treat it as a determinative factor. The ECtHR did not have any grounds on which to shift its attention from the official reasons of the applicant's dismissal to the public criticism, which, in its opinion, should have been protected.

The ECtHR decided that the interference with the applicant's right to freedom of expression was not necessary in a democratic society and found a violation of Article 10, taking into account its serious chilling effect on other employees of the University.

Dissenting Judges Mahoney and Wojtyczek opined that the ECtHR came to the wrong conclusion as it had misconceived the nature of the dispute. They argued that the majority's approach brought with it the risk of transforming the ECtHR into a higher-instance labour court adjudicating on the merits of labour disputes.[483] Evidently, this is not what the international court of human rights should be; in the light of the majority's decision in this case, the analysis on the merits of employment cases will add yet another layer of complexity and uncertainty to national labour law.[484]

However, the majority of the European Judges supported such a reading of the case. Prof. Dirk Voorhoof argued that this judgment is a well-balanced and transparently motivated example of how a disproportionate interference with the right to freedom of expression of an employee could be scrutinised by the ECtHR.[485] From labour law scholar's point of view, the excessive attention paid by the ECtHR to the disclosure of the information misled it into protecting the freedom of expression of the employee who has violated the employment contract instead of balancing this violation with the imposed sanction. This approach, in my opinion, infringes the principle of subsidiarity, which is a 'a necessary component of democratic rule and human rights law.'[486]

Scholars noted that subsidiarity requires international courts to exercise some deference to national courts through appropriately defined judicial standards of review.[487] The cases considered above demonstrate that on occasions, the failure to pay such respect to the domestic adjudication of the labour disputes can lead to an

482. This point, expressed in my comments on the Rubins judgment on strasburobservers.com was criticised by Prof. Dirk Voorhoof. See Dirk Voorhoof, Response to comment on Rubins v. Latvia: adjudication is not erroneous at all (14 April 2015) strasbourgobservers.com/2015/04/14/response-to-comment-on-rubins-v-latvia-adjudication-is-not-erroneous-at-all/ (accessed 20 June 2015).
483. ECtHR, Rubins v. Latvia, Dissenting Opinion Of Judges Mahoney and Wojtyczek, para. 16.
484. Frank Cranmer, 'Free Speech or Misconduct' in Employment? Rubins v Latvia. Law & Religion UK, 14 April 2015, http://www.lawandreligionuk.com/2015/04/14/free-speech-or-misconduct-in-employment-rubins-v-latvia/ (accessed 20 June 2015).
485. Dirk Voorhoof, *see supra* note 441.
486. Shelton Dinah, Subsidiarity and Human Rights Law. Human Rights Law Journal 27 (2006): 4.
487. Andreas von Staden, The Democratic Legitimacy of Judicial Review beyond the State: Normative Subsidiarity and Judicial Standards of Review. International Journal of Constitutional Law 10 (4) (2012): 1023–1049.

unjustifiable interference with the regulation of domestic employment relations. The protection of employee human rights is indisputably valuable; however, implementing such protection should not permit the *biased pursuits* of one's own self-interest and should ensure a harmonious and well-balanced regulation of the duties and rights of both parties of an employment contract. The international adjudication of labour disputes should respect the limits of subsidiarity and, in particular, the margin of appreciation of the states when making appointments to leading roles in the public sector. Otherwise, it risks its authority on the national level and bolsters the arguments of opponents of the ECtHR.[488]

§7.04 CONCLUSIONS

Strasbourg jurisprudence on Article 10 shows the ECtHR has developed a very detailed and profound approach to the protection of employees' rights to the freedom of expression and association. The principal achievements of the ECtHR in this area are as follows:

(1) It has demonstrated that the ECHR is an instrument capable of protecting the freedom of expression at the workplace, in respect of both public and private employees.
(2) It has interpreted the possible derogations set out in Article 10 in a restrictive way.
(3) It has urged the States to balance in all cases the duty of loyalty with the right for freedom of expression and association, putting great weight on the need to rigorously examine the necessity of the interference.
(4) It has developed a particular approach to the scope of the employee's duty of loyalty, creating a framework by which domestic courts may consider cases regarding the public criticism of one's employer, the disclosure of information in the public interest and a for the adjudication of cases on whistleblower protection.
(5) The ECtHR's conclusions have lead, in some cases, to significant changes in the national legislation in favour of employees (*Redfearn v. UK*[489] is an example which has been discussed earlier). The national cases mentioned in the first subsection of this part demonstrate that some domestic courts are

488. There is currently a heated debate over the limitations of the influence of ECtHR judgments in UK and Russia and there is even talk of withdrawing from the ECHR. These discussions were provoked by the judgments in respect of the prisoner's rights to vote and compensations to the YUKOS share holders, the judgments considered in this subsection might support the opponents of the ECtHR, providing evidence of the excess of powers. *See* Nicholas Watt, Owen Bowcott, Tories Plan to Withdraw UK from European Convention on Human Rights (3 October 2014). Available at: http://www.theguardian.com/politics/2014/oct/03/tories-plan-uk-withdrawal-european-convention-on-human-rights (accessed 17 July 2015); *See also*: Russian Constitutional Court permits Russia not to implement the decisions of the ECHR (KS razreshil Rossii ne ispolnyat' resheniya YESPCH). Available at: http://www.interfax.ru/russia/453542 (accessed 17 July 2015).
489. ECtHR, Redfearn v. United Kingdom, (47335/06) 6 November 2012.

> aware of these achievements and do refer to Article 10 of the ECHR. Raising this kind of awareness and the promoting the Strasbourg judgments domestically are vital to ensuring their greater impact and effectiveness. This is particularly the case in relation to whistleblower protections, because in many countries of the CoE there is no equivalent legislation offering adequate protections. Application by national courts of the framework elaborated in Strasbourg might encourage the enhancement of protection. Even in the absence of domestic legislation in monist countries, the reference to the ECHR and to the ECtHR's interpretation of Article 10 could grant certain protections to whistleblowers.

A survey of whistleblowers protection regimes in the Eastern European region revealed that in the majority of countries, the legislation lacked instruments for effective enforcement of such protection.[490] Amongst these countries, Poland, the Czech Republic, the Slovak Republic, Romania, Bulgaria, Slovenia, Estonia and Russia can be characterised as monist countries. Therefore, the ECHR as interpreted by the ECtHR may be directly applicable in those countries to protect employees' right to the freedom of expression.[491] The direct implementation of the ECtHR's legal positions is possible when national courts are aware of the jurisprudence and esteem it. Such deference can be better maintained if the ECtHR ensures that it only acts within the confines of its subsidiary role, according due respect to the national courts and refraining from considering employment disputes on merits.

490. See Sándor Léderer, Tivadar Hüttl, *see supra* note 408.
491. The list of monist countries was cited from Andrea Oil, Multilevel Regulations Reviewed by Multilevel Jurisdictions: The ECJ, the National Courts and the ECtHR In: Andreas Føllesdal, Ramses A. Wessel, Jan Wouters, editors. 'Multilevel Regulation and the EU: The Interplay Between Global, European, and National Normative Processes'. BRILL, 2008, p. 348.

PART IV
Potential of the European Convention on Human Rights: Wage Protection and Occupational Health and Safety

In contrast with the individual employment rights and civil liberties at work considered in the previous parts, neither the protection of wages nor the occupational health and safety ('*OHS*') of employees can be directly deduced from the provisions of the Convention.

However, the number of cases concerning issues of remuneration of public and private employees being brought before the ECtHR is growing as time passes. The ECtHR's approach to OHS matters has developed significantly in the most recent two years, based on the interpretation of several ECHR rights. These trends clearly demonstrate the permanent enlargement of the scope of the ECHR, which allows us to presume the possible value of ECHR provisions for the establishment of a decent wage and even for the protection from PSR although the ECtHR has never dealt with these issues. The research of these topics will be presented in the following two chapters.

CHAPTER 8

The Protection of Wages: Current Cases and Perspectives

Article 1 of Protocol 1 to the ECHR ('*A1P1*') provides:

> Protection of property:
>
> Every natural or legal person is entitled to the peaceful enjoyment of his possessions. No one shall be deprived of his possessions except in the public interest and subject to the conditions provided for by law and by the general principles of international law. The preceding provisions shall not, however, in any way impair the right of a State to enforce such laws as it deems necessary to control the use of property in accordance with the general interest or to secure the payment of taxes or other contributions or penalties.

The drafting of this article raised numerous disputes between the representatives of the States concerning the definition and precise scope of the right. In particular, the possibility of interpreting these provisions as providing a social right requiring the States to play a substantial and active role was one of the most controversial points.[1] It is interesting to note that the British representative was worried whether the article would infringe governments' power to implement social policies (e.g., to impose taxes on the wealthy). One of the drafters, Sir David Maxwell Fyfe, responded that, 'legislation, the object of which is to carry out a social policy in the general interest, would be saved'.[2] This statement illustrates the fact that the drafters initially supposed that the provisions of this article would have little impact on States' social policies. Fortunately, time has proven them wrong and the ECtHR has developed, over the years, a very particular approach to the protection of property rights, which has significant implications for social security laws[3] in the Member States and has contributed to the protection of wages. 'Wage protection' in the context of this part is

1. R.G. van Banning, The Human Right to Property. Intersentia (2002): 79.
2. *Ibid.*, p. 73.
3. S. Günter Nagel, Francis Kessler, Social Security Law, Council of Europe. Kluwer Law International, 2010; Mel Cousin, The European Convention on Human Rights and Social Security Law.

understood as comprising the issues relating to a decent wage, deductions from wages, its reduction, the lack of its payment and entitlements to additional payments.

§8.01 GENERAL APPROACH TO THE PROTECTION OF POSSESSIONS UNDER A1P1

The ECtHR's approach to cases under A1P1 is largely similar to the way it adjudicates cases relating to other qualified rights. In *Sporrong and Lönnroth v. Sweden*,[4] the ECtHR established three main rules: the principle of one's right to peaceful enjoyment of property; acceptable conditions for the deprivation of one's possessions; recognition of the State's right to control the use of property in accordance with the general interest and by enforcing such laws as they deem necessary for the purpose.[5] Having decided that there is an interference with property within one of these rules, the ECtHR will go on to consider whether such interference can be justified (i.e., serves a legitimate aim and was proportionate). At this stage, the burden of proof is on the state.[6]

As the provisions of A1P1 do not contain any definition of 'possessions', it must be explained how the Strasbourg bodies perceive this term. As early as in the *Marckx* case, the ECtHR acknowledged that A1P1 in substance guarantees the right of property.[7] A more complex approach has developed over the years and the ECtHR has formed an autonomous concept of 'possession'.[8]

In autonomous concept cases, the violation does not at first glance concern whether the state has secured the enabling conditions for the exercise of a right under the ECHR; the problem arises at a conceptual level, where the state has authoritatively qualified a ECHR right such that some instances of it are explicitly excluded from its extension, even though they should not be.[9]

It means that the notion of 'possessions' in the A1P1 is independent of the way it is formally classified in domestic law.[10] According to the ECtHR, 'possession' is not limited to the ownership of physical goods; certain other rights and interests related to

Intersentia, 2008; Ana Gómez Heredero, Social Security as a Human Right: The Protection Afforded by the European Convention on Human Rights, Council of Europe Pub., 2007.

4. ECtHR, Sporrong and Lönnroth v. Sweden (7151/75 and 7152/75) 23 September 1982.
5. *Ibid.*, para. 61.
6. Carss-Frisk Monica, The Right to Property: A Guide to the Implementation of Article 1 of Protocol No. 1 of the European Convention on Human Rights. Directorate General of Human Rights, CoE, 2001, p. 8.
7. ECtHR, Marckx v. Belgium (6833/74) 13 June 1979, para. 63.
8. The Inter-American Court of Human Rights has developed a similar approach and the protection of property has become an important tool for the economic, social, and cultural rights. *See* Lixinski, Lucas. Treaty Interpretation by the Inter-American Court of Human Rights: Expansionism at the Service of the Unity of International Law. European Journal of International Law 21(3) (2010): 585–604.
9. George Letsas. The Truth in Autonomous Concepts: How to Interpret the ECHR. European Journal of International Law 15(2) (2004): 279–305. 283.
10. ECtHR, Beyeler v. Italy (33202/96) GC 5 January 2000, para. 100.

assets can also be regarded as 'property rights' and thus be understood as 'possession'.[11] 'Possessions' can be 'existing possessions' or claims that are sufficiently established to be regarded as 'assets'.[12]

The ECtHR emphasised that A1P1 does not include a right to *acquire* property.[13] However, it considered in the light of this article several cases concerning the right to future income.[14] In such cases, the ECtHR stated that the claims of future income cannot be considered to constitute 'possessions' unless it has already been earned or is definitely payable.[15] In *N.K.M. v. Hungary*, the ECtHR had to decide whether severance pay constituted possession in the sense of A1P1. It held that this payment constitutes a substantive interest protected by A1P1 as it is undeniable that it 'has already been earned or is definitely payable'.[16] In *Stec and others v. UK*, the ECtHR held that an enforceable claim to a social security benefit can constitute 'possession' within the meaning of A1P1.[17]

The Strasbourg approach to 'possessions' was classified by Prof. Sermet as comprising three categories of property: acquired property; property falling under sufficiently established legitimate expectations; and property resulting from rights to restitution.[18] The second type of protected property is the most relevant to the protection of wages and will be further considered in greater detail.

[A] Legitimate Expectation

In the Grand Chamber judgment of *Kopecký v. Slovakia*,[19] the ECtHR went to some lengths to define the notion of the legitimate expectation in the context of A1P1, and acknowledged that a legitimate expectation might be protected under the ECHR only if the claim has a sufficient basis in national law, for example where there is settled case law of the domestic courts confirming it.[20] It further noted that no legitimate expectation can be said to arise where there is a dispute as to the correct interpretation and application of domestic law and the applicant's submissions in this context have been rejected by the national courts.[21] Therefore, as noted by one commentator, the ECtHR's

11. ECtHR, Gasus Dosier- und Födertechnik GmbH v. the Netherlands (15375/89) 23 February 1995, para. 53.
12. ECtHR, Lelas v. Croatia, (55555/08) 20 May 2010, para. 56.
13. ECtHR, Stec and others v. UK(65731/01, 65900/01) 12 April 2006, para. 53.
14. ECtHR, Centro Europa 7 S.r.l. and Di Stefano v. Italy (38433/09) GC 7 June 2012; Anheuser-Busch Inc. v. Portugal [GC] (73049/01) 11 January 2007; Tre Traktörer Aktiebolag v. Sweden (10873/84) 7 July 1989.
15. ECtHR, Anheuser-Busch Inc. v. Portugal, para. 64.
16. ECtHR, N.K.M. v. Hungary (66529/11) 14 May 2013, para. 35.
17. ECtHR, Stec and others v. UK, *see* more in S. Günter Nagel, Francis Kessler, Social Security Law, Council of Europe. Kluwer Law International, 2010, p. 40.
18. Laurent Sermet, The European Convention on Human Rights and Property Rights, vol. 11. Council of Europe, 1998, p. 17.
19. ECtHR, Kopecký v. Slovakia (44912/98) 28 September 2004, paras 45–52.
20. *Ibid.*, para. 52.
21. ECtHR, Anheuser-Busch Inc. v. Portugal (73049/01) GC 11 January 2007, para. 65; Sukhanov and Ilchenko v. Ukraine (68385/10, 71378/10) 26 June 2014, para. 35.

jurisprudence is clear that relevant expectations should be more than a reasonable hope.[22]

However, in the recent case of *Béláné Nagy v. Hungary*,[23] the ECtHR acknowledged the applicant's legitimate expectation to receive a disability pension once he had met the administrative requirements of the disability pension scheme as in force at the first material point in time.[24] Based on this argument, the ECtHR acknowledged the right of the applicant for the disability pension, despite decisions by the domestic courts not to grant this right.

This judgment demonstrates that it is not easy to draw the line between potential rights not protected by the article, and the legitimate expectation that the right will materialise, as protected by A1P1.[25]

The ECtHR's jurisprudence provides us with some guidelines in this respect. In *Aizpurua Ortiz and Others v. Spain*, the ECtHR acknowledged that the applicants, deprived of the right to access supplementary pensions acquired under an earlier collective agreement, *had at least a legitimate expectation* of continuing to receive this pension.[26] In *Kjartan Ásmundsson v. Iceland*,[27] concerning the abolition of a disability pension as a result of changes in the way the applicant's disability was assessed, the ECtHR held that the applicant could validly plead an individual legitimate expectation that his disability would continue to be assessed on the basis of his incapacity to perform his previous job and found the violation of A1P1.[28] These cases demonstrate that a legitimate expectation might be established in cases where the lack or reduction of payments were the result of external factors, in other words, when the applicant did not cease to satisfy the requirements to benefit from the payment as it was initially established.

In *Eskelinen and Others v. Finland*,[29] however, the ECtHR held that the applicants had not had a legitimate expectation of receiving an individual wage supplement (cold-area allowance) since the municipality that they worked for, had been removed from the group for which this allowance was to be paid. Therefore, the employees in this case were not removed from the remote and cold area, the municipality itself was cancelled from the list of such places, however, there is a doubt that the conditions of labour changed since that bureaucratic removal. If the conditions of labour had not

22. Alexander Orakhelashvili, The Interpretation of Acts and Rules in Public International Law. Oxford University Press, 2008, p. 275.
23. ECtHR, Béláné Nagy v. Hungary 53080/13 10 February 2015.
24. *Ibid.*, para. 47.
25. On this point *see also* Guðrún Gauksdóttir, The Right to Property and the European Convention on Human Rights: A Nordic Approach. Lund University, 2004, cited from Olsson Petra Herzfeld, Every Natural or Legal Person is Entitled to the Peaceful Enjoyment of His or Her Possessions: Article 1, Protocol 1 to the European Convention on Human Rights In: Filip Dorssemont, Klaus Lörcher, Isabelle Schömann, editors. 'The European Convention on Human Rights and the Employment Relation'. Oxford: Hart Publishing, 2013, p. 399.
26. ECtHR, Aizpurua Ortiz and Others v. Spain (42430/05) 2 February 2010, no violation of A1P1 was found as the interference pursued an aim in the general interest.
27. ECtHR, Kjartan Ásmundsson v. Iceland (60669/00) 12 October 2004.
28. *Ibid.*, paras 44, 45.
29. ECtHR, Eskelinen and Others v. Finland (63235/00) 19 April 2007, para. 94.

changed, would not that have been more in line with the ECHR to conclude that the applicants had a legitimate expectation of receiving additional payment?

This example demonstrates that the ECtHR assesses more strictly the legitimate expectation reasonably attributable to the applicant in cases concerning remuneration, than in respect of pension claims.

The concept of 'legitimate expectation' makes us question whether an employee's right to be reimbursed for lost wages in case of unfair dismissal might be protected under A1P1. This question was answered in *Baka v. Hungary*.[30]

In that case, the applicant alleged that the State had violated his right under A1P1 as a result of the premature termination of his mandate as the President of the Supreme Court. One of the effects of the termination was his losing the salary he would have been entitled to obtain had he not been terminated from such a position. The ECtHR pointed that the dismissal of the applicant from the post had indeed precluded him from receiving a further salary, however, that income had not been actually earned and was not definitely payable.[31] Surprisingly, the ECtHR did not look at the national law in order to establish if the applicant's claim 'had a sufficient basis in national law.'[32] Such a conclusion is, in fact, in contrast with its usual approach to legitimate expectations, which caused labour scholars to argue that the claim of future income can at least be accommodated in legal systems where unjustified dismissals generate damages based on future earnings or reinstatement.[33] At the same time, this judgment demonstrates the lack of coherence in approach to the protection of claims brought under A1P1. It also demonstrates the ECtHR's unwillingness to protect job property, defined by Davies and M. Freedland, as the interest which a worker has in the continuation of his employment.[34] However, it is necessary to reflect over the reasons why the ECtHR refused to protect the right to receive reimbursement for lost wages in this case, where, in its opinion, the dismissal violated Articles 6 and 10 of the ECHR.

This judgment makes us remember the cases where, for example, the ECtHR held that the withdrawal of a licence constituted the violation of A1P1 as the nature of these claims has certain similarity with the claims of lost wage.[35] In *Tre Traktörer Aktiebolag v. Sweden*,[36] it found that the economic interests connected with the running of the restaurant were 'possessions' for the purposes of A1P1. In the later case, concerning the granting of a fishing licence, the Commission pointed out that a licence-holder cannot be considered to have a reasonable and legitimate expectation to continue his

30. ECtHR, Baka v. Hungary (20261/12) 27 May 2014.
31. *Ibid.*, para. 105.
32. ECtHR, Kopecký v. Slovakia[GC] (44912/98) 28 September 2004, para. 52.
33. Olsson Petra Herzfeld, *supra* note 25, p. 397.
34. Davies, M. Freedland, Labour Law: Texts and Materials. London: Weidenfeld and Nicolson, 1984, p. 428.
35. It's worth noting that in cases concerning the decrease of income due to legislative changes the ECtHR has been reluctant to find the violation of A1P1: *see* X v. the Federal Republic of Germany (8410/78) 13 December 1979 (concerning notaries' expectations in respect of fees which had been statutorily reduced), Casotti, Florio and The Consiglio Nazionale Dell' Ordine Dei Consulenti Del Lavoro v. Italy (24877/94) 16 October 1996 (concerning the possible decrease in the income of labour consultants).
36. ECtHR, Tre Traktörer Aktiebolag v. Sweden (10873/84) 7 July 1989, para. 53.

activity if the conditions attached to the licence are no longer fulfilled or if the licence is withdrawn in accordance with the provisions of the law which was in force when the licence was issued. It further reiterated that expectations for future earnings could only be considered to constitute a 'possession', if it had already been earned or where an enforceable claim to it existed.[37]

Therefore, the Commission separated the economic interests of the licence holder and the expectation for future earnings. This approach of the Strasbourg bodies to the protection of the rights of licence holders make us question whether the application of Mr Baka, who, in the opinion of the ECtHR, had a reasonable and legitimate expectation to continue his activity as the President of the Supreme Court, would have been more successful if he had claimed that his economic interest in keeping the post was infringed instead of claiming rights to future income as he did. It is likely that the ECtHR would still refuse to find the violation of A1P1. The ECtHR's finding that the dismissal violated the ECHR generally provides the possibility to re-consider the case by the national court. The claim under A1P1 is always additional in such cases. The ECtHR's refusal to grant it might be explained by the reference to the margin of appreciation of the States and the subsidiary role of the ECtHR. It consciously leaves the issue of reimbursement for lost wages national courts to address.

§8.02 CASE LAW ON THE PROTECTION OF WAGES

The interconnection of property rights and labour rights is indisputable. It is curious that political theorists of an earlier era, such as John Locke, Adam Smith and Thomas Paine, argued specifically for the recognition of labour rights as property rights.[38] Davies and M. Freedland defined job property as 'the interest, viewed as proprietary in nature, which a worker has in the continuation of his employment as the result of legal measures or social systems which protect the expectation and security of continued employment'.[39] However, the ECtHR is far from recognising this 'property' right, and, as scholars justifiably note, there is not much to say about the protection of wages as property rights under the ECHR.[40] The Strasbourg Court has on several occasions stated that the provisions of the A1P1 do not guarantee the right to continue to be paid a salary of a particular amount and that it is entirely at the State's discretion to determine what benefits are to be paid to its employees out of the State's budget.[41]

The establishment of a wide margin of appreciation of the states in matters dealing with wage protection is a general peculiarity of the cases considered in the light of A1P1. Even in a case concerning the calculation of a minimum wage, the ECtHR was

37. ECtHR, Størksen v. Norway (19819/92) admissibility decision 5 July 1994.
38. Tonia Novitz, Labour Rights and Property Rights: Implications for (and Beyond) Redundancy Payments and Pensions? Industrial Law Journal 41 (2012): 137–141.
39. Davies. M. Freedland, Labour Law: Texts and Materials. London: Weidenfeld and Nicolson, 1984, p. 428.
40. Koch I. Human Rights as Indivisible Rights: The Protection of Socio-economic Demands under the European Convention on Human Rights. Martinus Nijhoff Publishers, 2009, p. 225.
41. ECtHR, Baka v. Hungary (20261/12) 27 May 2014; Panfile v. Romania (13902/11) inadmissible 20 March 2012; Vilho Eskelinen and Others v. Finland [GC] (63235/00) 19 April 2007.

reluctant to impose any restrictions: in *Nerva and Others v. UK*,[42] the ECtHR declared inadmissible the applications of waiters who argued that the employer's refusal to include the tips paid by cheque or credit card in calculating their statutory minimum remuneration violated their rights under A1P1. The ECtHR' reasoning in this judgment demonstrates that it tends to acknowledge the legitimate expectation of receiving a minimum wage; however, it prefers to leave the calculation of the minimum wage wholly within the margin of appreciation of the State.

The ECtHR left aside the nature of the minimum wage and the nature of tips.[43] Relying on the conclusions of the domestic courts, it found that the applicants could not maintain that they had a separate right to the tips and a separate right to minimum remuneration, and emphasised that the ECHR does not guarantee the right for a higher level of earnings. The ECtHR also noted that it was for the applicants to come to a contractual arrangement with their employer as to how the tips at issue were to be dealt with, from the point of view of their wage entitlements.[44] This statement vividly demonstrates the reluctance of the ECtHR to interfere with relations between private parties of employment contracts and with the establishment of minimum wage regulations. The decision was criticised by British scholars as permitting restaurants to pay down the statutorily mandated UK minimum wage[45] and for not regarding the worker as being entitled to a certain threshold level of remuneration as a matter of right.[46] Some commentators pointed out that such an approach to the minimum wage ultimately led to the inclusion of customers in the employment relationship, and to the legal precariousness of workers.[47]

It is interesting to note that trade unions have successfully campaigned to amend the UK Minimum Wage Regulations, so the amounts of money paid by customers as a service charge or tip should be subtracted from the total of remuneration which the employer pays to the worker. Those changes were adopted in 2009.[48]

[A] Wage Supplements

In *Vilho Eskelinen and others v. Finland*,[49] the ECtHR established a general rule that the establishment or annulation of wage supplements should be left within the margin of appreciation of the States. In this case, the applicants argued that the abolition of the

42. ECtHR, Nerva and others v. UK (42295/98) 24 September 2002.
43. Dissenting Judge Loucaides noted that the nature of tips, given directly to the waiters, demonstrated that the tips were a possession in the meaning of A1P1. *See* Dissenting opinion of Judge Loucaides, Nerva and others v. UK.
44. ECtHR, Nerva v. UK, para. 43.
45. Tafreshi Shawn, Here's a Tip, Change the Law-Nerva v. United Kingdom. Loyola of Los Angeles International and Comparative Law Review 27 (2005): 127. Available at: http://digitalcommons.lmu.edu/cgi/viewcontent.cgi?article=1581&context=ilr (accessed 20 August 2015).
46. T. Novitz, *see supra* note 38, p. 148.
47. Einat Albina, A Worker-Employer-Customer Triangle: The Case of Tips. Industrial Law Journal 40(2) (2011): 181.
48. Hugh Collins, Keith Ewing, Aileen McColgan, Labour Law. Cambridge University Press, 2012, p. 259.
49. ECtHR, Vilho Eskelinen and Others v. Finland [GC] (63235/00) 19 April 2007.

remote-area supplement to wages of police officers constituted the violation of A1P1. The ECtHR noted that the applicants did not have a legitimate expectation to receive an individual wage supplement as the entitlement to it had ceased. In *Smokovitis and Others v. Greece*,[50] concerning the payment of a research allowance to teachers employed on temporary basis, the ECtHR did find the violation of A1P1, deciding that the applicants had a 'legitimate expectation' to receive this supplement as the national courts had on multiple occasions stated that this research allowance applied to all staff.

In *Kechko v. Ukraine*,[51] the ECtHR found in favour of the applicant who claimed that the refusal to pay him a 20% increase in his salary, as required by law, violated A1P1. Therefore, in order to establish a legitimate expectation in remuneration claims brought under A1P1, such a claim must be supported by law or national case law, and, ideally be acknowledged by decisions of the domestic courts. This approach reflects the ECtHR's general reluctance to consider remuneration claims under A1P1 unless the circumstances of the case demonstrate very clearly that a debt in favour of the applicant arose in this context.[52]

In *Lelas v. Croatia*,[53] the ECtHR considered a claim about the refusal to pay a wage supplement from a very interesting perspective. The applicant, a serviceman, was entitled to receive a wage supplement for carrying out demining work. For several years this right had been acknowledged by his supervisor. When the applicant brought a claim before the domestic courts, they found that the relevant limitation period had expired and therefore refused his claim. It found that the statutory limitation period continued to operate regardless of any acknowledgment of the debt on the part of the applicant's supervisor, as the supervisor was not an authorised person to extend any statutory limitation periods. The ECtHR considered that the refusal to grant the applicant's claim was an interference with the applicant's rights under A1P1. It further considered whether such interference was lawful and came to conclusion that the failure of the domestic courts to refer to a legal provision justifying its finding that the debt should have been acknowledged by another official was incompatible with the principle of lawfulness and therefore contravened A1P1.

This judgment demonstrates that the ECtHR's approach to the protection of wage claims can expand to cover claims which have been refused by domestic courts. It is important that in such cases it seeks to establish whether such refusal corresponded to the criteria of accessibility and foreseeability as developed in the Strasbourg jurisprudence.

[B] Reduction and Deductions

In all the cases concerning wage reduction or deductions from wages, the ECtHR has either explicitly or implicitly referred to the wide margin of appreciation of the States in the organisation of the labour market. It is particularly wide in respect of working

50. ECtHR, Smokovitis and others v. Greece (46356/99) 11 April 2002.
51. ECtHR, Kechko v. Ukraine (63134/00) 8 November 2005.
52. ECtHR, Van der Mussele v. Belgium (8919/80) 23 November 1983.
53. ECtHR, Lelas v. Croatia (55555/08) 20 May 2010.

prisoners when the deductions from their wages have a compensatory role, for example, because the deductions were intended to cover expenses for board and lodging while imprisoned. Thus in *Puzinas v. Lithuania*,[54] the ECtHR found that the deduction of a 25% contribution from a prisoner's salary did not violate A1P1, and in *Stummer v. Austria*[55] it noted that the deduction of 75% of prisoners' wages 'appears rather high' but was not found to unreasonable overall. In *Davis v. UK*,[56] the Commission declared inadmissible the application of a prisoner who claimed that the deductions from his wage, used to provide entertainment and other facilities in prison, violated A1P1 of the ECHR.

In *Evaldsson v. Sweden*, the ECtHR established that the margin of appreciation should be limited by a positive obligation of the State to ensure the accountability of trade unions for received compulsory deductions from wages.[57]

As far as the reduction of wages is concerned, the ECtHR has tended to justify such interferences with reference to the public interest. In the last twenty years it has formed an approach to cases involving the reduction of benefits, finding violations in cases where such reductions were aimed at a limited number of individuals and decreased to such a significant extent so as to violate the 'safeguard against poverty for persons who lacked basic maintenance from another socially acceptable source'.[58]

[C] Austerity Measures

The recent case law on austerity measures demonstrates largely the same approach to the matters of reduction or deductions from wages. The proportionality exercise is the most significant part of the adjudication of applications under A1P1, and the ECtHR generally prioritises the general interest of the State in decreasing wages. In such cases, it tends to find violations if the applicant succeeds in demonstrating that as a result of the State's interference he or she has suffered from an individual and excessive burden.[59]

The estimation of the burden is very rigorous and this point, again, highlights the wide, but not unlimited,[60] margin of appreciation of the state in this sphere. Let us take as an example the ECtHR's reasoning in *Koufaki and ADEDY v. Greece*,[61] which

54. ECtHR, Puzinas v. Lithuania (63767/00) 9 January 2007.
55. ECtHR, Stummer v. Austria (37452/02) 7 July 2011.
56. EurCommHR, Davis v. The United Kingdom (27042/95) inadmissible 17 January 1997.
57. ECtHR, Evaldsson And Others v. Sweden (75252/01) 13 February 2007, para. 63. The case concerned compulsory deductions from the wages of those who are not members of the union.
58. Compare, for example, ECtHR, Goudswaard-Van der Lans v. the Netherlands (75255/01) 22 September 2005 and Kjartan Ásmundsson v. Iceland (60669/00) 12 October 2004.
59. This concept was developed in social security cases, *see*, for example, Kjartan Ásmundsson v. Iceland (60669/00) 12 October 2004; Goudswaard-Van der Lans v. the Netherlands (75255/01) 22 September 2005; Marija Božić v. Croatia (50636/09) 24 April 2014; Khoniakina v. Georgia (17767/08) 19 June 2012.
60. ECtHR, Da Conceição Mateus and Santos Januário v. Portugal (62235/12, 57725/12) 8 October 2013, para. 23.
61. ECtHR, Koufaki and ADEDY v. Greece (57665/12, 57657/12) 7 May 2013.

concerned cuts to pensions and salaries of public servants under national austerity measures.

It is interesting to note that, in contrast with the earlier case such as *Mihăieş and Senteş v. Romania,*[62] the ECtHR did not hesitate as to whether a salary cut might constitute an interference with possessions in the sense of A1P1; therefore it already represents a step forward. The State, justifying its interest in imposing austerity measures, noted that its goals coincided with those of the euro area Member States to ensure budgetary discipline and to preserve the stability of the euro area.[63] The ECtHR decided that the State did not, in this case, overstep its margin of appreciation and thus did not violate the ECHR.[64] The ECtHR did not investigate the first applicant's claims that the reduction of her wage, compounded by the rise in the price of basic essentials such as fuel and public service charges, had led to a drastic fall in her standard of living. Having found that the reduction was about 20%, the ECtHR stated that the extent of the reduction in the first applicant's salary was not such that it would place her at risk of having insufficient means to live on, and thus amounting to a breach of A1P1.[65] It also noted the observation of the Greek Court that the applicants had not claimed that they risked falling below the subsistence threshold. This observation might be interpreted as posing a 'subsistence threshold' to justify the proportionality of austerity measures.

Examining other 'austerity' cases permits us to ascertain with more certainty the permissible threshold by which wages may be decreased at a time of economic crisis. These cases concern both the reduction in pensions or wages and the taxation of severance payments received by public servants. It is particularly interesting to follow the ECtHR's reasoning when addressing the concept of what constitutes an excessive burden. Violation was found in a series of cases against Hungary, where the State introduced extremely high levels of taxation in respect of severance payments to be received by public servants (the level of taxation differed in these cases from 52% in *N.K.M. v. Hungary*[66] to 98% in *R.Sz. v. Hungary*[67]). In the cases concerning a decrease

62. ECtHR, Mihăieş and Senteş v. Romania (44232/11, 44605/11) 2 March 2012.
63. N. Napoletano pointed out that the coincidence between the objectives pursued internally with those pursued by the European Union strengthened the position of the Government. Napoletano N., Estensione e limiti della dimensione economica e sociale della Convenzione europea dei diritti umani in tempi di crisi finanziaria, in Diritti umani e diritto internazionale, 2014 2(8), p. 425.
64. It is interesting to note that the ECSR two months before the decision of the ECtHR decided that Greek austerity measures violated the ESC, its opinion, however, is not mentioned in the decision of the European Court. *See* ECSR, complaint No. 76/2012, Federation of Employed Pensioners of Greece (IKA-ETAM) v. Greece; ECSR, complaint No. 77/2012, Panhellenic Federation of Public Service Pensioners (POPS) v. Greece; ECSR, complaint No. 78/2012, Pensioners' Union of the Athens-Piraeus Electric Railways (I.S.A.P.) v. Greece; ECSR, complaint No. 79/2012, Panhellenic Federation of Pensioners of the Public Electricity Corporation (POS-DEI) v. Greece; ECSR, complaint No. 80/2012, Pensioner's Union of the Agricultural Bank of Greece (ATE) v. Greece, became public on 22 April 2013.
65. ECtHR, Koufaki and ADEDY v. Greece, para. 46.
66. ECtHR, N.K.M. v. Hungary (66529/11) 14 May 2013.
67. ECtHR, R.Sz. v. Hungary (41838/11) 2 July 2013, *see also* similar cases Á.A. v. Hungary (22193/11), P.G. v. Hungary (18229/11) 23 September 2014.

in pensions, the ECtHR found that the loss of 38% of a pension did not impose an excessive burden on the applicant, whilst the loss of 67% did violate A1P1.[68]

Inadmissible applications brought against Georgia, Portugal and Romania, where the pensions or other social benefits were reduced at a level less than 20% might be also referred to as, in the opinion of the ECtHR, a fair balance had been struck between the demands of the general interest and the requirements of the protection of the applicants' rights under A1P1.[69]

This brief overview demonstrates that the violation of A1P1 was found only in cases when the decrease in payment was more than 50%; therefore, it appears that the margin of appreciation of the State is in fact very wide in this context.

The ECtHR, however, pointed out in *Steffanetti and others v. Italy* that the fair balance test cannot be based solely on the amount or percentage of the reduction suffered.[70] In this case, it took account of the average and minimum pensions in Italy,[71] comparing them with the reduced pensions of the applicants. In contrast with *Koufaki*, the ECtHR referred to the related conclusions of the European Committee of Social Rights (ECSR) in respect of Italy. All these circumstances made the ECtHR conclude that the reductions at issue had imposed an excessive burden on the applicants.

Other 'austerity cases' show that the ECtHR only considers significant an applicant's individual background if the level of reduction is more than 50%; otherwise its reasoning in these cases tends to be very brief and largely similar from case-to-case.

The ECtHR's approach to the impact austerity measures have on human rights could arguably be more rigorous; however, it would be impossible for it to take that more rigorous approach without interfering too much with States' social policies, and without invading the margin of appreciation of States. The ECtHR's decisions that reductions of wages and pensions can constitute an interference with ECHR rights is a valuable conclusion per se. It might provide domestic courts with a new perspective of such cases, by demonstrating the possibility to consider austerity measures in the light of fundamental human rights. National courts, which are in principle better placed than an international judge to appreciate what is 'in the public interest',[72] might be more stringent in its assessment of the proportionality of the interference with social rights and might notice details which are imperceptible from Strasbourg. It is remarkable that this approach has already been taken by the Estonian Supreme Court,[73]

68. ECtHR, Stefanetti and Others v. Italy (21838/10 et al.) 15 April 2014.
69. ECtHR, Da Silva Carvalho Rico v. Portugal (13341/14) 24 September 2015; Mihăieş and Senteş v. Romania (44232/11, 44605/11) 2 March 2012, Da Conceição Mateus v. Portugal and Santos Januário v. Portugal (62235/12, 57725/12) 8 October 2013, Khoniakina v. Georgia (17767/08) 19 June 2012.
70. ECtHR, Steffanetti v. Italy, paras 58, 59.
71. *Ibid.*, paras 62–63.
72. ECtHR, Mihăieş and Senteş v. Romania (44232/11, 44605/11) 2 March 2012.
73. On the 26 June 2014 the Estonian Supreme Court declared the cuts in judges' pensions during the austerity period unconstitutional, *see* Representing Retired Estonian Judges in Challenge to Austerity Measures. Available at: http://www.ceelegalmatters.com/index.php/over-the-wire/legal-ticker-deals-and-cases-in-cee/item/689-representing-retired-estonian-judges-in-challenge-to-austerity-measures/689-representing-retired-estonian-judges-in-challenge-to-austerity-meas ures (accessed 20 October 2014).

Latvian[74] and Portuguese Constitutional Courts[75] in judging pension cuts in those States as being unconstitutional.

§8.03 THE INTERCONNECTION BETWEEN VIOLATIONS OF PROCEDURAL RIGHTS UNDER ARTICLE 6 AND VIOLATIONS OF THE A1P1 IN THE CONTEXT OF EMPLOYMENT

Article 6 of the ECHR has a particular value in the context of employment relations. The ECtHR has formulated certain requirements to the procedural rights of employees in labour disputes.[76] This facet of the ECtHR's jurisprudence was intentionally left outside the scope of the present research as it merits a separate profound analysis. However, the cases considered in light of both Articles 6 and A1P1 will be researched in this section so far as they complement the ECtHR's approach to the protection of wages.

The ECtHR has dealt with numerous applications concerning the non-enforcement of judgments awarding social security benefits or salary arrears, and has established that if an applicant is unable to obtain the benefit awarded by the judgment then that inability constitutes an interference with the right to the peaceful enjoyment of possessions.[77] It has affirmed that States may not justify the non-enforcement of such judgments by reference to lack of relevant funds.[78]

Ukraine and Russia appear the most before the ECtHR as respondent States in such cases. In spite of adopting the pilot judgments against Ukraine[79] and Russia[80] respectively, in which the ECtHR urged each of the respective States to set up an effective domestic remedy for the non-enforcement or delayed enforcement of domestic judgments, the problem has remained largely unresolved.[81]

74. *See* Judgment Of The Constitutional Court Of Latvia, 21 December 2009, in the case No. 2009-43-01 that held unconstitutional the reductions of pensions, referring on the judgment of the ECtHR and to the General comments of the ICESCR.
75. *See* the Constitutional Court Decision No. 353/2012, that declared unconstitutional the provisions of Budget Law on salary and pensions cuts for public servants, decision is available at: http://www.tribunalconstitucional.pt/tc/acordaos/20120353.html (accessed 20 October 2014).
76. ECtHR, Fogarty v. The United Kingdom [GC] (37112/97) 21 November 2001; Waite and Kennedy v. Germany [GC] (26083/94) 18 February 1999; Oleksandr Volkov v. Ukraine (21722/11) 9 January 2013; D.M.T. and D.K.I. v. Bulgaria (29476/06) 24 July 2012; Tripon v. Romania(27062/04) 7 February 2012; Mitrinovski v. 'The former Yugoslav Republic of Macedonia' (6899/12) 30 April 2015.
77. ECtHR, Mykhaylenky and others v. Ukraine (35091/02, 35196/02, 35201/02) 30 November 2004, para. 60; Fuklev v. Ukraine (71186/01) 7 June 2005; Adamović v. Serbia (no. 41703/06) 2 October 2012; Stošić v. Serbia (64931/10) 1 October 2013.
78. ECtHR, Mykhaylenky and others v. Ukraine, para. 52; Piven and Zhovner v. Ukraine (56849/00, 56848/00) 29 June 2004; The delay in payment also cannot be justified by such a reference, *see* Voytenko v. Ukraine (18966/02) 29 June 2004.
79. ECtHR, Yuriy Nikolayevich Ivanov v. Ukraine (40450/04) 15 October 2009.
80. *See* ECtHR, Burdov v. Russia(N1) (59498/00) 7 May 2002; Burdov v. Russia (N 2)) (33509/04) 15 January 2009.
81. *See* Peter B. Maggs, Olga Schwartz, William Burnham, Law and Legal System of the Russian Federation. 6th ed., Juris Publishing, Inc., 2015, p. 389; Ivanna Ilciienko, Pilot Judgement procedure of the European Court of Human Rights: Panacea or Dead-End for Poland, Russia and Ukraine. LL.M. Human Rights Thesis Central European University, published 29 November 2013; Available at: www.etd.ceu.hu/2014/ilchenko_ivanna.pdf (accessed 20 July 2015).

The ECtHR recently faced another problem concerning the enforcement of judgments in favour of employees – the execution of such judgments in the course of insolvency proceedings or in case of insufficiency of the employer's property. In this series of cases the leading positions are occupied by Russia, Ukraine and Serbia.

The inability of an employer to cover its debts, acknowledged by national courts, is the most pervasive problem. According to the well-established Strasbourg case law, the extent of state obligations in cases of non-enforcement of judicial decisions will depend on who the debtor is, in each specific instance.

The situation is often complicated by the processes of privatisation, which meant that owners could change over the course of time. In cases where the privatisation occurred before the domestic courts handed down its judgment awarding salary arrears, the ECtHR tends to refuse employee's applications alleging the lack of payment, pointing out that the State cannot be held responsible for the financial debts of a private legal entity.[82] In such cases, the State is not directly liable for debts of private actors unless it fails to act in order to enforce a judgment.[83]

If the State fails to act then the ECtHR is more likely to attribute to them a failure to meet their responsibilities under the ECHR, particularly if it can be demonstrated that the national authorities did not ensure that the procedures enshrined in the legislation for the enforcement of final judgments and for bankruptcy proceedings have been complied with.[84]

At the same time, the ECtHR has consistently held the States responsible for the non-enforcement of the judgments rendered against companies owned by the State, or where there has been a subsequent change in their respective capital share structure resulting in the predominance of the state-owned and socially-owned capital.[85] Thus in *Khachatryan v. Armenia*,[86] the ECtHR found the State liable for the breach of both Articles 6 and A1P1 due to the non-enforcement of a judgment which granted damages for salary arrears against a private company, the majority shareholder of whom was the State. The same conclusion was reached in numerous cases against Serbia as far as they concerned the non-enforcement of judgments in the circumstances of on-going insolvency proceedings of state-owned companies.[87]

The most important point of the ECtHR's judgments in these cases is the requirement to pay an employee the sums awarded in the final domestic judgments.[88]

Another significant point is the acknowledgment of the state's liability in cases where the employer's company lacked institutional and operational independence

82. ECtHR, Lepetyukhov v. Ukraine (5033/07) inadmissible 16 March 2010.
83. ECtHR, Anokhin v. Russia 25867/02 inadmissible 31 May 2007; Polacik v. Slovakia (58707/00) 15 November 2005.
84. ECtHR, Fuklev v. Ukraine (71186/01) 7 June 2005, para. 91.
85. ECtHR, Sekulic and Kucevic v. Serbia (28686/06 50135/06) 15 October 2013.
86. ECtHR, Khachatryan v. Armenia (application no. 31761/04) 1 December 2009.
87. ECtHR, Marčić and Others v. Serbia(17556/05) 30 October 2007, para. 60; Crnišanin and Others v. Serbia (35835/05 et al.) 13 January 2009; Rašković and Milunović v. Serbia (1789/07 and 28058/07) 31 May 2011; Adamović v. Serbia (41703/06) 2 October 2012.
88. *See also* ECtHR, Janković v. Serbia (21518/09) 18 November 2014; Tomović And Others v. Serbia (5327/11 et al.) 24 February 2015; Jovičić and Others v. Serbia (37270/11 et al.) 13 January 2015.

from the state.[89] This conclusion concerns certain types of enterprises where the state under national law retains ownership of the property of that enterprise, approves all transactions with that property, controls the management of the enterprise and decides whether the enterprise should continue its activity or be liquidated.[90]

Under Russian law, for example, such enterprises are not liable for the debts of their owners, and the owners are not generally liable for the companies' debts. In spite of such a clear national provision the ECtHR found has found Russia liable for the debts of such companies in respect of their employees.[91] In the recent case of *Liseytseva and Maslov v. Russia*,[92] the State was also found responsible for the non-enforcement of the judgment on the payment of salary arrears in respect of the employees of municipality-owned companies.[93]

The prerequisites of a successful claim are clearly formulated in the Strasbourg case law. The applicant is only required to file a request for the enforcement of a judgment awarding salary arrears with the competent national court or, in case of liquidation or insolvency proceedings against the debtor, to report his or her claims to the administrators of the debtor.[94]

In *Zouboulidis v. Greece*,[95] the Court touched upon another facet of rights under A1P1. The applicant, an official of the Ministry of Foreign Affairs, was refused additional payments which by law he was entitled to, as the limitation period for the claims against the State had already expired. In his application before the ECtHR, he alleged that the establishment of a reduced time-limit for claiming the debts owed by the State as well as the calculation of default interest from the date on which notice of the action was served on the State were in breach with A1P1. The ECtHR emphasised that the mere interest of a state's cash flow could not in itself be regarded as a public or general interest justifying interference with individual rights, through the application of the two-year limitation period and the granting of preferential treatment to the state in fixing the date from which default interest was charged. It found the violation of A1P1 and awarded just satisfaction in respect of the pecuniary damage sustained by the applicant in the sum of the debt calculated on the basis of general rules.

The cases considered above demonstrate that the number of the cases brought before the ECtHR under Article 6 and A1P1 is growing with years. Due to the fact that the ECtHR can require the State to pay salary arrears, this body turns out to be the most effective international body in the sphere of wage protection and provides invaluable support to the realisation of the fundamental right for remuneration, even though this right is absent from the text of the ECHR.

---

89. ECtHR, Bichenok v. Russia (13731/08) inadmissible 31 March 2015, para. 18.
90. ECtHR, Aleksandrova v. Russia (28965/02) 6 December 2007 the same line in Veretennikov v. Russia (8363/03) 12 March 2009 *see also* Filshteyn v. Ukraine (12997/06) 28 May 2009.
91. ECtHR, Shafranov v. Russia (24766/04) 25 September 2008.
92. ECtHR, Liseytseva and Maslov v. Russia (39483/05 and 40527/10) 9 October 2014.
93. *See also* ECtHR, Voronkov v. Russia (39678/03) 30 July 2015.
94. ECtHR, Živković v. Serbia (63694/10) inadmissible 30 June 2015; Lolić v. Serbia (44095/06) 22 October 2013; Nikolić-Krstić v. Serbia (54195/07) 14 October 2014.
95. ECtHR, Zouboulidis v. Greece (no. 2) (36963/06) 25 June 2009.

§8.04 THE POTENTIAL OF THE ECHR IN THE SPHERE OF WAGE PROTECTION

'Give him food and shelter, when you have covered his nakedness, Dignity will follow by itself'.
Friedrich Schiller (1798)[96]

It has already been mentioned above that the ECHR, in the opinion of the ECtHR, does not guarantee the right to acquire property. Scholars have added that there is currently no 'real substantial movement' towards the acknowledgement of the right to acquire property.[97] However, as also noted earlier, the ECtHR has started to use the notion of 'insufficient means to live' in the consideration of cases under A1P1. Therefore, there is a hope, that taking into account a general trend of expanding the ECHR to address social matters and the social policies of the states, the ECtHR could develop even further this concept of the sufficiency of the means to live. This concept, if further elaborated, might be used for the protection of the right for fair remuneration.

Why should the European ECtHR interfere with the issue of wages? There are already provisions in the International Covenant of Economic, Social and Cultural Rights (Article 7) and in the ESC. According to the approach adopted by the ECSR, fair remuneration must in any event be above the poverty line in a given country i.e., 50% of the national average wage.[98] This clear interpretation of the right for a minimum wage has, regretfully, a very limited practical impact. The protection of social rights through the ECSR has already proven ineffective, taking into account the peculiarities of the collective complaints system[99] and the non-binding legal status of its conclusions.[100] The same could be said in respect of the ICESCR, which only recently acquired its authority to consider individual claims.[101] None of the five claims brought before the

96. Cited from Christopher McCrudden, Human Dignity and Judicial Interpretation of Human Rights. European Journal of International Law 19(4): 655–724.
97. Olsson Petra Herzfeld, *supra* note 25, p. 385.
98. *See* Digest of the Case Law of the European Committee of Social Rights, 1 September 2008. Council of Europe. Available at: https://www.coe.int/t/dghl/monitoring/socialcharter/Digest/DigestSept2008_en.pdf (accessed 30 July 2015).
99. Churchill, Robin R., and Urfan Khaliq, The Collective Complaints System of the European Social Charter: An Effective Mechanism for Ensuring Compliance with Economic and Social Rights? European Journal of International Law 15(3) (2004): 417–456.
100. *See*, e.g., Virginia Mantouvalou, Panayotis Voyatzis, The Council of Europe and the Protection of Human Rights: A System in Need of Reform. In: Sarah Joseph, Adam McBeth, editors. 'Research Handbook on International Human Rights Law'. Edward Elgar Publishing, 2010. pp. 326–352; *see also* Jean Petaux, Democracy and Human Rights for Europe: The Council of Europe's Contribution. Council of Europe, 2009, p. 263; Bob Deacon, Global Social Policy: International Organizations and the Future of Welfare. SAGE, 1997, p. 83.
101. The possibility of individual claims was highly anticipated by scholars and their necessity during times of crisis has been consistently emphasised. *See* O'Connell. Vindicating Socio-Economic Rights: International Standards and Comparative Experiences. London and New York: Routledge, 2012, p. 44.

ICESCR since the adoption of the Optional Protocol to International Covenant on Economic Social and Cultural Rights concern the right to a fair wage.[102]

Turning to other possible avenues of protecting the right to a decent wage, we find that '[i]t is barely hinted at in the sphere of the so-called four pillars of the Decent Work Agenda promoted by the ILO on a worldwide scale since 1999, the guarantee of an adequate wage is completely absent from the first EU formulations regarding the objective of (more and) better jobs pursued by the EU since 2000 within the so-called Lisbon strategy'.[103]

In fact, the right to a decent wage was left outside the scope of the fundamental principles of ILO.[104] Although the ILO Constitution mentions the necessity of an adequate living wage, but ILO Conventions on wage protection do not mention this notion.[105]

In such circumstances, the potential in any ECtHR elaboration on the concepts of 'insufficient means to live' and the possibility of considering relevant claims under Article 3, which prohibits (among other things) inhuman and degrading treatment, could provide employees with a new avenue by which to protect their right to obtaining fair remuneration on an international level. It could also offer interpretive support to the national courts, dealing with these matters.

As the ECtHR has recently noted in its Grand Chamber judgment in *Bouyid v. Belgium*: 'The prohibition of torture and inhuman or degrading treatment or punishment is a value of civilisation closely bound up with respect for human dignity'.[106] In the same judgment it pointed out that respect for human dignity forms part of the very essence of the ECHR.[107]

The ECtHR has already referred to Article 3 in cases concerning social rights[108] and scholars predict the strengthening of this trend.[109] In fact, the concept of human dignity has become a very 'attractive' normative concept,[110] capable of justifying

102. *See* the list of pending cases on the official site of the Committee: http://www.ohchr.org/EN/HRBodies/CESCR/Pages/PendingCases.aspx (accessed on 23 September 2015).
103. Lo Faro, Antonio, Is a Decent Wage Part of a decent Job? Answers from an Enlarged Europe. WP CSDLE 'Massimo D'Antona'(2008): 18. Available at: http://aei.pitt.edu/13699/1/lofaro_n64-2008int.pdf (accessed 20 May 2015).
104. *See* ILO Declaration on Fundamental Principles and Rights at Work (1998); Zimmer, J. Michael, Decent Work with a Living Wage In: Roger Blanpain, Michele Tiraboschi, editors. 'Global Labor Market: From Globalization To Flexicurity'. Kluwer Law International BV, 2008, pp. 61–80 (the author proposed to complement fundamental principles by the right to living wage).
105. ILO Minimum Wage Fixing Convention, 1970 (N 131); ILO Social Policy (Basic Aims and Standards) Convention, 1962 (N117). It is interesting to point out that the calculation of adequate earnings is one of thirty criteria elaborated by the ILO for the estimation of decent work, *see* Anker R. et al., Measuring Decent Work with Statistical Indicators. International Labour Review (2003). T. 142. No. 2. pp. 147–178.
106. ECtHR, Bouyid v. Belgium [GC] (23380/09) 28 September 2015, para. 83.
107. *Ibid.*, para. 89.
108. ECtHR, M.S.S. v. Belgium and Greece [GC] (30696/09) 21 January 2011; Larioshina v. Russia (56869/00) 23 April 2002; Budina v. Russia (45603/05) 18 June 2009.
109. Tulkens Françoise, The European Convention on Human Rights and the Economic Crisis: the Issue of Poverty. EUI Working papers, AEL 2013/8; N. Napoletano, *see supra* note 63.
110. Weisstub Honor, Dignity, and the Framing of Multiculturalist Values In: David Kretzmer, Eckart Klein, editors. 'Concept of Human Dignity in Human Rights Discourse'. Springer Netherlands, 2002, p. 265.

before the national and international courts the expansion of certain rights. It is widely acknowledged that economic and social rights are essential to the concept of human dignity.[111] In two cases against Russia, the ECtHR stated a very important thing – that a wholly insufficient amount of pension and social benefits may raise an issue under Article 3 of the ECHR.[112]

Even though it is rather questionable whether the ECtHR might conclude the same in respect of a 'wholly insufficient' wage, these decisions impose a new, positive social obligation on the state in the context of Article 3, which, if further developed, might have deepened impact on employment law as well.

It is necessary to mention the general approach of the ECtHR to the violations of this article. According to the Strasbourg case law, degrading treatment violates Article 3 if it attains a 'minimum level of severity'. This threshold is reached where ill-treatment involves actual bodily injury or intense physical or mental suffering, or humiliates or debases an individual, showing a lack of respect for, or diminishing, his or her human dignity.[113] Applying this principle the ECtHR noted that the applicants in two cases against Russia failed to provide sufficient evidence that the low pension had caused damage to the respective applicants' physical or mental health.[114] The applications were declared inadmissible, even though the sum of the pensions were about EUR 15 in *Larioshina*, and about EUR 50 in the case of *Budina*.

Let us imagine a civil servant residing in a remote area of Russia, where there is no employment opportunity other than with the civil service, which pays about 35% of the average national wages.[115] As a result of not having sufficient funds to pay for medical treatments, the civil servant's health suffers. The civil servant, having unsuccessfully pursued domestic legal avenues, brings a claim to the ECtHR, claiming that the State violated its Article 3 obligations to prohibit degrading treatment. In this hypothetical case, the applicant would bring evidence of the damage to her health and will establish an irrefutable link between the damage and the fact that her low wage directly caused her inability to obtain medical treatment that could have arrested the harm suffered to her health.

Should the ECtHR approach this case in a bold way and find a violation of Article 3, or should it rather leave a wide margin of appreciation to the State in establishing the

111. *See* Art. 23(3) of the Universal Declaration of Human Rights, *see also* Oscar Schachter, Human Dignity as a Normative Concept. The American Journal of International Law 77(4) (1983): 851, Conor Gearty, Virginia Mantouvalou, Debating Social Rights. Bloomsbury Publishing, 2010.
112. ECtHR, Larioshina v. Russia (56869/00) 23 April 2002; Budina v. Russia (45603/05) 18 June 2009.
113. ECtHR, Price v. The UK (33394/96) 10 July 2001; V. v. UK (24888/94) 16 December 1999; T.M. and C.M. v. The Republic of Moldova (26608/11) 28 January 2014, para. 35.
114. ECtHR, Larioshina v. Russia (56869/00) 23 April 2002; Budina v. Russia (45603/05) 18 June 2009.
115. Recent reports of the Russian Federal State Statistics Service clearly demonstrate that the situation is wide-spread, thus only the possibility to commence a relevant application to the ECtHR remains hypothetical. *See*: The results of the federal statistical observation in the field of remuneration of certain categories of social workers in 2014 (Itogi federal'nogo statisticheskogo nablyudeniya v sfere oplaty truda otdel'nykh kategoriy rabotnikov sotsial'noy sfery i nauki za 2014 god). Available at: http://www.gks.ru/free_doc/new_site/population/trud/itog_monitor/itog-monitor4-14.html (accessed 20 July 2015).

remuneration of civil servants? Obviously, the first option is less probable. However there is an opportunity for the ECtHR to take that bolder option if it follows the tradition to refer to other international instruments (such as they did in the *Demir and Baikara* case). Thus might it find support for such an innovative interpretation of Article 3 in the provisions of the ESC and any relevant conclusions of the ECSR.

§8.05 CONCLUSIONS

It has been illustrated in this section that the ECtHR's jurisprudence on the wage protection is rather modest, but nevertheless contributes to the protection of employees' rights. It entitles them to bring claims concerning the lack of payment before the ECtHR, alleging the reduction of wages or excessive deductions. This possibility, even if it is subject to numerous conditions, is very important as it provides an additional chance to confront the state as an employer and make it respect fundamental social rights.

Human rights litigation based on property rights has an ideological purpose, insofar as it has the potential to make workers collectively aware of and reflect upon their legal entitlements and their moral claims.[116] In addition, the ECtHR's jurisprudence urges national courts to consider the issue of proportionality where an interference with the employee's rights is justified by the state on the basis of advancing the public interests. It proposes a concept of 'excessive burden' (even if it needs further elaboration), which permits one to outline the margin of appreciation of the states in the adoption of the austerity measures.

116. Novitz Tonia, Labour Rights and Property Rights: Implications for (and Beyond) Redundancy Payments and Pensions? Industrial Law Journal 41 (2012): 153.

CHAPTER 9

Occupational Safety in the Jurisprudence of the ECtHR: Current Cases and Perspectives

Occupational safety matters are traditionally dealt with in ILO Conventions and in the ESC. Domestic labour legislation stipulates detailed provisions on the safety of employees. However, the ECtHR has in some recent cases determined important gaps in the OSH protection of certain countries, by approaching this matter from the human rights point of view. The ECtHR developed its legal positions on OSH protection on the basis of a wide interpretation of the rights to life; respect for private life; and for fair trial.

In *Brincat and Others v. Malta*[117] it deduced from Articles 2 and 8 the right of employees to access information concerning risks they are exposed to and the right to protection from dangerous industrial activities. In *Pereira Henriques v. Luxembourg*[118] and *Howald Moor and others v. Switzerland*,[119] the ECtHR established requirements to investigate workplace accidents and the procedural rights of victims of OHS injuries.

These judgments are a result of the ECtHR's thorough research of the content of the positive obligation to protect employees from dangerous activities, which emerged in the 'environmental' cases, and the positive obligation to provide information about the risks and establishment of procedural rights of victims of OSH accidents or diseases caused by one's profession.

The research of OSH matters in the ECtHR jurisprudence will be set out in the following structure: the first section of this part will deal with cases where the content of these positive duties was elaborated. The second section will reflect on the potential of the ECtHR's legal positions for the development of protection from emerging PSR at domestic levels.

117. ECtHR, Brincat and others v. Malta (60908/11 et al.) 24 July 2014.
118. ECtHR, Pereira Henriques v. Luxembourg (60255/00) 9 May 2006.
119. ECtHR, Howald Moor and others v. Switzerland (52067/10 and 41072/11) 11 March 2014.

§9.01 POSITIVE OBLIGATIONS OF THE STATE IN THE FIELD OF OSH

As early as in 1994, in the case of *Lopez Ostra v. Spain*[120] which concerned severe environmental pollution, the ECtHR interpreted Article 8 as including the right to protection from dangerous activities. The scope of the corresponding positive obligation of the states was developed in *Öneryıldız v. Turkey*,[121] which concerned the death of nine relatives of the applicant caused by a methane explosion. In this decision, the ECtHR stated that where dangerous activities are concerned, 'special emphasis must be placed on the regulations geared to the special features of the activity in question, particularly with regard to the level of the potential risk to human lives'.[122] These regulations, in the opinion of the ECtHR, must govern the licensing, setting up, operation, security and supervision of the activity and must make it compulsory for all those concerned to take practical measures to ensure the effective protection of citizens whose lives might be endangered by the inherent risks.'[123] In later cases the ECtHR pointed out that in the context of dangerous activities, the scope of the positive obligations under Articles 2 and 8 of the ECHR largely overlap.[124] The general message of these judgments is that an industrial activity (set up by private or public funds) must operate under health and safety standards.[125]

In later cases, the ECtHR specified its approach to the standards of OSH protection. *Vilnes and others v. Norway*[126] concerned complaints by divers that they were disabled as a result of diving in the North Sea for oil companies during a pioneer period of oceanic oil exploration (from 1965 to 1990). The ECtHR, having considered in detail the finding of the national courts, decided that the respondent State had already gone to some lengths in their efforts to secure the divers' safety and health; taking a wide range of measures, and in so doing they acted consistently with their positive obligations not only under Article 2 but also under Article 8 of the ECHR.[127]

In particular, the ECtHR emphasised that the State had adopted a *regulatory framework* which showed that the authorities sought to protect divers' safety responsibly and to actively improve the protection of their safety; that the publicly funded supervision had not been organised in an irresponsible manner; that the authorities had in the main been aware of the North Sea divers' working conditions;[128] and that the State set up special compensation schemes under which divers were eligible to apply

120. ECtHR, López Ostra v. Spain (16798/90) 9 December 1994.
121. ECtHR, Oneryildiz v. Turkey (48939/99) 18 June 2002.
122. *Ibid.*, para. 90.
123. *See also* Guerra and others v. Italy (14967/89) 19 February 1998; Tatar v. Romania (67021/01) 27 January 2009, Budayeva and others v. Russia (15339/02 et al.) 20 March 2008, Fadeyeva v. Russia (55723/00) 9 June 2005. *See* more about the positive duties of the State in respect of protection from dangerous industrial activities in Xenos Dimitris, Asserting the Right to Life (Article 2, ECHR) in the Context of Industry. German Law Journal 8(3): 231–254.
124. ECtHR, Kolyadenko and others v. Russia (17423/05 et al.) 28 February 2012, para. 212; Budayeva and others v. Russia, para. 133.
125. Dimitris Xenos, The Positive Obligations of the State Under the European Convention of Human Rights. Routledge, 2012, p. 3.
126. ECtHR, Vilnes and others v. Norway (52806/09 22703/10) 5 December 2013.
127. ECtHR, Vilnes and others v. Norway, para. 232.
128. *Ibid.*, para. 224.

for substantial amounts of compensation.[129] Therefore, the ECtHR's paid special regard to the availability and quality of the OSH legal framework for the protection of the divers, the quality of supervision over OSH matters, and the ability to seek compensation for damages suffered as a result of performing this dangerous work.

In *Brincat and others v. Malta*, the ECtHR developed its views on the due realisation of positive duties of the State in the field of OSH. The judgment concerned twenty-one applications of former workers of the public ship repair yard who had been exposed to asbestos from the 1950s and 1960s to the early 2000s. The State was held responsible for breaching its positive obligations to protect the applicants' right to life and the right to respect for private life. A violation of the right to life was found where the employee's death was caused by exposure to asbestos. Where employees had suffered from different diseases, the ECtHR found a violation of the right to respect for private and family life. It is interesting to follow the arguments of the State and the way the ECtHR considered those submissions.

Malta stated that at the time of the relevant events, it was not aware about the danger of asbestos; however, it had nevertheless provided the workers with protective masks and entitled them to additional payment to work with asbestos. In addition, Malta had adopted special legislation as soon as it became aware of the dangers arising from exposure to asbestos.

The ECtHR did not agree that all three submissions absolved the State of their responsibilities. It emphasised the importance of setting OSH norms in the domestic legislation.[130] Evaluating the Maltese legislative framework for employee protection from dangerous activities, the ECtHR for the first time specified its view on features required of OSH law: they must be well-timed; contain practical measures of protection; and must be implemented in practice.

The ECtHR's view on practical measures was also clarified. The use of protective masks, which the State regarded as a protective measure, was not considered to be sufficient protection for workers. It is interesting to note that this consideration was based on an expert's conclusions drawn in a national case heard by a Maltese court in 1989. This case concerned the death of a worker in 1979 who was exposed to asbestos in the ship-yard. The ECtHR cited the findings of experts and decided that these masks were of 'inadequate quality' and 'did not take sufficient account of the state of scientific knowledge about the subject matter at the relevant time'.[131] This finding can be understood as imposing an obligation on the states to ensure OSH protection should correspond with the level of scientific knowledge in any given field at a particular time.

According to the ECtHR case law, the violation of the positive obligation of the State to protect rights under Article 2 or Article 8 of the ECHR might be found in situations where the State knew or ought to have known about the danger.[132] As the ECtHR stated in *Opuz v. Turkey*: 'The scope of positive obligations under article 3 must

129. *Ibid.*, para. 231.
130. Brincat and others v. Malta, para. 112.
131. *Ibid.*
132. *See*, for example, ECtHR, Keeffe v. Ireland (35810/09) 28 January 2014, para. 144 or Öneryildiz v. Turkey (48939/99) 18 June 2002, para. 62.

be interpreted in a way which does not impose an impossible or disproportionate burden on the authorities.'[133] In *Brincat* Malta argued that it did not know about the danger of asbestos. The ECtHR, however, found that Malta ought to have been aware of the problem of asbestos from the 1970s. This conclusion was based on three main pillars: (1) The ILO Convention and Recommendation adopted in 1986[134] and NOT ratified by Malta; (2) The decision by the domestic courts where the employer was held liable for the death of a ship-yard worker in 1979 as result of exposure to asbestos; and (3) The state of scientific knowledge of the medical problems connected with exposure to asbestos.

Although the ILO Convention on the use of asbestos was adopted only in 1986, the ECtHR took into account ILO activities in this sphere stating that:

> the adoption of such texts comes after considerable preparatory work which may take significant time, and in the ambit of the ILO after having undertaken meetings with representatives of governments, and employers' and workers' organizations of all member countries of the organization.[135]

The ECtHR concluded that Malta as an ILO member could not be unaware of the problematic issue of the use of asbestos even before the adoption of Convention No. 162.

Considering the state of scientific knowledge of the dangers of asbestos, it took account of the list, submitted by the applicants, which contained references to hundreds of articles or other publications concerning the subject at issue published from 1930 onwards.[136] The ECtHR found inconceivable that there was no State access to any such sources of information, at the very minimum, by the highest medical authorities in the country who had an obligation to remain abreast of scientific developments and to advise the Government accordingly.

The fact that Malta was found responsible for the damage to the employees' health – in spite of the lack of direct evidence that it was aware of the danger of asbestos – demonstrates that the ECtHR imposes very rigorous requirements in the field of OSH.

[A] The Scope of the Positive Obligation to Provide Information

The positive duty of the State to provide information about the risk that the person is exposed to was deduced from Article 8 of the ECHR, which guarantees the right to respect for private and family life. This wide interpretation did not originate immediately but was rather the result of a slow and developmental process. It began with the 'environmental' case of *Guerra and Others v. Italy*,[137] where the ECtHR indirectly mentioned the right to assess risk factors connected with the activity of a nearby chemical factory. In *McGinley and Egan v. UK*, the ECtHR was more firm and directly

133. ECtHR, Opuz v. Turkey (33401/02) 9 June 2009, para. 129.
134. ILO Asbestos Recommendation, R 172; ILO Asbestos Convention C 162 (1986).
135. ECtHR, Brincat and others v. Malta, para. 105.
136. *Ibid.*, para. 106.
137. ECtHR, Guerra and others v. Italy (14967/89) 19 February 1998.

stated that 'where a Government engages in hazardous activities ...respect for private and family life under Article 8 requires that an effective and accessible procedure be established which enables such persons to seek all relevant and appropriate information.'[138] The same conclusion was reached in the later case of *Roche v. UK*.[139]

The most significant development of the ECtHR's approach to a person's right to access information concerning the risks he or she is exposed to can be found in *Vilnes and others v. Norway*. Both the divers in this case, as well as the respondent State, were not provided with information about decompression periods used by private enterprises, as decompression tables were recognised as confidential. The ECtHR stated that the State's positive obligation to provide access to essential information enabling individuals to assess risks to their health and lives may, in certain circumstances, also encompass a duty to provide such information.[140] The State argued that at the relevant time it did not possess enough information about the influence of decompression periods upon the health of divers. The ECtHR held that:

> it would therefore have been reasonable for the authorities to take the precaution of ensuring that the companies observe full transparency about the diving tables used and that the applicants ... receive information on the differences between tables, as well as on their concerns for the divers' safety and health, which constituted essential information that they needed to be able to assess the risk to their health and to give informed consent to the risks involved.[141]

It concluded that there had been a violation of Article 8 of the ECHR on account of the failure of the respondent State to ensure that the applicants received essential information regarding decompression tables enabling them to assess the risks to their health and safety.[142] It is interesting to note that the decision of majority was criticised by dissenting judges as imposing an 'unrealistic burden' on the authorities due to the lack of medical information at the relevant time.[143]

In the *Brincat* case the ECtHR took a step forward, developing the scope of the right for OSH information under the ECHR. The ECtHR noted that the State, seemingly oblivious to the obligations arising from the ECHR, opted to consider that it was not their responsibility to provide information at the outset and that anyone in such a work environment would in any case be fully aware of the hazards involved.[144] It emphasised that Maltese legislation failed to establish a duty to provide information on the dangers of exposure to asbestos and that the State had not undertaken any research about asbestos specifically. Considering the State's submissions, the ECtHR found that neither the distribution of the protective masks nor the reference to the OHS activities could be regarded as a sufficient source of information. Thus, the ECtHR focused again

138. ECtHR, McGinley and Egan v. UK (21825/93, 23414/94) 9 June 1998, para. 101.
139. ECtHR, Roche v. UK (32555/96) 19 October 2005, para. 167.
140. ECtHR, Vilnes and others v. Norway, para. 235.
141. ECtHR, Vilnes and others v. Norway, para. 244.
142. *Ibid.*, para. 245.
143. Partly Dissenting Opinion Of Judge Nordén, Joined By Judge Lorenzen to the judgments in Vilnes and others v. Norway.
144. ECtHR, Brincat and others v. Malta, para. 114.

on the importance of the legislative framework and made clear that studies or reports on OSH dangers should form a part of the positive obligation to provide information.

[B] The Requirement to Investigate Occupational Accidents and the Procedural Rights of Victims

The ECtHR has stated on numerous occasions that the right to life involves a primary duty of the State to put in place effective criminal-law provisions to deter the commission of offences against persons which must be backed up by adequate law-enforcement machinery to prevent, suppress and punish breaches of such provisions.[145]

In the recent case *Bakanova v. Lithuania,*[146] the Court considered the failure of State authorities to duly investigate the death of the applicant's husband (V.B.) on board the ship where he had been working as mechanic. The case is rather particular as the death took place on a Lithuanian private ship during a voyage to Brazil. Brazilian authorities issued a death certificate mentioning an acute heart attack as the cause of death. The body, embalmed in chemicals and put in a zinc coffin, was then shipped to Lithuania, which it reached in two months.

The applicants claim to recognise the death of her husband as a work accident were dismissed in administrative proceedings and criminal proceeding were discontinued, although much evidence was brought to demonstrate the poor working conditions on the ship, such as breaking down of the main engine which caused leaks of dangerous gases. These gases might have been the cause of V.B.'s heart attack.[147]

Ms Bakanova alleged that the experts had not been able to definitely confirm that her husband had died of a heart attack, as his body had been quickly embalmed without an autopsy being carried out. She also pointed to shortcomings in the investigation, such as the absence of blood test results and toxicology tests, the lack of documents concerning safety at work on the ship, the fact that the ship's logbooks had not been obtained and that the ship had not been inspected after her husband's death.

The Court pointed that the investigation was required to consider the broader context of V.B.'s working conditions on the ship, in order to assess whether there was a link between the allegations of hazardous working conditions and his death.[148]

The Court found that the criminal proceedings were essentially relying on a fairly limited amount of evidence, and were accepting the fact that V.B. had died of heart attack and the Lithuanian authorities made no effort to instruct the owner of the ship to bring it back to Lithuania, where it could be properly examined. It also paid attention to the fact that, in spite of the applicant's claims, the documents relevant to the working conditions on the ship were destroyed after the purchase of the ship by another

145. ECtHR, Osman v. The United Kingdom (23452/94) 28 October 1998, para. 115; Keenan v. The United Kingdom (27229/95) 3 April 2001, para. 89; Slimani v. France (57671/00) 27 July 2004, para. 29.
146. ECtHR, Bakanova v. Lithuania (11167/12) 31 May 2016.
147. *Ibid.*, paras 15, 31.
148. *Ibid.*, para. 68.

company.[149] These circumstances lead to the conclusion that Lithuanian authorities failed to conduct an effective investigation into V.B.'s death and thus violated a procedural facet of Article 2. The requirements of the Court to the due investigation of the death are evidently relevant to the investigation of occupational accidents.

In *Pereira Henriques v. Luxembourg*,[150] the Court directly established the necessity of effective investigations in respect of occupational accidents. The applicants complained that there had been no effective investigation into the circumstances of the death of their husband and father, who was killed during such an occupational incident. They also argued that they had been denied access to a court (Article 6) that there was a lack of effective remedy (Article 13) because the Social Insurance Code of Luxemburg did not give the victims of occupational accident or their successors standing to sue for damages against an employer in relation to that accident, except in the case of accidents at work caused intentionally.

The ECtHR noted that authorities were required to take any reasonable steps available to them to ensure relevant evidence relating to the facts in question is taken, including such matters as, *inter alia*, testimonies, expertise and, if necessary, conducting an autopsy which provides a complete and accurate record of injury and an objective analysis of clinical findings, including the cause of death.[151] It considered that the prosecution, deciding not to appoint an expert, prevented the clarification of the cause of the occupational accident and found that the State's investigation was therefore not effective, violating the procedural aspect of Article 2 of the ECHR.[152]

It also found the violation of Article 13 as the State had failed to show that the applicants had had an effective remedy by which to seek compensation following the State's ineffective investigation.[153] The ECtHR emphasised that Article 13 requires, in addition to the payment of compensation where appropriate, a thorough and effective investigation capable of leading to the identification and punishment of the persons responsible for the death and including effective access for the complainant to the investigation procedure.[154]

Therefore Article 13, in conjunction with Article 2, imposes on States the duty to effectively investigate occupational accidents and to ensure the rights of victims or their next-of-kin to legal protections including access to relevant procedures.

In more recent cases, *Sidika İmren v. Turkey*[155] and *Mircea Pop v. Romania*[156] the Court found the violation of the procedural aspect of the Article 2 as the respondent States failed to ensure effective investigation of the circumstances of occupational accidents, which led to the death of the applicants' relatives.

In *Sidika İmren v. Turkey* the applicant, whose daughter suffered serious injuries as a result of a fire at her workplace and died in the hospital, complained of the

149. *Ibid.*, paras 70–72.
150. ECtHR, Pereira Henriques v. Luxembourg (60255/00) 9 May 2006.
151. *Ibid.*, para. 57.
152. *Ibid.*, para. 62.
153. *Ibid.*, para. 91.
154. *Ibid.*, para. 87.
155. ECtHR, Sidika İmren v. Turkey (47384/11) 13 September 2016.
156. ECtHR, Mircea Pop v. Romania (43885/13) 19 July 2016.

excessive length of the criminal proceedings, which had resulted in the offence in question becoming time-barred, as well as of the length of the civil proceedings.

The Court examined whether either of those remedies satisfied the State's obligation under Article 2 to provide an effective judicial system and found that neither of remedies was provided in a way coherent with the ECHR. Criminal proceedings were excessively long and did not establish the accountability of those responsible for the death of the applicant's daughter.[157] While civil procedure was not carried out with reasonable expedition. The labour court was mostly inactive for the first ten years of the proceedings awaiting the results of criminal procedure even though the civil courts in Turkey are not bound by the findings of the criminal courts.[158] In these circumstance the Court found the of the State's procedural obligation under Article 2.

The applicant in *Mircea Pop v. Romania* complained of a lack of effectiveness and delays of the investigation in criminal proceeding brought against the employer. The applicant's son, a welder, employed by a private company, was found dead at the workplace (a ship under construction where he worked alone). According to the medical certificate he died a violent death by electrocution. The labour inspectorate imposed a fine on the employer on the grounds that the accident had been caused by inappropriate use of the electric lamp, that the victim had not received work safety training and that he had not been provided with the appropriate security equipment. However, Mr Pop's criminal complaints were dismissed by national courts, which established that the *death had been caused by the victim's own negligence*.

Before the ECtHR the applicant alleged that the employer did not comply with the legal provisions relating to safety at work, especially in training and provision of safety equipment, and the authorities ignored this situation. He also claimed that the State did not appropriately investigate the circumstances of the accident.[159]

The Court found that the length of criminal proceedings was excessive as the applicant's claim was considered by local courts and by the Court of Appeal during more than seven years. It was also concerned with the fact that the first designated expert deplored the destruction of objects that could be used as evidence, and, although the Court of First Instance and the prosecutor established the need to appoint a new expertise, prosecutors did not respond to the refusal of the criminal expertise laboratory of Bucharest to perform it.[160]

The ECtHR was convinced that these facts prevented clarification of the circumstances in which the victim died on his workplace when he was performing tasks without safety equipment and, furthermore, equipped with defective tools, and found the violation of procedural aspect of Article 2.

It is remarkable that this case was not about claiming damages or about investigation of the occupational accidents for the purposes of obtaining social security benefits, as in *Pereira Henriques v. Luxembourg*. The Court itself pointed in 2011, that positive obligation to ensure effective investigation under Article 2 does not necessarily

157. ECtHR, Sidika Imren v. Turkey (47384/11) 13 September 2016, para. 62.
158. *Ibid.*, para. 64.
159. ECtHR, Mircea Pop v. Romania (43885/13) 19 July 2016, para. 64.
160. *Ibid.*, para. 83.

require the provision of a criminal-law remedy in every case. Dissenting judge Sajó criticised the decision of the majority, specifying that 'the Court should not encourage applicants to pursue criminal procedures in cases of death from negligence'.[161] In the opinion of this judge, 'insisting on and the initiation of criminal investigations in private litigation, under cover of the positive obligation of the State to protect the life, will only result in a poor use of limited resources in terms of investigations and prosecutions'.

The right to fair trial was also found relevant to OSH matters in several cases. The ECtHR has considered factors including the length of proceedings related to establishing the existence of occupational disease[162] and the impossibility to challenge conclusions of special medical commissions on the non-occupational character of an applicant's disease.[163]

In *I.D. v. Bulgaria*, the ECtHR found the violation of the right for fair trial as the Bulgarian courts were precluded from conducting their own examination of the causal link between the applicant's working conditions and her illness, and were not free to determine its occupational or non-occupational character after it had been declared not work-related by the special medical commissions.[164]

In *Howald Moor and others v. Switzerland*,[165] the ECtHR deduced from Article 6 a rule which is particularly important for OSH protection. The applicants were the next-of-kin of a worker who had been exposed to asbestos from 1965 until at least 1978. The worker died in 2005 from malignant pleural mesothelioma. They claimed that the limitation periods stipulated by the domestic law applicable at the time violated their right to fair trial, as there was no real opportunity for persons suffering from asbestos-related diseases to claim damages before the expiration of the limitation period.

The ECtHR considered that in cases where it was scientifically proven that an individual could not know that he or she was suffering from a particular disease, that fact should be taken into account in calculating the limitation period.[166] It held that the systematic application of the rule on limitation periods, to persons suffering from diseases which could not be diagnosed until many years after the triggering events, deprived those persons of the chance to assert their rights before the Courts and thus violated the right guaranteed under Article 6 of the ECHR.[167]

The ECtHR's view as expressed in *Moor* might enhance the chances of judicial protection of the rights of employees who were exposed to dangerous or harmful conditions at work, which have a long-term effect upon their health and who suffer from occupational diseases. It is important to note that the revision of the provisions of

161. *Ibid.*, dissenting opinion of Judge Sajó, para. 17.
162. ECtHR, Bykov v. Ukraine (26675/07) 16 April 2009; Vaas v. Germany (20271/05) inadmissible 26 March 2009.
163. ECtHR, I.D. v. Bulgaria (43578/98) 28 April 2005.
164. *Ibid.*, paras 46–50.
165. ECtHR, Howald Moor and others v. Switzerland (52067/10 and 41072/11) 11 March 2014.
166. *Ibid.*, para, 78.
167. ECtHR, Howald Moor and others v. Switzerland, para. 77.

the Swiss Code of obligations on limitation periods is on-going.[168] The analysis of the ECtHR's case law on OSH matters was based on several judgments, much fewer than in respect of discrimination or the protection of employee privacy in the workplace. However, judgments considered in this section clearly demonstrate that the ECtHR is willing to deal with OSH matters in light of the rights to life, to respect for private life and for fair trial. It has established the set of the basic positive duties of the States in the field of OSH, which are equally applicable to all the countries of the CoE. Such a wide coverage makes us question whether the ECtHR's approach might be helpful for the development of OSH protection, for example, in establishing protection from PSR in countries where such risks are not recognised yet.

§9.02 POTENTIAL OF THE ECTHR'S LEGAL POSITIONS FOR THE DEVELOPMENT OF PROTECTION FROM PSYCHOSOCIAL RISKS ON THE DOMESTIC LEVEL

PSR are acknowledged by OSH specialists and policymakers as one of the growing key challenges in Europe.[169] There are European Directives[170] related to the ability to treat harassment as discrimination, soft law instruments on stress and harassment.[171] Domestic approaches to the protection of employees from these types of risks, which are far from being exhaustively defined, continue to differ within Europe states. Most evidently, they differ within the CoE, where some countries have a well-elaborated mechanism of protection from harassment and stress (e.g., France, Belgium) while others have not yet recognised such risks as being inherent at the workplace (e.g., Russia, Ukraine).

The ILO has contributed to the scientific research of this topic;[172] however, ILO Conventions on OSH do not explicitly recognise PSR as inherent in the workplace.

Are there any international norms which could be used for the development of protection from PSR in the countries where such risks are not recognised? The ECHR stipulates such norms and certain legal positions taken by the ECtHR represent general pillars of protection from PSR, that might be used by the members of the CoE.

168. Peter Loser, Switzerland. European Tort Law Yearbook 3(1) (2014): 673–698.

169. *See* Survey of Enterprises on New and Emerging Risks (ESENER). European Risk Observatory Report: European Agency for Safety and Health at Work 2010. Available from: https://osha.europa.eu/en/publications/reports/esener1_osh_management/view. (accessed 20 March 2014).

170. Council Directive 2000/78/EC of 27 November 2000 establishing a general framework for equal treatment in employment and occupation; Directive 2006/54/EC of the European Parliament and of the Council of 5 July 2006 on the implementation of the principle of equal opportunities and equal treatment of men and women in matters of employment and occupation (recast); Council Directive 2000/43/EC of 29 June 2000 implementing the principle of equal treatment between persons irrespective of racial or ethnic origin.

171. European framework agreement on harassment and violence at work (2007); European framework agreement on work-related stress (2004).

172. Psychosocial Factors At Work: Recognition and control. Report of the Joint ILO/WHO Committee on Occupational Health. Occup Saf Health Ser. No. 56; 1986; Mental health in the workplace. Geneva: ILO, 2000; Global strategy on occupational safety and health. Conclusions adopted by the International Labour Conference at its 91st Session, 2003. Geneva: ILO, 2004.

In the only case which had direct relevance to PSR at work, *Doloupoulos v. Greece*,[173] the Court considered the claim of the bank manager, who had a psychiatric illness and severe depression which, in his view, were caused in part by harassing tactics on the part of his managers. He alleged that the State violated Article 2 and 3 of the ECHR as it did not include mental illness in the list of occupational diseases. The Court decided to consider the case under Article 8 as, in its opinion, the degrading treatment in this case did not attain a minimum level of severity in order to fall within Article 3.[174] It, however, did not consider in detail the alleged mistreatment of Mr Doloupoulos.

According to the applicant, the management of the bank had numerously transferred him without paying in full the benefits to which he was entitled, his work was assessed in an unjust and humiliating way and he was reproached for his absence despite the fact that the bank was aware of his illness. On 15 July 2011 the applicant collapsed at the entrance to the bank. He was immediately brought to the hospital where he was diagnosed of recurrent panic attacks due to anxiety-provoking work environment and received treatment during thirty days. In sum, according to the applicant, he was unable to work for 311 days.

The bank did not declare the applicant's illness to the Labour Inspectorate as psychiatric illnesses, including those linked to stress at work, were not regarded as occupational diseases.

Further investigations of Mr Doloupoulos complaint by the public prosecutor established that he had not brought proceedings against the bank in the civil courts in order to complain of a deterioration in his working conditions. The Court of Appeal dismissed applicant's claim as it found that there was no evidence establishing a causal link between his illness and the conduct of the bank's management.

The applicant also lodged a complaint for harassment with the Regional Centre for the Prevention of Occupational Hazards, claiming that bank managers and the company doctor had been responsible for his serious psychiatric illness because of the pressure they had placed him under at work and their behaviour towards him. Having considered this claim the Labour Inspectorate had issued a report stating that it was difficult to establish a link between a psychiatric illness and the working conditions.[175]

The Court stated that the application raised the question of a gap in domestic law: the lack of the recognition of mental illnesses as occupational diseases. It further pointed that it is not it's task to substitute for competent authorities and determine the illnesses that should be included in the list of occupational diseases. It estimated in the light of the Convention the decisions of the Greek courts. The Court attached attention to the fact that in none of domestic proceedings a link between the mental illness of the applicant and his work was established. It underlined that in spite of the absence of mental illnesses in national labour legislation the applicant had had avenues available to him by which to complain of the deterioration of his mental health at work and, if appropriate, to obtain compensation for non-pecuniary damage. He used this avenue,

173. ECtHR, Dolopoulos v. Greece (36656/14) 10 December 2015.
174. *Ibid.*, paras 35, 36.
175. ECtHR, Doloupoulos v. Greece, para. 53.

but his claim was dismissed.[176] These findings permitted the Court conclude that the State did not fail to protect the physical and moral integrity of the applicant and did not violate Article 8 of the ECHR.

In this first case on PSR at work the Court might have developed its views on the due legal framework of protection from harassment at work, it might have referred to comparative research of relevant legislations of other European countries and establish that the recognition of mental illnesses as an occupational disease is a growing trend in Europe and might have paid more attention to the applicant's argument, where he cited the ILO Recommendation N194, which recognised mental and behavioural disorders as occupational diseases.[177] The superficiality of the Court's review is comprehensible as the circumstances of the case and the results of the applicant's claims analysis by national courts demonstrate that the acts perceived as harassment by Mr Doloupoulos did not in fact constitute degrading or inhuman treatments.[178] Therefore this decision is not a missed chance to establish the human rights requirements to protection from PSR at work, but a first step towards this direction: it clearly demonstrates that such cases might be brought before the ECtHR both under Article 3 and Article 8.

Although there are no judgments of the ECtHR on the protection of employees from PSR to date, important premises for such protection can be found in the ECtHR's jurisprudence on Articles 2, 3 and 8 of the ECHR. In order to determine the possible approach of the ECtHR to workplace PSR we will analyse cases that have similar features and compare them with the national jurisprudence on protection from harassment and work-related stress.

Article 2

First, Article 2 of the ECHR should be referred to as the recent case law on OSH, discussed in the previous chapter, has formulated a very wide interpretation of this right, imposing on the State a positive duty to ensure employees are protected against occupational risks.[179] But can PSR be considered as inherent risks that endanger lives of employees? Though PSR are the most problematic types of occupational risks, being neither immediate nor evident or clearly predictable, still we can conjecture that cases of suicides at work (e.g., suicides in France Telecom, Orange and Renault[180]) or deaths from heart attacks caused by stress[181] clearly demonstrate the necessity of enlarging the notion of inherent risks.

176. *Ibid.*, para. 48.
177. *Ibid.*, para. 43.
178. The Court mentioned that the applicant had been in confrontation with his manager, was accused of providing a customer with illegal financing and that he was twice summoned before the bank's disciplinary board (para. 54) and his repeating application to Labour Inspections which were also found groundless (para. 24).
179. ECtHR, Vilnes and others v. Norway, Brincat and others v. Malta.
180. K. Willsher. Orange France Investigates Second Wave of Suicides Among Staff. The Guardian. 23 March 2014. Available from: http://www.theguardian.com/business/2014/mar/19/orange-france-investigates-second-wave-suicides (accessed 20 December 2014); Decision of the Court of Appeal of Versailles No. 10/00954, 19 May 2011.
181. Decision of the Italian Supreme Court of Cassation No. 9888, 5 October 1998; Decision of the Italian Supreme Court of Cassation No. 14085, 26 October 2000.

For this reason we consider that the ECtHR's legal position that the State is positively obliged to supervise activities which may cause danger for human life, together with the obligation to take practical measures to ensure effective protection from such dangers, must be taken into account by States subject to the ECtHR's jurisdiction when protecting employees from PSR as well as from any other occupational risks.

The ECtHR's approach developed in *Brincat* and *Vilnes* can be applied in cases where PSR threatens the lives of employees. This might be particularly important for the countries where there is presently no other mechanisms by which employees are protected from PSR, such as Russia, Ukraine or other Eastern European countries of the CoE.

Based on the ECtHR case law, the components required to effectively protect against PSR at work might be as follows: (a) the States' obligation to prevent dangers to life (where it ought to have known about those dangers); (b) the State's obligation to properly investigate the accident; and (c) the State's obligation to ensure there are appropriate avenues by which the victim (or their next-of-kin) may seek redress.

In my opinion, these positive obligations of the State should be fulfilled by recognising PSR as a part of occupational risks. Such recognition would extend the occupational health standards of monitoring and prevention over risks of employee's stress or harassment.

Let us imagine a hypothetical case of a public servant who suffered severe damage from work-related stress and did not succeed in obtaining remedy in her national courts. The ECtHR in such a case should establish whether the State knew, or ought to have known, about the risk of stress in respect of a particular employee. The answer to this question is obvious where the domestic law of the respondent state requires the risk of stress at the workplace to be assessed, as in Italy or France. The situation would be more complicated if the state did not recognise stress as an inherent risk in the workplace and did not provide any legislative framework for protection against such concerns. In my opinion, the ECtHR in such a case could refer to the comparative review of other CoE Member States' laws. Comparative research in such hypothetical cases could lead the ECtHR to the analysis of the European Framework Directive on work-related stress and the experience of its implementation in EU Member States.

This kind of research could reveal that the recognition of stress as an occupational risk is a gaining traction in European countries. In such circumstances, the ECtHR might decide that the State ought to have known about the risk of stress even in the absence of relevant legislation. In this context the ECtHR's judgment in the *Brincat* case is very helpful. The respondent State was held responsible for damages to the employees' health caused by their work with asbestos, even though the domestic occupational health provisions did not recognise the danger to health arising from asbestos exposure.

This theoretical example demonstrates the possible application of Article 2 to cases involving PSR at work. This article can be read as entitling employees to make an appeal to the ECtHR claiming the State's failure to ensure his right to a life that was challenged by PSR at work, such as stress or harassment. It seems possible for applicants who fail to obtain remedy in ordinary domestic criminal or civil proceedings, in cases of death or any other grave consequences of PSR, to lodge an application for review by the ECtHR. Such an application could be lodged, e.g., against Russia. Some shortcomings of Russian investigation processes have been acknowledged by the ECtHR.[182] Russian researches claim serious defects in the system of investigation and judicial approach to the cases of bringing to suicide.[183]

This theoretical possibility is more tangible when public employees are concerned. In these cases the State, as the contracting party responsible for the health and life of employees, has a negative obligation to abstain from actions that may endanger the life of dependents, as well as a positive obligation to ensure its effective protection.

Article 3

Article 3 of the ECHR, prohibiting degrading treatment or punishment, is usually deemed as providing an absolute right for protection from such actions.[184] It might be used as another pillar for protection of employees against workplace PSR.

It is important to analyse the ECtHR's approach to the cases of degrading treatment and punishment as it might be used for the protection of employees from such PSR as moral harassment (mobbing). This provision was initially designed to provide protection against degrading treatment by the State. But as the ECHR is used as a living instrument which must be interpreted in the light of present-day conditions, the ECtHR has reserved to itself sufficient flexibility to address the application of that article in other contexts which might arise.[185] The ECtHR's flexibility is expressed in granting protection from degrading treatment caused by private persons, e.g., in cases of violence against children or domestic violence.[186]

The notion of inhuman or degrading treatment is understood as such treatment that deliberately causes severe suffering, whether it be mental or physical.[187] In recent cases the ECtHR considered that emotional suffering caused by humiliation can amount to a breach of Article 3 of the ECHR.[188] In *Đurđević v. Croatia* it recognised the violation of this provision deciding that the continued harassment of a disabled person which caused the applicant to feel fear and helplessness amounted to degrading treatment.[189] In *Vincent v. France* the ECtHR held that non-intentional degrading

182. ECtHR, Denis Vasilyev v. Russia (32704/04) 17 December 2009.
183. Chukaeva N.G. Ugolovnaya otvetstvennost' za dovedeniye do samoubiystva ili do pokusheniya na samoubiystvo: problemy zakonodatel'nogo regulirovaniya [Criminal liability for bringing to suicide or to attempt to commit suicide: problems of legislative regulation] [dissertation]. Tyumen, 2011.
184. M.K. Addo, N. Grief, Does Article 3 of the European Convention on Human Rights Enshrine Absolute Rights? European Journal of International Law 9 (1998): 510–524.
185. O De Schutter, The Protection of Social Rights by the European Court of Human Rights In: P. Van der Auweraert, T. De Pelsmaeker, J. Sarkin, J. Vande Lanotte, editors. 'Social, Economic and Cultural Rights. an Appraisal of Current European and International Developments'. Antwerpen: Maklu, 2002, p. 217.
186. ECtHR, A. v. The United Kingdom (25599/94) 23 September 1998; O'Keeffe v. Ireland (35810/09) 28 January 2014; Opuz v. Turkey (33401/02) 9 June 2009.
187. ECtHR, Treholt v. Norway (14610/89) 9 July 1991; Toth v. Croatia (64674/01) 9 July 2002.
188. ECtHR, R.R. v. Poland (27617/04) 26 May 2011.
189. ECtHR, Dorđević v. Croatia (41526/10) 24 July 2012.

treatment can also amount to a violation with the ECHR.[190] According to the ECtHR's case law, ill-treatment must attain a minimum level of severity in order to fall within Article 3 of the ECHR. The assessment of this minimum is relative: it depends on all the circumstances of the case, such as the nature and context of the treatment, its duration, and its physical and mental effects and, in some instances, the sex, age and state of health of the victim.[191]

The requirement of severe suffering as a consequence of inhuman behaviour is the main point of difference between the ECtHR's interpretation of degrading treatment, and the notion of moral harassment set out, e.g., in the European directives on discrimination. National approaches to harassment based on other than discriminatory grounds differ: in France employees do not have to provide evidence on the severe consequences of harassment on employees' health,[192] but Italian Courts require employees to prove these consequences in case of mobbing.[193]

This brief comparison makes us presume that actions recognised as harassment or mobbing might constitute a violation of Article 3 of the ECHR if the ECtHR finds that the minimum of severity was reached. There are cases of degrading treatment that seem to have common points with the possible cases of harassment at work. Harassment at work provokes severe suffering as the victim is obliged to stay in the hostile environment. In the cases of vertical harassment the victim is obliged to fulfil the orders of his tormentor and strongly depends on him. These characteristics of harassment have similarities with cases of domestic violence where victims are often considered vulnerable, taking into account their dependence on the perpetrators.[194] These traits are also present in situations where applicants were in a vulnerable position by virtue of being under an authority's control, e.g., conscripted servicemen,[195] who could be compared to some extent with contractual servicemen. In these cases the ECtHR, taking into account the vulnerability of victims, narrows the margin of the appreciation left to of the State and imposes a stricter obligation to create effective protection of the rights under Article 3 of the ECHR.

Therefore, the applicant's vulnerability might strengthen the claim of protection against degrading treatment (harassment) before the ECtHR. There are cases where some employees were considered vulnerable, e.g., HIV-positive employees.[196] The

190. ECtHR, Vincent c. France (6253/03) 24 October 2006.
191. ECtHR, T.M. and C.M. v. The Republic Of Moldova (26608/11) 28 January 2014, para. 35.
192. L. Lerouge, C. Hebert. The Law of Workplace Harassment of the United States, France, and the European Union: Comparative Analysis after the Adoption of France's New Sexual Harassment Law. Comparative Labour Law Policy Journal 35(1) (2013): 110–113.
193. Decision of Italian Supreme Court of Cassation, Social Chamber No. 09-72541, 15 March 2011; Decision of Italian Supreme Court of Cassation, Social Chamber No. 09-42097, 25 January 2011; Decision of the Italian Supreme Court of Cassation No. 2038, 29 January 2013.
194. ECtHR, Opuz v. Turkey; Hajduova v. Slovakia (2660/03) 30 November 2010; Bevacqua and S. v. Bulgaria (71127/01) 12 June 2008.
195. ECtHR, Placì v. Italy (48754/11) 21 January 2014, Chember v. Russia (7188/03) 3 July 2008.
196. ECtHR, I.B. v. Greece (552/10) 3 October 2013.

ECtHR's estimation of an applicant's vulnerability depends largely on the circumstances of the case;[197] however it is rather evident that minors, disabled persons or pregnant women would fall within the category of vulnerable persons in cases about harassment at work. Considering the cases of degrading treatment committed by private individuals, the ECtHR observed that there could be no direct responsibility of the States for the acts of the private individuals.[198] However, the ECtHR's case law leads us to conclude that the States have an obligation to ensure effective protection from degrading and inhuman treatment, also against the violence of other individuals.

In *T.M. and C.M. v. The Republic of Moldova*, the ECtHR stated that States are obliged to maintain and apply in practice an adequate legal framework affording protection against acts of violence by others.[199] In *Opuz v. Turkey*, the ECtHR noted that the scope of positive obligations under Article 3 must be interpreted in a way which does not impose an impossible or disproportionate burden on the authorities, as not every claimed risk of ill-treatment can entail a requirement for authorities to take operational measures to prevent that risk from materialising.[200] For a positive obligation to arise, it must be shown that the authorities knew or ought to have known, at the time of the existence of a real and immediate risk of ill-treatment of an identified individual from the criminal acts of a third party, and that they failed to provide practical and effective protection.[201]

The ECtHR emphasised the importance of ensuring that acts of ill-treatment do not remain ignored by the relevant authorities and that national courts should not, under any circumstances, be prepared to allow life-endangering offences and grave attacks on physical and moral integrity to go unpunished.[202]

Considering the above-mentioned positive obligations of the State in the context of harassment at work, two points of particular importance might be revealed:

(a) The State's liability under Article 3 of the ECHR in cases of harassment is possible, if national authorities knew, or ought to have known, about the ill-treatment or the danger of ill-treatment. In countries where there is no legal framework requiring the protection against workplace PSR, employees could appeal to a competent authority asking it to investigate any relevant criminal offence. The absence of an adequate response on the part of those authorities might constitute the violation of the State's positive obligations.

    The application of Article 3 might be particularly interesting in cases concerning harassment of public employees. As the States have a negative obligation not to behave in inhuman or degrading manner, acts of harassment of subordinate public employees might be considered a violation of this article.

197. L. Peroni, A. Timmer. Vulnerable Groups: The Promise of an Emerging Concept in European Human Rights Convention Law. International Journal of Constitutional Law 4 (2013): 1056–1085.
198. ECtHR, Beganović v. Croatia (46423/06) 25 June 2009, para. 69.
199. ECtHR, T.M. and C.M. v. The Republic Of Moldova, para. 39.
200. ECtHR, Opuz v. Turkey (33401/02) 9 June 2009.
201. ECtHR, Muta v. Ukraine (37246/06) 31 July 2012.
202. *Ibid.*

This conclusion may be especially curious in the case of France. According to French case law, the employer has to secure the occupational security of employees ('sécurité de résultat'); this principle also applies to the protection from PSR at work.[203] In these circumstances the question arises whether the presumed responsibility of an employer, in cases involving the harassment of public servants, can be interpreted by the ECtHR as if the State ought to have known about all actions of harassment, which reached the minimum level of severity? The positive answer to this question might enable public employees to seek protection from harassment by applying to the ECtHR if domestic avenues for redress have been exhausted.

(b) According to the ECtHR's case law, inhuman or degrading treatment must be treated as criminal offences in domestic law. States may be found to have violated their obligations to ensure protection from inhuman or degrading treatment if the crime was reported to the relevant authorities and was poorly investigated or granted insufficient judicial protection was not adequate. These are the prerequisites for claiming State's liability for harassment under Article 3 of the ECHR.

Bringing to suicide and insults are recognised as criminal offences in the majority of the members of the CoE. However, harassment is a broad term and encompasses a wide spectrum of ill-treatments, which by themselves may not amount to criminal offences. European countries have different approaches to penalising harassment: in France, harassment at work is prohibited by Article 222-33-2 of the Criminal Code, which defines 'harcelement moral' in the same way as French Labour Code.[204] In Italy, there is no unique crime that would correspond with harassment, but there is case–law on articles of the Criminal Code prohibiting defamation (Article 595), violence or threat (Article 610), ill-treatment (Article 572). Article 572 of the Italian Criminal Code is particularly interesting as it was designed to protect persons from domestic violence and was entitled 'Maltreatment of family and household members'. This article punishes the mistreatment of family members or other cohabitants, or a person who is under the authority of the perpetrator or entrusted to him for the sake of education, supervision or custody, or in the exercise profession. In a recent case, the ECtHR considered that this article may apply to cases of harassment where the relationship between the employee and the chief are stringent, intense, frequent and characterised by strict subordination of victim to the perpetrator.[205] In Russia, the basis for prosecuting acts of harassment can be found in Article 117 of the Criminal Code,

203. Lerouge L. Suicide du salarié et faute inexcusable de l'employeur: quelles évolutions juridiques? Revue de droit sanitaire et social. 2012(2), pp. 373–387; Lerouge L. Droit de la santé-sécurité et risques psychosociaux au travail: où situer le système français au regard des systèmes étrangers? In: Lerouge L., editor. Les risques psychosociaux au travail en droit social: approche juridique comparée. France - Europe - Canada – Japon. Paris: Dalloz; 2014. pp. 4–19.

204. L. Lerouge, Workplace Bullying and Harassment in France and Few Comparisons with Belgium: A Legal Perspective. JILPT Report 12 (2013): 39–59.

205. Decision of the Tribunal of Milan No. 34, section Dist. Cassano d' Adda, 14 March 2012.

prohibiting cruel treatment; Article 128.1, prohibiting slander; and Article 138 on violations of privacy.[206]

The ECtHR's case law on domestic violence reveals that the investigation and judicial protection from ill-treatment has numerous shortcomings in the countries of the CoE, especially in the former Soviet bloc countries.[207] Therefore, the failure of the States to ensure due protection from inhuman or degrading treatment might also be a basis for the ECtHR to consider moral harassment.

Article 8

The ECtHR's interpretation of the respect for private life is a key for opening new dimensions of protection under this article. In cases dealing with domestic violence, the ECtHR has stated that the right to respect for private life covers the physical and psychological integrity of a person.[208] The requirement of a State's protection of physical and psychological integrity of the person is particularly important for establishing a system of protection from workplace PSR. It is also used in very open manner. The ECtHR's jurisprudence includes certain cases which have common points with the protection from PSR. For example, the concept of the physical and psychological integrity of a person was used in the case concerning the right to protect one's reputation[209] or in a case involving protection from menacing behaviour.[210]

This formulation is consonant with the text of the Italian Civil code (Article 2087) that requires employers to ensure the protection of the physical integrity and moral personality of employees. These words serve as a basis of judicial protection of employees from PSR in Italy. In particular, Article 2087 is widely used in the cases of mobbing[211] and in the cases of work-related stress.[212] Therefore we can hypothesise that the system of protection of employees from PSR in the countries where this type of occupational risks are not addressed in domestic labour law, might be founded upon the obligation of the States to protect the physical and psychological integrity of persons, the latter having been acknowledged by the ECtHR in numerous judgments.

The ECtHR's interpretation of Article 8 doesn't impose any general requirements in regards to the severity of the illegal conduct. For example, in *Hajduova v. Slovakia*,[213] the ECtHR found the violation of the right to respect for private and family life, as the State failed to protect the applicant from the menacing behaviour of her

206. D.V. Chernyaeva. Legal Framework for Workplace Mobbing and Harassment Prevention in Russia: Problems and Prospects. E-Journal of International and Comparative Labour Studies 2 (2014): 14–31.
207. ECtHR, Valiulienė v. Lithuania (33234/07) 26 March 2013; Eremia and Others v. the Republic of Moldova (3564/11) 28 May 2013; E.S. and Others v. Slovakia (8227/04) 15 September 2009; A. v. Croatia (55164/08) 14 October 2010; Kalucza v. Hungary (57693/10) 24 April 2012.
208. ECtHR, G.B. and R.B. v. The Republic Of Moldova (16761/09) 18 December 2012.
209. ECtHR, Somesan and Butiuc v. Romania (45543/04) 19 November 2013.
210. ECtHR, Opuz v. Turkey (33401/02) 9 June 2009.
211. Decision of the Italian Court of Cassation No. 18093, 25 July 2013; De Matteis A. Infortuni sul lavoro e malattie professionali. Milan: Giuffrè Editore; 2011, p. 553.
212. Decision of the Tribunal of Trieste 6 October 2010, Corsalini G. La responsabilita del datore di lavoro per infortunio conseguente a stress lavorativo. Danno e responsabilità. 2008, p. 1061.
213. ECtHR, Hajduova v. Slovakia (2660/03) 30 November 2010.

ex-husband – even though these threats were not carried out. This case leads us to suppose that Article 8 might be more applicable for claims of protection from PSR than Article 2 or 3 of the ECHR. The right of the employee to assess the risks to his health and life might be another pillar for protection from PSR. It was acknowledged by the ECtHR in *Vilnes* and further developed in *Brincat and others v. Malta* and might extend also to PSR. It can be interpreted as setting out corresponding positive obligations of the State to create a system of assessing these risks at the workplace and dealing with them appropriately.

The binding character of the ECtHR's judgments is the main peculiarity of the Strasbourg mechanism of human rights protection. According to its jurisprudence, the States are required to remedy the situation, providing individual redress and establishing general measures to prevent further similar violations. Once a case on protection from PSR is brought before the ECtHR, it might even prescribe the need for adoption of a special policy in respect of addressing workplace PSR.[214] It would be possible, for example, if the majority of European countries recognise workplace PSR and adopt legal frameworks aimed at addressing these risks. The ILO's activities in this field, in particular, the adoption of a Convention or Recommendation explicitly recognising PSR, could also contribute to the establishment of an evident tendency towards including PSR within standard OSH policies.

Another interesting facet of the right to assess the risk to one's health in the context of PSR can be found in *Roche v.UK*.[215] The applicant claimed the violation of Article 8 as he was denied access to information relating to his participation in the testing of nerve gas and mustard gas on military personnel during his military service. The ECtHR found the violation of the right to respect for private life noting that the anxiety and stress caused by his uncertainty could also be considered a violation of his right for respect of private life.

The ECtHR's reasoning in this case makes us think that stress and anxiety are seen as challenges to psychological integrity, though it was not expressed this way by the ECtHR. It is rather unclear whether the ECtHR considered the stress of the applicant as a separate violation or whether it was mentioned to constitute violation only to emphasise the aggravating circumstance of the case. In any case, the ECtHR's position on stress, read together with the necessity to protect the psychological integrity of a person, constitutes a certain basis for the possibility to apply to the ECtHR for protection from workplace PSR.

The right to establish and develop relationships with other human beings

The ECtHR's legal positions on the right to establish and develop relationships with other human beings[216] could also contribute to the development of protection from

214. Among judgments where the Court urged the respondent States to change national policy incompatible with the ECHR should be mentioned: ECtHR, Oleksandr Volkov v. Ukraine (21722/11) 9 January 2013; Lustig-Prean and Beckett v. The UK (31417/96, 32377/96) 27 September 1999; Markin Konstantin v. Russia (30078/06) 22 March 2012.
215. ECtHR, Roche v. The United Kingdom (32555/96) 19 October 2005.
216. ECtHR, Niemietz v. Germany (13710/88) 16 December 1992.

workplace PSR. The ECtHR's willingness to extend protection on activities of a professional or business nature is particularly important for the present research as it might provide us with the necessary basis for claiming protection from harassment at work even in cases where Article 3 would be inapplicable (e.g., where the minimum level of the severity of suffering was not reached).

The ECtHR has not defined the notion and the components of the right to establish and develop relationships. Applying the '*Demir and Baikara* method'[217] in the case of protection from workplace PSR, the ECtHR could take into account the fundamental principle of the ILO set out in the Declaration of Philadelphia. According to this document, employment policies must ensure the material well-being and spiritual development of employees in conditions of freedom and dignity. Therefore, freedom and dignity can be seen as fundamental characterisations of workplace relations. The lack of freedom or an infringement of dignity could be considered a violation of the right to establish and develop relationships. It is obvious that harassment at work would be in breach of this right, guaranteed by Article 8 of the ECHR.

These theoretical findings give us scope to argue the theoretical possibility of appealing to the ECtHR if national authorities fail to provide effective protection from workplace PSR. However, it is difficult to foresee if the ECtHR will be ready to interpret the ECHR with such boldness as to recognise PSR as a part of OHS risks.

§9.03 CONCLUSIONS

The present research of the ECtHR jurisprudence demonstrated that the provisions of the ECHR could be valuable in protecting the OSH of employees. The ECtHR's most important contribution here is its elaboration of the set of minimum positive duties of the States in this sphere.

This analysis of the potential of the ECHR in this field demonstrates that the ECtHR, based on existing case law, might support protection from workplace PSR. It would be more likely if with the course of time more European states will include PSR to the list of OSH risks.

Another important conclusion is the possibility to apply to the ECtHR in cases where PSR has caused severe damage and domestic courts have failed to provide remedies. Although these findings are purely theoretical, there is a possibility of their implementation in national practices in future. Taking into account the increasing European tendency to include PSR in the category of occupational risks and the growing awareness of the problem it causes, we can be rather optimistic in this regard and expect that the ECtHR's recognition of the right for protection from PSR will not be far away.

217. Lörcher K., The New Social Dimension in the Jurisprudence of the European Court of Human Rights (ECtHR): The Demir and Baykara Judgment, Its Methodology and Follow-up In: F. Dorssemont, K. Lörcher, I. Schömann, editors. 'The European Convention on Human Rights and the Employment Relation'. Oxford: Hart Publishing, 2013. pp. 3–47.

Conclusions

This study has attempted to provide a conceptual reading of individual rights at work, as guaranteed by the ECHR. It was an ambitious project to reveal the ECtHR's interpretation of the employees' rights, which is binding upon the States and might be referred to in the national courts of all the forty-seven CoE countries. The goal was also to demonstrate the growing applicability of the ECHR to the protection of the individual rights at work both on the domestic and international levels.

In the course of this study its scope was gradually enlarging; new facets of protected rights has emerged in the ECtHR's case law in the last three years, such as the possibility to claim reinstatement, the opportunity to bring a claim concerning occupational safety, or to protest wage cuts in the result of austerity measures. This research was much like exploring a treasure island, where jewels were found in the most unexpected places. Having begun with few famous cases, it was difficult to imagine how many labour law points of the ECtHR's reasoning were hidden from the eyes of labour law scholars. The constant monitoring of the ECtHR's case law during last three years made me affirm the ECtHR's trend of enlarging the ECHR scope and the ever-widening coverage of individual rights at work.

It was particularly interesting to follow the history of the development of the ECtHR' perception of certain rights; to feel 'the wind of change' in its approach to discrimination, the protection from unfair dismissal and many other points. The initial inspiration even strengthened as I researched hundreds of cases which provided priceless support to the protection of individual rights at work.

The applicability of the ECHR to the protection of both private and public employees' rights is one of the most important general conclusions of the present work. The ECtHR has elaborated a set of positive obligation of the State in the employment sphere, including requirements:

- to ensure effective protection from slavery and servitude and human trafficking, corresponding to the qualitative requirements elaborated by the ECtHR;
- to create a system of judicial protection and to guarantee the right to bring a civil action against discrimination;
- to adopt regulations protecting employees' privacy;

- to provide practical and effective protection of employees' privacy, preventing unauthorised access to the personal data stored by her employer;
- to ensure that all interferences with the employee's privacy (monitoring such activities as telephone calls, e-mail, correspondence, use of the internet from work premises, searches of personal items placed at the workplace, and private data) are lawful and proportionate to the legitimate aim pursued by the employer;
- to ensure the respect for private life and freedom of religion, expression and association of employees, fairly balancing these freedoms with the rights of employers when considering employment disputes;
- to provide protection against dismissal by private employers where the dismissal is motivated solely by the fact that an employee belongs to a particular political party;
- to ensure the proportionality of austerity measures to the general interest, avoiding placing excessive burdens on employees;
- to adopt a legislative framework to protect employees from dangerous activities, which must be well-timed and include practical measures of protection and effectively implementing these in practice;
- to effectively investigate workplace accidents and to provide victims or their next-of-kin with adequate avenues of redress;
- to ensure due judicial protection of the rights of persons who suffer from occupational diseases.

The most significant aspect of the ECtHR's approach to the protection of the rights at work is imposing a requirement on States to ensure proper balancing of employees' rights with the rights of employers, or with the general interest of the State and to estimate in all cases the proportionality of the interference to the legitimate aim pursued. The research demonstrated that the ECtHR urges the States to adopt the same approach to employment disputes considered on domestic levels and to take account of the fundamental rights of employees in the context of employment.

This study, being inspired by the evolutionary character of the ECHR, attempted to draw attention to the potential of the ECHR provisions. The reflections on the possible contribution of the ECtHR's legal positions to the protection of the right to a fair wage or to the protection from workplace PSR, despite being speculative, and possibly, being too optimistic, suggests that there is a clear legal basis for such developments.

The research highlighted the impact of the ECtHR's judgments on the national policies of certain States. This impact happens in three main ways: (1) through the adoption of general measures, required by a particular judgment; (2) through the application of the ECtHR's legal positions by domestic Supreme Courts; (3) through the reference to the ECtHR's jurisprudence by advocates and the trade union in domestic judicial proceedings. The impact from policy changes in the result of adoption of general measures is clear and absolutely tangible; it allows us to argue that the ECtHR has become a strong player in the field of employee rights protection.

However, the effect of the Strasbourg jurisprudence might be much more significant, if two other ways were followed and ECtHR's legal positions were referred to in domestic courts. In this regard it is pleasing to observe that the Italian Supreme Court of Cassation has issued a summary of Strasbourg jurisprudence relating to labour and social security rights.[1]

Virginia Mantouvalou once wrote that human rights law can show new paths for the protection of workers' rights.[2] The research demonstrated that the ECtHR does show these paths, notwithstanding they are little appreciated and rarely followed by labour law advocates.

Research carried out by Russian human rights organisations demonstrates that domestic courts are generally unaware of the ECtHR jurisprudence; however, human rights activists succeed in raising such awareness by steadily and continuously referring to ECtHR decisions in applications to domestic courts and throughout legal proceedings.[3] This experience shows that the lawyer's role is very important in introducing ECtHR values into the national legal system, particularly in systems where the ECtHR's legal positions are directly applicable.

In the course of the present study, several issues which were canvassed should be separately and thoroughly researched. One example is the ECtHR's approach to the estimation of the proportionality of interference with individual and collective labour rights as well as with the security rights, both of which deserve profound study. The comparative research of the impact of Strasbourg jurisprudence upon the domestic policies of the Member States are also of great interest. The research of the ECtHR's approach to inhuman and degrading treatment in the context of social claims would contribute significantly to the justification of the indivisibility of human rights.

1. Corte suprema di cassazione rel. n. 112, 7 giugno 2012. 'Il diritto del lavoro e della previdenza sociale nella giurisprudenza della corte europea dei diritti dell'uomo'.
2. Virginia Mantouvalou, Human Rights and Unfair Dismissal: Private Acts in Public Spaces. The Modern Law Review 71(6) (2008): 939.
3. Burkov Anton. The Impact of the European Convention on Human Rights on Russian Law: Legislation and Application in 1996–2006. Stuttgart, 2007. pp. 56–58.

Bibliography

Books

Akandji-Kombe, Jean-François. Positive Obligations Under the European Convention on Human Rights. a Guide to the Implementation of the European Convention on Human Rights. Human Rights Handbooks, No. 7. Council of Europe, 2007.

Ashchenko, A., Zaikina, Y., Ibadova, L., Okhotnikova, N., Chovgan, V. The Implementation of Judgments of the European Court of Human Rights in Ukraine (Ispolneniye resheniy Yevropeyskogo suda po pravam cheloveka v Ukraine). Khar'kov, Izdatel'stvo 'Prava Lyudini', 2014.

Bagley Constance, E. Managers and the Legal Environment: Strategies for the 21st Century, 8th ed. Cengage Learning, 2015.

Bates, Ed. The Evolution of the European Convention on Human Rights: From Its Inception to the Creation of a Permanent Court of Human Rights. New York: Oxford University Press, 2010.

Boehm, Franziska. Information Sharing and Data Protection in the Area of Freedom, Security and Justice: Towards Harmonised Data Protection Principles for Information Exchange at EU-level. Springer Science & Business Media, 2011.

Bouchet-Saulnier, Françoise. Droits de l'homme, droit humanitaire et justice internationale. Acte Sud, 2002.

Burkov, Anton. The Impact of the European Convention on Human Rights on Russian Law: Legislation and Application in 1996–2006. Stuttgart, 2007.

Brems, Eva. Human Rights: Universality and Diversity. Martinus Nijhoff Publishers, 2001.

Burkov, Anton. The Impact of the European Convention on Human Rights on Russian Law: Legislation and Application in 1996–2006. Stuttgart, 2007.

Campbell, T., Ewing, K., Tompkins, A. (eds), The Legal Protection of Human Rights: Sceptical Essays, Oxford: Oxford University Press, 2011.

Carss-Frisk, Monica. The Right to Property: A Guide to the Implementation of Article 1 of Protocol No. 1 of the European Convention on Human Rights. Directorate General of Human Rights Council of Europe, 2001.

Cian C Murphy, Penny Green (ed.). Law and Outsiders: Norms, Processes and 'Othering' in the 21st Century. Bloomsbury Publishing, 2011.

Cismas, Ioana. Religious Actors and International Law. Oxford University Press, 2014.

Christoffersen, Jonas. Fair Balance: A Study of Proportionality, Subsidiarity and Primarity in the European Convention on Human Rights. BRILL, 2009.

Chukaeva, N.G. Ugolovnaya otvetstvennost' za dovedeniye do samoubiystva ili do pokusheniya na samoubiystvo: problemy zakonodatel'nogo regulirovaniya [Criminal liability for bringing to suicide or to attempt to commit suicide: problems of legislative regulation] [dissertation]. Tyumen, 2011.

Collected Edition of the 'Travaux Préparatoires' of the European Convention on Human Rights: Preparatory Commission of the Council of Europe, Committee of Ministers, Consultative Assembly, 11 May-8 September 1949. Council of Europe. BRILL, 1975.

Conor, Gearty. Virginia Mantouvalou, Debating Social Rights. Bloomsbury Publishing, 2010.

Cousin, Mel. 'The European Convention on Human Rights and Social Security Law'. Intersentia, 2008.

Davidov, G., Langillc, B. (eds), The Idea of Labour Law. Oxford: OUP, 2011.

Davies, M. Freedland. Labour Law: Texts and Materials. London: Weidenfeld and Nicolson, 1984.

Deacon, Bob. Global Social Policy: International Organizations and the Future of Welfare. SAGE, 1997.

De Schutter, Olivier. The Prohibition of Discrimination Under European Human Rights Law Relevance for EU Racial And Employment Equality Directives. European Commission, 2005.

De Hert, Paul, Hans, Lammerant. Protection of Personal Data in Work-related Relations. STUDY. European Parliament, Brussels, 2013.

Di Pieter, van Dijk, Godefridus J., Hoof, Van Hoof, G.J.H. Theory and Practice of the European Convention on Human Rights. Martinus Nijhoff Publishers, 1998.

Donnelly, Jack. Universal Human Rights in Theory and Practice. Cornell University Press, 2013.

Dorssemont, Filip, Lörcher, K. The European Convention on Human Rights and the Employment relation. Hart Publishing, 2013.

Dworkin, Ronald. Taking Rights Seriously. Harvard University Press, 1978.

Dworkin, Ronald. Religion without God. Harvard University Press, 2013.

Ebert Franz, Christian, Martin, Oelz. Bridging the Gap between Labour Rights and Human Rights: The Role of ILO Law in Regional Human Rights Courts. ILO, 2012.

Eberle, Edward J. Dignity and Liberty: Constitutional Visions in Germany and the United States. Praeger, 2002.

Feldman, D. Civil Liberties and Human Rights in England and Wales. 2nd edn. Oxford: Oxford University Press, 2002.

Føllesdal, A, Peters, B., Ulfstein, G. (eds). The European Court of Human Rights in a National, European and Global Context. Cambridge University Press, 2013.

Forowicz, Magdalena. The Reception of International Law in the European Court of Human Rights. Oxford University press, 2010.

Freedland, Mark. Data Protection and Employment in the European Union an Analytical Study of the Law and Practice of Data Protection and the Employment Relationship in the EU and Its Member States. Oxford, 1999.

Gallagher Anne, T. The International Law of Human Trafficking. Cambridge University Press, 2010.

Gordon, L. Weil. The European Convention on Human Rights: Background, Development and Prospects. Leyden: A.W. Sythoff, 1963.

Goold, Benjamin J. Neyland, Daniel. New Directions in Surveillance Privacy. Routledge, 2013.

Greer, Steven C. The Margin of Appreciation: Interpretation and Discretion Under the European Convention on Human Rights. Council of Europe, 2000.

Guðrún, Gauksdóttir. The Right to Property and the European Convention on Human Rights: A Nordic Approach. Lund University, 2004.

Günter, Nagel, Francis, Kessler. Social Security Law, Council of Europe. Kluwer Law International, 2010.

Habermas, Jürgen. Between Facts and Norms. Cambridge: Polity, 1996.

Handbook on European Non-discrimination Law\\European Union Agency for Fundamental Rights, European Court of Human Rights. Council of Europe, 2011.

Harris, O Boyle, Bates, Buckley (eds), Harris, O Boyle and Warbrick Law of the European Convention on Human Rights. 2nd ed. Oxford: Oxford University Press, 2009.

Hendrickx, Frank. Protection of Workers' Personal Data in the European Union, 2002.

Heredero, Ana Gómez. Social Security as a Human Right: The Protection Afforded by the European Convention on Human Rights. Vol. 88. Council of Europe, 2007.

Hepple, Bob. Rights at Work Global, European and British Perspectives. London: Sweet & Maxwell, 2005.

Ilciienko, Ivanna. Pilot Judgement Procedure of the European Court of Human Rights: Panacea or Dead-End for Poland, Russia and Ukraine. LL.M. Human Rights Thesis Central European University, published 29 November 2013.

Indivisible Human Rights: The Relationship of Political and Civil Rights to Survival, Subsistence and Poverty. Human Rights Watch, 1992.

Kapuy, Klaus, Pieters, Danny, Zaglmayer, Bernhard. Social Security Cases in Europe: The European Court of Human Rights. Intersentia, 2007.

Katri, Lõhmus. Caring Autonomy: European Human Rights Law and the Challenge of Individualism. Cambridge University Press, 2015.

Klatt, Matthias, Meister, Moritz. The Constitutional Structure of Proportionality. Oxford: University Press, 2012.

Koch, Ida Elisabeth. Human Rights as Indivisible Rights: The Protection of Socio-economic Demands Under the European Convention on Human Rights. Martinus Nijhoff Publishers, 2009.

La Promotion de la Justice, Des Droits de L'homme Et Du Règlement Des Conflits Par Le Droit International edited by Marcelo Gustavo Kohen. Martinus Nijhoff Publishers, 2007.

Lagoutte, S et al. (eds). Human Rights in Turmoil. Leiden: Brill, 2007.

Langford, M. Socio-Economic Rights Jurisprudence: Emerging Trends in International and Comparative Law. New York and Cambridge: Cambridge University Press, 2009.

Lautenbach, Geranne. The Concept of the Rule of Law and the European Court of Human Rights. Oxford: Oxford University Press, 2013.

Lazarus, L., Goold B.J., Swiney, G, Public Protection, Proportionality and the Search for Balance. Ministry of Justice Research Series, 10 July 2007.

Legg, Andrew. The Margin of Appreciation in International Human Rights Law: Deference and Proportionality. Oxford University Press, 2012.

Lyutov, N.L. Rossiyskoye trudovoye zakonodatel'stvo i mezhdunarodnyye trudovyye standarty: sootvetstviye i perspektivy sovershenstvovaniya.(Russian labor law and international labor standards: conformance and prospects of improvement) Moscow: ANO «Tsentr sotsial'no-trudovykh prav», 2012.

Maggs, Peter B., Olga Schwartz, William Burnham. Law and Legal System of the Russian Federation. 6th ed., Juris Publishing, Inc., 2015.

Mendel, Toby, Etude mondiale sur le respect de la vie privée sur l'Internet et la liberté: d'expression. UNESCO, 2013.

Merrills, J.G. The Development of International Law by the European Court of Human Rights. Manchester University Press, 1988.

Moreau, M.A. (ed.) Before and After the Economic Crisis: What Implications for the 'European Social Model'? Edward Elgar Publishing, 2011.

Mowbray, A.R., The Development of Positive Obligations under the European Convention on Human Rights by the European Court of Human Rights. Hart, 2004.

Nihal, Jayawickrama. The Judicial Application of Human Rights Law: National, Regional and International Jurisprudence. Cambridge University Press, 2002.

Nussbaum, M. Women and Human Development. The Capabilities Approach. Cambridge University Press, 2000.

O'Connell. Vindicating Socio-Economic Rights: International Standards and Comparative Experiences. London and New York: Routledge, 2012.

Olinga, A.D. et Picheral C. La théorie de la marge d'appréciation dans la jurisprudence récente de la Cour Européenne des droits de l'Homme ». R.T.D.H. 1995 Reid Karen, A Practitioner's Guide to the European Convention on Human Rights. Sweet & Maxwell, 2011.

Orakhelashvili, Alexander. The Interpretation of Acts and Rules in Public International Law. Oxford University Press, 2008.

Özgür Heval, Çınar. The Right to Conscientious Objection to Military Service and Turkey's Obligations under International Human Rights Law. Palgrave Macmillan, 2014.

Pagallo, Ugo. La tutela della privacy negli Stati Uniti d'America e in Europa: modelli giuridici a confronto. Giuffrè Editore, 2008.

Petaux, Jean. Democracy and Human Rights for Europe: The Council of Europe's Contribution. Council of Europe, 2009.

Reforming the European Convention on Human Rights: A Work in Progress: a Compilation of Publications and Documents Relevant to the Ongoing Reform of the ECHR. Council of Europe, 2009.

Renucci, Jean-François. Article 9 of the European Convention on Human Rights: Freedom of Thought, Conscience And Religion. Human Rights Files, 2005, No. 20.

Resta, Giorgio. Dignità, persone, mercati. Giappichelli Editore, 2014.

Roca, Javier García, Pablo, Santolaya (ed.). Europe of Rights: A Compendium on the European Convention on Human Rights. Martinus Nijhoff Publishers, 2012.

Robin, Allen, Anna, Beale, Rachel, Crasnow. Employment Law and Human Rights, 2nd ed. Oxford University press, 2007.

Saul, Ben, David, Kinley, Jaqueline, Mowbray. The International Covenant on Economic, Social and Cultural Rights: Cases, Materials, and Commentary. Oxford University Press, 2014.

Sepulveda, M. Magdalena. The Nature of the Obligations under the International Covenant on Economic, Social and Cultural Rights. Intersentia, 2003.

Sen, A. Development as Freedom. First Anchor Books Edition, 2000.

Sermet, Laurent. The European Convention On Human Rights and Property Rights. Vol. 11. Council of Europe, 1998.

Scoglio, Stefano. Transforming Privacy: A Transpersonal Philosophy of Rights. Greenwood Publishing Group, 1998.

Spyridōn I. Phlogaitēs, Tom, Zwart, Julie, Fraser (ed.). The European Court of Human Rights and Its Discontents: Turning Criticism Into Strength. Edward Elgar Publishing, 2013.

Tobler, Christa. LImits and Potential of the Concept of Indirect Discrimination. European Commission, 2008.

Van Drooghenbroeck Sébastien. La proportionnalité dans le droit de la Convention européenne des droits de l'homme: prendre l'idée simple au sérieux. Publications Fac St Louis, 2001.

Van, Banning R.G. The Human Right to Property. Intersentia, 2002.

Velyvyte Vilija, The Right to Strike in the EU after Accession to the ECHR: A Practical Assessment. In: Mark Freedland, Jeremias Prassl, editors. Viking, Laval and Beyond. Bloomsbury Publishing, 2014.

Verstraete, Alain. Workplace Drug Testing. Pharmaceutical Press, 2011.

Vickers, Lucy. Religious freedom, religious discrimination and the workplace. Oxford: Hart, 2008.

Virginia, Mantouvalou (ed.). The Right to Work: Legal and Philosophical Perspectives. Hart Publishing, 2015.

White, Robin C.A., Ovey Clare. The European Convention on Human Rights. New-York: Oxford University press, 2010.

Whelan, Daniel J. Indivisible Human Rights: A History. University of Pennsylvania Press, 2011.

Xenos, Dimitris. The Positive Obligations of the State Under the European Convention of Human Rights. Routledge, 2012.

Yourow. The Margin of Appreciation Doctrine in the Dynamics of European Human Rights Jurisprudence. Martinus Nijhoff Publishers, 1996.

Yutaka, Arai-Takahashi. The Margin of Appreciation Doctrine and the Principle of Proportionality in the Jurisprudence of the ECHR. Intersentia, 2002.

Articles and Chapters

Addo, M.K., Grief N. Does Article 3 of the European Convention on Human Rights Enshrine Absolute Rights? European Journal of International Law (9) 1998.

Aksenova, Marina, Anchugov and Gladkov is not Enforceable: The Russian Constitutional Court Opines in its First ECtHR Implementation Case. Published 25 April 2016 at: opiniojuris.org/2016/04/25/anchugov-and-gladkov-is-not-enforceable-the-russian-constitutional-court-opines-in-its-first-ecthr-implementation-case/.

Allain, Jean, Rantsev v Cyprus and Russia: the European Court of Human Rights and trafficking as slavery. Human Rights Law Review (3) 2010.

Amy, Ludlow, The Right to Strike: A Jurisprudential Gulf between the CJEU and ECtHR. In: K. Dzehtsiarou, T. Konstadinides, T. Lock, N. O'Meara, editors. Human Rights Law in Europe: The Influence, Overlaps and Contradictions of the EU and the ECHR. Routledge, 2014.

Anker, R. et al., Measuring Decent Work with Statistical Indicators. International Labour Review T. 142. №. 2 (2003).

Arai, Yutaka, The ECHR and Non-discrimination. Amicus Curiae (7) 1998.

Arnaud, Stéphanie, Analyse économique du droit au respect de la vie personnelle: application à la relation de travail en France. Revue internationale de droit économique, 2007, vol. t. XXI, 2, issue 2.

Barnard, C., Hepple B., Substantive Equality. Cambridge Law Journal 59(3) (November 2000).

Baker, Aaron, The Enjoyment of Rights and Freedoms: A New Conception of the 'Ambit' under Article 14 ECHR. The Modern Law Review (69.5) 2006.

Bayefski, Anne, The Principle of Equality or Non-Discrimination in International Law. Human Rights Law Journal 11(1–2) 1990.

Bellamy, Richard, The Democratic Legitimacy of International Human Rights Conventions: Political Constitutionalism and the European Convention on Human Rights. European Journal of International Law (25:4) 2014.

Bielefeldt, Heiner, Freedom of Religion or Relief: Anachronistic in Europe? In: Zeynep Yanasmayan, Katayoun Alidadi, Jørgen S Nielsen, Marie-Claire Foblets, editors. Belief, Law and Politics: What Future for a Secular Europe? Ashgate Publishing, 2014.

Bojin, Liician, Challenges Facing the European Court of Human Rights: Fragmentation of the International Order, Division in Europe and the Right to Individual Petition. In: Spyridōn I. Phlogaitēs, Tom Zwart, Julie Fraser, editors. The European Court of Human Rights and its Discontents: Turning Criticism to strength. Edward Elgar Publishing, 2013.

Bossuyt, M., Should the Strasbourg Court Exercise More Self-Restraint? on the Extension of the Jurisdiction of the European Court of Human Rights to Social Security Regulations. Human Rights Law Journal 28(9-12): 2007.

Brauch, Jeffrey A., The Margin of Appreciation and the Jurisprudence of the European Court of Human Rights: Threat to the Rule of Law. Columbia Journal of European Law (11) 2005.

Brems, Eva, the Margin of Appreciation Doctrine in the Case-Law of the European Court of Human Rights. Zeitschrift für ausländisches öffentliches Recht und Völkerrecht 56 (1996).

Brems, Eva, Conflicting Human Rights: An Exploration in the Context of the Right to a Fair Trial in the European Convention for the Protection of Human Rights and Fundamental Freedoms. Human Rights Quarterly 27 (2005): 305.

Brems, Eva, Loures Peroni, Religion and Human Rights: Deconstructing and Navigating Tensions. In: Silvio Ferrari, editor. Routledge Handbook of Law and Religion. Routledge, 2015.

Bruun, Niklas, Prohibition of Discrimination: Article 14 European Convention on Human Rights. In: Filip Dorssemont, Klaus Lörcher, Isabelle Schömann, editors. The European Convention on Human Rights and the employment relation. Oxford: Hart Publishing, 2013.

Buyse, Antoine, The Truth, the Past and the Present: Article 10 ECHR and Situations of Transition. In: Antoine Buyse, Michael Hamilton, editors. Transitional Jurisprudence and the ECHR: Justice, Politics and Rights. Cambridge University Press, 2011.

Bygrave, Lee A., Data Protection Pursuant to the Right to Privacy in Human Rights Treaties. International Journal of Law and Information Technology 6.3 (1998).

Busby, Nicole, Rebecca, Zahn, The EU and the ECHR: Collective and Non-discrimination Labour Rights at a Crossroad? International Journal of Comparative Labour Law and Industrial Relations (2/2014).

Bratza, Sir Nicolas, The Relationship between the UK Courts and Strasbourg European Human Rights Law Review (2011) 505.

Caflisch, L., Labour Issues before the Strasbourg Court, Lecture available at: http://www.ilo.org/public/english/bureau/leg/include/home/caflisch.pdf.

Calo, Zachary R., Constructing the Secular: Law and Religion Jurisprudence in Europe and the United States. Robert Schuman Centre for Advanced Studies Research Paper No. RSCAS 94 (2014).

Caruso, Bruno, Changes in the Workplace and the Dialogue of Global Law in the Global Village. Comparative Labour Law and Policy Journal 28:3 (2007).

Caruso, Bruno, New Trajectories of Labour Law in the European Crisis. The Italian Case. Comparative Labour Law and Policy Journal 36 (2015).

Cavanaugh, K., Policing the Margins: Rights Protection and the European Court of Human Rights. European Human Rights Law Review 4 (2006).

Chaudary, Saadiya, Trafficking in Europe: An Analysis of the Effectiveness of European Law. Michigan Journal of International Law 33 (2011).

Chernyaeva, D.V., Legal Framework for Workplace Mobbing and Harassment Prevention in Russia: Problems and Prospects. E-Journal of International and Comparative Labour Studies 2 (2014).

Churchill, Robin R., Urfan Khaliq, The Collective Complaints System of the European Social Charter: An Effective Mechanism for Ensuring Compliance with Economic and Social Rights? European Journal of International Law 15.3 (2004).

Compa, L., Solidarity and Human Rights. New Labor Forum 18 (2009): 38.

Collins, Hugh, On the (In) compatibility of Human Rights Discourse and Private Law. LSE Law, Society and Economy Working Papers 7 (2012).

Coomans, Fons, Education and Work. In: Daniel Moeckli, Sangeeta Shah, Sandesh Sivakumaran, editors. International Human Rights Law. Oxford University Press, 2013.

Corsalini, G., La responsabilita del datore di lavoro per infortunio conseguente a stress lavorativo. Danno e responsabilità. 2008.

Cranmer, Frank, 'Free speech' or 'misconduct' in employment? Rubins v Latvia. Law & Religion UK, 14 April 2015.

Cullen, H., Silihadin v. France: Positive Obligations under Article 4 of the European Convention Human Rights. Human Rights Law Review 6 (2006).

De Matteis, A., Infortuni sul lavoro e malattie professionali. Milan. Giuffrè Editore, 2011.

De Schutter, Olivier, Bosphorus Post-Accession: Redefining the Relationship between the European Court of Human Rights and the Parties to the Convention. In: Vasiliki Kosta, Nikos Skoutaris, Vassilis Tzevelekos, editors. The EU Accession to the ECHR. Bloomsbury Publishing, 2014.

De Schutter, Olivier, The Protection of Social Rights by the European Court of Human Rights. In: P. Van der Auweraert, T. De Pelsmaeker, J. Sarkin, J. Vande Lanotte, editors. Social, Economic and Cultural Rights. An Appraisal of Current European and International Developments. Antwerpen: Maklu, 2002.

Dorsscmont, Filip, Collective Action Against Austerity Measure. In: Niklas Bruun, Klaus Lörcher, Isabelle Schömann, editors. The Economic and Financial Crisis and Collective Labour Law in Europe. Bloomsbury Publishing, 2014.

Dorssemont, Filip, The Right to Take Collective Action under Article 11 ECHR. In: Filip Dorssemont, Klaus Lörcher, Isabelle Schömann, editors. The European Convention on Human Rights and the employment relation. Oxford: Hart Publishing, 2013.

Ducamp, Sebastien, Cheryl Tama Oblander, Heather Benno. Recent Developments in EU Employee Data Privacy Law. Privacy & Data Security Law Journal April (2007).

Egan, Suzanne. Protecting the Victims of Trafficking: Problems and Prospects. European Human Rights Law Review 1 (2008).

Evans, Carolyn, Anna Hood, Religious Autonomy and Labour Law: A comparison of the Jurisprudence of the United States and the European Court of Human Rights. Oxford Journal of Law and Religion 1 (2012).

Ewing, Keith David, The Human Rights Act and Labour Law. Industrial Law Journal 27.4 (1998).

Ewing, Keith D., John Hendy, The Dramatic Implications of Demir and Baykara. Industrial Law Journal 39.1 (2010).

Flauss, Jean-Francois, European Court of Human Rights and the Freedom of Expression. Industrial Law Journal 84 (2009).

Feldman, David, The Developing Scope of Article 8 of the European Convention on Human Rights. European Human Rights Law Review (1997).

Ford, Michael, Two Conceptions of Worker Privacy. Industrial Law Journal 31.2 (2002).

Freedland, Mark R., Lucy Vickers, Religious Expression in the Workplace in the United Kingdom. Comparative Labor Law and Policy Journal 30.3 (2009).

Fredman, Sandra, From Deference to Democracy: The Role of Equality Under the Human Rights Act 1998. Oxford Legal Studies Research Paper No. 5/2006; Law Quarterly Review, Vol. 122 (2006).

Frowein, Jochen, European Integration Through Fundamental Rights. University of Michigan Journal of Law Reform 5 (1984).

Frowein, J.A., The Transformation of the Constitutional Law through the ECHR. Israel Law Review 41(3) (2008).

Frowein, J.A., How to Save Democracy from Itself? In: Y. Dinstein Domb, editor. Israel Yearbook on Human Rights. Martinus Nijhoff Publishers, 1996.

Fudge, J., Constitutionalizing Labour Rights in Europe, In: The Legal Protection of Human Rights: Sceptical Essays, edited by T. Campbell, K. Ewing & A. Tompkins. Oxford: Oxford University Press, 2011.

Fyrnys, Markus, Expanding Competences by Judicial Lawmaking: The Pilot Judgment Procedure of the European Court of Human Rights. German Law Journal 12 (2011).

Galetta, D., Il principio di proporzionalità dell uomo, fra principio di necessarietà nella convenzione europea dei diritti e dottrina del margine di apprezzamento statale: riflessioni generali su contenuti e rilevanza effettiva del principio, Riv. Ital. Dir. Pubbl. Comunitario. 3-4 (1999).

Garcia-Jourdan, Sophie, De La Transition Démocratique En Lituanie À La Consécration Du Droit D'exercer Une Activité Professionnelle Dans Le Secteur Privé. Revue trimestrielle des droits de l'homme 16 (2005).

Gerards, Janneke, The Discrimination Grounds of Article 14 of the European Convention on Human Rights. Human Rights Law Review 13:1 (2013).

Greer, Steven, The Interpretation of the European Convention on Human Rights: Universal Principle or Margin of Appreciation? UCL Human Rights Review 3 (2010).

Halberstam, Daniel, 'It's the Autonomy, Stupid!' A Modest Defense of Opinion 2/13 on EU Accession to the ECHR, and the Way Forward (20 February 2015). University of Michigan Public Law Research Paper No. 439. Available at SSRN: http://ssrn.com/abstract=2567591(accessed 13.04.2015).

Helfer, Laurence R., Embeddedness as a Deep Structural Principle of the European Human Rights Regime. European Journal of International Law 19 (2008).

Hendrickx, F., Aline Van Bever, Article 8 ECHR: Judicial Patterns of Employment Privacy Protection In: Filip Dorssemont, Klaus Lörcher, Isabelle Schömann, editors. The European Convention on Human Rights and the Employment Relation. Hart Publishing, 2013.

Henrard, Kristin, The Effective Protection of the Freedom of Religion: The ECtHR's Variable Margin of Appreciation Regarding Religion-State Relations and the Rule of Law. In: Marie-Claire Foblets et al., editors. Belief, Law and Politics: What Future for a Secular Europe? Ashgate Publishing, 2014.

Henrard, Kristin, A Critical Appraisal of the Margin of Appreciation Left to States Pertaining to 'Church–State Relations' Under the Jurisprudence of the European Court of Human Rights (2012). In M.C. Foblets, K. Alidadi & J. Vrielink, editors. Test of Faith? Religious Diversity and Accommodation in the European Workplace. Ashgate, 2012.

Hepple, Bob, Future of Labour Law. Comparative Labor Law Journal 17 (1995).

Hepple, Bob, The Aims of Equality Law. Current Legal Problems 61(1) (2008).

Heringa, Aalt Willem, Standards of Review for Discrimination. The Scope of Review by the Courts. In Titia Loenen, Paulo R. Rodrigues, editors. Non-Discrimination Law: Comparative Perspectives. Martinus Nijhoff Publishers, 1999.

Hins, Wouter, Dirk Voorhoof, Access to State-Held Information as a Fundamental Right under the European Convention on Human Rights. European Constitutional Law Review 3.01 (2007).

Itzcovich, Giulio, One, None and One Hundred Thousand Margins of Appreciations: The Lautsi Case. Human Rights Law Review 13:2 (2013).

James, Sarah, Social Networks at Work–Employment Law and the Facebook Generation. Human Resource Management International Digest 19.6 (2011).

Jacobs, Antoine, Article 11 ECHR: The Right to Bargain Collectively under Article 11 ECHR. In: Filip Dorssemont, Klaus Lörcher, Isabelle Schömann, editors. The European Convention on Human Rights and the employment relation. Oxford: Hart Publishing, 2013.

Kazanga, Isabel, et al., Prevalence of Drug Abuse Among Workers: Strengths and Pitfalls of the Recent Italian Workplace Drug Testing (WDT) Legislation. Forensic Science International 215.1 (2012).

Kennedy, David, The International Human Rights Regime: Still Part of the Problem? In: Rob Dickinson, editor. Examining Critical Perspectives on Human Rights. Cambridge University Press, 2012.

Khalif, Urfan, Protocol 12 to the European Convention on Human Rights: A Step Forward or a Step Too Far? Public Law 3 (2001).

Kiviorg, Merilin, Religious Autonomy in the ECHR. Derecho y Religión IV (2009).

Kirchner, Stefan, Vanessa, Maria, The Freedom of Expression of Members of the Armed Forces Under the European Convention on Human Rights in Jokšas V. Lithuania. Baltic Journal of Law & Politics 7.1 (2014).

Kolben, K., Labor Rights as Human Rights? Virginia Journal of International Law 50 (2010).

Langille, Brian A., Core Labour Rights - The True Story (Reply to Alston). European Journal of International Law 16.3.(2005).

Lawson, Rick, A Twenty-First-Century Procession of Echternach: The Accession of the EU to the European Convention on Human Rights. In: Filip Dorssemont, Klaus Lörcher, Isabelle Schömann, editors. The European Convention on Human Rights and the employment relation. Oxford: Hart Publishing, 2013.

Laurent, Sermet, The European Convention on Human Rights and Property Rights, Human Rights Files, No. 11 rev. Council of Europe, 1999.

Lavrysen, Laurens, Protection by the Law: The Positive Obligation to Develop a Legal Framework to Adequately Protect ECHR Rights. In: Yves Haeck, Eva Brems, editors. Human Rights and Civil Liberties in the 21st Century. Springer Science & Business Media, 2013.

Leigh, Ian, Andrew Hambler, Religious Symbols, Conscience, and the Rights of Others. Oxford Journal of Law and Religion 3(1) (2014).

Lerouge, L., Suicide du salarié et faute inexcusable de l'employeur: quelles évolutions juridiques? Revue de droit sanitaire et social. 2 (2012).

Lerouge, L., Droit de la santé-sécurité et risques psychosociaux au travail: où situer le système français au regard des systèmes étrangers? In: Lerouge L., editor. Les risques psychosociaux au travail en droit social: approche juridique comparée. France - Europe - Canada – Japon. Paris: Dalloz; 2014.

Lerouge, L., Workplace Bullying and Harassment in France and Few Comparisons with Belgium: A Legal Perspective. JILPT Report, 2013.

Lerouge, L., Hebert, C., The Law of Workplace Harassment of the United States, France, and the European Union: Comparative Analysis after the Adoption of France's New Sexual Harassment Law. Comparative Labor Law & Policy 35.1 (2013).

Letsas, George, The ECHR as a Living Instrument: Its Meaning and its Legitimacy (14 March 2012). Available at SSRN: http://ssrn.com/abstract=2021836 (accessed 20 September 2014).

Letsas, George, The Truth in Autonomous Concepts: How to Interpret the ECHR. EJIL 15 (2004).

Letsas, George, The ECHR as a Living Instrument: Its Meaning and its Legitimacy (14 March 2012). Available at SSRN: http://ssrn.com/abstract=2021836 (accessed 20 September 2014).

Letsas, George, Two Concepts of the Margin of Appreciation. Oxford Journal of Legal Studies 26. 4 (2006).

Lixinski, Lucas, Treaty Interpretation by the Inter-American Court of Human Rights: Expansionism at the Service of the Unity of International Law. European Journal of International Law 21.3 (2010).

Lock, Tobias, Beyond Bosphorus: The European Court of Human Rights' Case Law on the Responsibility of Member States of International Organisations Under the European Convention on Human Rights. Human Rights Law Review 10 (2010).

Lock, Tobias, EU Accession to the ECHR: Implications for Judicial Review in Strasbourg. European Law Review 6 (2010).

Lo Faro, Antonio, Is a Decent Wage Part of a Decent JOB? Answers from an Enlarged Europe. WP CSDLE 'Massimo D'Antona'. INT-64/2008 (2008).

Lo Faro, Responsabilità e sanzioni per sciopero illegittimo: cambia qualcosa in Italia dopo Laval? Giornale di diritto del lavoro e delle relazioni industriali, 3 (2011)Lord Hoffman, European Human Rights – A Force for Good or a Threat to Democracy? Lecture at the Dickson Poon School of Law, King's College London 17 June 2014, available at: http://www.kcl.ac.uk/law/newsevents/newsrecords/2013-14/assets/Lord-Phillips-European-Human-Rights--A-Force-for-Good-or-a-Theat-to-Democracy-17-June-2014.pdf (accessed 20 August 2014)

Lord Lester of Herne Hill, The European Convention on Human Rights in the New Architecture of Europe: General Report. Proceedings of the 8th International Colloquy on the European Convention on Human Rights. Council of Europe, (1995).

Lörcher, K., The New Social Dimension in the Jurisprudence of the European Court of Human Rights (ECtHR): The Demir and Baykara Judgment, its Methodology and Follow-up. In: Filip Dorssemont, Klaus Lörcher, Isabelle Schömann, editors. The European Convention on Human Rights and the employment relation. Oxford: Hart Publishing, 2013.

Lushnikov, A. Protection of Employee's Personal Data: Comparative and Legal Comments of Chapter 14 of the Russian Labour Code (Zashchita Personal'nykh Dannykh Rabotnika: Sravnitel'no-Pravovoy Kommentariy Gl.14 Trudovogo Kodeksa Rf) Upravlenie personalom. 17 (2009).

Lyutov, N.L., Diskriminatsiya v oblasti truda i zanyatiy: problemy opredeleniya (Discrimination in Employment and Occupation: problems of definition) // Trudovoye pravo v Rossii i za rubezhom 4 (2011).

Mantouvalou, Virginia, Hugh Collins, Private Life and Dismissal: Pay v UK. Industrial Law Journal 38.1 (2009).

Mantouvalou, Virginia, Labour Rights in the European Convention on Human Rights: An Intellectual Justification for an Integrated Approach to Interpretation. Human Rights Law Review 13.3 (2013).

Mantouvalou, Virginia, Servitude and Forced Labour in the 21st Century: The Human Rights of Domestic Workers. Industrial Law Journal 35.4 (2006).

Mantouvalou, Virginia, Human Rights and Unfair Dismissal: Private Acts in Public Spaces. The Modern Law Review 71.6 (2008).

Mantouvalou, Virginia, Work and Private Life: Sidabras and Dziautas v. Lithuania. European Law Review 30 (2005).

Mantouvalou, Virginia, Panayotis Voyatzis, The Council of Europe and the Protection of Human Rights: A System in Need of Reform. In: Sarah Joseph, Adam McBeth, editors. Research Handbook on International Human Rights Law. Edward Elgar Publishing, 2010.

Mantouualou, Virginia, The Protection of the Right to Work through the European Convention on Human Rights. Cambridge Yearbook of European Legal Studies 16 (2013–2014).

Martínez-Torrón, Javier, Limitations on Religious Freedom in the Case Law of the European Court of Human Rights. Emory International Law Review 19 (2005).

Mahoney, Paul, The Doctrine of the Margin of Appreciation Under the European Convention on Human Rights: Its Legitimacy in Theory and Application in Practice. Human Rights Law Journal 19.1 (2001).

Mahouney, P., Marvellous Richness of Diversity or Invidious Cultural Relativism? Human Rights Law Journal 19.1 (1998).

Mahoney, Paul, The European Convention on Royal Rights: Royalty, Aristocracy and the European Convention on Human Rights. In: Marcelo Gustavo Kohen, editor.

La Promotion de la Justice, Des Droits de L'homme Et Du Règlement Des Conflits Par Le Droit International. Martinus Nijhoff Publishers, 2007.

Maul, Daniel Roger, The International Labour Organization and the Struggle against Forced Labour from 1919 to the Present. Labor History 48.4 (2007).

McHarg, Aileen, Reconciling Human Rights and the Public Interest Conceptual Problems and Doctrinal Uncertainty in the Jurisprudence of the European Court of Human Rights. The Modern Law Review 62 (1999).

Mgrditchian, Greg, Employment & Social Media Privacy: Employer Justifications For Access To 'Private' Material. Rutgers Computer & Technology Law Journal 41 (2015).

Miller, Arthur Selwyn, Public Confidence in the Judiciary: Some Notes and Reflections. Law and Contemporary Problems (1970).

Mouly, J., J-P. Marguénaud, L'alcool et la drogue dans les éprouvettes de la CEDH: vie privée du salarié et principe de proportionnalité. Recueil Dalloz Sirey: hebdomadaire 1 (2005).

Mowbray, Alastair, A Study of the Principle of Fair Balance in the Jurisprudence of the European Court of Human Rights. Human Rights Law Review 10.2 (2010).

Mundlak, G., Labor Rights and Human Rights: Why Don't the Two Tracks Meet. Comparative Labor Law and Policy Journal 34 (2012).

Muzny, Petr, Bayatyan v Armenia: The Grand Chamber Renders a Grand Judgment. Human Rights Law Review 12.1 (2012).

Murzea, C., The European Court of Human Rights and Its Theories of Interpreting the European Convention on Human Rights. Bulletin of the Transilvania 5.1 (2012).

Napoletano, N., Estensione e limiti della dimensione economica e sociale della Convenzione europea dei diritti umani in tempi di crisi finanziaria. Diritti umani e diritto internazionale, 2.8 (2014).

Neuman, Gerald L, Import, Export, and Regional Consent in the Inter-American Court of Human Rights. The European Journal of International Law 19.1 (2008).

Nicholson, Andrea, Reflections on Siliadin v. France: slavery and legal definition. The International Journal of Human Rights 14.5 (2010).

Nordeide, Ragnar, Demir & Baykara v. Turkey - European Court of Human Rights Judgment on Rights of Trade Union Formation and of Collective Bargaining. American Journal of International Law 3 (2009).

Novitz, Tonia, Labour Rights and Property Rights: Implications for (and Beyond) Redundancy Payments and Pensions? Industrial Law Journal 41 (2012).

O'Boyle, M., Right to Speak and Associate under Strasbourg Case-Law with Reference to Eastern and Central Europe. Connecticut Journal of International Law 8 (1993).

O'Connell, Rory, Cinderella Comes to the Ball: Article 14 and the Right to Non-Discrimination in the ECHR' Legal Studies. The Journal of the Society of Legal Scholars 29.1 (2009).

O'Connell, Rory, Substantive Equality in the European Court of Human Rights? Michigan Law Review First Impressions 129 (2009).

O'Connell, Rory, The Right to Work in the European Convention on Human Rights. European Human Rights Law Review 2 (2012).

Oddný, Mjöll Arnardóttir, Non-discrimination Under Article 14 ECHR: The Burden of Proof. Scandinavian Studies in Law (2007).

Oil, Andrea, Multilevel Regulations Reviewed by Multilevel Jurisdictions: The ECJ, the National Courts and the ECtHR. In: Andreas Føllesdal, Ramses A. Wessel, Jan Wouters, editors. Multilevel Regulation and the EU: The Interplay Between Global, European, and National Normative Processes. BRILL, 2008.

Olsson, Petra Herzfeld, Every Natural or Legal Person is Entitled to the Peaceful Enjoyment of His or Her Possessions: Article 1, Protocol 1 to the European Convention on Human Rights. In: Filip Dorssemont, Klaus Lörcher, Isabelle Schömann, editors. The European Convention on Human Rights and the employment relation. Oxford: Hart Publishing, 2013.

Ornstein, Daniel, Social Media Usage in the Workplace around the World-Developing Law and Practices. Business Law International 13 (2012).

Pati, Roza, States' Positive Obligations with Respect to Human Trafficking: The European Court of Human Rights Breaks New Ground in Rantsev v. Cyprus & Russia. Boston University International Law Journal 29.1 (2011).

Pennings, Frans, Non-Discrimination on the Ground of Nationality in Social Security: What are the Consequences of the Accession of the EU to the ECHR? Utrecht Law Review 9.1 (2013).

Peroni, Lourdes, Alexandra, Timmer, Vulnerable Groups: The Promise of an Emerging Concept in European Human Rights Convention Law. International Journal of Constitutional Law 11.4 (2013).

Petkova, Bilyaria, The Notion of Consensus as a Route to Democratic Adjudication? Cambridge Yearbook of European Legal Studies 14 (2011–2012).

Pitt, Gwyneth, Keeping the Faith: Trends and Tensions in Religion or Belief Discrimination. Industrial Law Journal 40.4 (2011).

Postema, Gerald J., The Soul of justice: Bentham on Publicity, Law, and the Rule of Law In: Xiaobo Zhai, Michael Quinn, editors. Bentham's Theory of Law and Public Opinion. Cambridge University Press, 2014.

Purtova, Nadezhda, Private Law Solutions in European Data Protection: Relationship to Privacy, and Waiver of Data Protection Rights. Netherlands Quarterly of Human Rights 28 (2010).

Råman, Jari, European Court of Human Rights: Failure to Take Effective Information Security Measures to Protect Sensitive Personal Data Violates Right to Privacy–I v. Finland, no. 20511/03, 17 July 2008. Computer Law & Security Review 24.6 (2008).

Rodrick, Sharon, Open Justice, Privacy and Suppressing Identity in Legal Proceedings: 'What's in a Name?' and Would Anonymity 'Smell as Sweet'? In: Normann Witzleb, David Lindsay, Moira Paterson, Sharon Rodrick, editors. Emerging Challenges in Privacy Law: Comparative Perspectives. Cambridge University Press, 2014.

Rodrigues, Rowena, The Surveillance Industry in Europe In: David Wright, Reinhard Kreissl, editors. Surveillance in Europe. Routledge, 2014.

Rowe, Peter, Control Over Armed Forces Exercised by the European Court of Human Rights. Geneva Centre for the Democratic Control of Armed Forces. Working paper series 56 (2002).

Ryssdal, R., Data Protection and the European Convention on Human Rights. In: Data Protection, Human Rights and Democratic Values, Proceedings of the 13th Conference of Data Protection Commissioners held 2–4 October 1991 in Strasbourg. Strasbourg. CoE, 1992.

Samson, Klaus, The 'Berufswrlwt' problem revisited — Views from Geneva and Starsbourg in Les normes internationales du travail: un patrimoine pour l'avenir: mélanges en l'honneur de Nicolas Valticos edited by Juan Somavía. ILO, 2004.

Samuel, D. Warren, Louis D. Brandeis, The Right to Privacy. Harvard Law Review 4.5 (1890).

Sen, A., Tanner Lecture: Equality of What? delivered at Stanford University in 1979, available at: http://tannerlectures.utah.edu/_documents/a-to-z/s/sen80.pdf (accessed 23.11.2014).

Sen, A., Elements of a Theory of Human Rights. Philosophy & Public Affairs 32.4 (2004).

Sen, A., Europa e il mondo - Quale sviluppo nel prossimo futuro? Lettera internazionale (2005).

Sen, A. Capabilities, Lists, and Public Reason: Continuing the Conversation. Feminist Economics 10.3 (2004).

Sen, A., Work and Rights. International Labour Review 2 (2000).

Sen, Emploi A., Institutions et technologie: Quelques problèmes de politique générale. Revue international de travail. 135.3 (1996).

Schachter, Oscar, Human Dignity as a Normative Concept. The American Journal of International Law 77.4 (1983).

Schokkenbroek, Jeroen, The Basis, Nature and Application of the Margin-of-Appreciation Doctrine in the Case-Law of the European Court of Human Rights, Human Rights Law Journal 19.1 (1998).

Scott, Craig, Interdependence and Permeability of Human Rights Norms: Towards a Partial Fusion of the International Covenants on Human Rights. Osgoode Hall Law Journal 27.3 (1989).

Shelton, Dinah, Subsidiarity and Human Rights Law. Human Rights Law Journal 27 (2006).

Simpson, A W B., The ECHR: The First Half Century. 2004. University of Chicago Fulton Lecture Series. Available at: Http://Chicagounbound.Uchicago.Edu/Cgi/Viewcontent.Cgi?Article = 1017&Context = Fulton_Lectures (Accessed 30 October 2014).

Sjaak, Nouwt, Berend, R. de Vries, Introduction. In: Sjaak Nouwt, Berend R. de Vries, Corien Prins, editors. Reasonable Expectations of Privacy? Eleven country Reports on Camera Surveillance and Workplace Privacy. Cambridge University Press, 2005.

Sorensen, M., Do the Rights and Freedoms Set Forth in the ECHR in 1950 Have the Same Significance in 1975? In: Pierre-Henri Teitgen editor. Forth ECHR Colloquy. Rome, 1975.

Stoyanova, Vladislava, Article 4 of the ECHR and the Obligation of Criminalizing Slavery, Servitude, Forced Labour and Human Trafficking. Cambridge Journal of International and Comparative Law 3.2 (2014).

Sychenko, E., Contradictions of Anti-discrimination Protection of Employees in Russia and the Influence of European Court of Human Rights. In: Vladimir Lebedev and Elena Radevich editors. Labour Law in Russia: Recent Developments and New Challenges. Issue 6. Newcastle upon Tyne: Cambridge Scholars Publishing, 2014.

Sypris, Phil, The Treaty of Lisbon; Much Ado ... But about What? Industrial Law Journal 27 (2008).

Tafreshi, Shawn, Here's a Tip, Change the Law-Nerva v. United Kingdom. Loyola of Los Angeles International and Comparative Law Review 27 (2005).

Tiirmen, Riza, Freedom of Conscience and Religion. In: Marcelo Gustavo Kohen, editor. La Promotion de la Justice, Des Droits de L'homme Et Du Règlement Des Conflits Par Le Droit International. Martinus Nijhoff Publishers, 2007.

Tissandier, H. Risques psychosociaux et Cour de Justice de l'Union europeene [Psychosocial risks and the Court of Justice of the EU]. In: Lerouge L., editor. Les risques psychosociaux en Europe. Analyse jurisprudentielle (Droit communautaire, Allemagne, Belgique, Espagne, France, Italie, Pays-Bas, Royaume-Uni, Suède [Psychosocial risks in Europe. Jurisprudential analysis (Community Law, Germany, Belgium, Spain, France, Italy, Netherlands, UK, Sweden]. Paris: L'harmattan; 2013.

Tsakyrakis, Stavros, Proportionality: An Assault On Human Rights? Jean Monnet Working Paper 09/08.

Tulkens, Françoise, European Convention on Human Rights and Church-State Relations Pluralism vs. Pluralism. Cardozo L. Rev. 30 (2008).

Tulkens, Françoise, The European Convention on Human Rights and the Economic Crisis: The Issue of Poverty. EUI Working papers, AEL 2013/8.

Thilo, Marauhn, Freedom of Expression, Freedom of Assembly and Association In: Dirk Ehlers, Ulrich Becker, editors. European Fundamental Rights and Freedoms. Walter de Gruyter, 2007.

Van Hiel, Isabelle, The Right to Form and Join Trade Unions Protected by Article 11 ECHR. In: Filip Dorssemont, Klaus Lörcher, Isabelle Schömann, editors. The European Convention on Human Rights and the employment relation. Oxford: Hart Publishing, 2013.

Varju, Marton, Transition as a Concept of European Human Rights Law. European Human Rights Law Review 2 (2009).

Varelius, Jukka, Is Whistle-Blowing Compatible with Employee Loyalty? Journal of Business Ethics 85.2 (2009).

Van der Sloot, Bart, Privacy as Personality Right: Why the ECtHR's Focus on Ulterior Interests Might Prove Indispensable in the Age of 'Big Data'? Utrecht Journal of International and European Law 31(2015).

Van der, Vyver, Johan, D., State Interference in the Internal Affairs of Religious Institutions. Emory International Law Review 26 (2012).

Verstraete, Alain G., Anya Pierce, Workplace drug testing in Europe. Forensic Science International 121.1 (2001).

Veldman, Albertine, The Protection of the Fundamental Right to Strike within the Context of the European Internal Market: Implications of the Forthcoming Accession of the EU to the ECHR. Utrecht Law Review 9.1 (2013).

Velyvyte, Vilija, The Right to Strike in the EU after Accession to the ECHR: A Practical Assessment. In: Mark Freedland, Jeremias Prassl, editors. Viking, Laval and Beyond. Bloomsbury Publishing, 2014.

Vickers, Lucy, Religious Discrimination in the Workplace: An Emerging Hierarchy? Ecclesiastical Law Journal 12.3 (2010).

Vickers, Lucy, Freedom of Religion and Belief, Article 9 ECHR and the EU Equality Directive. In: Filip Dorssemont, Klaus Lörcher, Isabelle Schömann, editors. The European Convention on Human Rights and the Employment Relation. Hart Publishing, 2013.

Von Staden, Andreas, The Democratic Legitimacy of Judicial Review beyond the State: Normative Subsidiarity and Judicial Standards of Review. International Journal of Constitutional Law 10.4 (2012).

Voorhoof, Dirk, The Right to Freedom of Expression and Information Under the European Human Rights System: Towards a More Transparent Democratic Society. EUI Working Paper RSCAS 2014/12.

Waldock, H., The Effectiveness of the System Set up by the European Convention on Human Rights. Human Rights Law Journal 1 (1980).

Weisstub, Honor, Dignity and the Framing of Multiculturalist Values. In: David Kretzmer, Eckart Klein, editors. Concept of Human Dignity in Human Rights Discourse. Springer Netherlands, 2002.

Wildhaber, L., Hjartarson, A., Donnely S., No Consensus on Consensus? The Practice of the European court of Human Rights. Human Rights Law Journal 22 (2013).

Wildhaber, L., Protection against Discrimination under the European Convention on Human Rights-A Second-Class Guarantee. Baltic Yearbook of International Law 2 (2002).

Whitman, James Q., The Two Western Cultures of Privacy: Dignity Versus Liberty. Yale Law Journal (2004).

Xenos, Dimitris, Asserting the Right to Life (Article 2, ECHR) in the Context of Industry). German Law Journal 8.3 (2007).

Zimmer, Michael J., Decent Work with a Living Wage. In: Roger Blanpain and Michele Tiraboschi, editors. Global Labor Market: From Globalization To Flexicurity. Kluwer Law International BV, 2008.

Zorkin, V., The Limits of Pliability (Predel ustupchivosti) Rossyskaya gazeta, 29.10.2010.

Zoethout, C., #Margin of Appreciation, Violation and (in)Compatibility: Why the ECtHR Might Consider Using an Alternative Mode of Adjudication. European Public Law 20.2 (2014).

Zykina, T.A., The Right of Employees to Privacy (private) life (Pravo rabotnika na neprikosnovennost' lichnoy (chastnoy) zhizni). Pravovedeniye. 1 (2007).

Reports

Joint Report 'Trade Union Rights Situation in Turkey', presented on the 32nd meeting of the EU-Turkey Joint Consultative Committee on the 7–8 November 2013.

Report of the Constitutional Court of the Russian Federation for the XVIth Congress of the Conference of European Constitutional Courts.

Mark Worth, Whistleblowing in Europe Legal Protections for Whistleblowers in the EU. Report, 2013.

Psychosocial Factors at Work: Recognition and Control. Report of the Joint ILO/WHO Committee on Occupational Health. Occup Saf Health Ser. No. 56, 1986;

Mental health in the workplace. Geneva: ILO, 2000; Global strategy on occupational safety and health. Conclusions adopted by the International Labour Conference at its 91st Session, 2003. Geneva: ILO, 2004.

Survey of Enterprises on New and Emerging Risks (ESENER). European Risk Observatory Report: European Agency for Safety and Health at Work 2010.

Table of Cases

Title of the case (number of application) date of judgment/decision (day/month/year)

BCLR - BULLETIN OF COMPARATIVE LABOUR RELATIONS

Vol. Author/Title/Year/ISBN

1. Roger Blanpain, *Individual Employment Contracts: Collective Agreements,* 1970.
2. Roger Blanpain, *Social Planning,* 1971 (ISBN 90-312-0018-2).
3. Roger Blanpain, *Guaranteed Income Funds,* 1972 (ISBN 90-312-0019-0).
4. Roger Blanpain, *Employee Participation at the Level of the Enterprise,* 1973 (ISBN 90-312-0020-4).
5. Roger Blanpain, *Vastheid van Betrekking: Staking en Bezetting,* 1974.
6. Roger Blanpain, *Labour Law and Industrial Relations (International Bibliography),* 1975 (ISBN 90-312-0023-9).
7. Roger Blanpain, *Multinational Enterprises,* 1976 (ISBN 90-312-0024-7).
8. Roger Blanpain, *Worker's Participation in the European Company,* 1977 (ISBN 90-312-0044-1).
9. Roger Blanpain, *Women and Labour,* 1978 (ISBN 90-312-0077-8).
10. Roger Blanpain, *European Conference on Labour Law and Industrial Relations: Multinational Enterprises,* 1979 (ISBN 90-312-0091-3).
11. Roger Blanpain, *Job Security and Industrial Relations,* 1980 (ISBN 90-312-0147-2).
12. Roger Blanpain, Greg Bamber & Russell Lansbury, *Technological Change and Industrial Relations: An International Symposium,* 1983 (ISBN 90-312-0205-3).
13. Roger Blanpain, James Janssen van Raay & A. Moulty, *Worker's Participation in the European Community: The Fifth Directive,* 1984 (ISBN 90-654-4187-5).
14. Roger Blanpain, *Equality and Prohibition of Discrimination in Employment,* 1985 (ISBN 90-654-4215-4).
15. Roger Blanpain, *Restructuring Labour in the Enterprise: Law and Practice in France, F.R. of Germany, Italy, Sweden and the United Kingdom,* 1986 (ISBN 90-654-4283-9).
16. Roger Blanpain & E. Kassalow, *Unions and Industrial Relations: Recent Trends and Prospect: A Comparative Treatment,* 1987 (ISBN 90-654-4294-4).
17. Roger Blanpain & Marco Biagi, *Trade Union Democracy and Industrial Relations,* 1988 (ISBN 90-654-4394-0).
18. Roger Blanpain & Jelle Visser, *In Search of Inclusive Unionism,* 1990 (ISBN 90-654-4439-4).
19. Roger Blanpain, *Flexibility and Wages: A Comparative Treatment,* 1990 (ISBN 90-654-4461-0).

20. Roger Blanpain, Stephen Frenkel & Oliver Clarke, *Economic Restructuring and Industrial Relations in Industrialised Countries,* 1990 (ISBN 90-654-4488-2).
21. Roger Blanpain & Friedrich Fürstenberg, *Structure and Strategy in Industrial Relations,* 1991 (ISBN 90-654-4559-5).
22. Roger Blanpain, Amira Galin & Ozer Carmi, *Flexible Work Patterns and Their Impact on Industrial Relations,* 1991 (ISBN 90-654-4572-2).
23. Roger Blanpain, *Workers' Participation: Influence on Management Decision-Making by Labour in the Private Sector,* 1992 (ISBN 90-654-4600-1).
24. Roger Blanpain, Brian Brooks & Chris Engels, *Employed or Self-Employed,* 1992 (ISBN 90-654-4613-3).
25. Roger Blanpain & Tiziano Treu, *Industrial Relations Developments in the Telecommunications Industry,* 1993 (ISBN 90-654-4642-7).
26. Roger Blanpain & Marco Biagi, *Industrial Relations in Small and Medium Sized Enterprises,* 1993 (ISBN 90-654-4696-6).
27. Roger Blanpain & Marco Biagi, *Participative Management and Industrial Relations in a Worldwide Perspective,* 1993 (ISBN 90-654-4769-5).
28. Roger Blanpain, Jacques Rojot & Hoyt N. Wheeler, *Employee Rights and Industrial Justice,* 1994 (ISBN 90-654-4804-7).
29. Roger Blanpain & Ruth Ben-Israel, *Strikes and Lock-Outs in Industrialized Market Economies,* 1994 (ISBN 90-654-4841-1).
30. Roger Blanpain, Kazuo Sugeno & Yasuo Suwa, *The Harmonization of Working Life and Family Life,* 1995 (ISBN 90-411-0064-4).
31. Roger Blanpain & Laszio Nagy, *Labour Law and Industrial Relations in Central and Eastern Europe,* 1996 (ISBN 90-411-0298-1).
32. Roger Blanpain, *Labour Law and Industrial Relations in the European Union,* 1997 (ISBN 90-411-0527-1).
33. Taco Van Peijpe, *Employment Protection under Strain,* 1998 (ISBN 90-411-0528-8).
34. Roger Blanpain, Takashi Araki & Ryuichi Yamakawa, *The Process of Industrialization and the Role of Labour Law in Asia,* 1999 (ISBN 9-041-1104-7-X).
35. Roger Blanpain & Marco Biagi, *Non-standard Work and Industrial Relations,* 1999 (ISBN 90-411-1117-4).
36. Roger Blanpain, *Private Employment Agencies: The Impact of ILO Convention 181 (1997) and the Judgment of the European Court of Justice of 11 December 1997,* 1999 (ISBN 90-411-1118-2).
37. Roger Blanpain, *Multinational Enterprises and the Social Challenges of the XXIst Century: The ILO Declaration on Fundamental* Principles *at Work, Public and Private Corporate Codes of Conduct,* 2000 (ISBN 90-411-1280-4).
38. Roger Blanpain, Ryuichi Yamakawa & Takashi Araki, *Deregulation and Labour Law: In Search of a Labour Concept for the 21st Century,* 2000 (ISBN 90-411-1370-3).
39. Roger Blanpain, *The Council of Europe and the Social Challenges of the XXIst Century,* 2001 (ISBN 90-411-1543-9).

40. Roger Blanpain, *On-Line Rights for Employees in the Information Society, Use & Monitoring of E-Mail & Internet at Work*, 2002 (ISBN 90-411-1626-5).
41. Roger Blanpain, *The Evolving Employment Relationship and the New Economy: The Role of Labour Law & Industrial Relations*, 2001 (ISBN 90-411-1691-5).
42. Roger Blanpain, *Involvement of Employees in the European Union, Works Councils, Company Statute, Information and Consultation Rights*, 2002 (ISBN 90-411-1760-1).
43. Michele Colucci, *The Impact of the Internet and New Technologies on the Workplace: A Legal Analysis from a Comparative Point of View*, 2002 (ISBN 90-411-1824-1).
44. Roger Blanpain, *White Paper on the Labour Market in Italy: The Quality of European Industrial Relations and Changing Industrial Relations*, 2002 (ISBN 90-411-1841-1).
45. Roger Blanpain, Russell D. Lansbury & Young-Bum Park, *Impact of Globalisation on Employment Relations: A Comparison of the Automobile and Banking Industries in Australia and Korea*, 2002 (ISBN 90-411-1850-0).
46. Roger Blanpain & Antoine Jacobs, *Employee Rights in Bankruptcy:* A *Comparative-Law Assessment*, 2002 (ISBN 90-411-1942-6).
47. Roger Blanpain, Takashi Araki & Shinya Ouchi, *Corporate Restructuring and the Role of Labour Law*, 2003 (ISBN 90-411-1949-3).
48. Roger Blanpain, *Collective Bargaining, Discrimination, Social Security and European Integration*, 2003 (ISBN 90-411-2010-6).
49. Roger Blanpain & Luis Aparicio-Valdez, *Labour Relations in the Asia- Pacific Countries*, 2004 (ISBN 90-411-2239-7).
50. Roger Blanpain & Ronnie Graham, *Temporary Agency Work and the Information Society*, 2004 (ISBN 90-411-2252-4).
51. Roger Blanpain, *The Actors of Collective Bargaining: A World Report*, 2004 (ISBN 90-411-2253-2).
52. Roger Blanpain & Michele Colucci, *The Globalisation of Labour Standards: The Soft Law Track*, 2004 (ISBN 90-411-2303-2).
53. Roger Blanpain, Takashi Araki & Shinya Ouchi, *Labour Law in Motion: Diversification of the Labour Force & Terms and Conditions of Employment*, 2005 (ISBN 90-411-2315-6).
54. Roger Blanpain, *Smoking and the Workplace*, 2005 (ISBN 90-411-2325-3).
55. Roger Blanpain, *Confronting Globalization: The Quest for a Social Agenda*, 2005 (ISBN 90-411-2381-4).
56. Roger Blanpain, Thomas Blanke & Edgar Rose, *Collective Bargaining Wages in Comparative Perspective: Germany, France, the Netherlands, Sweden and the United Kingdom*, 2005 (ISBN 90-411-2388-1).
57. Roger Blanpain & Anne Numhauser-Henning, *Women in Academia & Equality Law: Aiming High - Falling Short?*, 2006 (ISBN 978-90-411-2427-6).
58. Roger Blanpain, *Freedom of Services in the European Union: Labour and Social Security Law: The Bolkestein Initiative*, 2006 (ISBN 978-90-411-2453-5).
59. Roger Blanpain, Frans Pennings & Nurhan Sural, *Flexibilisation and Modernisation of the Turkish Labour Market*, 2006 (ISBN 978-90-411-2490-X).

60. Roger Blanpain & Boel Flodgren, *Corporate and Employment Perspectives in a Global Business Environment*, 2006 (ISBN 978-90-411-2537-X).
61. Roger Blanpain, Shinya Ouchi & Takashi Araki, *Decentralizing Industrial Relations and The Role of Labor Unions and Employee Representatives*, 2007 (ISBN 978-90-411-2583-3).
62. Roger Blanpain, *European Framework Agreements and Telework: Law and Practice: A European and Comparative Study*, 2007 (ISBN 978-90-411-2560-4).
63. Roger Blanpain, Jim Kitay, Leanne Cutcher & Nick Wailes, *Globalization and Employment Relations in Retail Banking*, 2007 (ISBN 978-90-411-2620-1).
64. Roger Blanpain, Russell Lansbury, Jim Kitay, Nick Wailes & Anja Kirsch, *Globalization and Employment Relations in the Auto Assembly Industry: A Study of Seven Countries*, 2008 (ISBN 978-90-411-2698-6).
65. Roger Blanpain & Michele Tiraboschi, *The Global Labour Market: From Globalization to Flexicurity*, 2008 (ISBN 978-90-411-2722-8).
66. Roger Blanpain, Michele Colucci & Frank Hendrickx, *The Future of Sport in the European Union: Beyond the EU Reform Treaty and the White Paper*, 2008 (ISBN 978-90-411-2761-7).
67. Roger Blanpain, Linda Dickens, *Challenges in European Employment Relations: Employment Regulation, Trade Union Organization, Equality, Flexicurity, Training and New Approaches to Pay*, 2008 (ISBN 978-90-411-2771-6).
68. Roger Blanpain, Hiroya Nakakubo & Takashi Araki, *New Developments in Employment Discrimination Law, 2008* (ISBN 978-90-411-2782-2).
69. Roger Blanpain, Andrzej Marian wiątkowski, *The Laval and Viking Cases: Freedom of Services and Establishment v. Industrial Conflict in the European Economic Area and Russia*, 2009 (ISBN 978-90-411-2850-8).
70. Roger Blanpain, William Bromwich, Olga Rymkevich, Silvia Spattini, *The Modernization of Labour Law and Industrial Relations in a Comparative Perspective*, 2009 (ISBN 978-90-411-2865-2).
71. Roger Blanpain, Juan Pablo Landa & Brian Langille, *Employment Policies and Multilevel Governance*, 2009 (ISBN 978-90-411-2866-9).
72. Roger Blanpain, European Works Councils; *The European Directive 2009/ 38/EC of 6 May 2009, 2009* (ISBN 978-90-411-3208-6).
73. Roger Blanpain, William Bromwich, Olga Rymkevich & Silvia Spattini, *Labour Productivity, Investment in Human Capital and Youth Employment: Comparative Developments and Global Responses*, 2010 (ISBN 978-90-411-3249-9).
74. Greg J. Bamber & Philippe Pochet, *Regulating Employment Relations, Work and Labour Laws: International Comparisons between Key Countries*, 2010 (ISBN 978-90-411-3199-7). General Editor: Roger Blanpain.
75. Roger Blanpain, Desislava Nikolaeva Dimitrova, *Seafarers' Rights in the Globalized Maritime Industry*, 2010 (ISBN 978-90-411-3349-6).
76. Roger Blanpain, Hiroya Nakakubo & Takashi Araki, *Regulation of Fixed- Term Employment Contracts*, 2010 (ISBN 978-90-411-3356-4).

77. Roger Blanpain, William Bromwich, Olga Rymkevich & Iacopo Senatori, *Rethinking Corporate Governance*, 2011 (ISBN 978-90-411-3450-9).
78. Roger Blanpain & Frank Hendrickx, *Labour Law between Change and Tradition: Liber Amicorum Antoine Jacobs*, 2011 (ISBN 978-90-411-3424-0).
79. Roger Blanpain, Thomas Klebe, Marlene Schmidt & Bernd Waas, *Trade Union Rights at the Workplace*, 2012 (ISBN 978-90-411-3460-8).
80. Roger Blanpain, William Bromwich, Olga Rymkevich & Iacopo Senatori, *Labour Markets, Industrial Relations and Human Resources Management: From Recession to Recovery*, 2012 (ISBN 978-90-411-4004-3).
81. Roger Blanpain, Hiroya Nakakubo & Takashi Araki, *Systems of Employee Representation at the Enterprise: A Comparative Study*, 2012 (ISBN 978-90-411-4080-7).
82. Roger Blanpain & Frank Hendrickx, *Temporary Agency Work in the European Union and the United States*, 2013 (ISBN 978-90-411-4769-1).
83. Roger Blanpain, Toker Dereli, Y. Pınar Soykut-Sarıca & Aslı en-Tabaı, *Emerging Patterns of Work and Turkish Labour Market Challenges under Globalization: Readings on Labour and Employment Relations*, 2014 (ISBN 978-90-411-4983-1).
84. Roger Blanpain, Pablo Arellano Ortiz, Marius Olivier & Gijsbert Vonk, *Social Security and Migrant Workers: Selected Studies of Cross-border Social Security Mechanisms*, 2014 (ISBN 978-90-411-4770-7).
85. Roger Blanpain & Nikita Lyutov, *Workers' Representation in Central and Eastern Europe: Challenges and Opportunities for the Works Councils' System*, 2014 (ISBN 978-90-411-4746-2).
86. Roger Blanpain, Ulla Liukkunen & Chen Yifeng, *China and ILO Fundamental Principles and Rights at Works*, 2014 (ISBN 978-90-411-4984-8).
87. Roger Blanpain, *The Use of Languages and Employment Relations*, 2014 (ISBN 978-90-411-5606-8).
88. Roger Blanpain, Hiroya Nakakubo & Takashi Araki, *Protection of Employees' Personal Information and Privacy*, 2014 (ISBN 978-90-411-5608-2).
89. Roger Blanpain, Jan Wouters, Glenn Rayp, Laura Beke & Axel Marx, *Protecting Labour Rights in a Multi-polar Supply Chain and Mobile Global Economy*, 2015 (ISBN 978-90-411-5662-4).
90. Roger Blanpain & Stefania Marassi, *Globalization and Transnational Collective Labour Relations: International and European Framework Agreements at Company Level*, 2015 (ISBN 978-90-411-4748-6).
91. Roger Blanpain, Frank Hendrickx & Petra Herzfeld Olsson, *National Effects of the Implementation of EU Directives on Labour Migration from Third Countries*, 2016 (ISBN 978-90-411-6257-1).
92. Roger Blanpain, Frank Hendrickx & D'Arcy du Toit, *Labour Law and Social Progress: Holding the Line or Shifting the Boundaries?* 2016 (ISBN 978-90-411-6747-7).

93. Roger Blanpain & Frank Hendrickx, *Reasonable Accommodation in the Modern Workplace: Potential and Limits of the Integrative Logics of Labour Law*, 2016 (ISBN 978-90-411-6258-8).
94. Roger Blanpain, Frank Hendrickx & Bernd Waas, *New Forms of Employment in Europe*, 2016 (ISBN 978-90-411-6239-7).
95. Roger Blanpain, Frank Hendrickx, Hiroya Nakakubo & Takashi Araki, *The Notion of Employer in the Era of the Fissured Workplace: Should Labour Law Responsibilities Exceed the Boundary of the Legal Entity?*, 2017 (ISBN 978-90-411-8470-2).
96. Elena Sychenko, *Individual Labour Rights as Human Rights: The Contributions of the European Court of Human Rights to Worker's Rights Protection*, 2017 (ISBN 978-90-411-8629-4).

Made in United States
Orlando, FL
04 November 2026

90208072R00151